# SOCIOLOGY

# SOCIOLOGY
## Second Edition

## Joseph H. Fichter

**THE UNIVERSITY OF CHICAGO PRESS**
Chicago and London

*International Standard Book Number: 0-226-24633-7*
*Library of Congress Catalog Card Number: 70-143688*

The University of Chicago Press, Chicago 60637
The University of Chicago Press, Ltd., London

*Printed in the United States of America*

# Contents

# FOREWORD
# To Second Edition

EVEN IN A CHANGING AND PROGRESSIVE SOCIETY THE
basic principles of the sociological science remain the
same and an author must have a cogent reason for revis-
ing an already useful and serviceable textbook. In the
present case one may modestly remark that there has been
a certain demand for the product, as evidenced in part
by published versions in foreign languages—French, German, Italian, Portuguese, and Spanish (even a Latin version, which is reportedly circulating in mimeographed
form among European divinity students).

A respectable reason for keeping this book on the market is that it is neither a popularization nor a propaedeutic
to sociology. Like the first edition, this introduction to
sociology has been designed as a beginners' book. It is,
however, a sociological work and not a preliminary to the
study of sociology. There has been no attempt to produce
a simple and easy do-it-for-yourself type of introductory
explanation. The approach used here recognizes the complexity of the sociological system and the fact that the
serious student, even with the help of textbooks, lectures,
and instructors, is expected to work at the process of gaining knowledge. Technical terminology is defined and used
throughout, and the difficulty of the subject matter of
sociology is not camouflaged by an effort to "talk down"
to the student.

Sociology does not exist as an autonomous and cultivated enclave surrounded by the forest of other social
sciences; but the experience of two decades of teaching
this introductory course has emphasized the importance of
systematizing the relevant and pruning out the irrelevant.
The student of society should try to learn all he can about
biology, economics, ethics, history, geography, and psychology, but he should not expect to find such materials
all scrambled together in a sociology textbook. This book
tries to avoid also the various value slants that in a hid-

den or open way are lodged in many introductory sociology textbooks. Above all, it does not moralize from any
particular ethical point of view.

The feature that must perdure through all editions is
the conceptual framework on which the contents of sociology are arranged. Instead of the jumble of miscellaneous
and all-embracing items that characterize some introduc-

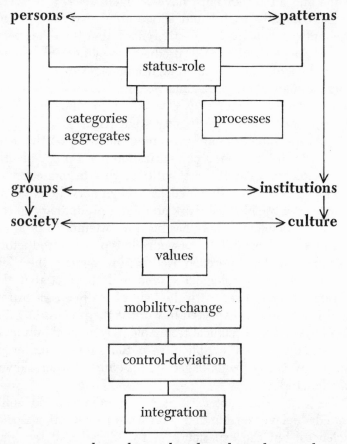

tory texts, we have here placed exclusively sociological
materials in a logical order. To systematize the relevant
sociological material means simply to collect, define, clarify, classify, and coordinate those principles of sociology
upon which there is fairly common consensus among the
most empirical of all social scientists, the American sociologists.

The manner in which the key concepts of sociology are systematized is shown in the diagram on the previous page. The book's first part starts with the minimum unit of society, the social person, and evolves to the largest collectivity, the total society. In this edition the separate chapters on categories and aggregates have been compressed into one, and a new chapter on communities has been added. Part II starts with the basic component of culture, a revised combination of overt and conceptual patterns of behavior, and evolves to the total culture. The third part analyzes the manner in which society and culture and their components are inescapably intertwined in the whole sociocultural system.

Since this book deals only with the essentials of sociological knowledge the brief bibliography following each chapter lists the most important relevant books. These lists do not include articles from sociological periodicals nor chapters contributed to edited books. Every instructor knows these materials and can make his own reading recommendations for pertinent materials. Students ought to be stimulated to read as widely as possible around each of the key concepts of sociology.

There are now available many excellent anthologies of outside readings to accompany the introductory textbook in sociology. Most of these volumes are a boon to college librarians, who have difficulty in providing sufficient copies of scientific periodicals for large undergraduate classes. They are a boon also to instructors, who find them a ready reference to preselected materials. Each chapter of the present textbook contains a series of "original readings" some of which are new to the second edition. This concentration on American sociocultural phenomena helps to bring the scientific principles alive, calls attention to the milieu in which the student himself lives, and avoids the exotic behavioral trivia which social scientists have turned up among primitives and other non-American societies.

The debt that this book owes to the great American sociologists, both living and dead, is obvious on every page. The fact that the contents are presented as a sociological system in a manner that the beginning student can grasp bespeaks a debt to the influence of the author's great professors: Gordon Allport, Clyde Kluckhohn, Talcott Parsons, Roscoe Pound, Pitirim Sorokin, Rupert Vance, and W. Lloyd Warner. A more immediate debt is owed to Professor Lawrence Bourgeois, an associate of many years at Loyola University of the South, whose scientific insights suggested whatever is best about the revisions of this second edition.

JOSEPH H. FICHTER

Cambridge, Massachusetts
June, 1970

# INTRODUCTION
# What Is Sociology?

SOCIOLOGY IS THE SCIENTIFIC STUDY OF HUMAN BEINGS in their relations with one another. People have always been interested in other people. Journalists and commentators are constantly gathering and disseminating notable happenings from daily life in society. Historians, for the most part, keep a record of how men behaved when they were on public view. Poets and storytellers focus on social relations and draw on their memory and imagination to reconstruct the manner in which they think people would act under certain circumstances. Philosophers and theologians speculate on how human beings should behave, and their interpretation rests on a fund of experience and previous knowledge.

The sociologist also specializes in people, but his task goes further and deeper because it is a scientific approach to social behavior. The sociologist may possess the abilities of the journalist and historian, and perhaps some of the insights of the poet and philosopher, but this is not enough. He differs from other social observers by the manner in which he gathers data and by the manner in which he analyzes the results of his observations. The sociological approach to group life is accompanied by a sociological interpretation of group life.

The term "sociology" was first used a little more than a century ago by Auguste Comte, a Frenchman, and popularized by Herbert Spencer, an Englishman. But they did not "invent" social behavior the way a chemist invents new products in a laboratory. Nor did subsequent generations of sociologists make "discoveries" the way the astronauts discovered the surface of the moon. Social behavior was always there. The subject matter of sociology—the phenomenon we study in this book—has had a persistence throughout human history.

The essential constituents of social life are as old as mankind, existing sometimes in relatively elementary and

1

simple forms, at other times in highly complicated and sophisticated forms. This twofold fact of essential continuity and basic similarity makes possible the scientific study of social life. Certain regularities and uniformities are always present. These can be observed, described, analyzed, and interpreted; and it is only after men have learned to do this that we can properly speak of a science of sociology.

During the past half century, especially in the United States, sociology has acquired a body of practical research information, has brought its theories down to earth, and has gained a central place in the college curriculum. The sociologists who have provided the materials for this book have done three things. First, they have asked questions of people. Second, they have observed methodically how people behave. Third, they have participated in various forms of group life. What makes this work scientific is that it has been systematic and controlled. Obviously, no social scientist can talk to every person, observe every behavior pattern, do everything that people do in society.

The key to the assembling of scientific knowledge is the scientific sample. The so-called "universe" of the teenage culture in America includes many millions of young people, but we can gain reliable knowledge of that culture if we study a properly proportionate segment of all teenagers. The same can be said about American family life, the business and industrial world, the political and military systems, the religious, educational, and recreational institutions.

The generalizations we make from such sampling methods are never completely accurate because there are always people who act differently from others. Nevertheless, these generalizations have high probability and provide us with knowledge that we are constantly rechecking. This means that there is a genuine predictability about the cultural and social behavior of human beings. The fact that we can occasionally recognize erratic behavior in some people means that the great majority of people conform to the expectations of their society.

THE CONTENT OF SOCIOLOGY

A definition of sociology must distinguish it from the other social sciences. Economics places its focus upon the material things that human beings require to live on earth —how these things are produced, exchanged, distributed, and consumed. Political science places its focus upon power and authority—the ways in which these are employed and distributed to make an orderly public life possible. Sociology focuses upon the fact of human "togetherness"; it studies the patterned regularities of social interaction as they exist everywhere in society. As a body of knowledge, it centers around the fact of human relations; anything that contributes to, or flows from, this human association is sociological.

No definition can provide anything more than an identification of the thing defined. When we say that sociology is the scientific study of society, or of human interaction, or of social behavior, we have merely given an indication of its contents. This whole book is a discussion and explanation of the definition of sociology, that is, it treats the contents of the science. As an introductory book, it must necessarily be a survey of basic and essential and general knowledge in this area of study. We shall not have time to describe the more specialized and highly technical and detailed studies made by individual sociologists.

When we say that sociology is a "scientific study," we do not mean merely that it is an intellectual exercise or that it is only a peculiar approach to certain human phenomena. It is both of these, but it is mainly a body of knowledge about society. The word "science" immediately implies that there is something (content) which is studied and that there is a way (method) of studying it. This book summarizes the basic content of sociology, and the way in which it presents the material for study indicates the method which sociologists employ.

The content of sociology is frequently called "social phenomena" but that is too vague. It is better to say that we are studying human interaction, for our daily experience of human relations—with family, friends, enemies, and strangers—is the basic stuff of the science. Not only do we make some kind of response towards all the people with whom we associate, but we make approximately the same kind of response over and over. This means that our social behavior is standardized and patterned.

The phrase "patterns of social behavior" expresses a primary idea in sociology. The unique, abnormal, private activities of people interest us only secondarily, because we pay attention to social relationships as they happen in repeated order. The travel experience of the astronaut who reaches the moon does not interest the sociologist so much as the regularized travel of passengers on commercial airlines. In essence, the sociologist studies the routine repetition of social behavior.

THE CONCEPTUAL FRAMEWORK

Social behavior occurs concretely, that is, personally, among flesh and blood people at a definite time and place. In order to understand this behavior, however, we must form generalized concepts that identify a similarity in the acts of behavior wherever they take place. We know what we mean by a system of education, even if school customs differ in China and Chile. We know what a family is, even if French peasants differ from American suburbanites in their family behavior. Broad conceptualizations of this kind indicate that the sociologist is able to think of a species of human conduct rather than just of specific human acts.

Social interaction occurs in concrete everyday life, but in order to analyze and understand this interaction, we must learn to conceptualize it. We must train ourselves to abstract essential generalizations from numerous specific occurrences. We are then able to distribute and arrange these generalizations or concepts, the content of the science, upon a logical framework. We shall see how these key concepts are interconnected in order to form a mental construct of the sociocultural system.

A quick and rough description will indicate the parallel structures of society and culture. For example, from our observation of people in society we recognize certain patterns of social behavior clustering around the social functions people are meant to perform. Such a set of patterns is conceptualized as the social role that the individual enacts. Your role as a student has been standardized and patterned quite differently from the role of your professor. Each acts in expected ways and towards the aims for which the actions are intended. But the conceptualization goes further. When you bring together all the patterned roles which center upon a certain social function, you have a social institution. Finally, all of the institutions combined as a totality and existing among a given people are conceptualized as the culture.

We must remember that we are studying not only social patterns, but also social persons. The student and the professor associate and interact in human relations, and this is observed wherever reciprocal social roles exist. These human relations occur in social groups in which people cooperate towards the fulfillment of social needs. Since these social needs are quite varied, we must conceptualize and classify a great variety of groups. The major groups in society employ corresponding major social institutions. The persons who are in educational groups, for example, follow the patterns and enact the roles consonant with the institution of education. When all of the groups are conceptualized as a connected and ongoing totality, we have the abstraction called society. This rough description shows that the particular society employs a culture peculiar to it.

ARE WE STUDYING REAL THINGS?

When we speak of the conceptual framework of any science, we speak, of course, of generalized abstractions existing in our minds. But if our concepts are not realistic, and if they do not correspond with the concrete social and cultural system in which human beings live, they cannot lend themselves to scientific study. The subject matter of sociology actually exists in the real order, but it is not the function of the sociologist, as social scientist, to eval-

uate the reality of social phenomena. He accepts them as
given data and leaves it to the philosophers to make final
declarations concerning their existence and essence.

What we are saying here is that human behavior has
many dimensions and that human beings can be studied
from many points of view. The physician is not a sociologist, and neither is the dentist or the psychiatrist or
the lawyer, although each of these specialists might be
helped by a background of sociological knowledge. What
we are doing here is to abstract the social dimension in
human behavior and to focus our attention upon it.

This question of social reality is of great importance
for the beginning student of sociology. He is likely to be
confused by certain contributions to sociological literature that go far beyond the field of sociology. These appear in speculative and pseudometaphysical discussions
that deny the existence of objective norms of behavior
and particularly of social values.

This problem of social reality is pertinent in the numerous and imaginative analogies which have been employed
to explain and describe social life. One reads, for example, that society and culture constitute an organism,
or a superorganism, that has its regular stages of birth,
growth, and decay. Mechanistic explanations have been
put forth to deal with stresses and forces as though people
in their human relations were so many parts of a gigantic
engine called society. Psychological explanations sometimes start with the premise that some sort of collective
consciousness is the central fact of social life.

An analogy is a comparison of two objects that are
partly similar and partly dissimilar. If similarities are pointed out by these descriptions merely as illustrative clarifi-
cations, they are relatively harmless, but the terminology
of social science has developed to the point where such
analogies in general are quite useless. Biological, mechanical, and psychological descriptions of society and culture
are in themselves erroneous. The objective fact is that
social reality cannot be reduced to the terms of biology,
physics, or psychology. But this does not mean that social

phenomena exist in a vacuum or that they are completely divorced from other aspects of reality.

## Distinction From Other Disciplines

Sociology has come of age as a science not only through the research and theory that have uncovered and systematized the facts of social life. In this process of development to scientific status, sociology has also gradually purified itself of its analogous interpretations. Without switching his scientific role, the sociologist has learned the basic facts about the analogy of being from the philosopher. Similarly he learns from other disciplines and builds up certain prerequisites of knowledge that prevent him from misinterpreting the genuine subject matter of sociology. These may also be termed "extra" requisites because they are outside the field of sociology and preliminary to it.

The distinction of sociology from other academic disciplines can be better appreciated through a series of illustrations. For example, the student of society must learn the facts of heredity from the biologist. There is no doubt that physiological heredity has an influence upon some aspects of cultural behavior. Similarly, it is a fact that the physical environment in the form of climate, terrain, and various other aspects of geography exert an influence upon behavioral patterns. The social scientist turns to the geographer for the necessary factual information from this science. Again the presence of human psychological aptitudes has an effect upon social behavior. The field of individual psychology is quite distinct from that of sociology, but it provides many important and fundamental teachings for the social scientist. This is true also in the area of ethics and morality, in which the experts have developed important principles and concepts.

Every educated person should have some minimum of knowledge in each of these various academic disciplines. No one can always and exclusively be a pure sociologist, and an adequate specialization in any particular field of knowledge requires a broad, general education.

The scientific role, limited to one area of knowledge, is only one of the many roles that the social scientist as a human being enacts within society. Sociology is a clearly definable science, an area in which a student may obtain specialized knowledge, but this specialization should be pursued together with a background of more generalized education.

The various auxiliary disciplines provide knowledge that the sociologist must accept in the form of assumptions. The factual information supplied by philosophy, biology, geography, psychology, and ethics is assumed by the sociologist to have been tested and proven in these fields. These facts are assumptions, not to the experts in these fields, but to the sociologist. The encyclopedic, all-embracing concept of sociology has long been abandoned. The social scientist does not take time out to prove that man has the power of self-direction, that objective moral values exist, or that the physiological structure of people differs in various ways. The student of society should know these things, but he should not expect to learn them from the sociologist.

IS ANYTHING CONSTANT?

The beginning student of sociology is often perplexed by the bewildering array of information he learns concerning the variety of behavioral patterns in different societies. He hears and reads so much about variations in social customs that he wonders whether there are any uniformities at all. As we proceed further into the study of sociology we shall perceive that certain constant elements must be present in every society and culture. As a matter of fact, the so-called principles of sociology, constituting the contents of this book, are the uniform, universal elements. A glance at the chapter headings will indicate what these are.

The student of society must learn to distinguish between the constant similarities and the changing differences. Every culture, whether primitive or modern, must contain the basic major institutions, and every society must have the corresponding basic major groups in which people function together toward social goals. One may say that it is the nature of social life that these uniformities be present. These fundamental institutions and groups —familial, educational, recreational, economic, religious, and political—are found wherever people live in organized social life. The components of institutions and groups, as described in this book, are also necessarily present everywhere.

The student of society ought not to look so hard for essential similarities of behavior that he is fooled by accidental similarities. Elections in Poland and elections in England, for instance, are roughly the same in outward appearance, but their social meaning is entirely different. The student also must not be tricked by accidental differences. The fact that an American greets people on the street informally while a Japanese bows to the people he meets does not mean that the Americans lack courtesy. The fact that in one society alcoholic drinks are outlawed and in another society wine is served at every meal does not make one set of people better than another.

We must recognize and accept both uniformity and variability, both permanence and change. The wide variation in the sociological constants in different places and among different people simply indicates that society and culture are extraordinarily flexible. In one society children receive all their formal education from their fathers or uncles. In another society, children are sent in groups to a person who is a specialist in education. The daily routine of an Arab watering his date trees in the Sahara seems far different from the activities of an Eskimo hunting seals in Alaska. The important point here is that educational and economic institutions are common to all cultures. The same fundamental social needs exist in every society, but the manner of satisfying them differs widely.

## Is Anything Worthwhile?

This problem of constants and variables is closely connected to that of the relativity of values. If there is so much change throughout the world and if people satisfy their needs in so many different ways, is there anything of enduring value in social life? The student is a moral person, and, in a sense, a citizen of the world. He is responsible and accountable for his own behavior and logically concerned about good and evil in society. This concern is obviously a matter of conscience—of ethics and morality. It cannot be satisfied, although it is often aroused, by the scientific study of sociology.

From a scientific point of view, sociology is not aligned with any particular moral system. Social science in itself cannot be democratic or totalitarian; it cannot be Christian or Mohammedan. The sociologist, as scientist, tries earnestly to avoid moral judgments about the cultures and societies that he studies and analyzes. He observes that value systems differ from one society to another and even from one group to another within the same society. If he says that one system is as "good" as another or that some are "worse" than others, he is making a value judgment which emerges from his moral role rather than his scientific role.

Social values are those items which the members of a society consider highly important and worthwhile, and according to which they tend to standardize their behavior. Probably no student of society can be completely impartial in his attitude toward values. It would be like playing a child's game to suggest, for example, that the scientific sociologist recognizes no moral difference between a gang of criminals and a committee of church vestrymen. Probably no sociologist can entirely purify his lectures and writings from the values he personally holds. He implies by the very adjectives he uses that he sees a moral difference between an "oppressive" system of child labor and a "free" system of management-labor relations.

This means, of course, that even the secular scientist, which every sociologist must be, cannot divorce himself completely from the culture in which he is himself involved. His own personal values in some way reflect the values of the culture in which he has been socialized.

It is important that the beginning student of sociology recognize this fact in his own attempt to be impartial and objective. We shall see more of this when we discuss ethnocentrism, which is the tendency to judge other groups by the norms and the values currently held in our own group. It is the very nature of personal and social life that people must hold values and act according to them, and this fact often impedes students of society from understanding and analyzing and appreciating different kinds of value systems.

Social values are the norms, or the measure, by which members of a society standardize their behavior. Among conservative French families, for example, the only "correct" way for young people to marry is according to their parents' wishes. In the United States, on the other hand, many young people feel that the only "correct" way to marry is according to mutual romantic love. The sociologist himself, exposed to the values of his society long before he becomes a scientist, is not so impartial as he would like to be. Even his most scientific behavior implies two value judgments: (*a*) scientific investigation is a worthwhile activity; (*b*) man in the group is a proper object of such investigation. A sociologist who grows up in a society that detests cannibalism and protects children tends to reflect these attitudes when he writes of a society that practices cannibalism and infanticide.

The question of what is ultimately worthwhile goes far beyond the limits of sociology. The question of the existence of a body of objective and irreducible value principles is not part of the study of sociology. In actual social life, however, there is everywhere a relativity of social values; what one society values highly another may spurn as worthless or even harmful. This the social scientist readily recognizes. He studies the social fact of existing values; he analyzes and interprets them. This is in itself an absorbing area of study: to understand how these values originate and develop, what function they perform, what effect they have on society, how widely people conform to them. To go beyond this and to attempt a judgment concerning their ultimate and immutable validity requires the assistance of the expert in ethics.

## SOCIOLOGY, A DIFFICULT SUBJECT OF STUDY

People accustomed to the mechanical conveniences of our modern generation tend to ignore the tremendous problem-solving activities that made these conveniences possible. It is exceedingly simple to turn on a television or radio set, to regulate an air-conditioning or deep-freeze unit, to dial a number on the telephone, or to walk up the steps into an airplane. The very simplicity of these actions gets the same results whether or not we are aware of the enormous system of coordinated technical knowledge and productive facilities which have made the action so simple for us.

Similarly, most people are unaware of all the factors and elements which make an ongoing sociocultural system possible. The student, like every social person, has been doing these things throughout his life; he has been following patterns of behavior, holding social values, and living in groups without giving much thought to these facts. It is sometimes surprising for him to learn that sociology is one of the most difficult areas of study into which the human mind can enter. This difficulty arises from three main facts: (a) the complexity of the subject matter of sociology; (b) the operation of multiple causality in society and culture; (c) the variability and impermanence of solutions to social problems.

**a.** *The complexity of sociology.* The beginning student usually does not recognize that society and culture are highly complex, even in the so-called primitive forms of group life. Patterns of behavior are inherited from previous generations, and the individual gradually gets accustomed to them without either analyzing them or comparing them with the accepted cultural patterns of other societies. It is only when he begins to study the variations and combinations of social thought and action possible to human beings that he comes to realize their variability and complexity.

Sociological analysis is difficult because there are so many elements of the social situation that have to be recognized simultaneously. For example, one cannot understand even the often-expressed concept of "social institution" unless he realizes that an institution is an intricate network of different but coordinated and related patterns of thought and behavior, which in turn are directed toward social ends and governed by social values. The institutions of a culture also intermesh, and it is difficult to understand one institution like the educational or familial without also having some knowledge of the other major institutions in the culture.

Another pertinent example is the intermeshing of the social roles of related persons in the same social situation. One does not enact the role of daughter in a vacuum. The ways of acting and thinking of a daughter in a family are related to the roles of other members of the family. There is a reciprocity of rights and duties, of expected patterns of behavior, between parent and child, between sister and brother. Although the roles of each necessarily differ from those of others, all the roles must necessarily be correlated. The individual social person is also a complex of multiple social roles. Each role differs somewhat according to the social group and situation in which it is enacted, but the person still remains an integrated human individual.

**b.** *Multiple social causality.* The same problem of multiformity and complexity is present to the social scientist concerned with ends and means, that is, with the reasons why things are done and the ways of doing them. It is obvious to any careful student of society that social facts do not "just happen." The theory that society and culture evolved by regular, progressive stages has long since been abandoned by sociologists. Nevertheless, various deterministic theories are still prevalent, especially among people who have not studied social science. Such ideas most often take the form of a theory of single causality, that is, attributing either the total sociocultural system or any part of it to one all-embracing cause. In normal conversation we often hear a simple, sovereign cause used as an explanation of social phenomena. For example, one hears that the social problem of American race relations is caused by the immorality of Negroes, or that warm climate makes people in the Southern states politically conservative, or that the introduction of automation causes secularization of our culture, or that Wall Street is responsible for economic recessions, or that a Communist conspiracy underlies all student unrest. The list of these simple, single, all-embracing "explanations" is almost inexhaustible.

The single-causality approach is probably the most widespread and most consistently occurring error in the social thinking of people. There seem to be two main reasons for this error. First, a single "explanation" is the easiest answer to the complex question of human relations. The lazy thinker grasps that which seems to him to be the obvious answer. Second, people often lack scientific knowledge about society and culture, and this ignorance is sometimes accompanied by arrogance and prejudice. The study of social science is an important antidote to both ignorance and arrogance.

Almost any question of human relations, from the simplest item of child care to the most serious decision of a corporation president, has behind it a whole series of interrelated factors. People do not act merely "on instinct"; they do not make "on-the-spot" decisions without a great deal of preliminary social and cultural experience. Even the theory that great men cause historical change has been tempered by the realization that leaders are themselves the product of their culture and can operate only within the limitations of the sociocultural environment.

c. *Impermanence of social solutions.* Besides the complexity and multiple causality of social phenomena, there is also the difficulty of change in the society and culture. Change is an ever-present social fact wherever human beings live together, and it is further complicated by the variability of both the rate and direction of change. Even traditional and conservative societies that appear to be almost static are constantly subject to adaptation and variation. In this sense, social change is in itself one of the sociological constants; it is treated in some detail later in this book.

The phenomenon of change presents a never-ending challenge to the sociologist. Unlike the geologist, who can demonstrate with fixed evidence the successive strata of the earth's crust, the sociologist finds that contemporary society does not stay "fixed." The demographers have learned this lesson in predicting population curves. The so-called "futurists" are on relatively safe ground when they foresee the state of technology at the end of the century, but they can only vaguely speculate on what sociocultural changes will result from the impact of increased technology.

The fact of change does not belie the presence of structure and order in society, but it does make more arduous the study of social problems. Many causes are at work bringing about this change, the most important of which appears to be man's own power of selection and decision. A free society is likely to be a more dynamic society because the individual social person has greater latitude in his patterns of social behavior. The ancient philosophical problem of unity and diversity in the world is here present in the modern scientific garb of the coordination of social function and structure.

Sociology is not social reform, but the essential principles of sociology are a prerequisite in any proposed solution of social problems. It is desirable, of course, that solutions be found for the problems of society and that certain universal principles of social life be established. But in the concrete social situations of real life we always find some individuals and groups who deviate, who will not "stay put" in nicely arranged categories, and who will not consistently behave according to the principles uncovered by social science. Just as there are no single causes of social phenomena, so also are there no permanent solutions to social problems; this is why blueprints for social utopias are of only minor sociological significance.

## SOCIAL ENGINEERING AND SOCIOLOGICAL RESEARCH

The student may take the attitude that he studies sociology only for its own sake, only because he wants to know more about society and culture. Beyond this he may seek knowledge of social life because this knowledge enriches his mind, gives him a more thorough understanding of other people, and provides a satisfying objectivity for judgment of others. There is no question of the fact that a tremendous storehouse of this kind of knowledge has been built up in recent decades from the scientific research of sociologists. The modern student can depend upon the validity of sociological information, and is no longer forced to choose among a series of mere speculations.

The student is also a moral person and citizen, an actor in the various social roles which his society demands of him. In this sense, mere knowledge does not satisfy him. As an intelligent and concerned person, he probably seeks the application of sociological knowledge to the social situations in which he finds himself. This is a transition that neither a textbook nor a professor, but only the student himself can make. A person can be an expert in sociology and still behave as a social deviant, just as a man with deep theological knowledge may be a great sinner, or a learned economist may spend his own money foolishly.

In general it may be said that study and research are almost always ultimately directed towards "doing the thing better." The emphasis in an introductory course in sociology must be on factual knowledge resulting from long research by social scientists. This is the scientific aspect of any study: to obtain exact and universally true information that one can study in a systematic way and about which one can have a high degree of certitude. The human and personal aspect of any study is to render it useful and fertile. Sociological study lends itself to helping the individual and his society achieve results in terms of better social relations.

The planned improvement of society is practically impossible without the scientific knowledge provided by sociology. The term "social reform" has gone somewhat out of fashion because of its apparently moralistic overtones. One speaks now of its synonym, "social engineering," which in turn may be objectionable because of its overtones of mechanism and manipulation. Whichever term one employs, the fact remains that administration and planning are essential elements in organized social life.

Social engineering, therefore, involves the intelligent application of sociological knowledge. Much of the social planning of the past has been done on the basis of shrewd guesswork and hit-or-miss experience. Every family, school, and church, every club, business, and municipality, works out plans for the future, seeks to solve its problems, administers its personnel, recognizes and pursues its social goal. This is nothing more or less than social engineering, and it is eminently more intelligent and productive to perform these functions on the basis of the exact and valid knowledge provided by sociology than on the basis of haphazard, trial-and-error experimentation.

## Why Study Sociology?

We assume that most readers of this book are college and university students. What we have said previously about social research and engineering helps to answer the question why sociology is an important area of study for them. Relatively few students become professional sociologists; but all students are participants in society and become more and more involved in various social roles after they finish their formal academic training. The more prominent and influential a person expects to be after his college years, the more useful and important will sociological knowledge be for him.

Most college students know sociologists as professors, and indeed four out of five sociologists are in the teaching profession. But even these tend to become specialists in research and consultation. They study human behavior in government, industry, schools, churches and neighborhoods. They concentrate on social problems of poverty, discrimination, drug addiction, and other forms of delinquency. In an increasingly complex and problem-filled society the sociological profession continues to attract new members and to grow in prestige and usefulness. The need for trained, professional sociologists is a continuing need of American society.

Since everybody must at all times live in society, associate with people, and enact social roles, it is obvious that sociological knowledge is a basic help in every career and vocation. Positions in law, journalism, teaching, salesmanship, business administration, preaching, politics — positions in which an essential occupational activity is "dealing with people"—require more than ordinary knowledge about human relations in society. Even normal participation in family life, the neighborhood, and community is more intelligent and successful when based upon scientific sociological knowledge.

The function of the sociologist is not to argue whether knowledge is more important than virtue, or vice versa, in the development of the "good society." Every responsible person is presumably interested in a better world, and in the last analysis social improvement is not achieved by merely willing it, or by having good intentions, or even by constantly practicing social virtue. There is a great difference between passive virtue and active virtue, between unthinkingly accepting change and intelligently promoting change.

Highly ethical people are certainly a desirable asset in society, but if they are ignorant of the technical analysis of roles and institutions, processes and functions, they will probably contribute little to intelligent social advancement. Reliable knowledge about social phenomena is an essential and basic prerequisite for a better society, and this is what a textbook in sociology is intended to provide.

## Suggested Readings

Bates, Alan P. *The Sociological Enterprise*. Boston: Houghton Mifflin, 1967.

Berger, Peter. *Invitation to Sociology: A Humanistic Perspective.* New York: Doubleday, 1963.

Chinoy, Ely. *Sociological Perspective: Basic Concepts and Their Application.* New York: Random House, 1967.

Inkeles, Alex. *What is Sociology? An Introduction to the Discipline and Profession.* Englewood Cliffs: Prentice-Hall, 1964.

Tomlinson, Ralph. *Sociological Concepts and Research.* New York: Random House, 1965.

# 1
# *Person and Society*

The conceptual approach to this introductory study of sociology is that social persons are the unit of society and that behavior patterns are the unit of culture. In this first section we proceed from the smallest unit, the person, through the various ways in which he is associated with others, to the total society.

We analyze first the social person and the process of socialization (chapter 1), then the social status of the person and the manner in which he obtains this position in society (chapter 2), then the various ways in which people are placed in social categories and aggregates (chapter 3), in groups and associations (chapter 4), and in communities (chapter 5). The final chapter of this first section deals with society as a whole (chapter 6).

# 1
# The Social Person

WHEN ONE APPROACHES A NEW FIELD OF STUDY IT
seems logical to begin with the smallest unit and to
expand the field from that point. Some sociologists suggest that the smallest unit of the total sociocultural system
is the social act, that is, the interaction, or relation, or
process, between two persons, between a person and a
group, or between two or more groups. Other sociologists
prefer to conceptualize the total system of human interaction as composed of three large segments: personality,
culture, and society. In either approach the central concern is the social behavior of human beings.

The starting point of sociology, therefore, ought to be
the social person—not the isolated individual, but the
person in his human relations with others. It is scientifically essential, then, to obtain a clear understanding of
the social person, his nature, potentialities, and abilities.
The whole picture of the social order, or of the sociocultural system, can be distorted if the image of man
is allowed to remain vague, or if it is in itself distorted.

The irreducible physical unit of social categories, aggregates, groups, and societies is man—the human being,
the human individual, the person. All of these terms are
synonymous and they are used interchangeably throughout this book. We sometimes hear about the analogous
"social behavior" of ants, bees, chickens, and primates.
However curious and interesting this may be, the sociologist is not directly concerned with subhuman levels of
life, with the gregarious instincts of herd life or brute
animals. Man is, of course, the only "social animal" we
are studying here, and his social behavior is not simply
a series of instinctive and predetermined responses to
environmental stimuli.

DEFINITION OF PERSON
The human being is recognized as different from sub-

human and nonhuman beings by his ability to think in abstract terms and to make choices and decisions. The person is a self-directing animal. He can recall the past, and reflect upon his own actions and reactions and on the meaning of his and others' behavior. He can do "paper work"; he can plan and arrange for the future. No other observable species can be called *homo sapiens*. The person is accountable for his own behavior and can develop a sense of responsibility toward others. *Homo sapiens*, though not always acting wisely, is also *homo socius*, though not always acting sociably.

Society and culture are scientifically meaningless without reference to these abilities and competencies of the human being. Experience and observation show, of course, that not all people are equally social, intelligent, and volitional. Not everybody uses his mind and his other abilities to the best advantage. Some, like imbeciles and idiots, are never able to develop these human qualities. Some become social outcasts, criminals, or other kinds of social deviants. Some remove themselves from the normal world by the use of drugs, or by deliberately withdrawing from society as a hermit, a monk, or social recluse. Nevertheless, the potientiality for normal, standardized social behavior is in all these people, and for this reason they too are persons.

The human being is a physical unit, individual, distinct, and identifiably separate from all other beings, human and nonhuman, animate and inanimate. On the other hand, this "oneness" of the human person does not mean that he must be studied from only one point of view. The human person has many aspects, or facets. He is a single and separate being, but he is also a composite and complex being.

As a *physiological* unit, the person is studied by biologists, anatomists, biochemists, and pathologists. As a *moral* unit, as one who can do right and wrong, he is studied by ethicians, moralists, theologians, and lawyers. As a *psychological* unit with conscious desires and subconscious drives, he is studied by psychiatrists, psychologists, and psychoanalysts. This variety of aspects does not refer to different kinds of persons, nor does it mean that the same person is actually divided into separate segments. The human being studied under all these different aspects is the same person studied by the sociologist, but under a still different aspect.

## THE SOCIAL PERSON

All human beings, as distinguished from nonhuman animals, are social persons. The terms "rational" and "social" are not synonymous, but one quality does not exist without the other. The very fact that we say an individual is a rational person necessarily means that he is a social person. Rationality and sociability are characteristics only of people. When we say that irrational animals can "learn" or that they are "social," we are speaking only analogously.

When a sociologist says that people are social, he does not mean that they are charming, urbane, accomplished, or refined. He does not refer exclusively to the social events or social leaders described in the society pages of the newspapers. The limitation of the words "social" and "society" to the recreational activities of people, or to the gracious and hospitable virtues, is a restriction of their full meaning.

The term "social" is derived from the Latin word *socius* which means companion or associate. The potentiality for being a *socius* and for learning how to behave like one is innate to the human person, a potentiality that is sometimes called "sociality." The person is social in the sense that he not only has an inclination to relate to others but also a need for human relations. Social science, therefore, studies people only under this one aspect. The student of society is interested in the ways in which persons are related to other persons. The fact that the person is a *sociological* unit, that he can be and is studied only under this aspect, must be kept in mind as a central point of reference throughout the reading of this book.

What is it that makes people act the way they do? Why are some nations highly developed while others are underdeveloped? Why are there still primitive tribes in an otherwise sophisticated world? One of the quick and erroneous answers to these questions has been the factor of *biological heredity*. This is the explanation proposed by racists, who maintain that some people are naturally superior and others inferior in both mental and physical capacities. There is indeed research evidence to show that individuals differ greatly in the kind of physique they have inherited from their parents and that this difference affects the way they behave in society. There is no evidence, however, to prove that races or ethnic and national groups are innately and biologically inferior or superior.

Another popular explanation lies in *geography*. This explanation suggests that the social character of people is the result of the climate in which they live, so that those in southern areas are less progressive than those in northern areas. There is supposed to be a difference in the personality of people who live in the mountains as compared to those who live on the plains or the coastlines. The best we can say here is that the physical environment does present a greater challenge to some peoples than to others. It is obviously difficult to carry on a normal and progressive social life in the jungles of Africa, the high mountains of South America, the frozen wastes of the Arctic Circle. These are moderating influences on society and culture even though modern man has had considerable success in adjusting to the forces of nature and in dominating them.

The third explanation, that of the *cultural environment,* seems to make the most reasonable and scientific sense. This explanation asserts that cross-cultural contact tends to develop people more quickly than relative social isolation. This is not simply the demographic factor, measured against the size of the population. An area that is overpopulated in relation to its resources may be as handicapped as an area where people are in social isolation. Historically, it seems important that the first civilizations developed along the shores of the Mediterranean Sea, where it was possible to have communication among different cultures. We shall later discuss in more detail the importance of the cultural environment.

NATURE AND NURTURE

It is obvious that there is a vast difference between a person at the age of thirty days and a person at the age of thirty years. Quite aside from physical, moral, and intellectual change, the older person is sociologically different. He has developed his capacities as a social person. He knows his way around in groups and societies; he knows how to behave in relations with other persons. To what do we attribute the development of these abilities?

Most sociologists speak of original nature as the "raw material" with which a person is equipped both actually and potentially at birth. Frequent speculation about the contribution of this original nature to the development of the mature social person, because it is for the most part merely speculation, does not provide adequate scientific knowledge. The scientific difficulty lies in the fact that one cannot properly measure the "natural" person completely unaffected by social factors.

The term "nurture" in its most general meaning refers to all the external influences affecting the individual person. It may include material and physical items, but more specifically for the sociologist, it refers to the social and cultural factors that help the individual to develop his "original" and natural social potentialities. We study the individual already present in society, whether as a relatively helpless infant or as a relatively self-sufficient adult.

It appears to have been futile to debate whether nature or nurture is more important in the socialization of the individual. The normal baby is certainly born with abilities to respond to external influences, but what these abilities are in their "raw state" concerns physiologists and psychologists more than it concerns sociologists. The latter are content to accept and study "given data," and these given data are the readiness and the abilities of persons to react to external influences. The most reliable scientific conclusion appears to be that both nature and nurture contribute to the socialization of the individual person.

## CREATURE AND CREATOR

The important point to remember is that the person responds and reacts. In other words, the human individual is not simply a pliable object which the society molds to its purposes. He is not merely a puppet of his culture, performing exactly and always in the way his culture demands. As an agent with the proven ability to discern and decide, the human being can alter his own behavior and can influence the society in which he lives. The great-man theory of history exaggerates this point, and American faith in leaders emphasizes it; what must be remembered is that both culture and society are man-made. If human beings did not have the ability to create and produce changes in their human relations, there would be no culture in the strict sense of the word. There would be no society of acting and interacting persons.

It is true also that persons are in many ways the products, the creatures, of their culture and society. Most individuals appear to be much more influenced by their social and cultural environment than they are influences upon it. We are not only socialized; we are socialized in particular ways. This fact has been dramatized by large numbers of farm laborers who migrate to industrial cities. They find the ways of the city people and the industrial workers strange, and they often have tragic difficulties in attempting to adjust their own behavior to the new cultural setting.

The reason for this difficulty is that the person from an isolated rural area is a cultural creation different from the person who has been conditioned by the big industrial and commercial city. This has been recognized in the universal stereotypes of the farm boy and the city boy. Even greater differences in the human cultural products are observed when we compare an Oriental with a Westerner. A Chinese is more similar to his fellow

Chinese than he is to an American. The similarity between a Chinese and an American may be in their "original nature"—the fact that both are persons, with intellectual, volitional and emotional potentialities at birth.
Their behavioral differences, however, develop in each
mainly because of the culture and society in which they
have grown up.

## SOCIALIZATION

Socialization is a process of mutual influence between
a person and his fellow men, a process that results in
an acceptance of, an adaptation to, the patterns of social
behavior. It does not mean that the person ceases to be
an individual. Just as we cannot say a person "becomes
human" when he learns to use his intellect, so we cannot
say that a person "becomes social" when he learns to
get along with other people. The human being is a social
person from the beginning of his life, but he undergoes
continuous adaptations and changes as long as he lives.
One sees this development not only in the different
stages between infancy and senility, but also in persons
who move from one culture to another, or from one
social status to another, or from one occupation to
another.

Socialization can be described from two points of
view: objectively, from that of the society acting upon
the individual, and subjectively, from that of the individual responding to the society. *Objectively*, socialization is that process by which the society transmits its
culture from one generation to the next and adapts the
individual to the accepted and approved ways of organized social life. The function of objective socialization is
to develop the skills and disciplines which are needed
by the individual, to instill the aspirations and values
and the "design for living" which the particular society
possesses, and especially to teach the social roles which
individuals must enact in that society.

The process of socialization is continuously at work
"outside" the individual. It affects not only children and
immigrants when they first come into this society, but

all people within the society all their lives. It acts upon people; it provides for them the patterns of behavior which are essential to maintenance of the society and culture. From the point of view of society, it is essentially a process of social control and a manner of providing some kind of orderliness in group life.

*Subjectively,* socialization is a process of learning which goes on in the individual while he is adapting to the people around him. The person takes on the habits of the society in which he lives. From infancy on, he becomes gradually "society broken." As an immigrant, the person becomes sociologically "naturalized" to his adopted society. It must be stressed that this is a lifelong process, that much of it is a kind of subconscious conformity, and that it is always particularized in time, place, culture, and society. It is important to note that a person does not become socialized in a haphazard, generalized fashion, as a sort of citizen of the world or as a general member of human society. The process makes him into a recognizable American, Mexican, Frenchman, or whatever.

THE SOCIAL FRAME OF REFERENCE

The accumulated experiences of the individual in his society form the background against which he undergoes new experiences. The sociologists say that the culture becomes "internalized," that the individual "embodies" it, and that in this way, "from the inside," it continues to influence his conduct. The culture is not something merely external to the individual. His whole social background tremendously and constantly influences the patterns of thought and behavior which the person follows at any given moment.

The ways of life he has learned, the ideas he holds, the values he treasures, all in some way come originally from outside him. These are the results, the products, the materials of the socialization process. The person tends to meet new experiences and to interpret current happenings in the light of these past experiences. In a sense, he tends to think and act according to the degree of conformity that he has achieved.

The social frame of reference has as its content the social experiences of the individual. These are the vantage points from which he looks out at the world; they are the points of reference and comparison against which he forms opinions and judgments, and according to which he behaves, often without any conscious reflection. This is the storehouse in which a person readily finds models for his behavior in the usual and frequently repeated situations of social life. It is also the storehouse out of which he draws models from the past when he is confronted with a novel social situation.

The life experiences that make up the social frame of reference can be analyzed roughly from three different aspects. (*a*) There is that which is common to all human beings, the sociological elements that are found everywhere: behavior patterns, human relations, status and role, institutions, and so forth. (*b*) Each of these is experienced by a person through his unique personality in a way that no other person can share. (*c*) The experience is specified by the culture and society in which it occurs. Thus, the social frame of reference is universal, unique, and cultural at one and the same time.

These three aspects of social experience can be demonstrated with numerous examples. Friendship and the primary group are found wherever human beings live in society; but each person experiences friendship in a unique (that is, never exactly duplicated) manner, in this time and place, with these particular persons. The manner in which friendship is demonstrated and symbolized differs from one culture to another. In one society, adult males who are friends greet each other with a kiss on the cheek, in another society with an embrace, and in still another with a handshake.

SOCIAL LEARNING

The subjective process of socialization can ultimately be reduced to the fact that the individual learns by contact with society. The process, however, refers not to individual knowledge, which also comes from contact with others, but to shared knowledge which has social signifi-

cance. From the point of view of society this process is
essentially one of social control, with the problem of
making the person comfortable in an orderly sociocultural
system. The question is not who learns or how he learns,
but what he learns. We need not discuss the innate biological and psychological drives that are characteristic of
normal human beings and account for the fact that people
want to learn. They are attracted to ideas, objects, or situations that satisfy the capacity for knowledge. The interaction between the learner and the thing learned is called
the response; it is what occurs when the particular drive in
the individual is coordinated with the object. Sociologically, we may also speak here of the importance of rewards and punishments—those things which strengthen
or make easier the response of the individual in striving
to learn.

This abstract terminology may give the impression
that each facet of the learning process is a single, separate
item. The fact is that, concretely, each is a complex aspect
of the whole process. For example, a boy wants to learn
the game of football so that he can become a star athlete
on the high school team. This desire to achieve local glory
and popularity constitutes a drive for learning, but it is
overlaid with other wishes—to get recreation, to release
physical energy, to prove that he is "tough." He must
learn the techniques of the game, the system of rules for
the team on and off the field, the various kinds of trick
plays. The response is his actual practice and performance, achieving perfection in the patterns of play and
in coordination with other players. The reward, too, may
be multiple—the actual winning of games, the appreciation of the coach, the applause of the spectators. When
he suffers the negative aspect, the penalties or punishment, he may find that these are also factors in the learning process.

From the point of view of social science, there are certain conditions and qualifications surrounding the process
of social learning. All of these have to do with the manner
of learning in relation to other persons. We are not con-

cerned here with original thinking and discoveries, the composition and invention of ideas, trial-and-error research in the privacy of one's study or laboratory. The process of learning in social situations is a process that occurs with and among people and therefore always involves social relations.

The two most important sociological processes of learning are imitation and competition. *Imitation* is the human action by which one tends to duplicate more or less exactly the behavior of others. It is commonly recognized not only in the way children behave like their parents but also in the way adolescents and even mature adults take on the charactersticis of people whom they appreciate and admire. It is a common experience that skilled and professional people provide a "role model" for the imitation of young people who want to follow the same occupation. There is also a great deal of social imitation in the conformity among peer groups, as well as in the common fashions of everything from clothing to housing to educational procedures.

*Competition* is a stimulative process in which two or more individuals vie with one another in achieving knowledge. It is peculiarly important in the social learning of children because it is often involved in the desire of the child to obtain the approval of others. It is also strong in the whole area of social status where people commonly attempt to "keep up with the Joneses." It seems significant that social learning is at its most competitive in highly developed and flexible cultures. Competitive learning is a clear indication that people tend to conform to the approved ways of behaving in society and to shun the ways which are disapproved.

It must be obvious from these brief remarks concerning the processes of imitation and competition that the essential prerequisites of social learning are contact and communication. The few authentic studies of socially isolated individuals, of children who were kept apart from society, show that association with others is an essential condition of social learning. Within certain limits, the number and kind of contacts and relations a person has during his lifetime are also a measure of the extent to which he becomes socialized.

## HINDRANCES TO NORMAL SOCIALIZATION

Normal socialization is the process producing at least the minimum learning that any person requires to get along in his particular society. The term "normal" must necessarily be left indefinite because the society does not demand exactly the same degree and kind of response from all of its members. More is expected from some than from others. Some are able and willing to respond more readily and quickly than others. No person can fully exploit all the potentialities of his society and culture for himself.

No matter how ambitious or brilliant a person may be, he is constantly limited by time and circumstances from realizing more than a fraction of the available cultural and social potentialities. The development of a highly specialized society has increased the number of possible roles and functions generally available, but it has decreased the number specifically available to the individual. Selection must necessarily be made among numerous roles, and concentration of effort is required once the choice has been made. It is seldom that a person completely fulfills his formally expected roles—familial, occupational, religious, and others. It is even more seldom that he realizes his potentiality in more than one occupation. The expert physicist, for example, cannot also have a successful career in music or in political science, although he may be broadly knowledgeable outside the field of physics.

There are other hindrances to the full development of the social capacity of the individual. A person may be simpleminded or lazy, sick or crippled, or handicapped in other physical ways. The social structure and its assignment of power and prestige may repress individual opportunities for learning, as when a small ruling class subjugates large masses of the people. The culture itself, with its beliefs and attitudes and values, may impede learning by emphasizing the traditional and the static. The physical and geographical environment of a society may make such demands upon the people that their energies are expended in mere survival.

## AGENCIES OF SOCIALIZATION

It may be said that the total society is the general agency for socialization and that each person with whom one comes into contact is in some fashion a special agent of socialization. Between the large society and the individual person there are numerous small groupings, and these are the principal agencies for the socialization of the person. The obvious beginning of the process for the newborn child is his immediate family group, but this is soon extended to many other groups.

Preschool influences act upon the child from many directions. The little circles and relationships in which he participates with parents, relatives, friends, and others are all important in showing him how to be "a good little child." Even in these early years, media like television, radio, and comic books begin to provide patterns of behavior. The neighborhood, the school, and in some instances the church, are important agencies of socialization for young people.

Other media of socialization have varying effects at different stages of a person's life. Since social learning is a continuous process at every age level, the person is constantly being checked in some drives and encouraged in others. Frustrations and satisfactions, strains and readjustments, all constitute experiences which are ways of learning. The mother who explains the differences in the way her various children have gone through their growing stages says indirectly that she herself has learned a great deal from these experiences.

All forms of adult groups and associations, in business and professions, in recreation and politics and religion, continually influence the change and development of the social person. The modern media of communication, like movies, television, radio, and mass circulation newspapers and magazines are more influential in forming social behavior than most people realize. Parents and teachers who are concerned about the impact of these agencies upon their children do not often realize that they themselves are following examples and suggestions and picking up opinions and attitudes through the same process. They are being subconsciously socialized.

## INDIVIDUALIZATION

We have seen that every individual internalizes and personalizes his social experience. This is what we mean by the individualization of culture. Patterns of behavior, in order to be scientifically observable and measurable, must be expressed by actual persons in concrete social situations. In spite of the imagination of fiction writers, we do not really know what a man from outer space is, how he behaves and acts with others. This is because no one has ever been able to analyze the patterns pertinent to such an individual. Similarly, only a person who has been a mother can ever actually fulfill all the role expectations of motherhood.

The social personality is never a perfect reflection of the culture and society in which it has been developed. It is physically impossible for two people, even twins, to have exactly the same experiences with the same people at the same time and in the same situation and to respond in exactly the same way. No pair, or cluster, of individuals can ever be completely identical, and no individual is ever completely predictable in his social behavior. Individualization, however, is not the opposite of socialization. It is merely the process which personalizes one's experience. This is simply another way of saying that everyone has a unique personality and that even social experiences and social relations are productive of differences between individuals within groups.

It is true that every person is both unique and social. Nobody lives in a vacuum, and the person is individualized by the adjustments he makes to the influences exerted upon him and by his own personal interpretation of what he has learned. A sociologist studies that which is social, common, and shared in many people rather than that which is unique, peculiar, and personal to the individual. The agencies of socialization have a similar effect upon a large number of people, and it is these similarities shared by pluralities of people that make possible the study of social science.

### THE SOCIAL PERSONALITY

We have said that a person is characterized by the ability to think and make decisions, that the human individual can be studied for different purposes from different points of view. The concept of the social personality, as a complex of various roles, is an extremely useful device of the sociologist. The individual is a social person from birth, but his social personality develops constantly through the socialization process. In general terms, the social personality includes all the ways in which the individual acts in relation to and with other persons. In specific terms, all these ways may be analyzed under the headings of the various social roles which he has developed and according to which he acts.

We shall later analyze social roles in greater detail. It suffices here to note that the person follows a patterned way of behavior in each of the major groups in which he participates. He is the father in his family, the vestryman in his church, the superintendent in his factory, a member of a parent-teacher association, of a country club, and of the local Republican party. These are more than just facets or aspects of his person. Each one of them requires him to enact a role corresponding to the objectives of the group and to his participation in the group. When we put all these roles together, study their origin, function, interrelation, and structure, we are studying the social personality of the individual.

## American Socialization and the Social Person

### 1. THE "SPOILING" OF CHILDREN

Americans of the older generation and foreign visitors to our country are horrified at the manner in which we bring up our children. Older and conservative people often complain that these children are being raised without courtesy or manners. Europeans and Asiatics sometimes suggest that our children are seen too often and heard too much, that parents are doting and indulgent, and that in some sense children rule the American home. As consequences of this trend in permissive socialization, they point to vandalism in the public school system, student strikes on the college campus, juvenile gangs in the large cities, draft resisters and dropouts among young adults.

It is to be assumed that the socialization of children in any society tends to be integrated with the patterns of thought, the goals, beliefs, values, and ideals of that society. This integration is never complete and perfect, but it helps to explain what may appear to be erratic and undisciplined behavior. In some ways adult patterns socialize the child, but in other ways the childhood patterns influence American adulthood. A consideration of the following items may help to explain the peculiar socialization of American children.

a. In the United States there has been traditionally a high evaluation of the individual personality. This is not likely to be confined only to adults or to be appreciated and applied suddenly at some transitional point in a person's life. Even the very young child is accorded this respect and appreciation.

b. There is also an emphasis on the future. Unlike most older populations of Europe and Asia, the American people have little regard for traditions as a guide to conduct. Children are the "wave of the future." In them lie the aspirations of many parents who themselves have not achieved success.

c. The relative isolation of the immediate family group prevents the child from developing diffused emotional ties to a large group of adult relatives. He gets his security and love from parents only and not from relatives of the larger kinship group, like grandparents, aunts, uncles, and cousins.

d. The inconsistency of adult standards of conduct tends to bewilder the child. This is especially noticeable around the ages of seven to ten when the child begins to question why he must tell the truth, go to Sunday school, and avoid certain "bad words," when his parents' conduct does not conform to their preaching.

**e.** The child has an extraordinary dependence upon the mother, who symbolizes love and security for him, while the father tends often to be a relative stranger. The bringing up of children in American society is seldom a function shared equally by both parents.

**f.** The scientific and rational tendency of the American culture is seen in the dependence of American parents on expert and pseudoexpert advice on child rearing. The natural and almost automatic rearing of children has been replaced by a desire to follow improved and scientific methods.

Research in this field of socialization is only gradually accumulating among American social scientists, and our analyses are still imperfect. The above trends, however, are fairly well marked in the American society. They are not meant to be a full explanation of the problem of "spoiling" children, nor are they universally applicable. There are many local, regional, and class differences in the bringing up of children.

The number of European immigrants has sharply decreased in the past quarter century, but insofar as some families in the United States behave according to the ideals of foreign countries, there are noticeable differences in socialization. This makes a problem for children of such families, especially when they discover that the home life of their school companions is quite different from their own.

To some extent the rural pattern of socialization differs from that of the urban family. The possibilities of larger kinship groups, of closer cooperation between husband and wife and between children and parents, the conservatism and traditionalism of the rural family—all this means a different kind of social apprenticeship for rural children. Much of what is pointed out as "different" in the socialization of black children stems from the manner in which black families were forced to adjust their patterns of living to the conditions of Southern rural poverty.

## 2. STANDARDIZATION AND INDIVIDUALISM

Universal public schooling, national coverage by news media, simultaneous release of television programs, are said to be producing a uniform mass culture. Added to this is a technological theory of analogous cultural automation. The American industrial economy has made possible a standardized process and product. From this technological fact a peculiar logical leap has been made to the behavioral notion that because Americans produce and consume standardized commodities Americans themselves have become standardized. Against this, one may argue that the result has really been greater diversification.

We are interested here, of course, in the question of whether the social person in America is a standard product, of whether there is even a remote similarity between the production of American goods and services and the American production of social persons. From the point of view of process, it would appear that only some extreme form of socialism and regimentation in the rearing of children from infancy could bring this about. This is so far from American reality that it is hardly even an academic question.

The standardization of the American people does not begin to approach that of the people in the older major nations of the world. Even the standardization of items of material culture has not progressed to the extent that casual observation may lead one to believe. From the point of view of the human product, that is, the American person, the following observations indicate that he is not a uniform and standardized person.

a. The enormous variety of our biological and physical stocks makes impossible standardization of physical features. There is probably no nation in the world where one encounters more differences in bodily features and types. Our people exhibit a total range of known skin color, facial characteristics, and hair types.

b. The offspring of intermarriage among the various racial and ethnic stocks is providing, at least temporarily, an even greater diversification of physical types. As this process continues over the generations, it must eventually produce a more or less standardized physical type of American. At the present time, however, we are many generations removed from this homogeneous product.

c. The number of different religious bodies in America is larger than that of any other country in the world. Although Christianity is the basis of many of our religions, the varied interpretations of it have resulted in more than 250 distinct and formal religious bodies.

d. The types of architecture differ enormously. This is noticeable, not only in factories, schools, churches, and office buildings, but especially in residential construction. The identifiable types of homes, like colonial, Georgian, southern, Spanish, ranch-type, and others are many; but the ingenious combination of styles often makes identification and enumeration almost impossible.

e. The trend to the single-family dwelling reflects individualization, not only in the material surroundings of life, but also in a further isolation of the families themselves. Even in the cities it is questionable that multiple apartment houses and public housing projects provide a community setting for the development of behavior conformism. The continuing migration of families to the suburbs tends to counterbalance the so-called mass living in cities.

f. The rich variety of available clothing styles for both men and women eliminates even the external appearance of standardization. Men's clothing, traditionally more conservative in color and cut than that of women, has developed a multiplicity of styles and combinations. Almost any American department store offers a greater choice than any European store in size and style of women's shoes, hats, and dresses.

g. From the sociological point of view the standardization of patterns of behavior is more important than all the foregoing. No doubt a recognizable "American type" of social person is gradually emerging, but American differences in this regard are often more striking than the similarities. Some of these differences are those between rural and urban people and between lower and upper classes, but the most dramatic of them are recognizable on a regional basis. Distinctive cultural variations still exist in the Deep South, New England, the Midwest, the Southwest and California.

Strangely and unexpectedly, the assembly line and the mass production system have had results almost opposite from what some theorists predicted. Instead of a deadly and uniform standardization, there has been differentiation of both the products and of the people who use them. In other words, the American industrial system, and this includes both the technological and the social organization of the system, has made possible a richer variety than has ever existed in the world before.

Because of refrigeration, transportation, and food preservation, the American is no longer tied to the seasons and cycles of nature. He can vary his diet in ways unknown to his ancestors and to most of his international contemporaries. Because of inventions and gadgets, he can live comfortably in the desert, in the cold of winter, or in the heat of summer. He can travel faster and by more ways than the people of other countries. Admittedly, these are external items; they do not touch immediately the character or the soul of the American. But these material things are the product of the kind of person the American is—pragmatic, imaginative, energetic, and rationalistic.

### 3. THE ADAPTIVE AMERICAN PERSONALITY

Analysis of the American character, that is, of the kind of representative personality found in the United States, has been attempted by both social scientists and popular commentators. Some of these analyses are serious and scholarly attempts, and some are highly impressionistic and biased caricatures. The social personality of Americans cannot be a matter of statistics, of the sheer numbers who conform to the definition, whatever it may be. Usually, when such an analysis is of any value at all, it centers upon a status type of American, like the upper-middle-class, urban, white person.

Whatever else this "typical" American person is, the scientific consensus appears to focus on his adaptiveness.

This is a logical deduction from the enormous dynamism of American society and culture, as well as a generalization based upon direct and empirical observation. Opportunities are so numerous, inventions are so frequent, aspirations are so optimistic, that the American is almost forced to adapt himself to the constantly changing situation. This readiness to shift, implied in the term "adaptiveness," is a central tendency of the ideal American-type personality.

**a.** The influence of the past, the patriotic reverence for a long and hallowed history, is often said to be the reason why a society and its social units become stable. It is absurd to suggest that the United States has no traditions or that our people are not influenced by them. The fact is that one of our most important cultural heritages is precisely the tradition of change and the willingness to change. This has been embedded as a high value, and it is reflected in the adaptive personality.

**b.** The influence of the future is not a contrary or opposite influence to that of the past. The American emphasis on progress is a constituent element of the body of social values that stretches back into American history. Neither progress nor the desire for progress appears to be slowing down in our society. In this sense, the American possesses a "future-directed" personality. An adaptation to future situations, whether foreseen or not, is an essential ingredient of the American character.

**c.** Dependence on self is a virtue strongly urged on American youth. This does not mean a rigid isolation as a lone wolf or as the captain of one's own soul and destiny. It is simply the confidence of the American that he can make the grade, that he must find within himself the resources to respond to every stimulus, or at least to the stimuli that he considers worthwhile.

**d.** Dependence on others is an expression of an American's self-confidence rather than a relationship of helplessness and subordination to others. The American feels that he should be accepted by anybody anywhere, that he can depend upon others to appreciate him, or at least to tolerate him. The typical American expects a great deal of understanding from other persons, without the need to philosophize and to explain his motivation.

e. The need of approval is probably more openly expressed and more widely extended in Americans than in other people. The American personality is expansive in this regard; it wants the appreciation of as many people as possible in addition to family and intimate friends. The American wants to be known as a "good guy," but he does not want to be "taken for a sucker."

f. The mobility of people in American society contributes to the development of the adaptive personality. This means not only social mobility but also the physical and residential movement of individuals and families. It is estimated that the urban family moves its residence approximately three times a decade. In the occupational sphere the shifting of jobs is a social phenomenon unique in its frequency and extent. The sheer amount of travel for pleasure and business has made the United States a nation on wheels and on the wing.

An analysis of this kind does not pretend to delve into the inner motives of the Americans in their constant process of adaption. It may be said, however, that the attitudes and values held by persons tend to conform with their outward expressions of behavior. The American personality has to adapt itself to the social and cultural factors. It must meet the social situation in which it exists.

Any discussion of the adaptive personality implies the important question of whether the social person is the means or the end. If the social person is the center of the society, the important, irreducible physical unit of the group, would one not expect that the institutions and values should be adapted to him rather than vice versa? This is probably an oversimplified question that cannot be fully answered in this form because of the complex relationship between the individual and the society.

Basic social needs are the same everywhere, but the ways of satisfying them differ. People tend to develop the kind of culture that suits them, and culture tends to develop the kind of people that can best utilize it. A dynamic culture will be employed by dynamic people. Adaptive persons will have an adaptive society. In short, adaptability is a central characteristic both of the American personality and of the American society and culture.

## 4. THE NEUROTIC AMERICAN PERSONALITY

It is commonly remarked by critics of the American scene that the fast pace of modern life is making us a nation of neurotics. The thesis is that speed itself somehow generates neurosis, that the inability to keep up the pace leaves people frustrated and nervous, that the ever-increasing tempo makes demands which should not be expected of normal human beings. As evidence for this the critics point to the growing number of neurotic and psychotic cases, the increasing use of drugs, the fact that hospital beds at any given time are occupied by more mental patients than physical patients, that psychoanalysts are more and more in demand.

There appears to be a logical fallacy, however, in the relationship between "speed of living" and the development of the neurotic personality. The neurotic person is one who is confused in his behavior. The sociological question of significance is not whether the modern tempo has quickened or whether change is inherent in the American culture and society. The question is whether the inner conflict of the personality reflects, is caused by, or causes an external sociocultural conflict.

Neurotic persons are considered abnormal because they do not react to other people and to their social and cultural environment in expected and approved ways. For a long time it has been the fashion to look inside the individual for the explanation of abnormal behavior—to delve into his psyche, to search his dreams and fantasies, to measure his instincts, to unravel his traumas and fixations.

If the explanation of the neurotic personality lies fully within the afflicted individual, this is not an area of study for the social scientist. If his condition is, however, a reaction to, and a reflection of, the culture in which he lives, the problem is of prime importance to the sociologist. Certainly one of the criteria we commonly use in judging people is whether their patterns of behavior are congruous with those we call accepted and normal patterns. The criteria are not what any particular individual would judge to be socially normal, but what the society itself generally agrees upon. What is perfectly normal in the American culture may be considered abnormal in the Turkish society, and vice versa.

The mental conflict at the basis of some neuroses among Americans appears to come from outside of the person himself. It appears also that only the relatively intelligent persons who recognize cultural inconsistencies and the relatively scrupulous persons who try to resolve them are the ones most likely to be affected. Some of these inconsistencies are the following.

**a.** The contradictory aspirations to success and to humility tend to drive persons in two opposite directions. This does not mean that a successful person cannot be humble. But the meek do not inherit the earth, at least not the American earth. To be successful you are expected to be aggressive and self-assertive, and the constant attempt to follow this line of conduct almost certainly prevents humility.

**b.** Emphasis on the motives of both profit and service makes it difficult to compromise between them. This is simply another aspect of the attempted balance between self-seeking and self-interest, on the one hand, and brotherly love and universal charity, on the other. In the economic sphere, the American often considers service a salable item and actually provides excellent service in order to make more profit on the commodity he is selling.

**c.** Both honesty and shrewdness are extolled as social virtues in the American culture. The semiprofessionalism of college athletes is a glaring example of this. The suggestion that a student should follow the honor system is made on the very campus where there is a shrewd circumscribing of the amateur code. Within certain limits, a person who "gets away with" dubious practices achieves a kind of prestige even while he convinces himself that honesty is the best policy.

**d.** Conflicting standards of sexual morality are unquestionably a source of puzzlement to young people. They are told to be decent and proper in their relations with the opposite sex, but they are barraged almost from infancy with sensual pictures, advertisements, stories, movies, and songs.

**e.** Both physical ruggedness and bodily comfort are held up as ideal American goals. The largest appeal in the advertisements of most products is the appeal to easier and more comfortable living. But, at the same time, bodily exercise, strength, good health, and sturdiness are highly valued.

A much longer list of these contradictory aspirations can be made or found in almost any introductory textbook in sociology. Why does such a system of values not result in a still greater increase in the neurosis of the American people? The main answer seems to lie in the fact that a person can be socialized to accept as normal both ends of the contradiction. The child is accustomed from his early years to the patterns of compromise in his elders and, ultimately, tends to accept them without any question. This is a prime example of the culture molding the individual. The culture overcomes logic. Since everybody is thinking and acting in these ways, the individual is inhibited from questioning the obviously approved system of behavior, contradictory as it may be.

The personality whose neurosis can be traced to the culture is exceptional as well as abnormal. He has sufficient insight to be troubled by inconsistencies, and in this he is an exception to most people in the society. He is abnormal from the point of view of the society because he does not conform always to its standards.

A final warning must be emphasized, and that is that the recognition of cultural inconsistencies and contradictions does not necessarily make a person neurotic. Most careful students of American society realize the presence of these trends, and it cannot be assumed that they are abnormal personalities. On the other hand, most persons are constantly subjected to cultural influences without being fully aware of them.

5. THE VIOLENT AMERICAN

One of the matters of concern to social scientists has been the apparent increase in the amount of violent behavior in the American society. During the past two decades the FBI statistics have charted an almost steady increase in the annual rate of crimes against persons, and the news media report with some frequency not only the violent actions of individuals and gangs, but also of destructive mobs in the city streets. In reaction to these events there has been a public outcry for the restoration of law and order in our society.

The great majority of Americans are opposed to this violence, feel threatened by it, and are not personally involved in it. Yet it is a large enough phenomenon to raise the question of causality. How do the violent people get that way? Is it a characteristic of the American personality, inhibited by most people but expressed by some? Since the personality is socialized in the midst of the culture, are there historical and sociological factors that help account for the violent Americans?

The following observations are meant to provide a broader perspective on the cultural setting out of which the violent American emerges.

a. The United States is a young country that seems in some ways reluctant to settle down to the maturity of civilized behavior patterns. There remains an apparent nostalgia for the vanished frontier and for the rough, violent men who pioneered the opening of unexplored territories. The fact is that this young country has experienced much violence: the extirpation of the Indians, the brutality of the slave system, the fratricide of the Civil War, the disturbances of labor strikes, the gang warfare of organized crime, and more recently a series of campus uprisings.

b. One of the peculiar facts of contemporary society is that it has not allowed American violence to lie buried in history. The communications media provide a steady flow of violence that seems to have increased in intensity. The news media are their own arbiters of good taste in this matter. So-called detective stories are often extremely detailed in their portrayal of violence. More pervasive than newspapers, magazines, and books is the influence of television, which daily reaches into most of the homes of Americans.

c. As a general rule we may say that the more civilized a society becomes the more self-control and the less violence its citizens will exhibit. The most violent behavior occurs among people who lack self-control in a society that lacks social control. This means that violence is both a symptom and a consequence of weakened social control. We have seen that the whole socialization process, from the point of view of society, is a mechanism for developing conformity to accepted norms of behavior. Where socialization is inadequate these controls tend to break down.

d. Certain values are built into the socialization of Americans. The culture contains a strong emphasis on personal freedom, private rights, individual enterprise, and equal opportunities. In some instances this emphasis is developed at the expense of the counterbalance of social duties, mutual obligations, and corporate responsibility. It appears that the typical violent person tends to ignore, or fails to find, the equilibrium between these two facets of his social personality.

e. America is a land of great promises, but there are Americans for whom these promises have not been kept. According to some social scientists, the frustration engendered by this situation explodes into acts of violent aggression. In this sense the violence is not simply blind and irrational. It comes out of a conviction that America possesses the resources—material, technical, and organizational—to fulfill the promises of a better life for all citizens.

f. Americans are socialized in the expectation of change and improvement. The dynamic quality of the American system may also contribute to the violence of our society. The question is asked: if we can ultimately change all things for the better, why not change them now? It may well be that the principle of deferred gratification operates better in an economy where the emphasis is on production than it does in an economy where the emphasis is on consumption. Impatience is then added to frustration to breed violence.

These comments indicate the complexity of the question of the violent American, and suggest that the forceful suppression of violence by the military or the police still leaves the roots of violence unexamined. The same can be said for the so-called "backlash" legislation that has the valid intention of restoring law and order. Any strong police state can ultimately prevent violence but at the same time fail to find and remove the causes of violence.

## Suggested Readings

Cooley, Charles Horton. *Human Nature and the Social Order*. Glencoe: Free Press, 1956.

Goffman, Erving. *The Presentation of Self in Everyday Life*. Garden City: Doubleday, 1959.

Kluckhohn, Clyde; Murray, H. A.; Schneider, D. M., eds. *Personality in Nature, Society, and Culture*. New York: Knopf, 1954.

Murphy, Gardner. *Personality: A Biosocial Approach to Origins and Structure*. New York: Harper & Row, 1947.

Shibutani, Tamotsu. *Society and Personality: An Interactionist Approach to Social Psychology*. Englewood Cliffs: Prentice-Hall, 1961.

Williams, Robin. *American Society—A Sociological Interpretation*. New York: Knopf, 1961.

Bennis, Warren, and Slater, Philip. *The Temporary Society*. New York: Harper & Row, 1968.

# 2
# Social Status

EVERY PERSON HAS HIS "PLACE" IN THE GROUPS AND
the society to which he belongs. Society is not a haphazard, accidental conglomeration of human beings; it
is an orderly arrangement of parts, and the social structure can be conceptualized as a kind of scaffolding on
which each separate part can be recognized. Although
persons and status always go together, it is possible to
think of them abstractly as separate concepts. Social
status is the place the person occupies in the social structure, as judged here and evaluated by the people in the
society.

Everybody "has" social status, and the term does not
refer merely to high prestige and rank, nor does it refer
to the subjective opinion the individual holds of himself.
A person's subjective evaluation of his own social status
may be correct or erroneous when it is tested by objective
criteria. Social status is the rank or position that the person's contemporaries objectively accord to him within
his society.

## ORIGIN OF STATUS

The scientific concept of status is not fixed by mere
volatile public favor or disfavor which may make a person very popular one year and reject him the next.
Furthermore, in the maintenance or change of one's social
status the person is not an inert subject of the society's
whims. How, then, does a person come to have one particular social status rather than another? Social scientists
have analyzed the origin of status and recognize the two
main ways in which social status can be fixed.

*Ascription* of status refers to the fact that the society
applies certain criteria of evaluation to the individual
without any action on his part. The clearest example of
this is the criterion of ancestry, since a person has no
choice whatever about being born into an Italian or

51

Irish family, a royal or peasant stock, the black or the white race. Although it is true that ultimately all status is ascribed to the individual by his society, we refer here only to those characteristics that are, at least originally, out of the control of the individual.

*Achievement* of status refers to the socially evaluated results of effort on the part of the individual. This achievement works in two directions. A brilliant physicist not only enhances his own social prestige by his performance but also reflects honor and prestige on his whole scientific profession. If royalty as an ancestral criterion decreases in social prestige in a particular country, it may be possible that an efficient and successful king will through his own achievement raise the social value of the royal status. Thus a person is not merely a passive recipient automatically placed in a social status. His own behavior raises or lowers his status.

Sociologists sometimes speak also of *assumption* of status in reference to the individual's voluntary choice of entrance into a new status. A person may choose law as an occupation instead of carpentry; he may choose to marry or remain single, to marry into a "better" family, to assume parenthood in marriage, to accept a political appointment, to join an exclusive country club. These are all examples of the voluntary assumption of status which attaches to the acceptance of new social roles. But it must be remembered that each of these roles requires preparation, and in this sense an aspect of achievement rather than of mere assumption is involved.

It must also be noted that there is an interplay and overlapping of the ways in which status originates for the individual. People are neither completely and passively at the mercy of society's judgment, nor are they completely and actively the creators of their own social status. In the ultimate analysis, social status refers not to what you do, or what you are, or what you think you are, but to what people in the society think you are.

A person may work very hard all his life in an ascribed lowly position and never achieve much increase in social status. On the other hand, he may step into an occupational opportunity that automatically carries high status. It is possible too, especially in the less competitive societies, for a person to be relatively indifferent to social success, do hardly anything to achieve it, and still enjoy fairly high social status.

### DETERMINANTS OF STATUS

When we talk about determinants, or factors, of high or low status, we do not mean that these items of themselves give status. Status is a mental construct, a degree of esteem or disesteem which people in a society display toward individual persons. Ancestry and wealth, for example, are not inherently status-giving items. The kind of ancestry and the amount of wealth help us to determine objectively the status of the person, but this is possible only because these items are given social significance by the way in which people in the society evaluate them.

There is considerable variation throughout the world, from society to society, in the significance of status symbols, or determinants. But since status is socially defined, that is, determined by factors outside the individual, there exist certain universal criteria of approval and disapproval, esteem and disesteem. In most general terms, these are contained in the social values, that is, the things that people consider important and worthwhile. In specific terms, these criteria can be broken down into a series of determinants, or factors, universally present, in combination and in varying degrees of emphasis, wherever people live in social collectivities.

In attempting to judge the social status of any individual as well as of any family or any social category, the following criteria must be employed; and they can be more or less objectively measured. No single one of these criteria is sufficient for the evaluation of status; they must be taken in combination.

a. Ancestry gives one a privileged or inferior position because the fact of being well-born or low-born has a certain value even in a professedly democratic society. The esteem or disesteem of a particular person's ancestry rests on several factors: legitimacy or illegitimacy of birth, reputation of the parents, the family's length of residence in the area. One's racial background is often given prominent consideration (whether one is Negro, Indian, Asiatic, or Caucasian); and one's ethnic or national background (whether English, Mexican, Italian, French, and so on), is also usually of considerable importance.

**b.** Wealth, in one form or another, is likewise a universal criterion of social status. It is a convenient, objective measurement because possessions are tangible items. They can be counted and graded. They allow the possessor to display the degree to which he can afford to live in style, comfort, and in general well-being. The source of one's wealth is also socially significant, since newly-acquired or ill-gotten wealth does not give so much prestige as inherited wealth or that obtained in a socially approved fashion.

**c.** The functional utility which a person serves is also an important criterion of social status. A person is ranked according to what he "does" in a society, and this again depends upon what the people think is worth doing. In a society where the economic institution is paramount, a person will be scored heavily on the basis of his gainful occupation. On this criterion alone, we may say that the president of a bank is socially valued higher than the janitor of a bank. It is also true that certain functional categories (like medicine or engineering) may be ranked higher than others (like school teaching or police work).

**d.** The amount and kind of education are determinants of social status in every society. In some societies there are sharp distinctions between the illiterate and the literate. In societies where formal schooling is compulsory, the gradations are numerous and more subtle but nonetheless real. A person with higher education also has higher social status. The college degree is a symbol of status, and the degree has even more social value if it is earned at a college or university with high social prestige.

**e.** The kind and degree of religion one professes are also determinants of social status. The general values of society always include some attitude toward the supernatural. In most societies this is an attitude of approval; in a few societies formal attempts have sometimes been made to lower the esteem of religion as a criterion of social status. In a society where only one large religious body exists, one's relation to, and position in, that body has great significance for social status. In a society where numerous churches and denominations exist, these religious bodies themselves tend to be rated on a hierarchy of status.

f. Biological characteristics are important criteria by which a society places any particular individual in a higher or lower social status. Sex appears to be a universal criterion in the sense that most societies accord the male a higher status than the female. Femininity is generally subordinated to masculinity as a social value. The differences of degree are vast from society to society, for in one place and time there may be a tendency toward equality of the sexes, and in another place and time the lines of inequality may be rigidly preserved. Age is also a universal physical criterion of social status, at least in the sense that adulthood is valued more highly than infancy. The application of this criterion also differs widely. In some societies aged persons are valued, respected, and almost venerated, while in other societies there is a notable accent on youth. Closely allied to both age and sex is the concept of physical beauty as appraised by the people. The standards of beauty are variable as to height and weight, bodily contours, facial profile, skin color, and hair type, but such standards do exist everywhere.

THE TRANSFER OF STATUS

Although the person and his status are always intimately connected, we have been analyzing them in the abstract as separable items. The description of the social person tells us *what he is*, while the description of the social status tells us what he possesses of value in the opinion of the society in which he lives. What we are saying is that the social status is transferred to the social person himself. That which the society approves or disapproves indicates also, in this transfer, those whom the society esteems or disesteems. In other words, people tend to evaluate the individual according to the items of value that he possesses.

Transfer of status may be demonstrated by several familiar examples. It is usually the head of the family, the husband and father, who represents to the outside world the social status of the family members. Generally speaking, we may say that the wife and children reflect and share his social status, so that in a sense his social status is transferred to them. Another example of status transfer is that of a person holding an important office in a society. A president or a premier, a cardinal or a bishop, may have great personal popularity based on his intelligence, integrity, charm, and competence. These are subjective qualities by which he achieves increased prestige, but in addition he is held in high esteem because of the office he occupies, and one may say that this status transfers to the person himself. There is both charisma of office and charisma of person, and these are mutually influential.

There is still another kind of transfer, one in which a person may be said to "cash in" on his status, or in which a group gets the advantages of status earned elsewhere. A banker becomes a trustee in a university; an industrialist is appointed ambassador; an athlete becomes public relations officer for a chain of food stores. In each of these cases the status of the person is transferred; his social prestige and value are carried over into a different area of behavior. Retired military and naval officers of high rank have been employed by large industries doing business with the federal government. They probably know little or nothing about industrial production but they are valuable because of their high status or rank.

## SOCIAL POWER AND STATUS

It is sometimes said that social power, the influence a person is able to exert over others in society, is a criterion of the status he possesses. Although one may think of social power as a quick and ready rule of thumb to measure social status, this influence is a consequent rather than a determinant of social status. It is obvious that people with high social status have much more influence in a community than people with low social status. Even the person who may be said to have "achieved power" has done so mainly because he first achieved the social position from which to exercise influence.

It appears that this is the main reason why some people seek to improve their social status; they do this not merely to enjoy a feeling of superiority or of self-satisfaction, but because the possession of high status makes it possible for them to get concrete results in their dealings with others. This is especially noticeable in a dynamic society where opportunities for upward mobility exist. The person who is a "nobody" socially may have great ambitions, but he is hindered in many ways in the fulfillment of his ambitions.

We need not at this point discuss the characteristics of leadership and personal influence in modern society. The personal ability to persuade others is given much attention by psychologists, but the student of society is interested in the social origins and effects of this leadership. It must be pointed out that although social power accompanies and accrues to status, the latter is not the only source of influence and power. An individual may achieve higher status through personal effort, and it is also through effort and ability that he may achieve social power. The "kingmaker," the "man behind the throne," the manager for a political figure, and similar persons frequently wield an extraordinary amount of influence. To the extent that such a person is widely known to the public he may be said to have status as well as power.

## TYPES OF STATUS

The quantitative concepts of higher and lower, more or less, better or worse, inhere in the very notion of social status and stratification; it requires no special insight to recognize a classification of persons on this basis. In fact, the whole concept of class and of social stratification refers to one's status in relation to the status of others.

This relative position is legitimated by the society itself; it is socially approved to the extent that the items of value it reflects are institutionalized and expressed by the society itself. Not only the person, but also the group in which he participates, is accorded social status.

The major and basic social groups are the familial, educational, recreational, economic, political, and religious. As we shall see further, these groups are structured by the arrangement of the positions of persons within them. This makes it possible for us to speak about a person's *group status*—family status, an economic status, a religious status, and so forth. Within the family, for example, the individual may have the status of grandfather or of infant daughter; within the school system that of college professor or second-grade pupil; within the church that of bishop or sacristan.

There is another way of looking at group status. Every large society differentiates among its major basic groups in the sense that it accords more social prestige to one group than to another. This question centers on the relativity of the social value placed on the major functioning groups. A woman may enjoy higher social status as an actress than as a wife and mother. A man may be accorded higher status because he is an architect than because he is a deacon in his church. It is unlikely, realistically, that a person will enjoy high status in all the major groups in which he participates.

KEY STATUS

Each person has as many statuses as there are groups in which he participates, but he has also one principal status. The determination of this key status for any particular individual depends not only upon the status that he has assumed and achieved but also, mainly, upon the values current in the society. In a society where economic values and institutions carry high prestige, a person's gainful occupation will usually indicate his key status. Ordinarily, the familial status would be the key status for a mother with growing children, but if she also happens to be a successful businesswoman she would be valued even more highly for her key economic status. This would obviously differ in a society where the family, or the church, or the state, was the dominant collectivity.

The key status is a useful sociological tool for the analysis of the total social personality. It is the largest "window" that a person opens to the world about him, and it is through this window that the society sees and interprets his other statuses. People are typed, and sometimes stereotyped, by their key status—as college student, Woolworth heiress, auto mechanic, home-run king. It is at this point that what a person does prominently, that is, his key social role, is closely linked with his key status.

It is sometimes said that social status is what people think you are and social role is what people think you do. Evaluation, measurement, and judgment by others enter into the concepts of role and status. There is a clear distinction between these two concepts, but in the concrete social situation they go hand in hand. A person does, or is expected to do, certain things in accord with his status; that is why we say that the achievements of the individual affect his status. Certain roles carry higher status than others, and a person's key status attaches to the role his society considers the most significant.

In general terms we may say that the social roles carrying the highest prestige, or status, are relatively scarce in a society. They usually require certain skills and abilities not shared by large numbers of people. There are few corporation presidents in comparison to the rank and file of employed persons, and the skills required in the role of corporation president are considerably greater than those required in the lower industrial positions. There is only one heavyweight boxing champion. To hold this title and to enjoy the status that accompanies it, the pugilist has to fulfill the requirements of the role. The key social role refers to the functions that accompany the key status, while the key status refers, at least in part, to the evaluation that people place upon the function.

## STATION IN LIFE

The complex analysis of the social person, as he is seen and judged by others, demonstrates that each individual has many statuses but that only one of these is adjudged his key status. The person is a social totality, and he has a "total social status" which some sociologists call his station in life. This is a combination of all his social statuses; it is the generalized position that emerges when all the criteria of status are combined to form a single evaluation of the person. Station in life is heavily influenced by, but is not identical with, key status. It does not refer merely to a person's position in his family, in industry, in political, educational, recreational, or religious groups, but to a combination of all these statuses.

The sociological reality of one's station in life is readily recognized in the fact that class status is a universal social phenomenon. It is the individual's known "class position." Most people in any society have a rough concept of the meaning of upper, lower, and middle classes, and they recognize that one's station in life is his position in one class or another. As a matter of knowledge at this point of our study, social class may be defined as a category of people whose station in life is roughly similar; they are on a similar status level; they are socially acceptable to one another more readily than they are to people on other social levels.

It is sometimes said that social class itself is a determinant of station in life; but this statement appears to be tautological. The two terms reflect each other and are at best two ways of looking at the same phenomenon. From the point of view of the person himself, his station in life places him automatically in one or another of the social classes. From the point of view of the class category, the evaluation of class depends upon the station in life of those persons who constitute that class.

## STATUS AND STRATIFICATION

Since social status is the rank of one person in relation to others, and since social class is the rank of one category of people in relation to others, it is logical for the same criteria to be employed in identifying both. In other words, ancestry, wealth, function, education, religion, and biological characteristics reflect social values around which people are clustered into classes. People who have low status, as measured by all these criteria, are people who "belong" to the lower class. Social class, like social status, is a generalized position emerging from extrinsic evaluation. It is a mental construct that results from social consensus, and it does not refer to inherent or developed moral qualities in the individual.

Social stratification refers to the horizontal "layers" or strata into which the people of a society are arranged. A social stratum is conceptualized in relation to other strata in order to include large numbers of people placed similarly. Since every person is unique, it is possible that the infinitesimal shadings of differences would allow a continuum from one end of the social hierarchy to the other. This attempt, however, would probably be as useless as it is difficult to realize. General similarities are recognized in any society, so that people conveniently fall into stratified categories. It has long been customary to speak of lower, middle, and upper classes, but in a highly-stratified society there are recognizable differences in each of these broad categories; for example, people do talk of upper-middle and lower-middle social classes.

From the point of view of status, every group is stratified, and from the point of view of class, every society is stratified. Thus stratification of some degree and kind is universally present in social life. Even a recreational club has leaders and active and passive members. The positions of subordination and superordination are obvious in schools, churches, factories, and wherever else people have systematic social relations. From the scientific point of view, the aspiration for complete democracy or for perfect equality among people has no chance of fulfillment. Similarly, the idealistic promotion of a completely classless society is both unrealistic and impossible.

It is nevertheless true in some Western countries that the effort to introduce equality of opportunity and democratic human relations has resulted in a rearrangement of the class structure. Numerous societies have traditionally maintained a system in which a relatively small, wealthy, and powerful upper class controlled the large mass of people in the lower class. The so-called "revolt of the masses" appears to be stirring currently in many of these societies. In the democratic, Western societies, the spread of political, economic, educational, and other opportunities to the largest number of people has resulted in the growth of a relatively stable middle class and of a more complex and multiple system of stratification.

Social stratification is a highly complex arrangement, which to be understood requires a careful analysis of the multiple criteria of status. The concept is rendered practically meaningless by adherence to a simple distinction between the rich and the poor, the capitalist and the worker, the haves and the have-nots. This kind of distinction is prevalent because wealth and income, or their lack, are readily recognized. It must be emphasized, however, that wealth and a man's position in the economy are not the only determinants of his social class. In almost any large population, there are people of "good family" who are relatively poor, and there are people of great means who strive unsuccessfully to "break into" the upper class.

## SOCIAL INEQUALITY AND MOBILITY

Social status would have no meaning if there were no inequalities among the persons in the society and no scarcities in the items that people value as the criteria of prestige. Since perfect equality in the distribution of these items is impossible, complete social equality is impossible. Thus, a status-less and stratum-less society is unthinkable. This statement is true from both the subjective and objective point of view. Subjectively, individual persons have different degrees of competence, intelligence, and energy, and this is important insofar as it helps them to achieve or assume status. Objectively and extrinsically the criteria of social status cannot be shared equally even in the most doctrinaire socialist society.

In most instances, a person's possession of these valued items may increase or decrease. He may decrease his wealth and increase his education; he may adhere more closely to, or fall away from, approved patterns of religious behavior. There is little he can do about ancestry, sex, or age, but people have been known to invent genealogies, to accentuate their physical beauty, and to make themselves appear younger or older than their years. Popular emphasis on one social criterion may change in relation to another so that there will be shifts in those items that people consider important. For example, the athlete or actress may have higher status in one time and place than in another. But these shifts of values and of emphasis on values are usually slow and unspectacular.

Status and class are relatively enduring and unchanging universal social phenomena. Social mobility refers to the shifting of a person from one status to another and from one class to another. Traversing the "social distance" between any two statuses is the manifestation of vertical social mobility. This means going up or down, being more esteemed or less esteemed in the opinion of the society; if the distance covered is large enough, it means going up or down from one class to another.

The amount and rate of social mobility vary greatly from society to society. An "open class" society is one in which the opportunities for social mobility are relatively numerous. This is especially characteristic of a dynamic, progressive society in which competition has a high value, closed aristocracies of birth are belittled, and individual prowess is applauded.

## Peculiarities of Status Relationships in America
### 1. THE CHANGING STATUS OF WOMEN
Since the turn of the century the American reading public has been constantly made aware of women's rights, of the influence of women in public life, of the striving for sex equality, of the subtle dangers of "Momism." There are many evidences that the social status of the contemporary American female is quite different from that of women in most other modern countries. The

periodicals, television and radio shows, newspaper columns, books, and lectures that have dealt with the "woman question" indicate that female influence is increasing and that women's status is being raised.

Female status cannot be measured except in relation to the status of males. It is a fact that gross sex inequalities abound at the higher occupational and professional levels. Separate women's organizations, or "auxiliaries," are still much in evidence. Indeed, the theme of the so-called "feminine mystique" is that in many ways women are accepting submissive domesticity. On the other hand, there has been a resurgence of organized effort to gain women's rights. The National Organization for Women (NOW) invites male membership and seeks the rational reform of institutions. Some groups in the Women's Liberation Movement see males as the oppressors, want to overthrow the capitalist system and the American structure.

Complete equality of the sexes has not been achieved. Nevertheless, demonstrable changes have occurred in the status of the American female, as indicated by the following observations.

a.  Probably the most far-reaching change of all is that in the economic status of women. The stereotype of the helpless female who knows nothing about finances, is careless with money, and is completely dependent upon males for material support has vanished from reality, although it still exists in fiction. Women have come to possess wealth, a very important criterion of social status. It is estimated that more than half of the corporation stock in the United States is registered in the names of women and that about 90 percent of the purchase of consumer goods is made on the decisions of women. Unlike the ownership of stock, the making of retail purchases indicates the control of wealth. The deference paid to women customers hinges around this fact, and this deference is tantamount to a rise in status.

b.  The functional utility of women to the society has also been an indicator of the rise of social status. Women are often called the "culture bearers" in the sense that they preserve the values of a society. This function in the family and in the community is of great significance. Functional utility has widened also in the area of gainful employment. The tremendous increase in service occupations in our industrial economy has been largely handled by women. The great majority of telephone operators, secretaries, stenographers, file clerks, retail-sales people, school teachers, and social workers are women. With the exception of heavy industrial labor and the upper occupational echelons, women have accepted and performed adequately most of the gainful occupations previously reserved for males. Women are not only employed, they are contributing useful functions highly valued by their society. This utility is a criterion of their increased status.

**c.** The change in the political status of women began when they achieved equal suffrage a half century ago. In addition, women have become active party workers in city, county and state politics, and have been delegates to the national conventions of the major parties. They have achieved cabinet membership, ambassadorships and consular posts in foreign countries, and congressional office. Politicians listen respectfully to the League of Women Voters and to various civic groups that press for political reform. Large numbers of women are employed in the agencies of federal, state, and local government.

**d.** The level of female education is rising. This too has contributed importantly to higher social status for women. More women are being formally educated in America than ever before, they are spending more years in higher education, the kind of education they are receiving is often not specifically feminine, and they are matriculating at and graduating from the traditionally best colleges and universities of the country. While the exclusive women's colleges continue to enjoy a high prestige, they are educating a decreasing proportion of American girls.

**e.** In our society's recreational groupings, women have demanded and obtained a greater freedom of activity. Most fields of athletic competition, including even pro-

fessional wrestling and horse racing, have been opened
to them. They patronize gambling places, taverns, and
night clubs. In some few larger cities, exclusively male
grills, clubs, and bars continue the attempt to stem the
"invasion" of women patrons. But other areas of recreation
make deliberate efforts to attract female interest and
women customers with special devices like "ladies' day"
at the ball park and cut-rate tickets for women's clubs.

f.   From another point of view the rise of women's status
is seen in the fact that females are often a symbol of male
social mobility. It is not historically unusual that the
successful male demonstrates his status by adorning and
exhibiting his womenfolk, but this has reached unprecedented proportions in the American society. The male
wants his wife to "have the best," and the result is a
curious mixture of social pressure, upward mobility, symbols of status, desire for comfort, and response to advertising. Clothing, household appliances, automobiles, and
female participation in luncheon and garden clubs are
not only demonstrations of the female rise in status, but
also reflections of the station of life of the head of the
family.

It must be noted at this point that women still suffer
large inequalities in our society. Women still find little
room "at the top" as business executives, bankers, and
stockbrokers. There are relatively few females in den-
tistry, law, and architecture. They are not widely employed as university administrators and professors. Hardly
any women enter the professional clergy, although there
is now a vocal minority seeking ordination in the relatively high liturgical churches.

From the historical point of view, however, all the
changes we have described have contributed to a higher
evaluation of women in the American society. This does
not mean that earlier American females were treated
with dishonor and disesteem. In fact, the scarcity of
women and the moral climate of the colonies and the
frontier helped to keep women on a pedestal. To a large
extent this was chiefly ascription of status. The fundamental difference at the present time in the rise of female

status rests in the fact that women have been granted the opportunities to achieve higher status.

## 2. THE AMBIGUOUS STATUS OF YOUTH

The American society is remarkable in the modern world because of its youth problems. Organized revolt on the college campus, the militancy of black youth in the cities, the increase of dropouts and conscientious objectors, adult worry about the restoration of law and order—all these indicate a peculiar and vexing social problem. It seems safe to say that no major society in the history of the world has had to grapple with a youth problem of such magnitude and complexity.

We have seen that a person's age is one criterion of his social status in any society. We are speaking here of the status of young people as a general population-category as well as of youth as a criterion of status. "Youthfulness" —the desire to stay young and look young—has an extraordinarily high value in the American culture. The cult of youth as a criterion of social status has become almost a fetish. Social pressure to "keep young and fit" is exerted even upon the aged in the style of clothes and cosmetics for both sexes. Dieting and slenderizing are not merely for health's sake; even older people are expected to maintain their enthusiasm and interest for sports. Often the "old grads" seem to be more devoted to the football heroes than are the college students themselves. Youth as a social status appears to be valued and appreciated by everyone except the teenager.

Some of the factors which make this ambiguity of status possible in our society are the following.

a. Youth in America is largely functionless except in a preparatory fashion. We have said that the utility of the function performed is an important criterion of social status. American youth has no specific function except to "grow up." This is what happens in a society that finds child labor uneconomic and keeps its adolescents in economic dependence. Young people are in a waiting period, rather than a transitional one, between dependent childhood and independent adulthood. In most societies, the great majority of boys and girls are gainfully employed by the age of fourteen or fifteen. They are doing something that is considered important and is taken seriously by their contemporaries and themselves.

**b.** From another point of view this is a period of extended adolescence. There is no sharp and formal distinction, no approved rites of passage, between the status of the child and the status of the adult. The male or female who is sexually mature and intellectually adult is ready to assume the responsibilities of adulthood. Culturally and socially, however, such persons are still in the status of boys or girls. This situation is fraught with strains and frustrations for everyone concerned. The refusal of adults to take adolescents seriously is often accompained by the refusal of adolescents to take adults seriously. There is more than flippancy in the youthful slogan, "you can't trust anyone over thirty."

**c.** Prolonged education of youth often leads to restlessness and ambivalence, although it ultimately gives the individual greater social prestige as an adult person. Because Americans value formal education so highly and try to provide educational opportunities for all, the young people here stay in school much longer than the youth of other countries. The American belief that anyone with talent should have an opportunity for college education has sometimes given the added meaning that anyone who can afford to pay for higher education should have it. Young people are expected and urged to continue their schooling even when they have no interest and less competence for further learning. It is little wonder that some high school and college students find an outlet for their interests and energies in an excessive pursuit of recreation, in vandalism, strikes, and riots.

**d.** Youth is more easily adapted to change than is adulthood. The process of socialization, especially the willingness to accept new and progressive ideas, is quicker and more extensive in youth, often resulting in a clash of values with older people. The "generation gap" is a logical phenomenon in a dynamic society. Because he is confused about his own status, the youth seeks greater varieties of self-expression. The dynamic aspect of American society and culture is nowhere so dramatically demonstrated as in our adolescents with their characteristic volatile fads and fashions and their slogans and catchwords.

**e.** American youth often has the duties of a child and the privileges of an adult. Dating, which has no direct connection with marriage preparation and which starts at fourteen or fifteen, involves the operation of automobiles and many adult forms of recreation, such as drinking, with the frequentation of taverns and nightclubs. The girl is encouraged by her parents to be "popular with boys" but also to keep herself chaste and decent. Even here the standards of popularity and decency are ambiguous and sometimes in conflict because the terms are understood differently by parents and children.

These circumstances indicate the lack of a clear-cut, universally acceptable youth status in the United States. There are differences from region to region, from class to class, from one ethnic group to another, but these differences do not constitute the basic ambiguity concerning the status. The ambiguity exists in the minds of youth and in the minds of adults. Neither can say clearly and in detail how the general criteria of status apply to youth and how the expectations of behavior are patterned. The fact is that youth is in "flux" in a way peculiar to this society itself rather than to the physical characteristics of youth.

This discussion should not lead to any alarmist conclusion about the future of American society. It is probable that our dynamic, open, progressive, adaptive society requires this kind of youth status. The fact that the majority of young men can meet satisfactory standards of military discipline and efficiency, and that they "settle down" later to become competent employees, dependable citizens, and responsible fathers and husbands; the fact that the majority of young females assume their adult roles in a satisfactory manner—all of this indicates that the ambiguity of the youth status does not spell doom for the American society.

3. THE CHANGING STATUS OF AMERICAN BLACKS

Race relations in the United States provides a "laboratory" in which the student of society can test the generalizations of social science. Here we are concerned only with the status of the American Negro, and particularly with the application of the criteria of social status. This "laboratory" has become more and more open to the gaze of foreign observers and has become a scene of intensified activity by Americans themselves.

What we have before us is the dramatic upward shift of a whole social category from slave status, that is, from a position below and outside the American citizenry. The continuous rise of the social status of Negroes is not a proof of the change in criteria by which status is judged. These criteria are universal in every society, but the emphasis on one or another of the criteria differs. A process of interaction has taken place. The evaluation of the Negro by whites has changed because of the achievement of status by Negroes, and this achievement has been made possible largely by white ascription of status to Negroes. In other words, the complete explanation does not lie either in the statement that "Blacks have pulled themselves up by their own boot straps," or in the statement that "whites have changed their attitudes towards Blacks."

The most dramatic feature of this analysis is the switch in values—together with a new terminology—instigated by the Black Muslims, promoted by the Black nationalists, and gaining popular strength in the Black Power movement. It is as though a new cultural identity has been established in the repudiation of white norms and criteria of social status. For these people it is old-fashioned to talk about "Negroes" and to have reliance on the civilrights movement.

The following remarks are indicative of the manner in which Black status differs from Negro status.

a. The popular slogan "Black is beautiful" refers not only to skin color, physical characteristics, and "natural" hair style. It refers also to African modes of dress, distinctive kinds of music, and even to the preparation of "soul food," which does not originate in Africa but in the rural South. The basic principle is a repudiation of Caucasian cultural standards, which are considered "decadent" by the strongest supporters of the Black movement.

b. Black leaders sometimes remark that all people in this country are hyphenated Americans and verify their cultural identity by recognizing their ethnic ancestry. There should be a recognition of Afro-Americans as distinct from Polish-Americans or Italian-Americans. Like these groups, the Blacks should have a second language and ought to learn Swahili.

c. The radical shift of status is traced partly to the religious radicalism of the Black Muslims, who repudiate not only Christianity but also the highest values of Western civilization. The influence of this radicalism is seen also in the so-called Black caucuses in the various Christian denominations. These groups are not necessarily separating themselves from the parent denominations, but they seek much more power and influence within them. Furthermore, they are demanding from the Christian churches millions of dollars in "reparation" for the historical sins committed against Black Americans by generations of white Christians.

d. The demands of Black capitalism are not genuinely radical. They are rather a recognition of the traditional American appreciation of the power of wealth in the achievement of social status. Pride of status is exhibited in the establishment of independent Black banks, insurance companies, chains of retail stores, and other economic enterprises. The argument is that Blacks as customers should promote the general wealth of the Black population.

e. The high social value placed on formal schooling in the United States necessarily raises the status of persons having such schooling. The percentage of Black Americans attending colleges and universities is higher than the percentage of all citizens obtaining similar education in any of the other major countries in the world. A new emphasis has been introduced, however, at the higher levels of schooling by the establishment of departments and programs of Afro-American studies. What seems more important is the deliberate effort of universities to recruit Black students to graduate and professional schools, from which they can enter the better-paying occupations in our society.

f.  There can be no doubt that the radical protest of Black Americans has accelerated all of these changes in status. Nevertheless, the consciousness of democratic and egalitarian values in the general American society has also greatly influenced the changes. This consciousness is partly a consequence of the way in which social goals are emphasized as a reaction to the world situation in which the free nations are at odds with the totalitarian nations. The practical acceptance of social values and ideals by the majority of Americans has worked constantly in favor of Black Americans.

When all of this has been said, we must recognize that the majority of Black Americans are probably still adherents of the American dream of upward mobility. From the institutional point of view they seem to recognize that the American criteria of status are still applicable to most of the citizenry. The Negro is shifting in large numbers from the emotional religious sects to more conservative and even liturgical forms of religion. He is participating in forms of recreation with higher status, like golf and tennis, and is accepted in professional and collegiate sports. Although the "search" for talented Blacks is given much publicity, the racial barriers to achievement of status are only gradually breaking down in the major economic, political, and educational groups; but the changes do add up to a new and higher social status for American Blacks.

4.  RELIGION AS A CRITERION OF STATUS

Religion is one of the major institutions found in every society. The extent to which religion may be used as an important indicator of social status depends very much on the values the society puts on religious participation and practices. The United States is said to be a secular society with a this-worldly culture; if this is true, one may assume that intangible supernatural items are less effective criteria for social status than measurable secular items.

It is probably true that social status has always been measured more by secular than sacred standards. Even in theocratic societies, the measuring rods of holiness—like poverty, humility, and charity—probably did not help appreciably to elevate a person to high social status. Family status, wealth, and education have apparently always been more significant values to the great masses of people. Religious status might add to or detract from general social status, but religion itself has not been one of the most emphasized criteria.

In the United States organized religion is considered respectable. Church affiliation is an asset for persons like politicians and businessmen who have to meet and please the public. There is probably no high public official who would admit to having no religion. Governors of states, and other high officials, have been known to get themselves baptized and to join a church. It is estimated that about 40 percent of Americans are not members of churches, but seldom does an American admit in an interview or on a questionnaire that he is an atheist.

a. The kind of religion to which one belongs reflects the social status of the individual and contributes to that status. The emotional, noisy, "shouting" religions may satisfy a need for some individuals, but they are followed mainly by people of low social status. The dozen major religious bodies of the United States vary in their influence depending largely on the region of the country where they exist and on the local membrship of the church.

b. The conservative and traditional churches which pursue their functions unobtrusively and do not put great demands upon their members are typical of the high-status religions. They represent a kind of haven for the energetic and harassed American. They provide reassurance and comfort, and satisfy the important American quest for security. It is as though everything else must change, but these upper-class religions must remain stable.

c. A tolerant church is also highly appreciated by those who are attempting to maintain or to achieve high social status. The fiercely evangelical and openly proselytizing church is a disturbing element; it makes a great ado over relatively "unimportant things" like theological doctrines. A broad-mindedness in doctrine which allows various interpretations represents an attitude that many Americans consider worth striving for.

d. Americans expect their churches to have a social welfare approach, but mainly in the sense of providing recreational facilities and congenial atmosphere for the membership. Churches with upper-class membership sometimes provide professional marital counseling and even psychiatric help for the members. They usually support certain "good works" for the unfortunate in other parts of the city. The individual can demonstrate his social status by contributing generously to these causes.

e. The opportunity for lay participation in the actual administration of a congregation, especially among the Protestant churches, also provides an avenue for upward social mobility. A person may gain social recognition through these activities when he finds himself blocked and frustrated in the secular channels of mobility. Many of the functions thus performed are in essence secular, but they seem to take on an aura of extra spiritual value because they are being done "for the church."

In the last analysis it may be said that religion in America conserves social status for the individual. This is probably more true in the smaller towns and in the growing suburbs than it is in the anonymous metropolitan areas. Religion is the slowest-changing major institution in the American culture. The religious groups, especially those with the highest aura of social prestige and respectability, tend to conform to, rather than to change, the secular milieu in which they exist. They help the individual himself to conform to his social status.

5. Achievement Versus Ascription of Status

America is called the land of unlimited opportunities, not only by foreigners who are anxious to immigrate, but also by many Americans themselves. It is part of our folklore that anyone can go as high as his competence will allow. The youngster is urged to compete seriously because there is "always room at the top." There may even now be progressive and hopeful parents who have aspirations that their newborn daughter may some day become president of the United States.

The realistic fact is that achievement of social status is quite carefully circumscribed by many limiting conditions, even in the United States. In the ultimate analysis, as we have seen, all social status is ascribed, because it depends upon the way in which the society judges the individual, his family, and his class. While there is room for achievement of status, there are also definite hindrances. Some of the more obvious hindrances to achievement of social status are the following.

a. A ceiling exists for industrial workers because the specialization of function requires highly trained and educated personnel. It is no longer realistic to think of entering a factory as a mechanic's helper and working up to the presidency. Specialists are being channeled in from the colleges on those levels to which and through which the ordinary skilled worker cannot penetrate. This is a structural limitation on ascending social mobility which will probably become even more rigid.

b. The quota system is sometimes used in areas which could be normal avenues for upward mobility. Because of racial, ethnic, or religious background some people are limited or excluded from certain preparatory schools, colleges, and universities and from some country clubs, resort hotels, and even residential areas. In these instances the achievement of social status is thwarted before it can begin. It is to be expected that these practices will tend to decrease to the degree that the American people become more liberal and tolerant.

c. Restrictive covenants in residential areas can no longer be validly defended in American courts, but there are innumerable gentleman's agreements not to sell choice properties to "undesirable elements" of the population. A good address is more than a mere symbol of social status or a place for comfortable and convenient living. It also involves the opportunity for social relations with those persons, and with that class, which are known to live in the neighborhood.

d. Limitations on marriage opportunities, while not so rigid in American society as in other societies, are nevertheless real. It is not only people of the upper class who warn their children to be careful about their dates; most American parents are concerned that their children "marry well." The American "in-law problem" is not merely a problem of psychological maladjustment between relative strangers; it is more often the attitude that the son-in-law or daughter-in-law is "not good enough," that is, is not of sufficiently high social status to satisfy the family.

e. Regional disparities often hinder the bright boy or girl from making the most of opportunities. This is partly a matter of rural isolation and partly a matter of relative poverty of some regions of the country. To achieve higher social status a person has to be in a location where facilities for self-improvement exist. This lack is most noticeable in areas where schools are inadequately staffed and the number of school days are kept at a minimum.

f. Identification with "foreign ideologies" of a leftist nature tends to restrict social respectability and achievement of status. Radical groups which now identify themselves as "Maoists" are as unpopular as those which once promoted Russian communism. There is still a kind of guilt by association that hampers people who are suspect of such affiliations and would otherwise have careers of high social status. This is, in effect, analogous to social ostracism and earlier kinds of religious excommunication.

These hindrances to the achievement of social status are to some extent variable. In some respects they appear to be increasing in intensity and in other respects decreasing. At any rate, they are an indication that the dream of opportunity for all is a restricted dream, that the nature of social stratification, and of the criteria upon which status is judged, ultimately implies inequalities. American society, like every other society, contains these inequalities, but they are not so numerous or so restrictive here as in many of the less dynamic societies of the world.

## Suggested Readings

Bendix, Reinhard, and Lipset, S. M., eds. *Class, Status and Power*. Glencoe: Free Press, 1966.

Baltzell, E. Digby. *Philadelphia Gentleman*. Glencoe: Free Press, 1958.

Linton, Ralph. *The Study of Man*. New York: Appleton-Century-Crofts, 1936.

Mills, C. Wright. *White Collar*. New York: Oxford University Press, 1951.

Stonequist, Everett V. *The Marginal Man*. New York: Scribner, 1937.

Warner, W. Lloyd. *American Life, Dream and Reality*. Chicago: University of Chicago Press, 1962.

# 3
# Categories and Aggregates

SOCIOLOGY, BY ITS VERY DEFINITION, STUDIES PEOPLE who are related to one another, and every social unit must contain persons who are somehow "together." A social *category* brings people together, not in physical, external reality, but in the judgment of the observer, who notes that they possess one or more common characteristics. A social *aggregate*, however, does not depend for its unity upon the mental construct of the observer. It is an assemblage or plurality of people who are in physical proximity, but without reciprocal communication.

All football fans in the country constitute a category; the crowd in the stadium watching the game is an aggregate; the football team itself is a social group. This example shows that the social group differs from both category and aggregate because it involves various degrees of interaction, communication, and social relations. From this point of view the aggregate must be conceptualized somewhere between the category and the group. In the former the people are not even physically present to one another; in the latter the people have enduring social relations.

## KINDS OF CATEGORIES

Similarity, or the sharing of common characteristics which differentiate some people from others, is the essential note in the definition of the social category. When we deal with categories we are not dealing with organized collectivities, yet we can study them as social units because of their common characteristics. Ordinary examples easily clarify this notion: children of preschool age, marriageable females, farm laborers, families on social welfare. The forming of categories is one of the most com-

78

mon mental processes in which human beings indulge. It is also basic to every science because it makes possible intelligent understanding of the qualities and behavior of people (or things) that are similar.

The social scientist does not bother to classify people according to every possible characteristic that they have in common. The list of shared items among people is almost inexhaustible, but most of these items are of little sociological significance. The chiropodist, and perhaps the manufacturer of corrective shoes, would be interested to know how many people in a country or state have flat feet. Health programs were advanced tremendously when it was discovered that there are only four types of blood and that all human beings belong to one or another of these four categories. But this type of information and this kind of categorization would have at best only secondary significance for the social scientist.

All social categories are statistical in the sense that the people who have the common characteristic can be numbered. But the counting of people is merely a preliminary step to the analysis of social phenomena, because statistics, no matter how sharply refined, say nothing by themselves. In any particular instance the importance of the social category depends largely on the purpose that the social scientist has in studying it. If he is analyzing patterns of political behavior, he may arrange his data into categories of voters and nonvoters, radicals and conservatives, male and female voters, or according to age, education, and occupation. In a more general way, however, the important social categories are those that are measured against the main criteria of social status. As we have seen, these represent the values of the society, and the categorization of people according to these criteria opens up important social insights.

## UTILITY OF CATEGORIES

There are two extreme attitudes to be avoided in the matter of social categories. The first is the notion that they are only statistics, and therefore are of no importance. The other extreme is the belief that sociology is nothing but the study of statistical categories. The fact is that social statistics provide necessary and basic information for the student of social science; without these data he tends to speak in vague generalizations.

In many instances the statistical category constitutes the "universe" being studied. This term means simply the total number of persons who are involved in the study. If we say that "a thousand babies were born in this town last year," we cannot say whether this is a significant number unless we know how many people live in the town. It would represent a much higher birth rate if the town's population were five thousand than if it were twenty thousand. The total selected population is the universe studied. The plotting of population trends requires the accurate numbering not only of the total population of a given area but also of the age, sex, and marital categories. In this way, the larger categories must be divided into meaningful subcategories.

The knowledge of social categories has practical utility in many ways. If we know how many children were born six years ago and how many fourteen years ago, we have fairly accurate knowledge of how many pupils will be entering elementary school and how many will be entering high school this year. Such knowledge can be even more specifically refined by school administrators if they study the mortality rates from infancy to fourteen years of age. This is precisely the kind of information upon which insurance companies depend in fixing the rates for their policies. They arrange people in various categories according to age, sex, race, occupation, state of health, and other factors. They study the morbidity and mortality rates among miners or construction workers as compared to those among salesmen and teachers, and are thus able to fix differential premiums.

It is obvious that a knowledge of social categories is important to politicians, public officials, manufacturers, religious leaders, educational administrators—in fact, to anyone who must plan in relation to large numbers of people. It must also be obvious that statistical categories in themselves tell us nothing. The analysis, interpretation, and comparison of categories must be made before any significant conclusions can be reached. The fact that statistics can be manipulated to prove a point is not an argument against the study and use of categories. The popular fallacy that statistics and lies are somehow synonymous simply means that people sometimes lie with words and at other times with numbers.

## CATEGORIES AND STRATIFICATION

We have seen that it is possible to form a category on the basis of any real item that is common to a number of people. The items of similarity are selected for many different reasons and for many purposes of study. Not all common characteristics, however, lend themselves to the formation of sociologically relevant categories. The student of social science is selective in the study of social categories, and this selectivity results from the values that the people in any given society hold.

A number of people possess the same characteristic, and are therefore similar to each other but different from other people. Social categories can be ranked according to the value of the characteristic around which they are formed. We have seen that a stratification of social status also depends upon a hierarchy of social values. It is not nearly so important to study the number of people with blond hair as to know the number of people who have completed their college education. A category of curly-haired blond females is not as important sociologically as a category of females who earn doctoral degrees.

Stratification in a sociological sense refers to the "layers" of social categories as they are ranked from highest to lowest in the esteem of the people in the society. This concept is most frequently emphasized in the discussion about social classes; the rough difference among upper, middle, and lower classes is recognized by everyone. The notion of stratification is understood also in the discussion about various kinds of minorities in the society. Any particular social minority is identified as a category because the people within it have a lesser share in the socially valuable items, whether the people are migrant farm workers or members of a racial minority. This "lesser share" immediately places these people in a lower social stratum than the people who are not in the minority.

## PRINCIPAL COMBINATIONS OF CRITERIA

The student of society cannot be satisfied to learn only those social categories that are based upon one criterion of status. This is, of course, the simplest kind of knowledge, but mere casual observation will indicate that each person shares numerous characteristics with other persons. The human being in society is not merely rich or poor, educated or noneducated, pious or impious; he is also of definite family background, does many things in society, and represents a certain biological type. This means two things: first, that any individual can be placed in as many social categories as there are characteristics he shares with others, and, second, that any combination of characteristics in him can be matched by similar combinations in other people.

It is this sharing of a combination of similar characteristics that accounts for the most important social categories in every society. It is on this basis of combined similar characteristics that a meaningful and scientific analysis of social categories can be made. It is also in this area that the unsophisticated observer makes most of his mistakes in stereotyping people, that is, in assuming that one set of characteristics must necessarily accompany another set.

The most important social categories, formed on the basis of combined similarities, appear to be the following. **a.** Social minorities are categories of people who share a combination of similar disadvantages. They are therefore esteemed "below" that level at which the normal, the average, the acceptable is fixed. We are talking here of a numerical minority, since in this sense almost any social category is a minority. Powerful numerical minorities have governed and controlled societies through force and military might; and numerically the upper class is a minority everywhere. To be a social minority, the category must be underprivileged. It may represent one-third, or two-thirds, or even more of a nation; or it may be a relatively small segment of the population. Its members are not necessarily persecuted or suppressed, nor are they always and deliberately prevented from attaining the privileges enjoyed by the rest of society. In a slow-moving society the status of minorities changes very gradually; in a dynamic society there is often a general tendency to assimilate minorities into the larger population.

The three principal categories of this type are the foreign-born, the racial, and the religious minorities. *Religious* minorities exist in every major society of the contemporary world. We view them here not as people who form social groups because they profess the same religious beliefs, but from the point of view of others who think of them as a social category. The extent to which a religious minority, like the Doukhobors, differs in its beliefs and worship from the accepted norms of the majority also measures the extent to which it has low social status. The religious criterion is the most visible one, but it is often accompanied by other criteria like foreign origin and occupational and educational levels.

The *foreign-born* form a major social category divided into many subcategories according to country of origin. They too, for the most part, constitute social minorities. The principal criterion on which they are judged is their ancestry, that is, their national or ethnic origin, especially if it represents peasant stock. But other criteria combine with the fact of foreign ancestry: the educational, with reference to language and literacy; the economic and religious; and even the biological characteristics if these differ markedly from those of the majority. The Irish immigrant in Liverpool, the Italian miner in Germany, the East Indian in South Africa, are examples of foreign minorities.

*Racial* minorities constitute those social categories that are principally characterized by the criteria of ancestral and biological differences from the majority. This type of minority combines the largest number of the criteria of social status we have discussed. The degree of wealth and education the members of this minority possess both affect and are affected by their racial background. The utility of their function in society, especially of their occupational activities, is also an important overlapping criterion of their social status.

**b.** Social classes are the most obvious examples in any society of the combination of criteria of social status. In fact, the social class cannot be objectively studied except as a social category that depends upon the value judgments prevalent among the people. Whether one speaks of roughly two or three social classes, or of the numerous social strata existing in the more complex societies, one must essentially include and combine all the criteria of social status. A class is a plurality of people who are categorized as a social unit because they are actually similar in several respects and who are "rated" at a certain level of stratification.

A person's class status has a much greater concrete effect upon him than do the more general statistical categories in which he may be included. The reason for this is twofold; first, because his class is a category based on multiple similarities that often make him potentially accessible in social relations with other people; and second, because the value of these similarities is determined by other people's opinion of them and, therefore, by the esteem or disesteem in which the person himself is held. We say that a person is affected by his class status mainly because of what other persons think of him and how they act toward him. They consider him "better" or "worse" because of his class status, and at the same time he belongs in a higher or lower social class because he has or does not have what people in general consider the better or worse social characteristics.

It is a problem of research methodology to discover, first, the actual social values the society holds, and second, which people in any given area possess the combination of characteristics thus evaluated. Involvement in, and study of, a particular society reveals frequent reference to the characteristics the people hold in high regard. Hearing the people themselves talk about one another helps one to "place" them in their objective social class. For example, in one locality the "better people" may be categorized by the fact that they are of Creole ancestry, send their children to church-related preparatory schools and private Eastern universities, and belong to certain exclusively Gentile clubs that have Greek and Roman names. In other areas the specific details of these general characteristics will differ, but they will still act as clues in the discovering of membership in the upper class.

Social scientists also frequently employ certain quantitative measurements in order to fix the class status of a person or family. The student of society soon learns that a certain section of the city, or one suburb rather than another, is considered the better residential area, that one type of dwelling reflects higher social prestige than another, that certain types of occupation and kinds of financial income have greater social approval than others. Such items can be counted, measured, balanced, and compared. The data are objective and comparable and can be interpreted to indicate the number and size of the various social classes.

c."Publics" are a more subtle type of social category that has increased in importance in urban and commercial societies. The public, like the social class and the minority, is conceptualized as a social unit in which persons possess certain common characteristics. There is one aspect in which publics are sociologically more significant than classes and minorities. This is the fact that they are the focus of attention, and the subject of persuasion, by those who address the various publics.

In the technical scientific sense, a public does not refer to the total general population or to an organized social group, although both of these meanings are sometimes applied to the term. A public differs from an aggregate because the latter is marked by physical proximity and the former is not. The television comedian is addressing himself to his public, a category widely dispersed throughout the country, while the stage comedian is addressing himself to his audience, an aggregate gathered together in the theater. This distinction may appear to be slight but it shows clearly the difference between two kinds of social units.

When a preacher, lecturer, writer, manufacturer, or politician is asked "which public are you appealing to?" the question implies the focus of attention upon one social category rather than another. Thus there are many publics. Even the "consuming public" to which the advertiser appeals has many subcategories, sometimes vaguely referred to as "discriminating people," "men of distinction," or those "who want the best," and sometimes, more specifically, as the teenagers, the housewives, the suburbanites.

The appeal to the workers, or to the proletariat, is not simply a reference to a class category. These people combine certain shared characteristics on the basis of which they are considered a public. The readers of mystery fiction or of detective stories, the fans of wrestling, baseball, or football, the intelligentsia, the "arty" people, in fact any plurality of people to whom appeals are directed, constitute a public. Each of these categories can be studied separately and each will demonstrate the presence of similarities of educational and economic levels, of functional utility, and also, often, of sex and age characteristics.

DEFINITION OF AGGREGATES

As we move from the analysis of categories to that of aggregates we note that the people in each of these social units are "together" in different ways. In the social aggregate they are together only in the sense that they are loosely assembled. Some of the more common examples of the social aggregate are the people within arbitrarily drawn boundaries, like school districts, police precincts, political wards, the various districts, sections or quarters of the city; the uptown, downtown, and midtown areas, the various urban zones. Those are not the only kinds of aggregates but they fit the description of the social aggregate.

A more complete definition of the social aggregate must include the following elements: (*a*) The persons who constitute the aggregate are relatively *anonymous* in that they are almost strangers to one another. (*b*) The social aggregate is *not organized*; it does not have a structure with a hierarchy of positions and functions. (*c*) There is only *limited social contact* even though the physical proximity may be very great. (*d*) There is at best only a *slight modification of behavior* on the part of those who are in the aggregate. (*e*) Most social aggregates are *territorial* and their social significance is limited by certain physical boundaries. (*f*) Most aggregates are also *temporary* in the sense that people shift in and out of them and from one to another.

The term "aggregation" is frequently used as a synonym for the term "aggregate," but this use is scientifically valid in only one meaning of the word. Aggregation used transitively refers to the process by which people are brought into a collectivity. From this point of view, people are aggregated when they move into a different neighborhood, when they come into the theater for a play, when they stop to watch the excavation for a new building. Aggregation is not synonymous with, or sociologically so important as, the processes of socialization and assimilation. Aggregation used substantively refers to the actual collectivity of people and has the same meaning as social aggregate.

It must be noted that aggregation represents only one focus in the study of people. The typical urban apartment building in which the occupants of the various dwelling units have at most a nodding acquaintance with one another is a modern example of a social aggregate. But this does not deny that the individual family which occupies each apartment is a group. The building contains an aggregate of groups. The individual person may be a unit in an aggregate and a unit in a group at one and the same time.

PRINCIPAL KINDS OF AGGREGATES

The dynamic aspect of human relations makes difficult the scientific classification of social aggregates. There is a certain degree of confusion and overlapping in the application of sociological terminology because there is confusion and overlapping in the concrete social system. People simply do not "stay put" so that you can say they are in each instance either in a group or an aggregate, nor are their forms of aggregation always so easily identifiable as may at first appear. In spite of these difficulties it is necessary to use terms as accurately as the changing social phenomena will allow.

The following classification of social aggregates into crowds, mobs, audiences, demonstrations, and residential and functional aggregates, is an attempt to cut through some of these terminological difficulties. We discuss only those clearly identifiable social aggregates that are sociologically significant. They demonstrate the two most important elements of social aggregates: the people in them are physically and proximately assembled, and they have among themselves a minimum of social relations and communication.

**a.** The *crowd* is an ordered, relatively noninteracting aggregate of persons. From the point of view of the totality it is neither coordinated nor is it performing any common function; it is simply occupying physical space. This does not mean, however, that the individuals who compose it are purposeless or bewildered. Each individual can probably "explain his presence." The crowd is peaceable and nonexcitable; it is amorphous and exhibits only a kind of external unity.

There are nevertheless recognizable different kinds of crowds, and the student of society can usually make distinctions among them merely through observation. The individuals in the Saturday night shopping crowd of a supermarket can be distinguished from the crowd waiting to cross the street when the traffic light changes, and from the people who are streaming into a football stadium.

**b.** The *mob* is a social aggregate liable to "get out of hand" because it lacks both internal and external control. It is disorderly rather than orderly. It tends to act as a social unit on a short-lived, large-scale basis. The persons making up this aggregate are usually charged with intense emotions. The term is almost always used in a pejorative sense, indicating that the mob is destructive, antisocial, and belligerent. It is usually a protest phenomenon.

Street riots are mob activities, sometimes touched off by small incidents, fed by rumors, and then incited by "ringleaders." Interaction among the separate individuals in the mob is at a minimum, but there is almost always some relationship between the leaders and the followers of the mob. This is an essential difference betwen the crowd and the mob. It is possible also to distinguish among the different types of mobs from a knowledge of the kind of protest which each is making. Mobs are aroused by racist feelings, by economic exploitation, by political upheaval, by religious fanaticism. Mobs have been known to form on the basis of outraged artistic sensibilities and in reaction to the decisions of referees and umpires in athletic contests.

c. The *audience* is a social aggregate of persons who deliberately assemble to watch and listen to a performance of some kind. We use the term only in strict reference to a physical collectivity within a limited spatial area. The people in an audience differ from the mob in that they are listeners and spectators rather than active performers in any joint behavior. They differ from the crowd in that they endure longer and their attention is more closely focused. Audiences are expected to react to a common stimulus, and they are sometimes judged on the degree and kind of reaction they give to this stimulus: appreciative or dull; boisterous or quiet; approving or disapproving.

Audiences may be classified more meaningfully on the basis of that which attracts them. All kinds of performances gather audiences: athletic contests of various kinds, lectures on innumerable topics, theater and movie productions, debates, beauty contests. Even the persons assembled in a church congregation, to the extent that they do not participate as a group in the religious services, are an audience.

d. *Demonstrations* constitute a social aggregate of persons who are deliberately assembled for the purpose of promoting some idea, belief, movement, or person. The people who make up the demonstration are not merely spectators or listeners; they actually participate in some kind of collective behavior in the presence of others. The demonstration is usually organized, but only in the sense that some previous planning has occurred, and the participants are only loosely assembled in relation to one another.

Demonstrations are a social phenomenon peculiar mainly to big cities. They are social aggregates differing from crowds, mobs, or audiences. The most common examples of the demonstration are mass meetings, political rallies, civil-rights marches, religious processions, and various kinds of parades. A demonstration may be a one-time occurrence like the celebration at the end of a war, a march of the unemployed, or a procession of silent prayer in protest against religious, racial, or other persecution. Other demonstrations, like ethnic and civic parades, have become celebrated annual occurrences in certain cities. The St. Patrick's Day Parade in New York, the Tournament of Roses, the Mardi Gras parades in New Orleans, are examples.

e. *Residential aggregates* can be recognized in all large cities. The relative anonymity and the residential mobility of some people in large cities tend to develop the social aggregate in any given urban section. To the extent that people live near one another but remain relative strangers, have practically no contact or interaction, and are unorganized, they remain a social aggregate. This is more likely to occur in the so-called transient areas with rooming houses, hotels, and large apartment buildings, than in the stable "old, settled" neighborhoods of family dwellings.

The concept of the residential social aggregate is clarified when it is contrasted to that of the urban ethnic community. The latter term implies association, contact, communication, and friendly exchanges among the people in a given residential area. The fact that many residential areas tend to be aggregates only is demonstrated by the frequent effort of civic and religious leaders, of politicians and businessmen, to create or reawaken a "community consciousness" through which people will identify themselves with their residential area. A genuine social neighborhood already possesses this sense of community.

**f.** *Functional aggregates* are constituted by people to whom territorial boundaries are more or less arbitrarily assigned. For example, police precincts, school districts, and postal zones are arranged conveniently for certain functional purposes, but they can in no technical sense be termed groups or communities. Similarly, it can be said that the total aggregate of people who function in a shopping district, a financial center, or a theatrical district, lack the characteristics of a social group. Because of a discernible function performed in these areas, it is logical to distinguish them, as aggregates, from residential areas.

THE PERSON AND THE AGGREGATE

The impression is sometimes given that the aggregate is a herd of passive social animals which are not exercising their abilities as rational beings. It must be obvious from what we have said so far that this is not the case. The social aggregate, as a midway point between the conception of a social category and the actual solidarity of a social group, empirically "contains" people. The individual person has a relation to the aggregate in which he is a unit, and this relation is seen in several ways.

**a.** The person is necessarily present in a social aggregate. We have seen that physical proximity is necessary before an aggregate is created; it is also true that no one, especially no city-dweller, can avoid social aggregates. He is in them and part of them at all times. His mere physical existence at some address in some section of the city places him in a residential aggregate and in several functional aggregates. Whenever he moves about the city he is certain to be in crowds and audiences of one kind or another. He has little choice about remaining isolated.

**b.** Since social aggregates are unstructured, the individual has virtually no social status within an aggregate. Social status depends upon recognition and judgment of others, and a person's status is always a position in relation to other positions. If he does have status within a mob, for example, it is only in the sense that there is a vague understanding of the difference between leaders and followers in the mob. The aggregate in which the person is a unit, however, may influence his status in a group which is outside the aggregate. Insofar as he chooses to be in different audiences, to be a fight fan rather than an opera-goer, or a ready participant in street riots, his social status may be affected.

c. There is a small degree of patterned behavior to which the person conforms as a part of a social aggregate. Women in a shopping crowd may jostle one another in a manner unthinkable in a church congregation. The patterns of behavior at an athletic contest are much more relaxed than they are at a symphony concert, and they even differ from one type of sport to another. It must be noted that the modification of social behavior results from the type of social aggregate in which the person finds himself and not from the interaction with the other people who happen to be in the aggregate.

d. It may be said that in social aggregates a person exhibits collective behavior rather than social behavior. This distinction means that his behavior in the presence of others is simultaneous and often similar to that of others, rather than for, or against, or with the others. Social behavior implies communication, contact, and interaction, and this is precisely the type of behavior that occurs in groups but not in aggregates. Collective behavior does, however, have a social effect. The presence of an attentive crowd at a construction site may inspire workmen to steadier, more consistent, and more productive work. The roar of the crowd and the applause of the audience are often purposeful and effective.

e. The individual person tends to submerge his identity in the social aggregate. This is not necessarily a deliberate decision on the part of the person himself, but rather a resultant or concomitant of the nature of social aggregates. Anonymity and lack of personal knowledge of other people may be noted especially at demonstrations such as rallies and parades, where the voice of the individual is hardly heard or where he does not care to express it.

**f.** It is a well-known fact that personal responsibility diminishes in social aggregates. To be "part of the crowd" or to "follow the mob" means that the individual is largely surrendering his own accountability for the collective action. Much of what is done by the person in these situations is spontaneous and unreflecting. The "spirit" of the crowd is often contagious in temporary gatherings of people, while in the residential aggregate personal lack of responsibility increases because of the very transitoriness and anonymity of one's residence.

## Some American Categories and Aggregates

### 1. CLASS CONSCIOUSNESS OF AMERICANS

The oversimplified interpretation of the democratic way of life in America has resulted in such statements as "Everybody is as good as everybody else," or "We don't have social classes like Europe and South America," or "We cherish our traditions of freedom and equality." These are sometimes the remarks of the naive and sometimes of the opportunistic, or they reflect often a state of wishful and unrealistic thinking. Every society exhibits differences of social status among individuals and some sort of stratification of social categories. In this country, we have, apparently, a peculiar combination of an actual stratified society and a general reluctance of most Americans to admit the presence of stratification.

Social consciousness in this context refers to an awareness of social status and strata, not to an awareness of social problems, or to an attitude of civic duty or patriotism. Following are some of the reasons why class consciousness is minimized in American society.

**a.** Except on the most formal occasions Americans tend to disparage or to ignore honorific titles. They are noted for familiarity in social intercourse and for breaking down formal barriers even with strangers. The term "Mister" fits every adult male, but even here subordinates and employees use terms like "Boss" or "Chief" to avoid the stiffness of the title. Social peers use first names among themselves and persons in superior positions also address others by their first names. There is no distinction between formal and familiar in the second person pronoun. This type of familiar social address is unthinkable in most other major societies.

**b.** The diffusion of an egalitarian ideology is a most important means of minimizing class consciousness. The child is taught in his early school years about self-reliance, independence, and equal opportunities. He learns a great deal about his own rights, and this emphasis upon rights of the individual is widespread in the adult society. Slogans of equality are the stuff of which political speeches are made, and the various movements in support of equal rights which have dotted our history have been important determinants of attitudes.

**c.** Achievement of status is more valued than ascription of status. The American tends to admire and respect the individual who has made his own way, who has achieved success and made a name for himself. The person is regarded as an individual rather than as a representative of a social stratum related to other social strata. This means that the criteria of social status, as possessed in more or less degree, are recognized as personal differences rather than as social and class distinctions.

**d.** The availability of material symbols of status tends to compensate for lack of actual high status. The fact that automobiles, television sets, refrigerators, and other items can be bought on the installment plan, that reasonable imitations of "exclusive" clothing styles can be purchased, and that there are few traditional types of apparel which identify a person's class—these are all weighty factors in minimizing the recognition of class differentials.

**e.** The relative lack of exclusion or segregation in public and commercial facilities tends to decrease the physical separation of social classes. Except in places where racial or ethnic discrimination is practiced, the American, if he has the price of admission, may sit in the best seat at the opera, the race track, or the championship boxing match. He has access to libraries, parks, and public gardens, to transportation and communication facilities. When there are exclusive affairs, or memberships by invitation only, he usually likes to think that this is done on the basis of the private right of those who are excluding him, not because of his own lower social status.

f. By and large, the American is treated, and expects to be treated, as an equal in political, legal, and military procedures. Jury duty, the vote, military service, the right to bring suit and to stand a fair trial, the right to police and fire protection and service—all these are intended to apply impartially to all Americans. The fact that they are not always so applied must be noted by the student of society. Yet, relatively speaking, these practices are widespread and their value is emphasized. This tends to give the American a feeling that he is living in a classless society.

These few evidences concerning the de-emphasis of class consciousness among Americans are also evidences of the importance of conceptual categories. Even though the class structure exists as a concrete reality, and even though class status has immediate, personal and objective consequences for individuals, there is still a tendency to belittle or even ignore its reality. What people try to believe constitutes in itself a social fact of great significance. Because of the all-pervading ideology of democracy and all that it implies, people attempt to lessen the implications and consequences of the actual stratification of class categories.

## 2. Unequal Treatment of Social Categories

We have seen that the very definition of social status and strata implies an unequal possession of socially valued items among the persons in different social status categories. This is true in every society, including the American, where the cultural creed professes the basic dignity and equality of all human beings. Inequalities of social status, however, do not always imply inequitable or hostile relations between the persons of different status. There are innumerable examples of reciprocal relations of kindness, generosity, friendship, and love between people of higher position and those of subordinate status. This is seen in certain situations across class lines, and even across racial, ethnic, and religious barriers. It is seen in the play activities of very young children who have not developed an awareness of status, and also in the relations of some adults who try to recognize the personal qualities of intelligence, character, and virtue wherever they are found.

In spite of these exceptions there are several glaring examples of unequal treatment accorded to certain social categories in America. Not included in the following list are criminals who are said to have "forfeited" the right to equal respect.

a. The social status of women has been steadily rising, but it is still true that most women employees performing work equal to that of men do not receive equal pay. This is now a violation of the law. Females as a social category are also discriminated against in some ways by organized religion, labor unions, political parties, and university systems. In some respects, however, they are favored over males, as in the laws that protect them from nightwork, regulations providing rest facilities and sick leave, and customs preventing them from doing heavy industrial and mining work.

b. Illegitimately born children and dependent orphans form a category of socially disadvantaged persons. Through no fault of their own they are in a position of social inferiority. This status is gradually changing. American society's increasing awareness of these children, together with the more intelligent approach of social workers, philanthropists, and social reformers, has mitigated their condition to some extent. In most instances they are receiving temporarily, immediate material aid, even if this does not effectively raise their status.

c. The category of child labor in some urban slums, but especially among the migratory farm workers in rural areas, is also the object of inequitable treatment. The industrialized segment of the American economy does not need child labor, and the organized unions have opposed its use. Child-labor laws were designed to prevent exploitation of children by unscrupulous employers and to provide time and opportunity for normal schooling.

**d.** Upper-class people in every community are the objects of favorable discrimination by the several agencies of public service. The police treat with more deference the adult traffic violator or the potential juvenile delinquent from an upper-class family. The streets are cleaner and better lighted, the pavement is more quickly repaired, the fire department responds more readily, and the garbage is more neatly and regularly collected in those sections of the city which are the better residential areas.

**e.** The most obvious objects of negative discriminatory treatment have been the racial minorities, especially the American Indians, the Oriental immigrants to some extent, and the Negro Americans. The civil-rights movement finally achieved the removal of discriminatory legislation that had existed in many states since the novel legal doctrine of "separate but equal" was introduced at the end of the last century. Nevertheless, there remain strong customs and folkways at the local and regional levels that are prejudicial to American racial minorities.

There are other and smaller social categories, including certain religious minorities, dependent people of no income, the physically and mentally handicapped, and even some political categories, that receive unequal treatment from the majority in the American society. Those we have mentioned provide sufficient evidence that there are many levels of unequal treatment, and that social distinctions have certain concrete effects even in our democratic society.

3. Lack of American Mass Movements

Theoretically, one might suppose that a society characterized by large numbers of different social aggregates would also have a history of mass movements, but the United States is notable for its lack of them. Aggregates are people in the mass, and when the American aggregate organizes it usually becomes some kind of association. It does not form with other aggregates into a "people's

movement." The conditions for mass movements appear
to be present in our society, but all attempts to create
such movements have been short-lived.

Historically, of course, the United States has experienced all kinds of movements, but they have been social
movements of a relatively specialized nature. They have
not included the masses as a whole, the heterogeneous
aggregations of people in our country. There has not
even been a class movement in the sense in which the
Marxists define the working masses. The only attempt
to organize all the working people of America was that
of the Knights of Labor, who invited to membership all
who had gainful occupation, including business and professional men and women. This attempt was unsuccessful.

The women's movement for political suffrage was one
of the specialized movements that declined when it
reached its objective; but there is now a resurgence of
a women's movement for equal rights. Farmers' protest
organizations, the large-scale labor movement, the several
branches of the Black Power movement, are by definition
and purpose specialized and limited, and show no signs
of crystallizing into a solidary mass movement. College
students have made the broadest effort to "mobilize everybody" in the peace movement but with little success. It
is historically and sociologically significant that these
specialized movements tend to succeed one another rather
than to occur simultaneously.

The following are some of the factors that, taken in
combination, help to explain why there has been no viable
mass movement in America.

a. The institutional adaptiveness of our culture to the
reasonable demands of the people tends to satisfy the
needs for which mass movements are organized. The
major political parties are generally willing to take
seriously the demands of the people and to react favorably to them. The readiness of all three branches of the
federal government to reinterpret the laws in the light of
modern social developments has forestalled the formation
of mass movements.

**b.** The relative success of the democratic process has provided pragmatic confidence that "something can be done." Although Americans are notoriously apathetic voters in comparison with the people of some other countries, the "threat" of the polls has often influenced the elected officials. Reliance on their representatives, who must make an accounting to them in the next election campaign, accompanies the political inertia of the great masses of people.

**c.** Specialized movements succeed largely through lobbies and pressure groups, which concentrate on piece-meal advantages and particular issues. These are often specific and "vested" interests, rather than the general interest or the common good that a mass movement would be presumed to promote. This means of promotion is an indication of the rational and pragmatic approach characteristic of the American people.

**d.** The mass solidarity which accompanies mass movements has not emerged in the American society mainly because of the successive waves of immigration. The population has been subdivided by differences in language, education, and religion, and in ethnic, racial, and national background. This cultural pluralism, unique in the history of the world, has hindered cohesion of thought and action. While some of these differences are gradually disappearing, they have been historically effective as a preventive to mass movements.

**e.** There has always been a lower class of immigrant people who were more eager to establish themselves as Americans than to reform American society. These people have never been simultaneously numerous enough, well enough acquainted with the American society, and in sufficient effective communication with other Americans to form the basis of a mass movement. Rural Negroes and whites in the South, and in some places Puerto Ricans, Cubans, and Mexicans who have moved into the large urban centers have replaced the earlier immigrants with somewhat the same effect.

**f.** Because of the upward mobility of gifted individuals, much of the organizing talent that could have formed and led mass movements rose above the ranks of those who would most benefit by such movements. Each generation has "sent upstairs" the potential leaders of mass movements. This opportunity for advancement in social status has been one of the greatest advantages for the individual, and the development of individualism is an antidote to effective mass action. This is why intellectuals step in to provide both ideology and leadership in revolutions.

**g.** The material success of America, which provides a constantly rising standard of living for more and more people, has cut the ground from under many of the causes around which social movements build. This standard of living is not the same as government-provided "bread and circuses." Even where there is public assistance to the underprivileged masses it is disguised either as temporary relief in emergencies, or as the opportunity for "self-help." The basic American principle is still that people should acquire material objects through their own effort in their own economic roles.

These conditions explaining the absence of a mass movement in the United States are not necessarily enduring or permanent. Since social aggregates continue to multiply, it will be interesting to observe the future trends. The population becomes more homogeneous as people of differing ethnic, racial, and national backgrounds continue to intermarry. There are serious complaints that the system is no longer as open, dynamic, and adaptive as it once was, and that the political-military-industrial "complex" is managing the society to the disadvantage of the masses. There is no guarantee that the combination of factors offsetting mass movements will continue.

### 4. DEMONSTRATIONS AS SOCIAL AGGREGATES

Every society has its own way of staging public demonstrations. Folk festivals and religious processions, often carefully planned in advance, bring the people out into the streets. So do unpremeditated riots accompanied by shooting, looting, and vandalism. The American protest demonstration, sometimes in the form of a protest march, lies somewhere between the orderly parade and the disorderly street riot.

A kind of protest pattern has been established in the recent past that seems to mark these demonstrations as peculiarly American. Their more obvious features may be discussed briefly as follows:

a. The largest and nationally promoted protest demonstrations insist on the strategy of passive *nonviolence,* which appears to be based on an ideology of human love, the notion that one must not hate one's persecutors. The majority of protestors still adhere to this theme, but it has been repudiated since the late 1960s by a minority of radical extremists. The minority which advocates and promotes violence is often a close-knit group that tries to influence the behavior of the larger collectivity constituting a social aggregate.

b. Intentional *civil disobedience* is also often characteristic of such protest demonstrations. This too is a high ideological principle which asserts that unjust laws contradict the higher moral law and need not to be obeyed. The practical objective has been to call attention to both laws and customs that have prevented Negroes from obtaining equal access to public facilities like schools, parks, libraries, hotels, and restaurants. There has sometimes been deliberate defiance of court injunctions and police orders not to stage a march.

c. The fact that *mass arrests* by the police followed these instances of nonviolent civil disobedience underlines another principle of the protest demonstration. The willingness to go to jail, to be fined and otherwise penalized, provided a public test for both the morality and legality of discriminatory practices. If public officials ignored these demonstrations, and if the demonstrators demanded amnesty, the main force of the protest would have collapsed.

d. For most people involved in these demonstrations, participation is *transitory and anonymous,* and it is mainly for this reason that this phenomenon can be called a social aggregate. This is particularly true of the massive demonstrations in Selma, Montgomery, and elsewhere, the poverty march in Washington, the demonstrations for peace in many large cities. On these occasions people came from all over the country, many of whom would not meet again except perhaps on some similar rare occasion. These were like a crowd on the march, or at a rally.

e. While the largest demonstrations are transitory and spontaneous for the largest number of people involved in them, there is also always a small *organizing nucleus* of people who promote and plan the event. This is evident in protest demonstrations that are regularly repeated. It is most evident when a small nucleus of students succeeds in "occupying" a campus building and in rallying a large aggregate of students in demonstrations.

The point of view of the above discussion has been that of the social aggregate, the fact that large numbers of otherwise unrelated persons are assembled at a given time and place. The organized purpose, another aspect of these demonstrations, must be considered separately because it implies that a social movement is under way. Structure and function are involved in movements that promote justice and peace and that protest racism, poverty, and militarism.

5. Population as a Category

The declining birth rate in Western countries was the population problem about which social scientists and others were concerned in the 1930s. Since that time the death rate has declined, especially in the underdeveloped countries, and the demographic problem is now expressed in terms of the population "explosion." A low birth rate coupled with a lower death rate necessarily results in a steadily increasing population. The population problem, as Thomas Malthus knew a long time ago, also involves the means of subsistence for the population, or the study of human ecology.

Demographers are able to deal with the aggregate masses of the population by converting them into social categories. This work is presociological in the sense that it tells nothing about human relations although it does provide a great deal of basic information about the people who have human relations. Demography is a preliminary step to the study of sociological phenomena. The largest source of data on which categories can be arranged is the national census. Some countries maintain a "live" census that is constantly kept up to date, while other countries take a census only every ten years and collect only limited amounts of information.

Following are some of the characteristics of the population categories provided by the United States census.

a. Whatever the reasons may be, the census gives us practically no information that would be useful in the study of three major institutions—political, religious and recreational. In other words, we must seek elsewhere to discover how the population falls into subcategories in its political affiliation and activity. All attempts by statisticians to include a question on religion have been thwarted. Although leisure-time activities are rapidly increasing among the American people, the census tells us practically nothing about them.

b. On the other hand, census statistics are ample and of great value for the study of three major institutions: economic, educational and familial. We have detailed data on occupation and income, home ownership, number of rooms, kind of heating and plumbing, ownership of automobile, radio, television, refrigerator. People answer questions about their marital status and the number of children they have and whether they have boarders in their home. They are asked about the amount of education they have had and whether their children are attending school.

c. The sociological value of census data increases the more the categories are refined. A typical example is the breakdown by age categories. Among those who are fourteen years of age and older, most are in the labor force, more are males than females, and they are distributed in many occupations and on a range of annual income. But many are not in the labor force, and of these some are retired, many are enrolled in school, and most of the women are homemakers. Most of those in the age category five to thirteen years are enrolled in school. A third age category, that of preschool children, is a helpful index of population growth.

**d.** If it were not for census data we would have enormous difficulty in studying the internal migration of the American people. In successive census counts we have been able to measure the exodus from rural areas and the growth of suburbs; we have seen which large cities increase and which decrease in population. Significant sociological questions can then be asked. Why did these people move as they did? What kinds of people moved— what was their age, sex, occupation, race? What effects did the migration have on the social structure of the places to which and from which they moved?

**e.** The most popular graphic presentation of census data is the population pyramid which compares males and females by "layers" of five-year age cohorts. This becomes more valuable with extended comparisons, from one census year to another, of foreign-born and native-born, Negroes and whites, rural and urban, and many other sets of population. It suggests age and sex differences in mortality rates, and raises questions about "hollow" cohorts.

**f.** The only way accurate and exclusive categories can be known is by the tedious process of counting people, and this is what the Bureau of the Census does. The question of accuracy is often raised because the decennial census asks some questions of a 25 percent sample of households, and claims high probability rather than complete accuracy on these items. In a changing population it is important to know what is happening during the ten-year period between census-taking. This is solved by the Current Population Survey which occasionally samples about thirty-five thousand households on relevant questions.

The sociological value of census categories lies in the questions they raise and in the help they give to test hypotheses. The statistical fact of declining rates of both births and deaths forces the sociologist to ask why this is occurring and what effect it is having on the American society. Shifts in occupation and income call for explanation. The cross-tabulation of census data has enormously improved the basic store of information from which the sociologist can start to build his analyses and interpretations.

## Suggested Readings

Amory, Cleveland. *The Proper Bostonians*. New York: Dutton, 1947.

Barber, Bernard. *Social Stratification*. New York: Harcourt, Brace, 1957.

Cox, Oliver Cromwell. *Caste, Class and Race*. New York: Monthly Review Press, 1959.

Le Bon, Gustave. *The Crowd*. London: Unwin, 1917.

Ortega y Gasset, Jose. *The Revolt of the Masses*. New York: Norton, 1932.

Wrong, Dennis H. *Population*. New York: Random House, 1962.

# 4
# Groups and Associations

THE PERSON CAN BE A UNIT IN VARIOUS KINDS OF collectivities, but not all of these are social groups. People in a group associate with one another; they experience patterns of interaction among themselves. The briefest definition of the group is "human beings in reciprocal relations." We have seen that this is not the case with categories and aggregates. The aggregate is in physical proximity, but without interaction, and is not a group.

We need not dwell here on such imaginative speculations about the dim origins of group life as the evolution from animal hordes to human societies, the theory of the social contract, and other poetic inventions. We are interested only in factual data about contemporary social life, the specific group that has a beginning in time, continues for a while, then goes out of existence. Group life and social relations are coextensive with the existence of persons. Like categories and aggregates groups are universally present wherever people live. Where there are persons, there are groups; and where there are no persons, there are no groups.

## CHARACTERISTICS OF THE GROUP

The sociological meaning of the term "group" is much more detailed and technical than we have indicated. A more descriptive explanation of the group must include the following.

a. The social unit called a group must be identifiable as such, both by its members and by outside observers. This does not mean that every member must be known personally to every other member or to nonmembers. Secret societies, lodges, and fraternities have a recognizable existence, although their membership may be exclusive and hidden. The groups in any large city are so numerous that no individual could have personal knowledge of all of them; but they are knowable, that is, it is possible to find out about them.

**b.** The group has a social structure in the sense that each component, member, or person has a position related to other positions. Social stratification, or the ranking of social status, is present even in the smallest informal groupings. There is always at least a trace of subordination or superordination even in the most equalitarian groups.

**c.** The various members enact their social roles in the group. This is what group participation signifies and it is the aspect under which participation is studied. When the members cease to enact their roles, the group ceases to exist. A group in which there is no personal action of a patterned sort is sociologically unthinkable.

**d.** Reciprocal relations are essential to the maintenance of the group. In other words, there must be contact and communication among the members. There is no such thing as a one-way social process. This must be a mutual or reciprocal process, even if it is limited to only two persons in the group at any one time.

**e.** Every group has norms of behavior that influence the way in which the roles are enacted. These need not always be written rules or regulations or a constitution; but they are usually certain patterns of behavior which are understood and followed by the members. There is necessarily a modification of the behavior of the individual when and because he is in the group.

**f.** The members of the group share certain common interests and values which in some instances may be carefully spelled out. In other instances these may be only vaguely defined, but that they are present is seen in the fact that a conflict in values will almost invariably split the group.

**g.** Group activity, if not the very existence of the group itself, must be directed towards some social goal or goals. In other words, all groups are to some degree purposeful.

This answers the specific question of why, or for what reason, the group exists.

**h.** A group must have relative permanence, that is, a measurable duration over a period of time. This is one of the important marks distinguishing a social group from a transient social aggregate.

Taking all these characteristics together, we can now give the following complete definition of the social group. A group is an identifiable, structured, continuing collectivity of social persons who enact reciprocal roles according to social norms, interests, and values in the pursuit of common goals. It may be noted that a total society, like the American or French or Mexican society, is a combination of all the groups existing within it. Groups within a society are distinguished from one another mainly by their central functions, while major societies are distinguished from one another mainly by their cultures.

RECRUITMENT TO THE GROUP

If a group is to maintain itself in existence it must have ways of recruiting new members. People come originally into the conjugal family group by birth or adoption and into the extended kinship group by marriage. All other groups admit new members through one or a series of qualifying elements. There may be a merely informal understanding that a person is welcome to join a friendship circle. In other groups he may be elected or appointed or invited to membership. He may have to pass certain tests or examinations, conform to rituals and ceremonies of the group, and in some instances pay an initiation fee.

The question of recruitment to the group is not the same as the study of the formation or the origin of groups. It is obvious that people live in groups because they are social beings. In many instances they simply discover themselves taking part in the activities of groups without reflecting on the manner in which they happen to be in these particular groups rather than others. On the part of the individual there is often an almost nonrational and subconscious entrance into the group. A woman may become casually acquainted with her neighbors and bring herself and her husband into an informal friendship clique, or she may take the deliberate steps necessary to join the organized League of Women Voters.

In some instances there are deliberate campaigns for membership, a kind of "pressure to join" voluntary associations. The religious sect tries to convert people to itself, the local church congregation invites people to membership. The Parent-Teacher Association tries to get all parents of school children to participate in its activities. In a sense, the help-wanted ads in the newspapers are invitations to join occupational groups. Americans are sometimes thought of as a nation of "joiners" with a vast variety of groups and organizations; this tends to be the pattern for the middle class in a democratic, open, and pluralistic society.

## CLASSIFICATION OF GROUPS

Social groups are so complex and varied that their classification must necessarily be multiple. We have said above that the major groups in a society can be identified and classified by their central social function, but this is simply one of numerous approaches. The ways in which groups can be differentiated and arranged are as numerous as the points of view from which they can be studied. Many of these approaches are useful only for the purposes of a specific study.

Some of the "easier" classifications may of themselves be of little sociological value. Ranging all groups on a continuum of size, for example, from the smallest to the largest, is not particularly significant, unless the numbers of people are related to some other sociological characteristic. Arranging all groups on a basis of permanence, from the oldest and most enduring to the newest and most quickly changing, may be an interesting exercise in historical perspective, but to be scientifically important permanence and impermanence must also be linked with other features of group life.

Every social group must have the characteristics already defined, and it is possible to classify all groups on a continuum according to each of these characteristics. Some of these are more important than others. One may classify all groups according to *structure,* placing them on a continuum from the most rigidly to the most loosely structured; or according to *social roles,* from those that make the most demands on the members to those that make the fewest; or according to *reciprocal relations,* from those in which communication is most frequent and intimate to those in which it is the least. One may classify groups according to the *standards of behavior* expected of the members; according to the kinds of *social values* they share; and according to the kinds of *social goals* toward which they direct their behavior.

Another sociological classification is often made in the broad distinction between the in-group and the out-group. As the terms indicate, the in-group is made up of those who belong with us, while the out-group is people who are strangers to us. This is of significance to the isolated primitive tribe, the urban juvenile gang, the small exclusive country club; to these groups all others are "outsiders." Sometime the reference is to those who are "in favor" at any given time, as the close advisers to a president, while others, although associated with the government, are out of favor.

Another peculiar phenomenon of some sociological significance is the reference group, which serves as a kind of behavior model for many people. It is peculiar in the sense that the person deeply influenced by it may not be included in its membership. A rough example is that of the salesman who may be guided in his own behavior by the influence of any one of three reference groups: the orders of his employers, the expectations of his customers, the informal practices of his fellow salesmen. A more common and complicated example is that of the parish clergyman who may be guided in his behavior by the expectations of his congregation, although these expectations in turn may be in conflict with the practices of his fellow clergymen and the regulations set down by his ecclesiastical superiors. From this point of view, the reference group is an important instrument of continuing socialization in the roles that people enact in their group life.

## COMMON BASES FOR GROUPS

One of the most widely used systems of group classification, and perhaps the simplest to grasp for an introductory understanding, is that of the four common bases for group association. This is a common-sense approach rather than a scientific one, but it has the advantage of providing a quick, broad, and universal outline of group life. This most general classification embraces the largest number of groups in the fewest categories. The four bases upon which all people associate in group life are: (*a*) common ancestry, (*b*) territory shared in common, (*c*) similar bodily characteristics, and (*d*) common interests.

**a.** Common ancestry is traditionally the strongest tie that binds human beings in their social relations, although its importance has been greatly lessened in modern, complex, and large-scale societies. The groups based upon common ancestry are sometimes called "blood" groups, those in which members are related by birth, marriage, or adoption. Both the immediate conjugal family, consisting of parents and children, and the consanguine family, including cousins, aunts, uncles, and so forth, are of this type. In primitive societies the extended kinship group is often called the clan or tribe. The persistence of ethnic groups like Greek-Americans or Polish-Americans is largely attributed to an appreciation of common ancestry.

**b.** Territorial proximity is also a very broad basis for social groups. Since all groups are necessarily existent in time and space, it is obvious that they must somehow be limited to a physical location. The sociological neighborhood that is not merely a social aggregate, and the true community, are modern examples of territorial groups. Insofar as the persons within a political division, like a village, a suburb, or a township, constitute a collectivity in reciprocal relations, they may also be studied under this category. Many different kinds of groups such as athletic teams, parent-teacher groups, and civic clubs, are identified with the name of the place in which they exist.

c. The classification of groups based on bodily character-istics is widely used in modern society, and the listing of groups under this heading would be interminable. In isolated, primitive societies, the similarity of biological characteristics is closely allied to the facts of common ancestry and common territory. In complex, modern societies common racial features are still a basis of either imposed or voluntary social grouping, but other charac-teristics lend themselves to a great deal of voluntary association. For example, youth clubs, various female organizations, men's lodges, fraternities, and clubs show that age and sex are frequently used as a basis of group formation. Physical strength and aptitude are also com-mon bases for groups of football players, wrestlers, and other athletes.

d. The sharing of common interests is the basis for a great variety of modern social groupings. In fact, the "interest group" is sociologically more significant than most of the other groups discussed above because com-mon interest implies the willingness to function together in the pursuit of a common goal. The multiplication of scientific, business, and professional associations is merely one indication of the tremendous number and variety of this kind of group.

It must be emphasized that these four bases for social groups do not represent four exclusive classifications. They are abstractions from concrete reality—a way of looking at the same persons under different aspects and according to the varying relations they have with their fellowmen. There is, in fact, an overlapping of persons, a multiple membership of the individual in the various types of groups discussed. It would be difficult to find a normal adult who is not in some way a member of all four types of groups.

## THE MAJOR GROUPS

The most satisfactory and sociologically significant

classification of groups is that based on the major universal social functions that human beings in group life must perform if society is to continue in existence. Human beings everywhere and at all times must cooperate in some way to satisfy the social needs implied in familial, educational, economic, political, religious, and recreational activities. These essential needs and functions are sometimes called the social and cultural prerequisites in the sense that without them no society could continue to exist. It is obvious, therefore, that they are universal, and empirical studies have shown that they are also variable.

The universality of these major social groups has been established without question by social scientists. But although these groups are found in every society, without exception, this does not mean that each is given equal emphasis within any particular society. They are all essential to the continuance of the society, but in one place emphasis may be put upon one group or another. Nor does this universality mean that every social person is simultaneously enacting a social role in all of them in any given society.

Most adults in every society join with others in the fulfillment of familial and recreational needs. The father of a family may also be a member of a poker-playing group. All children submit to the socialization process and are, at least for a time, participants in informal and formal educational groups. The businessman plays a role in his parish church and his political party; and the economic, religious, and political groups engage the attention of varying numbers of people. The significant fact is that some people in every society must at all times be performing the central functions of these major social groups.

The diversity and variability of these major groups have also been scientifically established. The fact that these social needs, functions, and groups are present in every society does not mean that they are present in the same way. Different forms are emphasized in different societies, and greater variations are permitted in some societies than in others. Marriage is almost everywhere monogamous, but polygamy is practiced in some places; the economic groups in an industrial society differ from those in an agricultural society. The variety of recreational and religious groups is tremendous throughout the world. The way societies structure their groups for educational and political purposes varies greatly. Somehow or other every society manages to reproduce itself, educate its new members, provide material sustenance and means of relaxation, maintain public order, and satisfy the religious needs of people.

The advantage of classifying groups in this way is that every group which has a clearly defined central social goal can be included under one of these headings. Many groups have multiple functions, of course, but even these groups can be arranged for purposes of study under the principal activity in which they engage. The following is a brief resume of the groups which come under each of the six major headings.

a. The family group is made up of those persons engaged in satisfying the basic needs of family life: the arrangements for sex relations, the birth and care of children, and mutual affection of the members. In some societies, the concept of family extends vertically and horizontally to include all who are in any way related by marriage, birth, or adoption. In some places and at some periods of history the family is synonymous also with the word "household" and includes domestic servants, retainers, serfs, and even slaves.

b. The educational groups are those in which the essential social function of transmitting the culture to succeeding generations is performed in formal and informal ways. In simple societies this is often done within the family itself, but in more complex societies there is a great variety of schools, institutes, academies, and scientific and learned associations. No matter where and how it is done, the fact is that this function is recognized as a social activity performed by people together.

c. The economic groups are those in which the members produce and distribute the material goods and services necessary for the physical maintenance of life on earth.

Here again there is a great difference between the society in which the family members cooperate to sustain themselves and a society in which the division of labor has become highly specialized. All kinds of business and professional associations are primarily economic, although they may have other subfunctions like scientific research, the training of employees, or the maintenance of lobbies for political purposes.

d. The political groups are all those which perform the function of administering and governing, of maintaining the public order, of making, interpreting, and enforcing the laws. The political parties, the whole court system, the penitentiaries and jails, the military units of all kinds, must be included under this heading. The central function of the political groups can always be recognized even though certain governmental functions may become quite diffused and diverse. Large modern governments must concern themselves with almost everything from soil conservation and atomic research to hospital administration and radio communication.

e. The religious groups are constituted by those persons who share in a patterned and social way the relationship between God and man. The piety and private worship of the individual is affected by the kind of religious bodies present in the society, but the social scientist focuses upon the groups of people who share similar religious values and enact common religious behavior patterns. Most of these groups perform also other subfunctions, running parochial schools and sectarian colleges, operating social work agencies, and even providing playgrounds and other recreational facilities.

f. The recreational group is made up of persons who are satisfying in a social way the need for relaxation. Recreation does not mean simply play and athletics and physical exercise. A great variety of activities are considered recreational, and are carried on by serious aesthetic organizations as well as hobby clubs. The term "commercial" recreation indicates that the economic factor may play an important part in the formation and maintenance of recreational groups, and there can be no doubt that the entertainment "industry" in modern societies is big business.

## GROUPS AND ASSOCIATIONS

It has become customary in sociological literature to make a distinction between primary and secondary groups. Both of these are genuine social groups in the strictest technical definition of the term, but the tendency has been to identify the secondary groups as associations. This distinction is not merely an instrumental and conceptual device that enables us better to understand the composition of society. It is a distinction between two general types of groups that actually exist in large numbers.

When we discuss the various kinds of societies in the next chapter we shall see that some societies are characterized by a predominance of primary groups while others emphasize secondary groups, or associations. The type of society which places an emphasis on primary groups carries a long list of labels, each depending on the taste and point of view of the social scientist who is describing the groups. A society of primary groups is called communal, established, *gemeinschaftlich*, mechanical, closed, solidaristic, familistic, folk, and traditional. An Irish fishing village, a town of wood-carvers in Bavaria, a community of Louisiana trappers, a rural French-Canadian village, exemplify these primary-group characteristics.

Unlike the distinctions among the social groups which focus upon a single essential social function, the distinction between the primary and secondary groups is based upon a combination of characteristics. If we consider the terms which contrast with those given above for the primary type of society, we have a rough description of the secondary type of society. A society which emphasizes secondary groups is called associational, adaptive, *gesellschaftlich*, organic, open, anomic, contractual, complex, industrial, and dynamic. As we learn more and more about groups and societies, it becomes increasingly clear that modern urban America is developing all these characteristics.

Two important facts must be pointed out here. The first is that both the primary and the secondary groups fit the definition of the social group given above. This is true even though the secondary group is more frequently identified simply as an association. The second is that the identification of these types of groups is mainly a matter of the partial presence of certain characteristics. They are "types" in the sense that the represent the two poles of a range of groups. If all groups in a society were placed on a continuum, some would appear to be in a transitional stage, sharing some of the characteristics of both the primary and secondary groups.

The difference between the primary and secondary groups is mainly, but not exclusively, in the kind or reciprocal relations and communication that exists among the members of the group. When these social relations are intimate, personal, face-to-face, and frequent, they are characteristic of the primary group. The social relations in the secondary group, or association, are obviously on a different level. They are relatively impersonal, informal, and less frequent, and are characteristic of larger and loosely organized groups.

PRIMARY GROUPS

The primary group is a relatively "tight" collectivity of people who have frequent face-to-face relations, a feeling of solidarity, and a close adherence to common social values.

The face-to-face group is primary in the sense of being fundamental for the individual person. His earliest and most formative experiences are with the primary family group. Here he has his most effective and long-lasting lessons in socialization. Much of his social personality results from this contact and communication. The intimate groups with which he associates all during his life are also primary in the sense of being closest to him. They are made up of the people he loves and trusts and admires. They are the ones with whom he has his most worthwhile social experiences. They make life worth living. These groups are primary, too, in the sense that the individual's "true" personality is revealed in them. He may be more constrained to enact the rigid expectations of his social roles in the secondary associations, but in the primary groupings he is more "himself."

The social person's primary group is called the "in-group" only in the strictest sense of the term. In it he has a feeling of belonging, a consciousness of cohesiveness, which tends to place all other people in out-groups. This distinction between in-group and out-group is not synonymous with that between the primary group and the secondary association. In relation to any particular individual the various out-groups may be either primary or secondary depending upon their composition and characteristics. They are simply the groups with which any individual person has no social relations at all. The family of a migrant farm worker may be a close-knit unit, but it is probably an out-group to most other people. The person in an Appalachian "hollow" may consider the people in the nearest town an out-group, as well as all kinds of occupational, political, and religious groups to which he is a stranger.

SECONDARY GROUPS

The secondary group, or association, is a looser collectivity than the primary group. Individual persons enter into secondary relationships voluntarily and purposively and often, in an unspoken way, "contractually." These relationships are regulated by law and justice, by formal customs and agreements. They are more careful and calculated; a person has to "watch himself," has to be "on his best behavior." When a man asserts among his business associates that "my word is my bond," he is attempting to inject into a secondary group the highly regarded mutual trust and understanding characteristic of the primary group.

It must be noted that the social person, with the possible exception of the very youngest child, belongs simultaneously to both primary groups and secondary associations. The immediate family is a person's primary group, but the large, extended kinship to which he belongs is his secondary group. The people with whom the adult associates most in his church are his primary group, the other members of the parish or congregation form his secondary group. In his economic relations he associates more closely with some than with others; the former are primary, the latter secondary.

It is a mistake to assume that only the familial and recreational groups can be primary groups. This assumption occurs because sociological literature frequently gives only close family and the play group as examples of primary groups. Nevertheless, the fact remains that, as in most sociological classifications, the dividing line between primary and secondary groups is not in every specific case clear and distinct. Some primary groups may be in the process of becoming looser secondary associations; some secondary groups may be in the process of "closing ranks," limiting membership, and developing primary social relations. The Communist cell, as a close-knit action group, is an example of the deliberate formation of a primary group within the structure of a larger secondary association.

## ASSOCIATIONS AND AGGREGATES

From another point of view the secondary group, or association, stands midway between the primary group and the social aggregate. The same person is found in all three of them; in the primary group he is close to others, in the secondary group he is organized with others, and in the social aggregate he has only casual and fleeting contacts with others. The difference between a spatial neighborhood and a social neighborhood is largely a difference between a social aggregate and a secondary group. In the first the people hardly know one another; in the second they tend to live a community life.

The student of society must be careful to distinguish not only between the primary and the secondary group, but also between the secondary group and the social aggregate. We have seen that these aggregates, such as crowds, mobs, and audiences, are marked by transitoriness, fluidity, lack of organization and of continuing reciprocal relations. This is not true of secondary groups, which are relatively large associations of people, like a university, a city parish, a factory, a country club, a local political party. Human relations in these groups are less personal and intimate than they are in primary groups, but the people are formally organized and are identified as members of the association.

It is commonly asserted, and with fairly objective and sufficient evidence, that any urban industrialized nation tends to become a society of associations and aggregates. This generalization must be accepted and interpreted with caution. If it means that the people are spending more time in secondary groups and in aggregates than ever before, the statement can be well substantiated. But two points must be emphasized in reference to this generalization. The first is that both primary and secondary groups exist side by side, and that the person belongs to both simultaneously by virtue of his membership in any of the major social groups. The second is that primary groups do and must exist in any ongoing society. The degree to which the primary groups are strong and numerous is an index of integration and solidarity in the total society. If its primary groups are weak and insufficient, the society itself tends to disintegrate.

## Characteristics of American Group Life
### 1. THE DECLINE OF PRIMARY GROUPS

It is apparent to even the casual observer that social aggregates and secondary associations are increasing in American urban society. Since people are limited in their time, energy, and abilities, this increase in other forms of human relations almost necessarily implies a decrease in primary relations. It is not necessary, however, merely to deduce this fact. One can observe all about him, and in his own experience, the measure to which his time, energy, and abilities are employed in secondary rather than in primary groups.

Primary groups are as essential to the continuity of the American society as to that of any other society. There is a minimum level, which we have not reached and probably cannot know empirically, at which the decline of primary groups seriously threatens the existence of a society. When we talk about the decline of primary groups in our society, we are discussing a sociologically serious trend, but we are not implying the absence of primary groups—a sociological impossibility. On the other hand, it is true that urban Americans are adaptive and resilient, and they have accustomed themselves in many ways to the social change which emphasizes secondary associations.

The following are some of the indexes and factors in the decline of primary groups in the American society.

a. Americans are geographically the most mobile people (except for nomadic tribes) in the world. This population mobility has reached the point where an estimated 20 percent of the people change their residence within any given year. Primary groups develop through stable, continuous relations with the same persons. When a family moves its residence, the members of the family continue their primary relations among themselves but tend to break off and change relations in the nonfamily groups.

b. The discontinuity of generations is also a factor in the decline of primary groupings. In American society the newly married couple is expected to leave the parental family and to shift for itself. While this throws the members of the young conjugal family closer together and theoretically ought to strengthen their primary relationships, it tends also to take away the support of the many primary groups formerly surrounding them in the parental home and neighborhood.

c. The high incidence of divorce in American society is one of the indexes of the decline of primary relations. Whether it is also a cause of this decline is not clear. No human relation is more intimate and personal than that of marriage, and the breakdown of the marital relation is synonymous with the breakdown of the primary relation between the people involved. Nevertheless, it must be noted here that most divorced people remarry and that their second marriages are relatively stable and permanent arrangements.

d. While we have classified primary groups under the major social groups specified according to function, it is also true that there is a dispersal of social functions in many primary groups. The primary school group that shares in religious and recreational as well as educational functions is likely to be more cohesive than one that concentrates only on learning. The primary familial group in which members share economic, recreational, educational, and religious activities is likely to be more cohesive than one that allows these functions to be performed away from home.

e. The urbanization of church life is also a characteristic of American society. Theoretically the high values of religion, with its emphasis on love and fellowship, should strengthen the primary relations. As the city church becomes larger, however, it tends to become a secondary group. It is estimated that while 40 percent of Americans are not expressly affiliated with the churches, many of those who are formal church members participate only casually and sporadically in religious services and groups. This does not mean that the percentage of church membership is declining but that the intimate primary religious groups are declining in number and significance.

f. The decline of the social neighborhood in the inner city means the decline of those friendly personal relations that characterize primary groups. This appears to be part of the price we pay for population density and the general anonymity of urban life as well as for the residential mobility mentioned above.

g. The growth of specialized commercial services has helped to break down the primary group. The person pays to have something done for him, rather than to do it himself in the company of others. He does this frequently for sports and entertainment, but also for the various services in restaurants, barber shops, launderettes, supermarkets, and other places. The efficiency and promptness of these services are very attractive to the individual city-dweller.

In the midst of these facts concerning the decline of primary groups, there is a paradox which requires interpretation. This is the multiplication of the primary relations of the individual. A person associates with different persons in each different primary group. For example, the urban male may associate with one group of males in the shop or office, another group in the tavern, still another on the bowling team, in the church congregation, the political club, and of course, his own family. This kind of multiple social relationship is a corollary of the decrease of the multiple functions in the family itself. Usually there is a certain amount of crossing over and sharing of members in the different primary groups, but to the extent that the individual participates in completely separate groups, he tends to weaken his primary relationships.

## 2. AMERICAN PRESSURE GROUPS

The pressure group is an organized collectivity of persons seeking to promote their own special interests in the total society. Every self-conscious group tends to do this in some respect, to seek higher status, to be well regarded by others. But the special-interest group is identified by its use of social pressure, its attempts to gain power and advantages in relation to other groups. There is often a "conflict of interest" between two or more groups and this is what gives the pressure group its peculiar characteristic in the American society.

The pressure group is usually a secondary association built upon a broad base of membership and represented at its top by expert, efficient, and hard-driving smaller groups of individuals. The function of these groups is to promote the interests of their memberships, insofar as they are active in the political arena and influence government and legislatures, they are called lobbies. The government is sometimes thought of as a mediator among the pressure groups, but it is more often the agency from which favorable action is requested.

It is not accidental that a pluralistic, democratic society like the United States should have a large number of pressure organizations of great variety, including the following.

**a.** Business groups probably exert more pressure, spend more money, and have a greater effect on American society than any other type of pressure group. This is to be expected in a society dominated by economic values and activities. The National Association of Manufacturers and the United States Chamber of Commerce are the best known and most powerful of these groups, but there are also innumerable trade associations in the various industries and businesses of the country.

**b.** Professional and occupational groups also exert tremendous social pressure, sometimes against the business groups and sometimes in cooperation with them. The best known are the American Medical Association, the American Bar Association, and the various organized labor unions. Furthering their particular interests, they influence Congress and the state legislatures, publish newspapers, sponsor radio and television programs.

**c.** In some respects the farm groups are even more successful in building up power in the American society. Because of their rural background, and the nostalgic sympathy of most Americans for that way of life, the farmers are often not thought of as an organized pressure group. Many of these groups are not representative of the family farmer, but of the corporate farmers who specialize in industry-like production of citrus, dairy, and other foods. The cattlemen and wheat growers have especially powerful lobbies.

**d.** The pressure groups for military veterans make a strong moral claim for attention from the nation. The peace movement and various antiwar demonstrations have dulled the patriotic prestige of veterans' organizations. Nevertheless, the American Legion, the Veterans of Foreign Wars, and other similar organizations still make their demands felt at the state and federal level. Political leaders have been especially sensitive to these demands.

**e.** Pressure groups representing various minorities are also characteristic of American society. These operate mainly in promotion of the rights of racial and ethnic minorities that are constantly fighting for recognition. The Black

groups, and to some extent the Jewish defense groups, have become more prominent than the older hyphenated American groups representing minorities of various nationality backgrounds. This is the main area in which there are also strong antiminority pressure groups, designed especially to "protect" America from subversion.
**f.** The term "pressure group" is not often used in reference to American religious bodies, but each of the twelve major churches uses organized means to gain influence in both national and regional activities. This activity is seldom mere propaganda or proselytizing for new members, but seeks to influence legislation and to guard against presumably threatening activities.

It is clear that pressure groups do not by themselves exhaust all the agencies and channels that represent special interests in the United States. There are individuals who are socially powerful because of their high status, and there are also broad "impersonal" interests that permeate a climate of opinion, such as the vague "state's rights" movement, or the promotion of federal subsidies for education, or the various left- and right-wing economic and political groups.

The number and variety of these groups of "special pleaders" constitute a network of contravening, if not conflicting, forces. They indicate the complexity of American society and invalidate simple overall interpretations of its conflicts like "capital versus labor" or "the businessman versus the farmer." These dichotomies express at best only a small segment of the mosaic of American group life, often bypass a great amount of cooperation among groups, and de-emphasize the twofold relationship of the pressure group to the political system and to the general population.

## 3. American Women's Clubs

Adult American women have more leisure time, more money to spend, more freedom of movement, and a greater variety of interests than the women of any other major modern society. Since they are social persons living in an urban society which multiplies its social aggregates and associations, it is to be expected that females will organize themselves in numerous kinds of groups. Association of persons along sex and age lines is not something recent or novel; female groupings have existed in all societies.

In an earlier period, women's clubs were often organized for church activities, and since religious bodies have traditionally separated the males from the females, the old from the young, the married from the single, this was an almost automatic and enforced type of association. At a later period, as women demanded more freedom and equal rights, they also banded together voluntarily to seek and defend these rights. The suffragette movement focused mainly on voting rights; the more recently established National Organization for Women (NOW) seeks complete equality with males in all areas of American life.

The classification of large secondary female organizations indicates that women have grouped themselves around almost as many and varied interests as men have. These are not merely "ladies' auxiliaries" to associations primarily masculine in membership; they are also separate groups in professional, business, military, academic, political, and religious activities. The various sisterhoods, missionary aid societies, and temperance leagues are like the older religious-interest groups. Women are notoriously poor members of labor unions, but they have been relatively successful in groups dedicated to civic and political reform.

We are concerned here, however, with informal primary groups of middle-class women that flourish in the city and suburbs. Typical of these groups are the women's clubs dedicated to self-improvement and congeniality with a vague consciousness of "do-goodism." Most of the members are over forty years of age; their children are in their late teens; they are not gainfully employed, and tend to have extra time on their hands. More often than not, these are the women with whom foreign visitors come into contact and from whom they take back to their countries an unflattering stereotype of American womanhood.

What makes for this phenomenon? What are the elements which account for the emergence and continuing increase of this type of primary group?

**a.** These women's clubs fulfill a need for their members. The married woman in this category has performed her social function in bearing and rearing children. She is not needed for the economic support of her home; she has not been trained toward activities of a solitary or meditative nature; her housework requires a minimum of time and effort; she feels a need for social relations outside the home.

**b.** Because these clubs are relatively exclusive, membership in them is a reflection of one's social status. They differ in status from one another, but the women who belong to any particular club are of relatively the same social stratum. This social accessibility indicates for the most part that their husbands are also in the same social class. Membership for the woman helps maintain the status of the family.

**c.** This type of women's club always puts an emphasis on congeniality. Whether it is a luncheon club, a garden club, a bridge club, or any other kind, the members must be able to "get along" well together. Friendliness is more important as a personal quality than charm or poise. The members are genuinely fond of one another and meet on a basis of face-to-face relations.

**d.** Hardly any of these groups are primarily maintained for an ameliorative purpose, but almost all of them have some charitable project as one of their activities. They may donate to a hospital, promote help for handicapped children, sponsor an opera guild, or encourage any of the numerous activities for civic betterment of the community.

**e.** The central purpose, however, is almost invariably recreational. Even though the ladies feel that they must be "doing something for somebody," their acknowledged goal is relaxation and enjoyment—to have in a temperate and moderate way "a good time." This may be paradoxical, since it is the very surplus of leisure time and the relief from pressing social duties that make possible the proliferation of these women's groups.

**f.** Although the social relations within these groups are primary and informal, the group almost always has a formal structure. There is a chairman, secretary, and treasurer, dues are collected, new members are formally invited. Often, of course, the business meeting, or that portion of a meeting devoted to business, is at best a perfunctory affair.

It must be pointed out that this description is not applicable to all the various kinds of female organizations that flourish in our society. It refers only to that type of women's club which is so often unfairly caricatured. One cannot dismiss these organizations as innocuous groupings of people who are wasting their time. They have a definite place in our kind of urban society, and it is difficult to see what kind of group and activity could replace them.

## 4. URBAN YOUTH GANGS AS PRIMARY GROUPS

Another social phenomenon current in urban American society is the gang. Social scientists sometimes speak of the "gang age" because the members of these groups are mainly teenagers. The gang usually grows out of a spontaneous play group within a closely limited urban area. These groups are for the most part boys' gangs, although there are a few instances of similar girls' groups, and of girls' auxiliaries to the boys' gangs. The term "street gang" has come to have a negative connotation, as though all behavior of the participants were suspect and delinquent.

The fact is, however, that there are many more "good" gangs than there are "bad" gangs. The function of the gang is essentially recreational in nature. It is a friendship clique, a primary group of young people who like to associate with one another and who are for the most part given to harmless pranks. The "tough" gang with which the police are concerned is usually found in the crowded slums and adjacent areas where social and economic conditions are largely disorganized.

Youthful recreational groups are present in all societies in one degree or another. But the "tough" American street gang is unique in its large numbers and in the peculiar importance attached to it by its members and by the society in general. Following are some of the factors that contribute to its formation. It must be noted that no single cause is adequate, nor can any single solution be offered for the social difficulties which arise from these gangs.

a. Population density and substandard housing are characteristic of the urban areas where gangs develop. This means, of course, the constant overcrowding of homes. If there were only a few overcrowded dwellings in a city block, this would not be a large factor, but when each apartment of each building is overflowing with people, it is natural for the young people to spend much of their time on the streets.

b. Family disorganization accompanies urban overcrowding. The economic conditions, the presence of boarders, the lack of privacy, the feeling of young people that their parents, especially the father, are failures—all of these tend to weaken the emotional security a youth needs. The family fails to meet the minimum standard of living which the American society expects and values. The socialization process, through which the youngster is expected to develop into a responsible citizen, does not work to good advantage in this situation.

c. One of the reasons for the restlessness of American adolescents in general is their relatively functionless status; and in a crowded city young people are likely to seek status in disapproved ways. In other societies, where the great majority of teenagers become gainfully employed and are already started on their economic careers, juvenile delinquency is minimized.

d. It is a recognized fact that the American youth seeks status through peer approval more than through parental approval. This means that the "natural authority" of the older generation is weakened, and the young person tends to follow the patterns of behavior of his contemporaries. The youth seeks an outlet in the gang and prefers the approval of the gang to that of his parents and family.

e. The confusion of behavior standards is highlighted in the juvenile gang. The schools and churches with which the youth has some contact represent to him a standard of behavior that seems unrealistic because it is so far out of line with what he sees in his everyday experiences. The propositions for the "better life" offered in the whole system of American advertising are also, to his mind, completely out of his reach. Many of the behavior patterns he sees around him every day are very different from those said to be in existence in the "outside world."

f. Meanwhile the tremendous flood of movies, TV programs, comic books, pictures, and pulp magazines that portray crime and violence represents to the gang member a style of behavior which seems more suitable to his own life situation. The models of delinquent behavior, ostensibly censured by the society at large, are offered to him in detailed patterns of action performed in surroundings and by characters he recognizes. The youth certainly has access to the more "positive" representations in these media of communication and entertainment, but these often seem to him lifeless and unreal.

g. The lack of approved recreational facilities in the crowded urban areas is also a conditioning factor in the formation of gangs. Supervised recreation cannot be the single solution where all these other conditions exist. The fact is that a combination of boredom and tension is an important psychological factor in the formation of gangs and in the type of behavior which they pursue. Adequate playgrounds and meetings places, organized sports and dances, would help to relieve the tension and boredom.

It must be noted that the youth gang is simply a socially abnormal instance of the universally present primary group. There are leaders and followers in these groups, a code of behavior which the members consider important, frequent and informal social relations, a feeling of belonging, an attitude which stresses the welfare of the group. These are in many ways intensified characteristics of the primary group.

## 5. Associations of American Labor

In some ways the United States is a highly organized society. We have seen the various bases upon which people tend to associate with one another, not only the major social groups found in every society, but also the various subgroupings peculiar to each society. Americans often form groups and join existing groups on the basis of similar economic function. People who are gainfully employed organize to protect their interests and to promote their particular function. This is as true for physicians, lawyers, nurses, and teachers as it is for manufacturers, distributors, white-collar workers, and industrial workers.

The American labor unions, as social groups, have some of the characteristics found in all organizations of gainfully employed people. But the term "labor union" appears to have been limited by social usage mainly to groups whose members are organized manual workers. Teachers and social workers, bankers and physicians, for example, do not like to call their professional associations "labor unions," even though one of the primary functions of these groups is the economic protection of their members.

Unlike labor organizations of most other major societies, American labor unions have limited themselves mainly to immediate economic gains. They have acted as pressure groups, have exerted political influence, have issued statements on contemporary, social, and world problems. They have not, however, formed a political party and have no serious ideology other than that of the American capitalist system. They have no interest in "taking over" either economic or political management in the society or in establishing a proletarian and "classless" society.

Following are some of the features of American labor unions, which include in their membership a little more than one-fourth of all gainfully employed persons in our society.

a. The labor unions are secondary associations in which the social relations of members are largely standardized and impersonal. In any union local there are unquestionably primary groups made up of the most active and interested members, and in any national union the top officials in frequent contact with one another also form a primary group. But the very nature of large-scale industry in America has required a parallel large-scale organization of labor in which primary groups do not flourish.

**b.** Worker solidarity—the dedicated cooperation of members—is largely a myth in these unions. The aspirations of workers, like those of most other Americans, are directed towards higher social status and better material standards of living. The "middle-class mentality" of American workers has been the despair of communist and socialist labor leaders. The worker has a certain loyalty to his union and is often willing to endure the suffering of strikes, but this loyalty appears to be built on gratitude for benefits received and on the hope of more to come, rather than on a personal attachment to, and solidarity with, his fellow workers.

**c.** The growth of bureaucracy within the large labor unions parallels a similar development in government and industry, and even in educational and religious structures in America. Policies are determined at higher levels and subordinate officials are expected to execute them. Bureaus of special functionaries have emerged so that the top officials are surrounded by labor lawyers and strategists, labor accountants and economists, public relations experts, and other specialists.

**d.** The democratic process has imposed peculiar difficulties on the maintenance of labor unions. The voter apathy characteristic of the American people is seen also in unions. Factory-wide and industry-wide voting on particular issues has been facilitated by the cooperation of management and government. But the conduct of local meetings and the election of officers are hindered by the mass apathy of workers. Labor leaders depend upon popular elections for their continuance in office. Unlike a salaried manager, they cannot dictate to their membership; they are constantly forced to prove their worth and must periodically test their position, like the politician, by "going to the people."

The labor unions, as a whole, are often thought of as a solid phalanx moving the country irresistibly closer to the socialist or welfare state. This opinion is generally held by people who do not seem to realize that organized labor is a product of the American society and has developed alongside of other characteristic social structures. Unions are sometimes opposed by persons who pretend to be defending "free enterprise" and "rugged individualism" without realizing that these have long since disappeared from the American economic scene. The fact is that labor unions follow pretty closely the patterns of secondary associations as they have developed in the United States.

## Suggested Readings

Blau, Peter M. *Bureaucracy in Modern Society*. New York: Random House, 1956.

Cooley, Charles H. *Social Organization*. Glencoe: Free Press, 1956.

Homans, George C. *The Human Group*. New York: Harcourt, Brace, 1950.

Tönnies, Ferdinand. *Community and Society*. Translated and edited by Charles P. Loomis. New York: Harper & Row, 1962.

Thompson, Victor. *Modern Organization*. New York: Knopf, 1960.

Whyte, William F. *Street Corner Society*. Chicago: University of Chicago Press, 1955.

# 5
# Communities

THE TERM "COMMUNITY" IS ANOTHER OF THOSE SOCI-
ological words which has come to have a variety of meanings. The many meanings of this word are as confusing
as those other commonly used words, like culture, family,
and institution. We sometimes hear that there is a "family
atmosphere" if one works for certain kinds of companies.
People often use the word "institution" to refer to some
unusual person or situation. The word "culture" frequently refers to refinement and manners. If the behavioral
scientists have made any contribution to analytical concepts in our time they have done so by providing technical
precision for the language of human behavior.

It would be arbitrary, however, to insist that a word
means only what the sociologist says it means. We need
not quarrel with those who talk about the total human race
as the family of God in which we are all brothers and
sisters, or as the world community of which we are all
members. In other broad usages of "community" we know
what is signified by large general alliances like the North
Atlantic community, or the European economic community. Sometimes the term is applied to a loose social category
based on ethnic, racial, or religious similarity, like the Jewish community of New Orleans, the Black community of
Chicago, the Irish community of Boston.

## THE LOSS OF COMMUNITY

Sociologists who are concerned with broad historical
change attempt to explain the basic problems of modern
social life by saying that we have suffered an all-pervasive
"loss of community." This means that there has been a shift
of emphasis from one general kind of social organization to
another, a shift that provides a sociological explanation for
contemporary Western values, behavior patterns, social relations and institutions. This must not be interpreted as

134

simplistic, single-factor casuality, although some observers seem to find the single solution to our social problems in a global return to community.

In this broad application to group life, the concept of community embraces four elements: (*a*) close personal relations with other persons, that are sometimes called primary, face-to-face, intimate relations; (*b*) an emotional, sensitive involvement on the part of the individual in the social functions and affairs of the group; (*c*) moral dedication, or commitment, to the values that are considered high and significant by the group; (*d*) a sense of solidarity with other members of the group.

There are, of course, groups of people in the modern world who exhibit these qualities, but these are small primary groups. The difference is that these qualities are not characteristic of a total culture, as the historians claim they were before the advent of the industrial revolution, the large-scale capitalist system, mass urbanization and metropolitanism, and secularization. The anthropologists who look for societies in which community qualities are pervasive go to so-called underdeveloped areas, as Le Play did in Europe, Redfield in Yucatan, Warner among the Australian aborigines, and DuBois among the people of Alor.

This generalized concept of community is, then, a question of overall organization, but especially of the manner in which the social person relates to the larger social structure. It is improbable that large, complex democratic societies can be reorganized for the total restoration of community. There was a sense in which the totalitarian systems of nazism, communism and facism, attempted to restructure the people into a national community. The degree of success they achieved came at an exorbitant price in human lives and values; and their failures are part of the public record.

In order to comprehend the sociological significance of community we shall examine this phenomenon at three levels: social solidarity, social relations, and social structure.

## VALUE OF TOGETHERNESS

The sense of community, as a feeling of togetherness, is a desirable goal that social groups try hard to achieve and maintain. Labor unions seek solidarity among the workers; Protestant congregations try to develop fellowship among the members; family magazines attempt to inspire a feeling of togetherness in the home; Black racial groups often talk about "soul brothers" as an index of belonging. Many other terms are used almost synonymously, like social cohesion, harmony, esprit de corps, consensus, to indicate a kind of ideological attitude that binds and unites people.

The sociological significance of togetherness, or solidarity, has been much discussed by modern social scientists. They suggest that human beings, in seeking an antidote to frustration, anxiety, insecurity, and loneliness are trying to reach the goal of community. It is as though freedom has made modern man afraid, as though individualism has brought alienation from his fellowman, as though independence has destroyed man's social security. This general social malaise, the sense of social isolation in the midst of growing populations, is supposed to be cured by developing a sense of community.

The apparent weakening of the sense of community, or of social solidarity, which is expressed in a feeling of estrangement and alienation, is a matter of reflection among all social scientists. It was one of Sorokin's dominant themes; he attributed the condition to individualism and called it the characteristic "atomization" of society. The condition is also attributed in part to the bigness and remoteness and impersonality of the social structure. When radicals rail against the establishment, the institution, the power structure, they are picturing a cold social machine which is destructive of close social relations.

It is a paradox that the loss of a sense of social solidarity is accompanied by the loss of a sense of personal identity. This peculiar and contradictory phenomenon is symbolized among American youth by the hippie dropout. He rails against the confinement and institutionalization of society and expresses his alienation by becoming further alienated. Identity with the community, or social solidarity, is supposed to foster self-identity; and it is difficult to understand the logic of self-isolation as an antidote or solution for the problem of a lack of community.

## COMMUNITY RELATIONS

Community, as a social process, is a form of conjunctive human relation, or interaction, in which people are drawn together and become more integrated. This is not simply an attitude or an ideology of solidarity; it is solidarity at work at the level of everyday human behavior. The achievement of cooperation between employer and employee is an example of this process; so is the teamwork that gets results in all kinds of group efforts. When the annual United Fund campaign is conducted, its main slogan is the call for the conjunctive process of community effort. In this, and in other instances, every citizen is asked to participate to further the common cause.

The opposite of the community process is the disjunctive process of conflict. College students and liberal intellectuals, and even many clergymen, have been in conflict with the national administration because of its military programs and policies. Black nationalists in America have been in conflict with the white power-structure at the municipal, state, and federal levels. Many other examples could be cited, both historical and contemporary. The peculiar fact is that the success of the peace movement depends upon the internal cooperation of its members; the condition for progress in the Black Power movement is the effective cooperation of all segments of the movement.

Only by an extension, or a misunderstanding, of the meaning of community process can one say that the community "gets things done." Results come from people who are expending individual effort in the common cause, but who are acting in concert with others. This need for individual effort is best illustrated when the common goals of a local community become specified, so that some persons focus on improved schooling, others on fiscal reform, others on public services, and so forth. The talents of individuals are employed cooperatively for the commonweal.

From the point of view of community, what characterizes the integrative social relation is the extent to which the individual cooperates positively in all his major groups. In measurable terms this means that the total amount of cooperative relations increases in the larger society. Obviously, we are not talking about the imposition of the social process either by threat or payment. Community as a social process is accompanied by community as a sense of voluntary social solidarity.

## COMMUNITY STRUCTURES

The third way of looking at community, as social structure, is probably what most people have in mind when they use the term. Here we are talking about a group of people whose behavior patterns, social relations and roles are structured and organized. This fits the general definition of a social group as a collectivity of people in reciprocal communication. Aside from its spirit of solidarity and its demonstration of social cooperation, the community is specified by its locality. It is a territorial group of people.

In common sociological usage the community is essentially "bound to the ground" in the sense that the people live permanently in a given area, have a consciousness of belonging to both the group and the place, and function together in the chief concerns of life. The community is always considered in relation to a physical environment. The community is essentially a cluster, or network, of smaller groups, but in its totality it can itself be identified in many ways as a large social group. The members of the community are conscious of the needs of people in and out of their immediate group, and they tend to cooperate closely.

It is important to realize that these three ways of looking at community (solidarity, relations, and structure) do not always operate in a complementary fashion, and this is especially true of community as social structure. No sociologist would claim that the kind of social solidarity found in the total folk village (the kind of solidarity that the German sociologist Ferdinand Tönnies called *Gemeinschaft*) is found also in the total metropolis. It is only in an arbitrary way that we can distinguish the social structure of the folk village from that of the city. In other words, the social structures of folk village and city differ only in degree, but the folk village exhibits the social solidarity we call community, while the city does not.

Ordinarily we think of the modern community as a kind of neighborhood, and of the neighbor as a nearby resident in a given place. Neighborliness is a characteristic of communities in the rural, folk, and peasant societies. It is not a usual characteristic of the urban, metropolitan, and national societies, which are complex and associational. To some extent, however, the term "community" still applies to old city neighborhoods in which the people still have similar ethnic, economic, and educational backgrounds and have lived together for a long time. The modern suburbs, which are newer neighborhoods, often make a deliberate attempt to foster community spirit among the people, and in some instances these neighborhoods too may be technically described as communities.

The structure of a social collectivity refers to the organizational arrangement of its components. We have said that sociological analysis—as distinct from demographic, economic, or political analysis—focuses on the structural elements of community. From the point of view of status and stratification, this structure is relatively "flat" with little social distance or social mobility from bottom to top. Although there are functional subgroups in the typical territorial community, these are informally organized at a level of personal relations. The whole mood or organizational life tends to be "natural" and familistic, rather than contrived and contractual. To use an old phrase, there is a "consciousness of kind," an awareness of shared similarities, among the people of the community.

Up to now we have provided a descriptive analysis of the concept of community, showing what is meant by the elements of social solidarity, relations, and structure. Analysis must go further, however, in attempting to explain the "why" of community—the factors, or reasons, for the formation of community. Research in various parts of the world has revealed three main factors of community: the economic, or occupational; the ethnic, or ethnocentric; and the religious. Let us look briefly at each of these factors.

### THE ECONOMIC FACTOR

Some social scientists are reluctant to describe the community as an urban or metropolitan phenomenon mainly because of the diversity of economic and occupational activities in densely populated places. Occupational specializations, even though coordinated successfully, are necessarily a wedge of social differentiation. The community tends to be a stronger and more effective social system when it exists in small villages removed from urban complexities and specializations. This simple type of society is one in which community is likely to flourish. Here the people are more likely to cooperate in all the major functions of a social life, especially in economic pursuits.

*Kibbutz* is the Hebrew word for social group, but it has now come to signify the special kind of community deliberately established in some parts of modern Israel. The common occupation of all members, male and female, including children and youth, is agriculture. The ideal of equality between the sexes is demonstrated in the sharing of farm work by both men and women. This common occupational activity is considered so essential for the maintenance of the community that family life is secondary. Children are separated from their parents a few days after birth, are raised separately in children's quarters, and permitted to visit their parents at only specified times. There is no family hearth or living room, and adults eat their meals in common dining halls. Multiple factors give support to the communal life of the kibbutz, but the central factor is the common economic occupation of the inhabitants.

The extreme egalitarian nature of the kibbutz is not a central feature of most "natural" and less ideological communities. Nevertheless, in the so-called underdeveloped regions of the world a common occupation is a central feature of community. This is seen in the primitive coastal villages of Polynesia where the community supports itself by fishing, in a coal town of West Virginia where mining is the principal source of income, in the interior of Yucatan where the main occupation of the community is farming. The common economic function allows for little social mobility, and this lack of stratification tends to reinforce the community.

This matter of basic economic and occupational similarity is peculiarly absent from the suburbs where the residents tend to pursue their gainful employment outside the immediate area. The head of the family goes to his work in the city and there performs an economic role which is little related to the immediate interests of the suburban community in which he lives. It is an exaggeration, however, to call these places simply "bedroom" communities, even when referring only to the working commuter. In spite of a lack of a common occupation, these suburbs are the daily living quarters of most of their people. In all other aspects of social life the suburbanites tend to center their social behavior and social relations in their own physical community. Homes, schools, churches, recreational and civic facilities, and the major social functions that these represent and perform, are located in the specific territory where the community exists.

## THE ETHNIC FACTOR

The persistence of cultural islands in the midst of large cities has not escaped the notice of sociologists. The people who live in such circumscribed urban neighborhoods have been called "ethnic villagers" by Herbert Gans, who studied the group life of Italian-Americans in a large city. Like the Puerto Ricans in the Lower East Side of New York City, these people tend to find work outside their immediate neighborhood and are occupationally similar only in that most of them have lower-status jobs. Their way of life is culturally, or ethnically, dissimilar from that of other people in the larger city.

The cultural items that distinguish ethnic villagers are those that generally characterize immigrant enclaves in American cities: a language other than English, close family ties and primary relations, organizations that are loose and informal, the continuation of religious and recreational patterns from the "old country," a preference for "national" foods. There is also a degree of clannishness that provides mutual support and is expressed negatively in suspicion and distrust of outsiders.

The ethnic variable combines with religious and occupational factors to explain the maintenance of the Amish communities in America. The Old Order Amish are a relatively rigid religious sect with types of dress and rules of conduct that immediately set them apart from modern Americans. They refuse to conform to secular education and recreation, exclude radios and television from their homes, and do not use automobiles and tractors. Deviants are excommunicated from the community. Farming, an occupation in which they are successful, has almost sacred significance to them.

One must not get the impression that ethnic communities are for the most part eccentric and "unpatriotic," or unacceptably foreign to the American culture. Such communities are sometimes accused of seeking the privileges of freedom in the American society without accepting the obligation of conformity to the American culture. One can push too far in ethnocentrism by insisting on the complete application of the melting-pot theory. These people are indeed socially exclusive and internally cohesive, but there is also a pluralistic ideology in American culture that allows for their continued existence in this country.

## THE RELIGIOUS FACTOR

The promotion of fellowship among the members of a local church congregation is often thought to "build community." It is indeed true that many small Christian churches emphasize primary relationships and attempt to provide solace and comfort that would offset the secular frustrations suffered by people in the "outside-world." The local staff of the church helps to socialize children and provides pastoral care for families. The members of the local church are most often of relatively the same socio-economic status, as measured by education, occupation, and income.

The religious base of community is, therefore, only one factor of fellowship, although it may be considered the most important factor in the minds of both clergy and laity. The individual members and the families that belong to the church are obviously enacting other social roles in other social groups: as citizens in the political order, as employees in the economic order, and in various other activities. There are also people in the same neighborhood who belong to other churches. For these various reasons the local church congregation cannot be called a community in the technical sense of the term.

There is, however, another kind of religious community that more proximately fits the technical definition. These are the groups of church functionaries existing to some extent among the Lutherans, more among the Anglicans, and most in the Roman Catholic church. They are called religious congregations, or orders, and they are made up of celibates of either sex. These people are organized specifically in the name of religion; their community life is regulated around religious practices; they are full-time employees of their church.

Most of these religious groups are actively engaged in services to the larger society, as in schools, hospitals, nursing homes, and various forms of social welfare. Their motivation and solidarity are basically religious, but they are not "separate" and self-contained as is the case with the territorial community. Perhaps only the contemplative and strictly monastic orders, which are completely withdrawn from the "world," can be called complete communities in the more technical sense of the word. Even here, the term community would not refer to the entire religious order, but only to the local group, like the abbey at Gethsemani, Kentucky, made famous by the Trappist monk, Thomas Merton.

## SURROGATE COMMUNITIES

The classifications of social groups ought to emerge from what we observe in the repetitive social life of people. The academic tendency is to polarize types of social collectivities into primary and secondary groups as though there were no groups that share some characteristics of both types. We contrast the communal type of society with the associative type, as though there were no societies somewhere on a continuum between these two. Similarly, we have described the territorial community as a kind of miniature of the total territorial society.

There is another meaning of community that must be recognized by the social scientist because it exists in the minds and habits of many people. For want of a better term, we may call this the surrogate or substitute community, in the sense that it provides a substitute for the natural and almost automatic community by setting up a contractual, contrived, or artificial group life. All of these descriptive words indicate a deliberate attempt to "recapture" the essentials of traditional community: the spirit of camaraderie, moral commitment, emotional involvement, close personal relations with others.

We tend to classify groups by their functions and goals in relation to other groups, but it seems true to say that functions in almost any group are multiple and complex. The substitute community of which we are speaking places great emphasis on the congeniality of its internal human relations, which it does not simply consider a by-product of its announced function. For example, an honor sorority or scholastic fraternity on any large campus seems to be this kind of community. Church affiliates who live in different parts of the city but who come together in religious fellowship for worship services constitute this kind of surrogate community. The focus of these collectivities is announced as a selective kind of interest, goal, or value, but the underlying bond of unity is the desire for congenial relations.

The members of the surrogate community are, therefore, not totally committed to multiple social functions, as are the multiple and related subgroups of the traditional territorial community; nor are these members narrowly circumscribed by a fixed physical neighborhood. Their mutual relations are not frequent enough to place them in the usually accepted definition of the primary group. These negative comments—saying what the thing is not—indicate that the surrogate community lies somewhere between the close-knit community and the loosely structured secondary association.

## Variations of American Community Life

### 1. THE RURAL COMMUNITY

It is a commonplace remark in sociological literature that urbanization in America is increasing at the expense of the rural way of life. In a country as large as the United States there still remain millions of physically isolated farm families. There are also tens of thousands of small rural villages, or hamlets, that are unincorporated. It is difficult to ascertain such statistics because the United States Bureau of the Census provides no information about such small collectivities. Nevertheless, there has been much research on rural life in America, and we are able to describe some of the characteristics of the rural community.

a. The people living in the modern American rural community are becoming less and less isolated from the mainstream of American life. The increased use of the telephone has provided a personal form of communication with others, but the main source of social contact has been the radio and, increasingly, television. Through these media the wider culture patterns of the society have been brought into these rural homes. This has been the principal channel both of modernization and of breaking physical isolation.

**b.** Except in the most remote rural areas personal contact has been increased by the improvement of public roads and the multiplication of both private and public means of transportation. Bus service has penetrated into places which were never reached by railroad trains. This has allowed access by "outsiders," but more importantly it has provided a physical mobility among the people themselves in the rural community. With the automobile it became possible to increase the frequency of primary, face-to-face relations with larger numbers of neighbors.

**c.** All comparative demographic research shows that the rural birthrate continues to be higher than the urban birthrate. Sociologically this implies that there is less emphasis on the conjugal family and more on the extended kinship group. There are no high-rise apartment buildings in the rural community, and the general type of dwelling is a one-family house which is usually large enough to accommodate grandparents. Relatively speaking, the members of the family continue as a close-knit unit.

**d.** The educational opportunities of young people in the rural community are no longer limited to the "little red schoolhouse." It has become customary for several communities to combine their resources, sometimes with state and federal aid, to provide high schools of improved quality. There has also been a spectacular growth in the number of junior colleges and, to some extent, community colleges which make higher education available to rural youth.

**e.** While there is a core population of permanent residents which remains relatively stable, there is also a kind of shifting population in the rural community. One current in this movement is the steady exodus of young adults who seek employment opportunities elsewhere. Depending upon the scenery, especially coastal and mountain communities, there is an influx of the so-called "summer colony" of temporary residents. A third kind of population shift occurs in some places where migratory workers are needed for large-scale harvesting.

**f.** Shared occupational pursuits and interests have always been important factors in the social cohesion of the community. It has been said that farming is a "way of life" in the rural community. This implies that not only the members of a given family but all of the farmers in a given area share the problems involved in the vagaries of weather, the fluctuations of market prices, the choice of crops to plant, the fertility of the soil. Actual work on the farm is not done solely by the father, the "breadwinner" of the family, but involves to some extent and in different tasks the farm wife and children.

What we have said here is descriptive of a sociological type, the rural community, which allows of wide variations. These descriptive items are variable on a list of other sociological elements: there are differences between owners and tenants, dairy farmers and wheat farmers, areas where there is a concentration of social minorities like Negroes, Mexican-Americans, Orientals. The relative isolation of the rural community is not the same in western Massachusetts as it is in central Nebraska. Changes are occurring in rural communities, but the rate of change is more rapid in some than in others.

## 2. THE BEDROOM COMMUNITY

For many Americans the quest for community life has been answered by buying a house in the suburbs and settling down to what is often called the "bedroom," or dormitory, community. We shall see that the search for a place to sleep is probably the last reason why a family moves to the suburb. The growth of the residential areas adjacent to large cities has been phenomenal, and the increase of sociological research in the suburban way of life has provided many generalizations of value to the student. Following are some of the data from these studies concerning the suburb as a community.

a. Probably the most noticeable factor in the typical suburban community is the relative homogeneity of the residents. For the most part these people are middle-class Americans in their values and patterns of behavior. Social conformity is recognized in their style of life, in the kinds of homes they own, in the aspirations for their children, in their forms of recreation. Any given suburb tends to attract the same social class of people, and most suburbs can be put in the range from upper-middle to lower-middle.

**b.** Despite this demonstrable conformity and homogeneity, the expressed intention of families moving to the suburbs —especially from the city—is to obtain freedom of space— a lawn, a garden, some outdoor space around the house. This means that the suburb is not a place of multiple-unit apartment buildings. It is a place where the family has some privacy, where both the parents and children have a sense of freedom.

**c.** There tends to be a demographic as well as social-class similarity in the suburban community. Younger families are attracted so that the median age of the population is below that of the city. There are relatively few self-supporting unmarried persons in the community. The suburbs tend also to be racially similar, and the resistance to racial integration is stronger in them than it is in other communities.

**d.** These suburbs are sometimes called "parasite" communities because most of the gainfully employed persons obtain their income from the larger city. Social cohesion due to the occupational factor is not present. There is, however, an occupational similarity in the sense that large numbers of the residents hold so-called white-collar jobs that place them neither in the higher managerial positions nor in the class of industrial or manual workers.

**e.** The quality of neighborliness, or community spirit, is often deliberately fostered by formal and informal organizations in the typical suburb. Proportionate to the population there are probably more "social clubs" available to the residents than there are in either the rural community or the densely populated cities. These are accompanied by various noneconomic subgroups that focus on educational, religious, and political functions in which residents are able to demonstrate their concern for the "good" community.

**f.** The male adult suburbanite who says that the main reason for living there is "the wife and kids" provides a sociological insight of some importance. From his point of view, the suburban community is, and should be, family centered. He endures the inconvenience of daily travel to and from the city, but also tends to cooperate in the group activities that benefit his wife and children.

As for all sociological generalizations, one must realize for this one the existence of many exceptions. There are wealthy as well as poor suburbs. Newspaper accounts and novels sometimes highlight juvenile and adult delinquency, the use of drugs, sexual excesses, and other moral deviations among suburbanites. Social and moral aberrations may be found more in some cities than in others. The large and growing numbers of suburban communities in the United States also tend to exhibit a range and variety of such behavior patterns.

### 3. THE ETHNIC COMMUNITY

The flood of immigrant colonizers to America, starting with the Spanish settlers, the French traders, the English Puritans, was directed at specific localities. Subsequent national groups, like the Germans, Irish, Italians, Scandinavians, Greeks, and Poles, fit into this same selective, separate, and concentrated pattern. After the original groups became settled, a link of communication with the homeland was established so that few subsequent immigrants came as complete strangers. They went where their relatives and friends were already settled. In spite of enormous mobility, both social and territorial, this pattern of ethnic separatism is still subject to the scrutiny of the modern American social scientist.

What are the characteristics of such ethnic communities and why do they persist in American cities today?
a. The clustering of people of the same ethnic background is one of the clearest demonstrations of man's natural desire for community. His own people are familiar to him; the larger society is alien to him. The dread feeling of alienation, of being a rootless stranger, comes from a lack of personal ties with people one knows and understands. These ties are ready-made for the newly arrived immigrant because they have been deliberately fostered and preserved by the people living in the community.

**b.** It is often said that Puerto Ricans keep to themselves, as do Chinese, Mexicans and others, because they have not been made welcome by "old stock" Americans who are Anglo-Saxons or who like to think of themselves as such. Imposed residential segregation is contrary to American principles of democracy and is subject to fair-housing laws in many states; but it does exist in ways often more subtle than outright. It is a fact also that one ethnic community may close itself against others, so that Poles do not welcome Irish, and vice versa.

**c.** In many instances the urban ethnic community has secondhand housing, streets, stores, schools, and public facilities. The members of the community are occupying neighborhoods out of which others have moved, out of which the old settlers fled because they too were uncomfortable with persons who were not "their kind." Occasionally too, members of the ethnic group break out of the community, moving upward socially by virtue of some standard of American success. From the point of view of class status, however, the ethnic community tends to remain at the same level.

**d.** The ethnic neighborhood may be considered a way station for succeeding waves of national categories. Germans, Irish, Italians, and others, are at different levels of upward mobility with the expectation of becoming absorbed into the large American middle class, and thus ceasing to be hyphenated Americans in ethnic communities. The key concept is the occupational and economic status of the "ethnics." While there are exceptional individuals, most members of the community have relatively low-paying jobs.

**e.** The ethnic community is not a disorganized slum. Social relations and groups, especially those centered around kinship and leisure-time activities, are routinized on a personal and informal basis. The strength and endurance of community life are fortified by these kinds of group relations, and also by an attitude of distrust and exclusion of "outsiders." Social cohesion or solidarity is an essential characteristic of the ethnic community.

f. Whatever may be said about the details of life among these people, it is the ethnic culture as a whole that is the soul of the community. The common native language is retained by many of the older people; common religion is often an important factor; even the common food habits help to foster this cultural continuity. Culture, the "native" ways of life, are maintained in the midst of the "foreign" ways of American life. The ethnic community will endure as long as it resists complete cultural assimilation.

Many decades have passed since the quota laws were established to restrict immigration; during that time, dwindling numbers of immigrants were expected also to dilute the strength of ethnic communities. The persistence of these communities is not so much a failure of the Americanization process as it is an indication that cultural pluralism is a prominent aspect of American society. Ethnic diversity underscores that pluralism despite occasional antagonism by superpatriotic old-line Americans.

More important from a sociological point of view is the ethnic demonstration of the need for community life. As with the traditional rural community, and the more recently established suburban community, there is a multiple institutional base for the ethnic community. The major difference is that this community continues to be a kind of cultural island in the larger American culture.

4. THE COMMUNITY CHURCH

Discussion of the communal type of social collectivity often gives the impression that the community just "happens" because of historical developments and the presence of certain variables like similar status, common occupation and ethnic background. We have seen, however, as in the new suburbs, that the community can be contrived, that it can be planned with rational attempts to maintain and reinforce its socially desirable qualities. The concept of the community church is an example of such planning—a deliberate form of organization that both reflects and promotes solidarity.

The impetus for the establishment of community churches came from two typically American sociological experiences. The first is the internal migration of people, and the second is the sectarian diversity of American Protestantism. People moved out of the rural areas which then became "over-churched" with each denomination suffering from a dearth of finances, membership, and clergy. As people moved into new suburbs they represented different denominations, and the religiously diverse population could not support a separate church for each of them.

Following is a list of the main considerations that prompted the development of the community church.

a. Among many Protestant churchgoers—if not always among their clergy—there was a "leveling" of doctrinal and theological diversities. Theological disputes that had once been a reason for denominationalism or sectarianism no longer seemed quite so compelling. The importance of the creedal system in general was diminished as people began to say that "one religion is as good as another," or as the notion spread that "it really doesn't matter what you believe as long as you are sincere."

b. This theological notion that there are many roads of belief leading to salvation was accompanied by the notion that the Christian way of life need not be specifically denominational. The generalized moral virtues, especially those of love and justice, should be practiced by all good people. Even the worship services, which emphasized hymns and sermons, often had a sameness from one church to another. The moral behavior that the church promoted and the patterns of worship services lost much of their denominational specificity among the main-line Protestant churches.

c. The central rationale for the development of the community church was ecumenical in its ecclesiastical terminology and solidaristic in its sociological terminology. Perhaps the argument was a rationalization that came out of necessity, but it also was an opportunity to express the basic unity of mankind, to develop a focus for fellowship that would cut across denominational differences. The goal was fellowship and the declared factor of community was an assimilation into a broad, common faith and practice.

**d.** There was, however, an important financial factor at the base of these considerations. Small congregations, especially if they were decreasing in rural areas, found it uneconomical to maintain a separate church and could not provide sufficient salary to attract a resident pastor. They could share the cost of a minister who could function part-time for each autonomous church; or they could take the more logical step of merging the "gathered" congregations into a community church. The same financial argument was used in the new suburbs where the membership of a single denomination was not large enough to support a separate church.

**e.** A peculiar problem arises in the decision that the community church must be nondenominational. This cuts off the potential financial support from the parent body at the state or national level. It also creates a personnel problem. Clergymen, after all, are trained by and for service in a specific denomination and, while it is not unusual for a minister to switch denominational affiliation, it is personally risky for him to become nondenominational. Unless large numbers of community churches merge, or federate, and thus become a new and separate denomination, they will continue to experience this double problem of finances and personnel.

**f.** The establishment of the community church in the inner city emphasizes a service orientation to the needy rather than a cohesive orientation to the membership. The traditional function of evangelizing, bringing the gospel message to the unchurched, has given way to a concern about social welfare. The stance of openness to all comers tends to dissipate the goal of exclusive fellowship that is sought by members of the typical community church. A church with this stance fits in this nominal classification, however, because it has an interest in and serves the larger community.

The difficulty in understanding the technical sociological definition of community is exemplified by this discussion of the community church. The quest for Christian fellowship is seen in the genuine *koinonia,* a relatively small group of people who share common religious values and close personal relations, and who are committed in a selfless way to the cause of the gospel. The Church of the Savior in Washington exemplifies the *koinonia* up to a point; so does a local village of Old Order Amish religionists; and even more the monastic communities of religious orders.

In the final analysis it must be said that the community church, as existing in modern America, is supportive of the larger concept of social solidarity. It is probably most successful if other elements are also shared that are nonreligious. If the congregation is united only on religious grounds and is exclusive not only of other people but also of other solidaristic factors, it will simply be a haven for those who want to escape into the comforting arms of religion.

## 5. COMMUNITY ACTION PROGRAMS

The functional advantage of "togetherness" in the community is in the conviction that most people can, want to, and will cooperate for civic improvement. This is, of course, a relative expectation when we talk about community action in American cities. The community that goes into action represents a minority of citizens who suffer grievances, are trying to redress wrongs, and face opposition from some segments of the population.

There are three levels on which community action programs can be analyzed. First, the individual person who participates in the program has the opportunity to alleviate the feeling of alienation, frustration, and helplessness that is common to big cities. Second, common effort toward a common goal, especially if it has some hope of succeeding, helps to develop a sense of solidarity. Third, progress toward the goal is an expression of social power, of the conviction that the members of the community do have a voice in their own destiny.

The procedures and problems of community action programs are open to analysis in the following series of examples.

a. In some areas of large cities there has been concerted effort to achieve community control of the public schools. The argument is that the people, especially the parents, know what is best for their children, and want to have a voice in selecting not only the curriculum but also the school personnel. The strongest opposition to these demands comes from the professional educators, especially those in the teachers' union, but also from the bureaucrats of the public school system and from the city board of education. Both sides allege that there is agreement on the common goal: the improvement of the schools in the community.

b. The so-called "poverty program," instituted by federal legislation and supported by public funds, was intended to encourage community participation. The mechanism whereby the people could be sharers in the decision-making was at best cumbersome, and in some instances was completely ignored. Efforts to implement community control of the poverty program were opposed mainly by politicians who insisted on the right to appoint administrators to manage the program. The argument was that if the poor really knew what was best for themselves they would not remain in poverty.

c. Community action has been instituted in an effort to alleviate some aspects of the urban housing problem. The problem is particularly acute where there is overcrowding of dwelling units, where absentee landlords neglect the tenants, and where people can buy property only at exorbitant prices. The individual person or family must organize with many others before a solution can be reached. In this instance the effort is to break the economic power of the landlords and of real estate agencies, a power which often has the support of lawyers, politicians, and legislators.

d. Another kind of community action program is sometimes found in places where there is one dominant industry. Underprivileged minorities charge that there is discrimination in hiring and upgrading their workers. Even if there is an organized labor union in the plant its policies may also be discriminatory. The approach then is to arouse and unite the community in public protest against these conditions and to insist upon equitable contracts. The main opponents are the industrialists in the area, but they are often joined by the "best citizens," the people of social authority and power who feel that they know what is best for the community.

e. Quite different from these four examples is the community action program promoted by people who seek civic improvement and social change. This has been exemplified by numerous community surveys directed by a professional organizer but carried out by citizen volunteers. Theoretically, the best results are obtained when the largest number of volunteers participate in the four essential stages of planning, seeking the facts, making the decisions, carrying out the improvement. This kind of program has been manageable in smaller towns and suburbs rather than in large cities.

Community action programs are a relatively modern phenomenon that has arisen in answer to several social needs in urban living. It is an attempt to deal with concrete problems that have escaped the impersonal mechanism of the larger society. It recognizes the presence of various "vested interests" in the power structure that resist change. It attempts to offset the individualism and social apathy that characterize many citizens. It represents the voluntary association of people who say "we'll do it ourselves."

## Suggested Readings

Gans, Herbert. *The Urban Villagers*. New York: Free Press, 1962.

Hillery, George A. *Communal Organizations: A Study of Local Societies*. Chicago: University of Chicago Press, 1968.

Nisbet, Robert. *The Quest for Community*. New York: Oxford University Press, 1953.

Sanders, Irwin T. *The Community: An Introduction to a Social System.* New York: Ronald, 1966.

Vidich, Arthur J., and Bensman, Joseph. *Small Town in Mass Society.* Garden City: Doubleday, 1960.

Warren, Roland. *The Community in America.* Chicago: Rand McNally, 1963.

Reissman, Leonard. *The Urban Process.* New York: Free Press, 1964.

# 6
# Society

IN THE PREVIOUS CHAPTERS WE HAVE NOTED THE MANY ways in which human beings are related to one another and the many aspects from which the same social person can be scientifically studied. People are thought of as united in various kinds of social categories. They are loosely associated in numerous social aggregates. People engage in many types of reciprocal relations in a number of different kinds of groups. The broadest technical meaning of the term "society" must include all these types of social units as subunits within society.

The earlier sociologists, and before them the social philosophers, studied and discussed society "in general" and often confused a given society with its political system, or state. They made broad generalizations concerning human conduct and social forms drawn from mankind "as a whole." The modern sociologist is much more precise and modest in the limits of his science. He seeks to make the group the focus of study and builds up general knowledge out of concrete situations.

This shift of emphasis in the study of society means that social science has gained in exactitude and that sociological generalizations now have a greater scientific validity. The real significance of this change of focus is that even society "as a whole" is now more clearly understood and more thoroughly studied than ever before. Proceeding from the particular to the general has always been essential to the scientific approach, and in this case it has succeeded in removing some of the vagueness from the broad sociological generalizations of an earlier day.

## SOCIETY AND SOCIETIES

Before analyzing the technical definition of society, it is useful for us to exclude confusing and misleading interpretations and usages of the term. For all practical purposes it is scientifically meaningless to define society as the total population of the world, as human society, mankind, or the human race. All human beings, of course, share certain characteristics which identify them as social persons, but this fact merely unites them in the broadest of social categories. It does not bring them together in any observable or measurable way.

There exist certain universal similarities in the different societies all over the world. The demonstrable existence of these universals (like status, role, patterns, structures, relations, functions) makes it possible to develop social science in the strict sense of the term. These generalized phenomena are present in widely separated and distinct societies. In each society they constitute a network, or social system, which is identified as an ongoing concern. The whole human race is not so constituted, and to speak of mankind as a world society is to attempt a meaningless extension of the technical term "society."

On the other hand, it is common usage in the English language to apply the word "society" to various secondary associations. One need not be a purist to appreciate the confusion this engenders, and one finds it in the most unexpected places. When the first edition of this book was published, the American Sociological Association still called itself the American Sociological Society. The Society for the Scientific Study of Religion, like the Society for the Prevention of Cruelty to Animals, is in technical terminology an "association," a secondary group of persons pursuing definite social goals. The National Association for the Advancement of Colored People, like the National Association of Manufacturers, is more technically, and therefore more correctly, named.

It must be pointed out that there are numerous synonyms for the term "association" or "secondary group." Not only do the various "societies" fit this term, but many federations and unions and leagues are also secondary groups. The Women's Christian Temperance Union, the National Hockey League, the American Federation of Labor, and many other similar social organizations are secondary groups or associations, not societies.

## DEFINITION OF SOCIETY

Ultimately the irreducible physical unit of the society, as of the social aggregate and the social group, is the social person. From the point of view of the persons who constitute it, a society is the largest number of human beings who interact to satisfy their social needs and who share a common culture. This rough definition differentiates the society from the group since the latter embraces only a segment of a society and because the common culture of a society is much broader than that of a single person or group.

Pursuing this line of reasoning a little further, one may say generally that the group is made up of persons and the society is made up of groups. The study of any particular society focuses upon the groups rather than upon the persons. Since all persons in some way participate in all the major groups, it is obvious that all the basic groups are interconnected. Although individuals are more involved in some groups than in others, the personnel of any major group is roughly the same as that of any other major group. In enacting social roles, the people participate in all the primary and secondary associations that make up these major groups. Thus a society may be defined as a network of interconnected major groups that are viewed as a unit and that share a common culture.

## CHARACTERISTICS OF SOCIETY

A more complete definition of society includes the following elements.

a. The people within the society constitute a demographic unit, that is, they can be seen as a total population. This does not mean that they are merely a large social category, although it is true that one of the valuable approaches to the understanding of any society is a study of its varieties of social categories.

b. The society exists within a common geographical area. In the highly organized modern world, this usually means that certain physical limits fix the boundaries of a nation in which a complete society exists. It is possible, however, that separate societies exist within a nation, so that the word "nation" is not synonymous with "society." The French Canadians constitute a society with a separate culture that distinguishes them from other Canadians.

c. The society is made up of functionally differentiated major groups. There are, as we have seen, the six major groups of persons, found in every society, through which the basic social needs of the people are satisfied. It is obvious that a society cannot be made up of only schools, or only factories, or only churches.

d. The society is composed of culturally similar groups of people. Usually they speak a common language, but the cultural similarity lies much deeper, in general consensus on major and ultimate values, and it is characterized by relatively similar behavior patterns.

e. The society must be recognized as an overall functioning unit. The total organized population is in a dynamic continuity of multiple and coordinated action. There is a certain amount of cooperation, so that the society can be said to act as a whole, even though, as mentioned above, there are internal functional differentiations.

f. The society must, finally, be recognized as a separate social unit. This characteristic is probably implied in the other elements already mentioned, but it must be emphasized that each society is culturally distinct from all other societies. In the modern world this often—but not always—means that the society is politically a sovereign independent unit.

The complexity of a society makes a simple definition meaningless, or at best confusing. If we combine the observations we have just made, we can make the following definition. A society is an organized collectivity of people living together in a common territory, cooperating in groups to satisfy their basic social needs, subscribing to a common culture, and functioning as a distinct social unit.

## ESSENTIAL FUNCTIONS OF SOCIETY

When a society functions in a normal and adequate manner, things are done more efficiently and satisfactorily than they can be done by individuals alone. We know from our own experience that a person would be handicapped, slowed down, and frustrated if he were expected to do everything alone, without the aid of others. It is clear, therefore, that society exists for people. It has a number of general functions which operate through all of the more specifically defined functions such as those of the major groups. These *general* functions are as follows.

a. Society brings people together in time and place so that it is possible for them to have human relations with one another. This temporal and spatial condition is a prerequisite for the operations of society.

b. It provides a systematic and adequate means of communication among people, so that through language and other common symbols they are able to understand one another.

c. It saves time and energy for individuals by developing and preserving common patterns of behavior which the members of the society share and enact.

d. It provides a system of stratification of status and classes so that each individual has a relatively stable and recognizable position in the social structure.

The more *specific* functions of society revolve around the group response to the primary and basic social needs of people. Through the universal system of the major groups the society performs the following essential functions for the persons within it.

a. Society has an orderly and efficient way of renewing its own membership. Through courtship, marriage, family and kinship groups it provides a systematic and approved way of bringing new human beings into its membership.

b. Society provides for the socialization, development, and indoctrination of its members through its patterned and organized system of formal education.

c. In its various economic groups society produces and distributes the material and physical goods and services needed to sustain the life of individuals.

**d.** The basic human need for external security and order is satisfied by society through its political administration and various civic groups.

**e.** The religious and spiritual needs of people are provided for by society through its various forms of organized religion.

**f.** Every society also contains social groups and systematic arrangements through which it provides relaxation and recreation for its members.

When we speak of a society's functions, we obviously do not mean to make any crude personification of society. From the point of view of the individual person, it is the "other people" acting out their roles and performing their multiple functions who are doing the things that society "does." The society is, after all, composed of people through whom it "helps" an individual to be born, raised, and educated. Without society he would not get adequate material support, political protection, or religious and recreational opportunities.

Structure and Function of Society

It has been customary for sociologists to distinguish between the static and dynamic aspects of society. For analytic purposes it is important to make this distinction, but for an adequate understanding of society we must realize that these two aspects are always factually together. Even when we study the so-called static aspect of social structures, we must realize that structure is always in movement with regard to time, direction, and the persons within it. On the other hand, while functions are by definition dynamic, they are also necessarily structured, arranged or ordered, and in that sense static.

The *structure* of a society refers to the arrangement of its parts or units. If we look at the total society as a composite of the major groups, we note that there is an orderly relationship and interdependence of these major parts. We see that the whole structure, that is, the largest structure, is made up of these various interrelated, interdependent, and mutually responsive groups. This view emphasizes order, arrangement, and organization; it tends to be static and fixed. In its complete analysis, it discerns the status of the person within the various subgroups, the position of these subgroups in relation to the major groups, and the coordination of all the major groups in the society.

If structure answers the question "How is society arranged?" *function* answers the question "What does society do?" This refers to the dynamic aspect of society —the social operations, processes, and activities. We have reviewed briefly the several general and specific functions of society. The social groups that compose society do many things, and they represent society continuously changing, shifting, and developing, going on in time and space, and performing actions through, with, and for social persons.

The universally demonstrable fact that total society is functionally differentiated into the various major groups indicates that differentiation is essential. The specialization which develops within each of the major groups is further evidence of this fact. Trends toward overspecialization in structure and function are often consciously counterbalanced by the people of a society when they attempt to coordinate and to integrate their social activities. Coordination is essential in the all-inclusive total society so that the various functions are fulfilled cooperatively and not at cross-purposes.

## CLASSIFICATION OF SOCIETIES

There are many ways of classifying societies, and each is probably valid according to the point of view from which the society is discussed. Some of these ways require no great depth of analytical understanding; for example, if one places the known societies on a continuum of size, from the largest to the smallest, he is not learning a great deal about any one society. It appears more meaningful to classify societies according to their rate of growth or decline; a rapidly increasing population has a quite different kind of society from the one in which the population is rapidly decreasing.

On the more abstract level of important differences among societies, most social scientists agree that the principal distinguishing characteristic is the culture each society possesses. Societies are distinguished from one another more by their different cultures than by their differing structures and functions. We shall discuss culture in some detail in subsequent chapters of this book. Society and culture are closely allied, and it is only by the process of abstraction that we can talk about them separately. A simple example of the cultural differences that distinguish two types of society is the comparison of preliterate and literate societies.

## CLASSIFICATION BY LITERACY

Two "levels" of culture are indicated here. The preliterate society is often called the primitive society because the ability to communicate by written language is a major step towards modernization. All the major groups fulfilling the essential social functions are present, although in relatively simple and overlapping forms. The primitive or preliterate people communicate effectively through oral language; their great social handicap is that they do not have the use of a written language. They have no written records, and therefore the development of a formal educational system and the compilation of scientific information are very difficult.

The student of society must be careful not to base his understanding or explanation on any single factor, but it is obvious that literacy is an important factor in the classification of societies. Literacy is a major difference between the primitive and the civilized society. The literate society enjoys a tremendous advantage in its use of concrete symbols to preserve its ideas and its history. Even among literate societies, the varying degrees of development are often measured by the proportion of the population that can read and write.

Literacy, or its lack, is a cultural factor and its effect upon the type of society indicates the close relationship between social and cultural phenomena. Language, whether by gesture, by sounds, or by written and spoken words is an essential instrument of social relations. As the instrument of language becomes more sophisticated, more meaningful, and more widely usable, it tends to "carry" with it a more sophisticated and complex culture. This in turn means a more developed society. One sees this point by merely comparing Czarist Russia, where the literacy rate was low, with the contemporary Soviet Union, which now has a high level of literacy.

## CLASSIFICATION BY DOMINANT GROUP

A more subtle and significant classification of societies is that which marks the dominance of one major group and institution over the others in the society. Historically this typology has fallen into four major categories. Even a casual knowledge of the larger societies of the world indicates that each is now, or has been in the past, dominated by one of these major groups.

a. The *economic* dominated society is one in which the industrialist and businessman enjoy high social status; commercial and material values have great influence on the behavior of people; and more time and energy are spent in economic groups than in others. Americans have heard much about the "military-industrial complex" since the Second World War.

b. The *family* dominated society is one in which there are close kinship ties and great honor for the aged and for deceased ancestors, and where social status is measured more by the criterion of ancestry than by any other norm of status. The tribal societies of Africa have been strongly influenced by the kinship ties of people.

c. The *religion* dominated society is one in which the central focus is on the supernatural, on the relationship between man and God, or Gods, and in which the other major groups are accordingly subordinated to the religious. An outstanding example is the manner in which religion in India has influenced the caste system and all other aspects of group life.

d. The *political* dominated system is that which is customarly called totalitarian, in which power is monophasic and the state enters into the regulation of all other groups and institutions. Maoist China seems more "complete" in this regard than some of the Latin American dictatorships, and is the more recent of a series of historical examples.

We are speaking here, of course, in terms of relative dominance and precedence of one major group and institution over the others. There can be no question of a society which is exclusively economic, or religious, or familial, or political. All of these, together with the educational and recreational groups, must somehow be present in every society. In some societies great emphasis is placed upon leisure-time groups and activities, and in some high value is placed upon education, but it is improbable that any total society has ever been dominated by either of these major groups.

## COMMUNAL AND ASSOCIATIONAL SOCIETIES

A still different classification of societies, also of great sociological relevance, is that distinguishing the simple, communal type, and the complex, associational type. From what we have said in a previous chapter it is clear that the former type is dominated by primary groups and the latter by secondary associations. This is not the same as the distinction between preliterate and literate societies, although it is true that the preliterate society also tends to be simple and communal, while the complex associational type would not become highly developed unless it had the advantage of literacy.

The following elements characterize the simple, communal type of society, and from this list can be deduced the opposite characteristics which identify the complex, associational type of society.

a. The simple, communal society has little specialization and division of labor. In this sense it is preindustrial, subsisting mainly from some general occupation like farming, trapping, fishing, or cattle-raising. Most of the people gainfully employed engage in the same occupation, and many of the subsidiary maintenance functions are performed within the family circle.

b. Kinship ties are strong in this type of society; in fact, it is sometimes called a familial society because of the importance placed upon the family as the center of most social activity. Often enough, it is a patriarchal society, and with this emphasis it is usual for old people to be given close attention and respect.

c. Although there is leadership and authority, and differential status based on age, sex, and function, the communal society has relatively little social stratification. There are criteria of social status but there is little difference in the possession of those items upon which status depends.

d. Because there is minimum social mobility in the simple society, it is often called a closed society. Status tends to be fixed and relatively permanent according to family; the stranger finds it difficult to be accepted and is often looked upon with suspicion.

e. There is relatively strong social solidarity among the members of the simple society, especially in relation to other societies. Since their social functions are not highly specialized, the people are able to cooperate more easily in their performance.

f. The simple society tends to adhere to traditional values and to patterns of behavior inherited from the past. Social change is at a minimum, and innovations are difficult. Socialization of individuals is therefore less complicated, and problems of adjustment to the cultural environment are at a minimum.

g. The people in this type of society tend to be governed by informal custom more than by formal law. This does not mean that custom is more lax than law. The local political administration is unsophisticated and operates on a sense of what is right and wrong rather than on a carefully spelled-out reasoning process.

**h.** All these characteristics indicate that the simple, communal society is relatively small in numbers; it has little contact with the outside world and a great deal of permanence. It is likely that the characteristics we have described could hardly develop in a society only recently established, open to the crosscurrents of strange and novel ideas, and growing rapidly in numbers.

It cannot be stressed too often that the distinction between the communal and associational types of society is a matter of degree. For example, it is not a matter of presence or absence, of stratification, mobility, or solidarity. These characteristics, and others mentioned above, must be present in every society, but the manner, extent, and degree of their presence make it possible to recognize the difference between the two types of society.

The complex, associational society can be easily described by a list of characteristics in contrast to those given above. It tends to be mechanized and industrialized with a wide variety of occupational functions. People are mobile, both vertically and horizontally, because there are great variations in social status and family ties are not enduring. Solidarity is less automatic and effective than in the simple society. An elasticity in values is accompanied by greater rigidity in the system of maintaining public order.

## Peculiarities of American Society

### 1. RELIGION AND SOCIETY

Church historians, apologists, and theologians have long studied American religion, but it is only recently that social scientists began thorough studies of religious groups in the way that they have analyzed the five other major groups. The relative neglect, especially of comparative research, was probably due to the bewildering variety of religious groups and institutions as well as to the large percentage of unaffiliated Americans. A resurgence of ecumenical tolerance and cross-creedal respect seems to have aroused the scientific curiosity of sociologists about the manner in which organized religion fits into the total American society.

Religion and society are said to have a unique relationship in the United States. The frequent talk and writing about American "separation of church and state" seem peculiar to the people in England, Sweden, and Israel, where religion is state-established, and to people in Belgium, Holland, and Germany, where there are formal, contractual agreements between the state and the religious bodies. The American notion of separation between religious and political systems appears to be poorly understood even by many Americans.

Religious groups are an integral part of the American society, and religious and political persons, functions, roles, and groups meet at many points. In order to put this relation between religion and society in clearer perspective, we may consider the following points.

a. Although various statistics show that the organized religious bodies in America claim only about 60 percent of the population as members, practically all Americans "affiliate themselves" to some form of religion. Only a very small percentage acknowledge themselves to be atheistic or irreligious or without any religious denomination. This is not to say, of course, that most Americans are pious or that they freqeuntly attend religious services.

b. Religion is held in high repute in official and public life—days of prayer are proclaimed; chaplains are appointed for military services. Politicians favor religious leaders and tend to curry favor from the main religious bodies. They try to avoid religious controversy; religion has not been a serious issue in a presidential campaign since the anti-Catholicism of 1928.

c. Religious affiliation is seldom an obstacle to economic success. There are, of course, personal preferences and prejudices at work in economic competition, but the general attitude in American business and professional life seems to be that "if a man does his job, it does not matter what his religion is." This is partly because of the deliberate emphasis on religious toleration and partly the consequence of a culture which emphasizes occupational values and gainful employment.

**d.** In spite of the multiple fragmentation of organized religion in the United States, there are certain religious beliefs common to the culture. Monotheism includes the belief in a God who punishes and rewards human beings for their conduct here on earth; and there is some sort of general belief in salvation and the future life. There are also sacred notions, not necessarily supernatural, concerning the dignity and inviolability of the individual as well as his responsibility to society.

**e.** In spite of this general acceptance of a basic core of religious beliefs, there are many doctrinal differences among the major religious groups. This is actually more noticeable than the widely advertised separation of church and state. The difference between religious fundamentalists and liberals is in the interpretation of theology itself, while the difference between the progressives and the traditionalists is in the application of religion to life. These points of view reflect the varying approaches that are present everywhere in the dynamic American society.

**f.** The general American values of pragmatism, optimism, and progressivism are also influential in most of the major religious groups. The local congregation is often managed like an enterprise which has to show by its books that it is succeeding. The concrete and the practical are shown in the emphasis on social service and morality over any deep concern with doctrinal and theological discussions, arguments, or sermons. The perfectability of man is stressed much more than his sinfulness.

**g.** An important point is that in our pluralistic society people of differing religious affiliations meet and cooperate in all the major groups except religion. In other words, there is no exclusive identification of one religious body with one political party or with one economic system. The necessity for people of all religious bodies to participate in all the nonreligious groups and to accept the mores in each of these groups brings about a social integration which cuts across any social solidarity based on religious values and beliefs alone.

Every college student can probably from his own knowledge and experience point out exceptions to each of the statements made above. Unquestionably, there are Americans who have a tendency to religious bigotry, refuse to associate with people of other religions, and condemn all who are not members of their own religious in-group. There are sects which emphasize the sinfulness of man, decry materialistic culture values, and try to dissociate themselves from "secular" society. These must be considered exceptions; they do .not reflect the general trend toward a closer integration of religion into American society and culture.

There are many other aspects of American social relations and groups which show that there is no unrealistic divorce between religion and society in America. It is true that our society is not dominated by religious groups, that the central sacred values tend to be only indirectly supernatural, and that a kind of secular expediency exists even in the religious bodies, but all this says is that religion in America is different from religion in other major societies. It means that the religious groups have been Americanized; it does not mean that they have been excluded from, or segregated within, the American society.

2. REGIONALISM AND AMERICAN SOCIETY

It is a commonplace that in any large country a series of "sectional societies" can be identified within the framework of the larger national society. This is true also in the older European countries where regional idiosyncrasies have been imbedded in the local traditions and where there may be a continued adherence to local styles of clothing, forms of recreation, kinds of religious rituals, and even particular dialects. In the United States, too, we talk about types of Americans—the Texan, Midwesterner, New Englander, Southerner, Westerner, and others—as though these types of persons represented different cultures and belonged to different societies.

The specific characteristics that represent regional differences in other countries, like dress, religion, and language are not reliable sociological indexes for an understanding of regional differences in the United States. Social scientists here have emphasized the ecological differences, that is, the different relations of the people to the physical environment, and have based their comparisons mainly upon those material items which can be objectively quantified. This is not to say that each region so described can in a technical sense be termed a separate society.

The following points are important in considering the rapidly changing picture of American regionalism.

a. There is still a tendency to identify a region by the principal economic functions in the area. We speak about the industrial North and cotton South, the cattle states, the corn belt, the wheat states. This indicates not only the kind of gainful occupation that the people pursue, but also the main economic interest they have in relation to other parts of the country. It does not mean that the people in any particular area are exclusively engaged in these economic functions.

b. The spread of urbanism, in the sense of urban behavior patterns, is a tremendous factor in minimizing regional differences. This is, of course, a function of the communication and transportation systems, which reach out into all parts of the country. National networks of radio and television, the movies, and magazines have tended to break down parochial and regional ideas; national networks of airlines, trains, and buses and the individual use of automobiles have brought all the regions physically closer together.

c. Mechanization has been a particularly significant factor in decreasing the economic differences between the cities and the rural regions. It has brought a change in the financial status of farmers and has given the eight-hour day to many farm laborers. It has also facilitated the migration of surplus farm labor to industrial areas. In general, rationalization and specialization of labor have accompanied the mechanization of agricultural processes.

d. The kinds of minority categories which exist in different parts of the country have been a means of identifying regions. Human relations and social structures have been influenced by the presence of Negroes in the Southeast, French Canadians in New England, Orientals on the West Coast, Germans and Scandinavians in the Midwest, Mexicans in the Southwest, and Irish, Italians, and Jews in the metropolitan areas. The continuation of "mixed marriages" and the subsequent biological mingling of the people, as well as the migration of minority persons to other regions and a gradual rise in social status, are breaking down this regional identification.

e. The composition of the population from the point of view of age, sex, and marital status is strikingly different in the various regions of America. The Southwest still has a young population and one in which the rate of natural increase is great, as compared to other regions. The eastern industrial and commercial areas have an excess of marriageable females, while the big western farming areas have a surplus of young unmarried workers; regions like Southern California and Florida tend to attract older and retired persons.

f. It is probably still valid to distinguish regions on the basis of whether they are primarily communal or associational, although this distinction is gradually disappearing. Regions in which the population is predominantly urban tend to emphasize social relations in the secondary groups, while those which are predominantly rural emphasize the primary groups. But the general associational character of American society is reaching out into all parts of the country, so that this is becoming less a regional and more a national characteristic.

There are other indexes for the identification of regions, but they appear to be less valid. Traditionalism and conservatism are said to mark certain parts of the country, but there are many indications that these attitudes are no longer peculiar to one region alone. The political emphasis on "states rights" in the Southeast has led to the erroneous assumption that states in other parts of the country do not insist upon their rights with equal practical vigor. In general, it may be said that regionalism is not so significant or tradition-bound in the United States as in other major countries and that it is here moving fairly rapidly in the direction of a total and integrated American society.

### 3. "SOCIETY" IN AMERICA

One of the most confusing and common misusages of technical sociological termonology is that which identifies "society" with the upper-class category and "social functions" with the type of meetings, parties, dances, teas, and weddings which are described on the "society page" of the daily newspaper. This is an unfortunate conflict between technical meanings and popular usages, and it is important for the student of social science to understand the difference between the two.

Upper-class "society" in the United States is a peculiar phenomenon which is not exactly duplicated in any of the major modern societies of our times. The emphasis placed upon it and the interest shown in it by many Americans are an indication of the actual existence of social stratification in our country. This emphasis and interest may appear odd in a society which also stresses egalitarianism, the democratic process, and the movement of various groups and categories for equal rights.

Some of the distinctive features in the functioning of "society" in American are the following.

a. In the richest nation in the world there are very few persons who can be termed "the idle rich." There appears to be cultural disapproval of "doing nothing," and the normal, adult American male would be embarrassed to have a reputation of this kind. Even if his chief preoccupation is actually self-indulgence, he usually insists upon having a downtown office or a nominal position on a business board of some kind. Wealthy men of ability often identify themselves with foreign service, with government agencies, with philanthropic and civic organizations.

b. The use of titles of nobility or aristocracy, which persists even in European countries that have become democratic, is remarkable for its absence in the United States. These titles indicate distinguished ancestry, and while Americans are conscious of ancestry as a criterion of social status, they do not recognize it with titles. There are not enough descendents of the Mayflower or of the American Revolution to make these distinctions socially realistic. Earned titles, like general, governor, professor, doctor, and others, are of course in common usage, but they stress personal achievement rather than class identification, and they are not hereditary.

c. The criteria for acceptance into "society" are variable; they are not equally stressed in all parts of the American society. The criterion that is most often mentioned as an American ideal is that of personal occupational achievement, which is undoubtedly also one of the main channels of upward mobility. The actual possession of inherited wealth, however, is considered in some social strata as more important than personal achievement. The care which upper-class parents take in scrutinizing the "proper" marriage choice of their children indicates that "pure lineage" is often more important than even wealth or achievement.

d. "Society" people are often identified by the modes of conspicuous consumption they can afford. Through these they become known as "prominent society leaders." But upon analysis these activities—sponsoring or attending debuts, garden parties, opening nights, and so forth—are seen to be conservative and competitive and fairly strictly patterned. Daring innovations are not in good taste. This conservatism is reflected especially in the political and economic areas, in which these people are most often anxious to maintain the status quo.

e. While the actual social position of "society" people is attached mainly to the male head of the family, the maintenance externally of that position appears to be the concern of the adult females. Within certain limits it is the women who are the "social arbiters," the bearers and exhibitors of the family status, the guides of their menfolk in the intricacies of "society." It is a common joke in American society, and not only among the upper class, that the woman has to coerce her husband to attend the opera, art exhibits, and other "cultural" programs.

f. Consultation of the social register, in which the names of "society" leaders are recorded, still persists in some places; but the gossip columnists and the editors of society pages are gradually replacing the social register as an index of the people "who count." These newspaper employees often have a thorough knowledge of the degree to which individuals actually possess the various characteristics that serve as criteria of social status.

It must be noted that the descriptions mentioned above are relative to time and place. The criteria of upper-class status and the manifestation of this status are given variable emphasis. The upper social strata of Charleston and New Orleans are recognizably different from those of Kansas City and San Francisco, and the "society people" in these areas differ again from those in Chicago and New York. It is probably true to say that density of population makes a difference in the immediate influence and actual leadership of these upper-class people. In the smallest towns they are not able to exhibit the characteristics of "society." In the middle-sized cities they probably enjoy much greater social influence than in the large metropolitan areas.

### 4. AMERICAN SOCIETY AND INTERNATIONAL RELATIONS

The relative power positions of large nations has shifted dramatically during this century. The decline of England and Germany, and the rise of Japan and Russia, have all been connected in some way with the emergence of the United States as a major international influence. The simplistic earlier policy of "no foreign entanglements" definitely disappeared during the two world wars, but has reappeared in a more sophisticated form as a result of American military intervention in Korea and Vietnam.

In the long history of mankind this emergence of the American nation seems sudden and dramatic, and it exhibits certain unique characteristics. The change has necessarily had an internal effect upon Americans, and it has helped to form and readjust the attitudes of other people toward us. Americans are as favorably inclined as the people of other major societies toward the preservation of international justice, peace, and welfare. America, called the youngest of the nations, is in fact the oldest of the large continuing democracies. The position of leadership is, however, still an unfamiliar one; thinking and dealing in international relations are still strange to most American citizens.

There is no technical sense in which we can speak of a world society. The United Nations, born in San Francisco and with headquarters in New York, is a secondary group, or association, of representatives from independent countries. American relations across national boundaries existed before the UN. They are not only political, but also economic, religious, educational, and recreational. Various kinds of international organizations of scientists, professionals, businessmen, sportsmen, students, workers, and others have also tended to bring the people of America closer to those of other nations, but all of this does not constitute a world society.

The following considerations are meant to throw into perspective the position of American society in relation to other nations.

a. Americans for the most part have accepted only reluctantly the responsibilities attached to the position of world leadership. There is almost always some local and regional pressure not to "meddle in foreign affairs," or to stop "wasting the taxpayers' money," or to "bring the boys back." These are an indication of the intensely nationalistic attitudes of some Americans. The frustrations of the Vietnam War, as well as the excitement of the so-called "space race" with Russia, rekindled some of this isolationism, which is not, however, as widespread as it once was.

**b.** In a sense world supremacy has been thrust upon us. Unlike most of the major societies which in the past have gained world ascendancy through imperialism, the United States did not reach its current status of world leadership through the direct conquest of other nations. Like other nations, unwise decisions were sometimes made for military and economic intervention, and the charge of "aggressive imperialism" has been made against the nation on several occasions. For the most part, however, Americans have been concerned about consolidating the internal social structure, developing resources, and populating the frontiers. A large segment of the people insists on the slogan, "we can't police the whole world."

**c.** Colonialism is generally as unpopular as imperialism among Americans because the United States has had no need either for economic exploitation or for population expansion. Here again, "exploitive colonialism" has been charged against American business interests in under-developed countries. It is an interesting fact that Alaska and Hawaii were never considered permanent colonies and were eventually accepted as integral states of the Union. The Philippines, under American protection for more than a half century, became an autonomous nation. These examples indicate the general reluctance of Americans to imitate old-fashioned systems of colonialism.

**d.** Sociologically, the most significant official attitude in international relations is the American program of economic and technological aid to other countries. The Marshall Plan for the rebuilding of Europe after the Second World War was a program unprecedented in the history of civilization. This is not simply an example of unselfish love of others, nor is the continuing program of aid to underdeveloped countries. Such aid is based on a conviction that prosperous and contented people do not foment unrest or submit themselves to "subversive" influences. It is based also on the economic hypothesis that prosperous international trade cannot exist between poor nations and rich nations when the latter merely exploit the former. In simplest form it may be said that

Americans believe that what technological progress has
done for America it can do for any nation.

e. It is a sociological axiom that threats of external danger or aggression contribute to social solidarity within a
society. If these threats are genuine, as they were when
this country was involved in the two world wars, internal
solidarity tends to increase. At other times, as in the
period of so-called "cold war" with the Communist countries, the fear and expectation of such threats tend to
arouse socially disruptive suspicions among the people.
Chauvinists will probably always hunt for spies and
traitors who are suspected of "un-American activities,"
but the majority of Americans seem capable of distinguishing between genuine and spurious external threats to
their country.

f. Another important social factor has been the gradual
internal cultural assimilation of the American people.
Large discrepancies of social status continue to exist, but
what is significant is that these are recognized as social
problems that can be solved. The acclaimed position of
the American nation as the protagonist of democracy and
of the dignity and rights of individuals has made us
sharply conscious of the underprivileged and depressed
minorities in our midst. Many factors, like organized protest and legal action, industrialization and urbanization,
have helped to break down these discriminatory barriers,
but our position as the democratic model for the world
has accelerated this change.

There is a certain amount of ethnocentrism in some of
the international attitudes of Americans. Pride in the fact
that many people of different cultural and ethnic backgrounds have been able to get along more or less peacefully leads some naive Americans to deride the traditional
nationalistic animosities on other continents. The United
States is the largest democratic society the world has ever
seen. While nations with smaller populations, like Switzer-
land and Canada, have also been successful democracies,
many Americans tend to identify democracy with our
country. They are boastful of our success, and see no
reason why we should not help others to imitate us.

## 5. COMPLEXITY OF AMERICAN SOCIETY

The complexity of an object refers to both its structure and its functions. A child's toy airplane may be pressed out of a single piece of metal and it may not fly; an actual airliner is an intricate mechanism of many parts, and it has multiple functions. A simple agrarian society is said to have relatively few "parts" in its social structure and to have relatively generalized functions shared by most of its people. A complex industrial society, on the other hand, has multiple stratification of statuses, classes, and forms. Its functions are numerous and specialized, and each person tends to focus his time and energy on his own key role in the society.

The beginning student in social science often has difficulty in understanding this point in reference to American society. He sees that many actions are simplified in modern urban life. He goes to the supermarket and exchanges his money for a loaf of bread, a can of corn, and a package of sliced bacon. He reflects that this is much simpler than the many actions his grandparents had to perform in growing the wheat, corn, and hogs, and in processing them before they were edible. Many other examples show how simple life is today: travel by air, communication by telephone, easily available means of recreation, and a comprehensive educational system.

This simplification of the individual actions of people would be impossible, however, without the complexity of modern society. An intricate system of interdependent actions lies behind the placing of any packaged commodity on the shelves of the supermarket. This involves financing at every step of the way, communication and transportation, advertising and marketing, as well as the actual physical and mechanical labor of numerous specialized persons. A complicated system of interdependent actions must also occur before the customer has money in his hand with which to purchase the product.

While economic processes are a good example of complexity, one should not forget that a complex society is complex in all its major groups and institutions. The following is a brief indication of how complexity pervades the whole American society.

**a.** The political groups in our society, especially the federal government, exhibit a tremendous amount of complexity. Efforts at simplifying the government have been directed toward the elimination of so-called fringe functions and the coordination of various bureaus. The term "bureaucracy" is usually applied politically, although it exists in all the major social groups. The need to guide and to regulate the giant associations and structures of our society has itself resulted in supercomplexity of government.

**b.** The economic groups are so obviously complicated that this hardly requires a demonstration here. The division and interdependence of labor in the processes of gathering raw materials, manufacturing and distributing them to the consumer have become more and more specialized and detailed. The complicated problems of the giant corporations are matched by those of the giant labor unions. Plans for the future and files on the past are essential adjuncts to a capitalist economy, and they add to its complexity.

**c.** The educational system in American society is also highly complicated. New means of socialization—television, radio, and printed materials—as well as the shifting and expansion of youthful peer groups have added to the problem. Specialization reaches down into the elementary schools, is seen in the variety of curriculums in high schools, and achieves its most complicated forms in the university and graduate systems. The various associations of schools and colleges and of professional educators, and the development of technical, trade, and adult systems present a bewildering array of educational groups.

**d.** Recreation, which on the surface appears a simple matter of relaxing and having a good time, is also increasingly complex in American society. The great variety of commercial entertainment implies an intricate system by which this is presented and sold to the public. The attempt to distinguish between professional and amateur athletes presents problems even in the field of collegiate sports. The practice of leaving home for two- or three-week vacations involves tremendous competition among resort places attracting travelers and vacationers.

e. The religious bodies in American society are also highly complex. The number of different cults, sects, denominations, and churches is greater than in any other major society in the world. Systems of worship range from the simplest to the most elaborate. The problems of internal administration in the largest religious bodies have become so numerous and complicated that they require trained, scientific management.

f. It is a commonplace that life in the American family has changed tremendously since grandfather's day, moving from simplicity to complexity. The multiple common functions once performed by a group in the large kinship circles are now performed by individuals, many of whom are agents for parents. Tensions and strains in the conjugal family come largely from the increased demands placed upon the individual by economic, civic, recreational, and other agencies. There are many complicated decisions that must be made concerning children in regard to their schooling, extracurricular activities, physical training, and choice of vocation and occupation. Various social relations and functions must be constantly maintained with persons outside the family.

This brief survey is a mere indication of the tremendous complexity of American society as a whole. Complexity is not synonymous with confusion; American society tends to take a deliberate and scientific approach to individual functions and structures. There is a general recognition by Americans that multiplication and differentiation must be accompained by interdependence and coordination. A serious breakdown in one major group, like the economic depression of the thirties, affects drastically all the other major groups. Complexity is not something random, haphazard, or confused. It is orderly and intricate and requires social competence, adaptability, and knowledge on the part of Americans.

## Suggested Readings

Davis, C. A. *American Society in Transition*. New York: Appleton-Century-Crofts, 1969.

Galbraith, John Kenneth. *The Affluent Society*. Boston: Houghton, Mifflin, 1958.

Levy, Marion. *The Structure of Society*. Princeton: University Press, 1952.

Lipset, Seymour Martin. *The First New Nation*. Garden City: Doubleday, 1967.

Parsons, Talcott. *Societies: Evolutionary and Comparative Perspectives*. Englewood Cliffs: Prentice-Hall, 1966.

# II
# *Patterns and Culture*

The previous section has given us only a partial view of group life. Sociology would be a static science if it studied only what social persons *are;* it must study also what these persons *do.* One must be able to abstract and generalize the patterns of behavior performed by the people in society. In this part we proceed from the minimum unit, the culture pattern, through the various ways in which it is combined with other patterns to form the total culture.

We study first the patterns of behavior (chapter 7), then analyze the manner in which these combine into roles (chapter 8) and processes of interaction (chapter 9). Patterns, roles, and processes are the content of institutions (chapter 10), which in turn constitute the total culture itself (chapter 11).

# 7
# Patterns of Behavior

THE STUDY OF SOCIOLOGY AS A SCIENCE IS POSSIBLE ONLY because people in society think and act in certain similar patterned ways. A pattern is anything shaped or formed to serve as a model or guide in forming something else. The behavior pattern is shaped or formed through the constant repetition by many people of the same item of behavior. A personal idiosyncratic habit is formed when an individual constantly repeats the same act in the same way. Analogously we may say that when many people in a society do the same thing in relatively the same way over a long period of time there develops a nomothetic social habit. This repetitive way of thinking and acting is a cultural pattern.

People go to church on Sundays, they eat three meals a day, they buy automobiles on the installment plan, they stand at attention when the national anthem is played. These are a few of the myriad patterns of behavior that constitute the total culture. The people keep doing these things in the same way because that is the way they learned that these things should be done. We define the behavior pattern briefly as a uniformity of acting and thinking (and feeling) that regularly recurs among a plurality of people. It is the basic and irreducible unit of roles, institutions, and cultures. It is the generalized, standardized, and regularized behavior of people that serves as model or guide for what is acceptable and what is not acceptable conduct in any society.

Behavioral patterns are not only external activities; they are also common ways of thinking and believing in a culture, and they contain the creeds, meaning, values and attitudes of a culture. People take pride in the accomplishments of astronauts; they share preferences for certain kinds of food; they have common attitudes about the importance of education; they have similar opinions about what is worth doing or having. These are the recurrent patterns of cultural thought and feeling that express the meaning of human life in society.

We are concerned here not with every thought and feeling of every individual, but with only those "ways of thinking" that are so frequent and so widely shared that they may be termed cultural patterns. They are the content of what is sometimes erroneously called the "mind" or the "consciousness" of a society or group. The individual and fully socialized member of the society is supposed to be characterized by these thought patterns. It is generally believed that people in the same society tend to think alike, as is noted in such statements as "he thinks like a Japanese," or "like an American," or "like a Southerner." The content of such judgments is often in error because of ignorance of other cultures, but the fact of attitudinal or "thought" similarity is a valid scientific truth.

## THE RANGE OF PATTERNS

From the sociological point of view, there is much that people do that is not worth studying or analyzing, and for this reason it is necessary to limit the focus of our study. This can be done by examining the four elements of the definition. The culture pattern is (a) customary behavior that is repeated frequently; (b) it is performed in relatively the same way by many people; (c) it acts as a guide, model, or norm for the people in the group or society; (d) it is possessed of some social significance. For example the distinction can be made between sleeping as an unlearned biological pattern and as a cultural pattern. The use of beds with mattresses and springs, and the custom of retiring before midnight, turns a mere physical necessity into a culture pattern.

There are vast differences in the social significance of patterned behavior; not all forms of social conduct are of equal importance either to the individual or to the society in which he lives. Behavior patterns can be placed on a continuum from the culturally significant to the culturally trivial according to three qualifications. These norms of measurement are *universality*, that is, the amount and degree of conformity by the people in the society;

the amount of *social pressure,* or the degree to which the society sanctions the behavior in question; and the *social value* of the pattern, or the importance that the society places upon it.

In other words, people are greatly influenced to do those things everybody else is doing, the things that society considers so important that it will punish those who do not conform and reward those who do. No one of these three elements is the sole index of the importance of a cultural pattern. For example, almost all Americans eat with their right hand and almost all Europeans with their left hand. While there is a kind of pressure by example to conform to this pattern, it is not so highly valued that a violator will be visited with dire penalties. Attending religious services and voting in local elections are said to be highly valued behavior patterns, but large numbers of the adult American population do not do these things and in general there appears to be no widely applied social pressure that they should do so. Other patterns have more strength. A combination of conformity, pressure, and sanctions makes Britishers drive on the left side and Americans on the right side of the road.

PRINCIPAL TYPES OF PATTERNS

The range of patterns could allow a continuum of finely shaded distinctions of all social behavior, but for practical purposes social scientists have defined three general categories and identified them as mores, folkways, and usages. These classifications are at best a rough division of behavior patterns ranging from the most to the least universal, compulsive, and important. The dividing line among these three categories is often fuzzy because there are also variations within each category. Some patterns appear to overlap two categories when judged by the criteria social scientists employ. Some changing or shifting patterns cannot always be exactly pinpointed on the continuum that goes from the strongest mores to the weakest usages.

a. Mores are usually defined as the "must-behavior" of a society, the basic and important patterns persons enact because they feel obliged to do so. These are patterns considered essential to the welfare of the society. For example, acts of loyalty and patriotism are valued so highly in modern society that the traitor is looked upon with horror and loathing. The proper care and treatment of children are considered so important that the kidnaper, the molester of little children, the mother who abandons or neglects her children are heavily penalized. Religious worship is so highly respected (even though many do not formally practice it) that the person who desecrates a religious site is considered guilty of a terrible crime.

The prevailing mores are accompanied and reinforced by social convictions, ideologies, and core values. It is the American "way of thinking" that gives meaning and support to the American "way of acting." Freedom of thought and expression is guaranteed by the Constitution, but there is also a strong suspicion that only subversives would think differently, or question the "principles" of free enterprise, hard work, democracy, education, and religion. Here again, the strength of conceptual mores can be gauged by the outrage of citizens over their violation. It is possible to recognize the "must-thinking" in society.

**b.** William Sumner introduced the term "folkways," as well as "mores," into the sociological lexicon. Folkways are widely practiced patterns of behavior that are less obligatory than the mores. They are considered the "thing to do"; they are taken for granted as highly desirable cultural patterns, but there is no strict enforcement of them. For example, large numbers of weddings are performed at a church service and are followed by a reception for the bride and groom and by a honeymoon, but these three behavior patterns are not essential to the welfare of the society. The wearing of a wedding ring by a married man is perhaps becoming a folkway, while the married woman's wedding ring has almost the strength of the mores. The pressure that brings about conformity to folkways is usually a negative and informal kind, like ridicule, sneering, snubbing, and gossip.

Conceptual patterns can also be recognized at the level of folkways. Certain ways of thinking, while taken for granted and generally approved, are not strictly and universally enforced. The common notion that adolescent males should compete in athletics, that parents should take an interest in their children's schoolwork, that citizens should have an attitude of respect for high public officials, that there ought to be loyalty among members of a family—all these are conceptual patterns on a lower level than strong social convictions.

c. Usages are seen as the least compulsive among the social patterns of behavior. Most of them revolve around the various etiquettes and conventions current in a society. They are proper and fitting modes of conduct, voluntary and customary but not obligatory. Following are examples of cultural usages that have no great binding force but are widely practiced: addressing even casual acquaintances by their first name, euphemistic reference to bodily functions (especially near children), shaking hands among friends, applauding at a public performance.

The common ways of thinking at this level allow great latitude and are "mere opinions" rather than deep convictions. They allow for differences of opinion mainly because the object to which the opinion is directed does not involve a significant social value. It does not matter very much to the society in general whether the individual person agrees or disagrees, but the well-socialized person is expected to conform. Mental conformity to the "correct" conceptual usages indicates "good breeding," and these ways of thinking are usually found in the popular books on etiquette in any society. The empirical study of these categories of conceptual patterns is still in its infancy, but every observant member of society recognizes the difference between the concepts he *has* to believe and those about which a wide divergence is permitted. A preference for one brand of cigarette over another, for one type of television show, for one kind of beverage, does not deal with the more important values of society. On the level where wide differences of opinion are allowed we find the least important of the conceptual behavior patterns.

VARIATIONS IN BEHAVIOR PATTERNS

The study of behavior patterns is complicated by the dynamic aspect of any culture. It is clear from what we have said about the indexes of universality, social pressure, and social value that there is no immutability or absoluteness about social behavior. The intensity or strength of each of these indexes varies in the range of patterns from mores through folkways to usages. There are other perspectives from which this relativity of cultural patterns can be viewed. These are variations of behavior in the time, place, and social stratum in which they occur.

a. The passage of time brings a shift in behavior, and the temporal changes in cultural patterns are best observed in large dynamic societies. Mores are always durable and traditional but even they exhibit occasional additions and fluctuations. Driving a car on the right-hand side of the road was probably a folkway during the early days of the automobile, but orderly street traffic has become so vitally important that this custom has become one of the mores. A shift in the other direction is that of Monday washday, which has probably been reduced from a folkway to a mere usage. Divorce and remarriage, gainful occupation of married women, buying on the installment plan, the use of credit cards, extension of public education, annual paid vacation for wage workers, are all examples of shifting behavior patterns over a period of time.

Ways of thinking are apparently more traditional and more deeply imbedded in the culture than are ways of acting. Ideologies are more tenacious than techniques. Yet the social thinking of American people is now very different from that of the early twentieth century. The social philosophy of the people, their opinions and ideologies, have changed. Attitudes toward collective bargaining in industry, social security for the aged and the practice of child labor; beliefs concerning inferiority of immigrants or inherent differences of nationalities and races; opinions concerning the relation of the federal government to education, health, and welfare—on all of these subjects there have been changed patterns of thought over the last half century.

**b.** Regional variations in social behavior indicate the presence of fairly well-defined subcultures within even a relatively well-integrated society. Everyone realizes that local custom varies from place to place. This does not refer to the differences of culture between widely separated countries like Ireland and Mexico, or Portugal and Thailand, but to differences within the same society. Patterns of recreation differ regionally between rural and urban areas. Coeducational high schools are more available in some places than in others. Patterns of political participation differ widely, as do patterns of racial discrimination and segregation. Most noticeable is language —the choice of words and their pronunciation.

Obviously there are variations in social thinking from one region to another within the same country. The difference in thought patterns is apparent between the "Down-easterner" and the Texan, the people from Georgia and the people from Iowa. Political, religious, educational, and economic attitudes are shown to vary greatly when samples are taken for opinion polls in different parts of the country. Part of the explanation for the existence of a kind of subculture in the Southeastern region lies in the "state of mind" that is characteristic of the people there.

**c.** Behavior patterns vary also according to social status. In general it may be said that middle-class people in America, defined by the criteria we have already discussed, are those who best recognize, accept, and conform to standardized patterns of social behavior. In considering class variations, however, the degree of conformity is not so important as the kind of patterns performed. For example, attendance at symphonies, concerts, and operas is not a widespread behavior pattern in the lower strata of society. Playing golf and having a membership in a country club are folkways among rising young business executives and upper middle-class families.

It is an oversimplification to say that the way of life differs from one social class to another only because of what people can afford financially. Nor is it merely a matter of occupation. The ditchdigger and the stockbroker do not have the same "outlook" on life, but the distinction between their ways of thinking has been brought about by numerous divergent social experiences. The whole frame of reference resulting from the socialization process colors the conceptual patterns of behavior, the attitudes, opinions, judgments, and preferences that differ from one social class to another. For example, most lower-class whites have positive attitudes on the poverty program and negative attitudes on Negro civil rights; but the opposite is the case with upper-class whites.

## PATTERNS ARE HABIT-FORMING

Patterned and repeated behavior of any kind is a convenient shortcut in the conduct of human life. We are all creatures of habit, and this simple fact adds tremendous efficiency to our daily living. If there were no patterned conduct, personal and social, the whole process of living would be slowed down and would probably become psychologically intolerable. For the most part, cultural patterns are "ingrained" in people and do not require much forethought or afterthought. They are the rote behavior of people. Children pick them up almost subconsciously so that when they mature they think of them as things that "come naturally."

This does not mean that cultural patterns are simply instinctive or unreasonable and irrational. They are learned and habitual, and in some ways nonrational in the sense that they are performed without much reflection or deliberation. People are aware of the proper modes of behavior, and elders in the society make a conscious effort to instill this behavior in youngsters. But the individual does not have to stop, reflect, choose, and invent the manner in which he is going to respond to every social situation. Cultural patterns are the ready-made responses existing in the society. The individual has learned them through imitation and suggestion; he respects them because there is a weighty tradition and social authority behind them, and he performs them as though they were "second nature" to him.

At the conceptual level the habitual aspect of social patterns is seen in attitudes, stereotypes, and prejudices. Attitudes are a learned orientation toward some socially significant object, person, or category, and it involves an habitual readiness to act externally in a certain way. The attitude may be favorable or unfavorable. It may correspond to reality, or it may be erroneous and prejudicial. Stereotypes are prejudicial attitudes.

An enthusiastic young coed may hold the favorable attitude that "American men are so handsome." This is a prejudice. It is also a stereotype. The stereotype combines an attitude of either favor or disfavor with a number of prejudgments concerning the same person or class or category of persons. The result is a "mental picture" of others that is both inaccurate and incomplete. The stereotype is a preconception rather than a conception of a social category; it attributes to a whole category of people certain characteristics that are not really present at all. It is discovered most often in the habitual labels placed upon ethnic, racial, and religious categories of people. Popular concepts of the "national character" of people of other countries are almost all stereotypes. In short, steretotypes are caricatures rather than true pictures.

Custom reinforces custom. Patterns of social habits constitute the customary behavior of the society. Unlike personal habits, social habits are regularized, standardized, and shared by many people, but like personal habits they are learned, repeated, and developed. By and large it is almost as difficult for a person to change his social customs as it is to change his personal habits. Once they have been acquired by the individual in the society, they persist and endure. This persistence and this durability are, of course, strongest in the mores and weakest in the usages.

PATTERNS AS NORMS OF BEHAVIOR

The terms "behavior pattern" and "behavior norm" are

closely allied. Up to this point we have been stressing the fact that the pattern is something shaped or formed by repetitive behavior of large numbers of people. The behavior pattern, however, is not only a form of conduct. The normative aspect of the pattern lies in the fact that it is used as a model or guide in forming something else. It is an elementary fact of logic that the same object can be looked at from different points of view. The ways of behaving are, from another point of view, the norms of behaving.

This is no mere exercise in logic or play on words. When we say that people are expected to behave in certain ways when they are in a supermarket or a church, at a lecture or a rally, riding in an airplane or driving a car, we are saying that they know ahead of time what modes of behavior they should follow. This does not mean that everybody always conforms, and it may be useful to distinguish between the "ideal," normative expectations of behavior and the "real," actual forms of behavior. Everyone knows that principles of conduct, the way things *ought* to be, do not always match up with the actualities of conduct, the way things *are*. In a democratic society there exists an ideal and expected pattern of racial equality, but in this same society there exist people who practice patterns of racial discrimination.

The behavior norms, as expectations of conduct, vary in strength, permanence, and durability, which, as we have seen, are measured by the three indexes of universality, pressure, and value. The mores, which are the strongest patterns of behavior, are also the most important norms guiding social conduct. Folkways and usages are also standardized expectations of behavior but are not so imperative or compelling. In this respect patterns are, or ultimately become, accepted norms of conduct and they tend to become a large part of the normative system of any society. They are the rules of behavior to which most people subconsciously respond by doing what is right and proper in any social situation.

## Explicit and Implicit Norms

The behavior pattern is, therefore, an *implicit* norm of conduct because its universal performance indicates universal, subconscious acceptance and brings about a social pressure so that people conform to it. This is an abstract and subtle form of social control which we shall discuss in a later chapter. These implicit behavioral norms, however, do not constitute the total system of regulations governing social conduct.

There exist also certain *explicit* behavioral norms in every large modern society. These are found in the formal body of laws, promulgated and enforced throughout the society, and in the clearly stated ethical principles the members of every society share. It would be a serious scientific error to suggest that these laws and principles are "nothing more" than ideal behavior patterns or that they simply evolved out of the institutionalized customs of the society. In many instances formal laws are promulgated, and ethical principles are proclaimed, precisely for the purpose of changing long-standing patterns of behavior. In the United States, the so-called "labor laws" and the "race laws" result from such a purpose.

The principles of social conduct about which experts in ethics and law speak are based on what is right and wrong and not merely on the fact that large numbers of people have acted for a long period of time in certain similar ways. Unless a culture is seriously disorganized and a society is on the verge of disintegration, there is always a certain consistency and coordination between the explicit legal and ethical norms of behavior and the implicit patterned norms of behavior.

The obligatory norms of social conduct must, therefore, be seen under a twofold aspect: (*a*) consciously formulated laws, principles, rules and maxims that emerge from rational deliberation and are explicitly offered and identified as behavioral standards; and (*b*) nonrational and subconsciously accepted norms that are imbedded in the recurrent uniformities of thought and action approved by the society. The latter more often and more deeply influence actual social behavior than do the former. All the informal, primary, face-to-face groups in any society operate by the nonrational norms, while explicit laws and written regulations appear mainly in the larger, secondary associations of people.

## BEHAVIOR PATTERNS ARE STRUCTURED

It must be clear from what has been said up to now that patterns of behavior are not just a list of random items that occur with some regularity. Social behavior is structured or organized. The various items of conduct, the ways of acting and thinking, are interrelated and coordinated; they fit together. This structure is demonstrated in the following explanations that may serve as both a review and a preview of the conceptual framework employed in this sociological analysis.

a. Behavior patterns are structured within any given social role. For example, all the separately recognizable parts of the mother's role, whether it is feeding the child, dressing him, planning for his nursery school, expressing warmth and affection, teaching him to walk and talk—all these are coordinated in the maternal function of child care. The role is a sense-making combination of behavior patterns that must be logically arranged and related.

b. The so-called role relations also demonstrate the structure of behavior patterns. This structural aspect is seen in the reciprocal relations between husband and wife, mother and child, teacher and student, employer and employee, salesman and customer, mayor and citizen. If behavior were not coordinated within the social role of each person, and if the individual did not recognize and respond to the correlative behavior patterns in other persons, any systematic arrangement of social life would be unthinkable and impossible. The physician who deals with his patient as an employer deals with his employee would soon have no more patients; the husband who treats his wife the way a lawyer treats his client would probably soon have no wife.

**c.** The principal social processes or important types of social interaction also show the structural aspect of behavior patterns. While it is true that these patterns are enacted by the individual, they are most often performed with one or more persons. The social process of friendly cooperation illustrates this fact. There are certain minimum requirements, ways of acting and thinking, "rules of the game," which constitute friendship and which are already existing in the culture before two people meet and become friends. Each person "senses" the expectations of these behavior patterns, realizes that they interlock, and if he wants to be a good friend fulfills them.

Another illustration is that of competition, which is a highly valued social process in the American culture. Even competitors who are friends know that competition differs from friendship; and the difference is found in the patterns of behavior that constitute each. The content of the process is the combination of ways of thinking and acting that each competitor displays in responding to the other.

**d.** Behavior patterns are further organized and systematized into institutions. For example, the various forms of behavior that occur regularly at a religious worship service are coordinated with one another and are directed toward the goal of the religious institution. This is true even though many of the generalized actions and meanings in the situation may not be fully understood by the participants. In the political sphere, compaigning, voting, propaganda, law enforcement, and civic administration are institutionalized, and all the patterns of such political behavior are structured in a coordinated way.

**e.** Finally, culture is the organized total system of all the behavior patterns of the people. The learned social behavior of a whole society, all the repetitive shared ways of thinking and acting, constitute the "pattern of living" of a people. Structure or organization is inherent in the very notion of behavior pattern. We shall study the larger cultural aspects of this structure in subsequent chapters of this book.

## Some American Behavior Patterns

### 1. PATRIOTISM AND ETHNOCENTRISM

Americans are becoming more and more conscious of their national existence; even naturalized citizens are proud to be Americans, and some who are only one generation removed from foreign ancestry develop a fiercer and more vocal patriotism than the descendants of old American families. The student who is himself a patriotic and loyal American is often puzzled by discussions of ethnocentrism and wonders whether he is being unfair to his own country in trying to develop scientific objectivity toward other countries.

Ethnocentrism is a tendency, usually one of superiority, according to which we judge foreigners and out-groups by the norms, values, and standards to which we have become socialized. This is one of the greatest obstacles to scientific objectivity, and is a source of patterns of prejudice, intolerance, discrimination, and stereotyping. The important point to note is that the patriotic person need not be ethnocentric. One can appreciate the social values of another culture without repudiating his own; at least one can attempt to understand these foreign forms of behavior without judging all members of the out-group as stupid and unintelligent.

Most Americans pride themselves on being fair, reasonable, and objective—in fact these are high values in our culture—but there are numerous ethnocentric attitudes expressed by Americans. Following are a few of the many non-American cultural patterns that are derided by some Americans.

a. The lack of formal schooling and the extent of illiteracy that characterize the masses of people in most countries of the world are often confused with lack of intelligence. The high social value of universal compulsory schooling in the United States is erroneously employed as a norm to measure the intelligence of those people in other countries who have not been so favored.

b. The relatively closed class-system existing in many countries is criticized as a defect by Americans who value upward social mobility. We often assume that the ambitious efforts in social climbing constitute a universal value and that there is something wrong with people who adapt themselves to a permanent social status. People who do not try to "better themselves" in an economic and material way appear somehow to have defective characters.

c. The practice of gesticulating when talking, which appears to be customary among some Latin peoples, seems to many Americans ridiculous, if not uncouth. Because we have acquired the pattern of talking without using our hands, we come to the conclusion that this is the best way of carrying on a conversation. Similarly, we make a negative judgment about the rapid talking and the excitable tones of voice frequently used by some non-Americans.

d. Many Americans consider the habit of tardiness among some peoples to be an affront and a sign of laziness. "Time is money" is a peculiarly American notion, and since we value time and punctuality highly, we find it difficult to understand people whose pace is leisurely and unpunctual.

e. Americans often recognize the problems in their own family system but still criticize the parent-child relationship in many foreign countries and among immigrants. They feel that foreign children are often repressed and subject to inhuman restrictions, particularly if they are adolescent girls. Americans' belief in individualism, freedom, and competition influences their judgment of human relations in other cultures. These values are used by Americans in giving sympathy to the children of foreign parents.

These are simple examples of American attitudes toward foreign culture patterns. They show that the American is often suspicious of what is strange to him. He distrusts foreign behavior patterns because he does not accept the social values according to which they are formed. He askes about foreigners, "Why don't they do things more naturally?" This question really means, "Why aren't they American in their ways?"

Americans are often surprised to find that foreigners have the same ethnocentric attitudes toward us. This

sometimes shocks us because most of us have assured
ourselves that our patterns of behavior are the very best
possible. This attitude is ethnocentrism in its severest
form, and it is characteristic of some people in all cultures. The ethnocentric person distrusts everything foreign
and often considers foreign culture patterns subversive
of his own society. He greatly lacks scientific objectivity.

2. PATTERNS OF LAWLESSNESS

American urban society has become notorious for its
widespread patterns of lawlessness, exemplified by organized crime, racketeers, and syndicates. We are not concerned here with individual acts of crime, or with occasional outbursts of mob violence. Lawlessness is a social
problem but it also appears to be in conflict with the basic
statements we have made about normative patterns of
behavior. The point of confusion for the beginning student
is that criminal behavior, even though it is patterned, is
inconsistent with approved norms and guides of social
behavior.

Most Americans are law-abiding most of the time. People are conformists in most of their routine activities; if
this were not true, an organized and orderly society would
not be possible, and social science could not exist. The
possibility of a continuing and functioning society is pred-
icated on the fact that most people act and think in
expected patterns. The interesting fact about habitual
criminals is that most of the time their behavior patterns
are the same as those of everyone else in society. There
are, however, certain consistencies of behavior that set
the criminal apart from other persons.

a. The criminal follows norms of behavior. He is lawless
only in the sense that he consistently disregards some of
the legal norms the society at large accepts and approves.
In his world he is expected to remain secretive about himself and his associates and to look down upon the police
informer or "stool pigeon." He is expected to honor his
word, keep his promises, and to treat fellow criminals
with respect and appreciation.

**b.** Only a small proportion of career criminals are lone wolves. In other words, much criminal activity is socially organized. This organization is present not only in the large-scale gangs that traffic in dope and other illicit merchandise but also in the human relations that exist wherever two or more criminals work together. There are reciprocal role relations and interdependence among these people even when they join only temporarily to do a single job.

**c.** The professional criminal specializes. He becomes successful and proficient in some kind of activity that he has repeated many times. This is why it is possible for the police to "type" criminals and, ironically, to locate them more easily. Success in one line of endeavor creates certain observable consistencies of behavior that the police come to expect of the individual criminal. They do not search for a swindler among bank robbers and burglars.

**d.** From an institutional point of view crime is an economic or occupational pattern of behavior. The major incentive for the criminal is economic gain, a way of making a livelihood. Crimes resulting from the personal vice of habitual drunkards, dope addicts, and sex offenders are not included in this discussion of professional criminals. The explanation of the lawlessness of these deviants is probably found in psychological rather than in economic motives. Career criminals are therefore identified mainly by crimes against property and secondarily by crimes against persons.

**e.** Criminal behavior is a cultural product, the result of social experiences. Criminals exchange information—the young man learns from the veteran and expert; new ideas are generated and tested. Just as the normal, law-abiding citizen is constantly going through the process of socialization, so also is the career criminal influenced by his social and cultural environment.

These general patterns of behavior are characteristic of the professional criminal, whose principal gainful occupation is the violation of other people's property. They do not account for all crimes, nor are they an explanation of the many variations among American criminals. Numerous studies have shown, for example, that the southern states have a higher rate of criminal violence than other regions, that crimes against property are in higher proportion in urban than in rural areas, that age, sex, and intelligence differ according to the type of crime committed.

Whether Americans are less law-abiding than the people of other societies is a question which we cannot fully answer at this point. We have been dealing here with the "professional" criminal and must remark that there has been much expressed about "amateur" lawlessness, civil disobedience, disorder on the street and campus, the extent to which the law is broken in the use and traffic of drugs. Social attitudes toward lawbreakers, the competence and social status of law-enforcement officers, and the policies of prevention, punishment, and reform are all variables that must be considered in the scientific study of lawlessness.

## 3. RECREATIONAL PATTERNS

The institution of recreation exists in every society, but the emphasis on recreational patterns differs enormously. In some societies full-time recreation is considered the prerogative only of children and the idle rich. The notion in some societies that work is evil and leisure is good is countered in others by the notion that work is highly ethical and that leisure activities are morally suspect. It is obvious that the actual patterns of recreation in any society are influenced by the attitudes people take toward leisure and work.

In the American culture both work and leisure are highly valued. The shorter work-week has provided increased leisure time for more and more Americans, and the higher level of income has made it possible for Americans in general to pay for more recreation. This combination of leisure and money has helped to develop a number of distinctive features in our recreational patterns. In this analysis we omit consideration of creative work and hobbies and of literary and artistic activities, even though these are important patterns, and we discuss only the "play" aspects of recreation.

**a.** The commercialization of athletics has probably gone further in this country than in most other countries. Not only are the performing athletes full-time professionals, but large numbers of trainers, coaches, managers, and agents, as well as many subsidiary functionaries, make their living from sports. Recreation for them is business, and recreational patterns and roles are economic. Large profits accrue to the most successful participants in baseball, football, basketball, hockey, boxing, and wrestling.

**b.** The organization of so-called "big-time" athletics means that many Americans become spectators rather than active participants in sports programs. On many college campuses intramural teams are de-emphasized. The pattern of movie attendance and television watching is a further indication of the way Americans take their recreation as passive spectators. Just as the commercial aspect of recreation requires spendable income, so the spectator aspect requires leisure time.

**c.** The American attitude toward nature as a servant rather than as a mother has tremendously influenced the perspective of recreational patterns. Nature, in the form of mountains and plains, streams, lakes, and seashore, is something to be used and enjoyed, not merely to be looked at and revered. Even though the wanton exploitation of natural resources has given way to a national policy of conservation, the American attitude still remains a pragmatic one. Even the decorative aspects of nature must be useful to us.

**d.** The modern means of transportation have also had an increasing effect on our recreational patterns. Americans are the most traveled people in the world, and their country has been called a "nation on wheels" and may soon be called a "nation on wings." This traveling has contributed greatly to the development of institutionalized recreation. Motels, roadhouses, and outdoor movies have evolved because of the use of the automobile. Vacation travel by bus, railroad, and airplane has brought Americans to places in our country that were once inaccessible. Our various kinds of transportation — and the means to make use of them—help to explain why, unlike most Europeans, we have never accepted hiking as a popular form of recreation.

e. Certain forms of traditionally masculine recreation, such as fishing, hunting, and camping, are now gradually being practiced by both sexes and all ages. These forms are a continuation of our pioneer rural traditions and to some extent, also a reaction to the confinement of city living. Values concerning better health, fresh air, and outdoor exercise are brought together in these forms of recreation.

f. Social awareness of the benefits of recreation has resulted in the systematic organization of playgrounds and public parks. These are provided by society as a means for healthy physical development and also as an antidote to deliquency. The emphasis on sports in America is not only commercial and professional. There is a social responsibility for the voluntary and amateur recreational needs of the people.

There are many artistic and literary aspects of the American recreational institution that we have not discussed here. There is some question whether the serious pursuit of art can be interpreted as relaxation and recreation. In many ways these patterns reflect specializations in the American culture, and they probably require a separate analysis. They imply canons of good taste and preferences about which there is much dispute, and they are on a level apart from the outdoor play and sports we have discussed above.

It is important for the beginning student of society to realize that recreation is not merely a by-product of a culture or an activity in which people indulge when they have nothing better to do. Recreation in some form or other is found in every society. It is one of the basic universal institutions. It is an increasingly important institution of our culture as the American society continues to provide more leisure and a higher standard of material living for its people.

4. Opinion Polls and the American Public

The opinion poll in its current form is a peculiarly American mechanism. In other societies both past and present, there have been inquisitive persons who tried to discover what other people thought. It remained for American social scientists to devise and improve sampling techniques, forms of questions, and methods of presentation through which they could investigate conceptual patterns. This does not mean that they have arrived at a perfect way of discovering the opinions and attitudes of people or that any of the pollsters claim complete accuracy for their work.

Nevertheless, opinion polls are here to stay. Judging from the frequent publication of polls in newspapers, from articles about polls in magazines, and from quotations from polls on radio and television, the American people are not only deeply interested in them but also have a certain amount of faith in them. A correct understanding of the validity and reliability of opinion polls requires a consideration of certain facts.

a. The opinion poll represents a sample of the personal expression of opinion by the individuals interviewed. It would be inconceivable that every man, woman, and child in the United States could be interviewed on any issue. Since our population is made up of many social categories, the poll tries to obtain a numerically representative sample from each of them. The most far-reaching poll is that constituted by the national elections, which involve somewhat more than half of the eligible voters and a much smaller percentage of the total population.

b. Opinion polls are static representations of thought patterns. They represent the opinion of those questioned at the time they were questioned, just as the decennial census presents static facts as of April 1 in the year of the census. Polls taken in successive weeks on the same issue indicate that opinion shifts from time to time, but the change occurs usually in a small proportion of the interviewees. Even with these shifts of opinion, however, it is possible to recognize definite trends of opinion in a population over a period of time.

c. Viewed with scientific objectivity, the opinion poll is not a prediction of future behavior patterns. It is true that manufacturers make use of opinion polls as indicators of trends in consumption, but they depend much more heavily on the polls that survey the actual use of their products, that is, the actual behavior patterns of customers. We must carefully distinguish between the use of opinion polls as a propaganda and advertising device that attempts to persuade people to do certain things, and their use as a precise instrument for the prediction of behavior. The latter use is not fully reliable because all the variables cannot be known and controlled.

d. The validity of some opinion polls is questioned because people often have a tendency to give expected answers, especially when the questions concern important social values. People who indulge in extramarital relations are likely to give the opinion that they favor marital fidelity. Few atheists admit to an outright denial of the existence of God. It is often difficult to distinguish between true opinion and expected opinion.

e. The results of opinion polls are always presented statistically, but the misinterpretation of these statistics sometimes gives a false impression. For example, if on a particular question a poll registers 60 percent with no answer, 10 percent negative, and 30 percent positive, it is misleading, if not dishonest, to claim that "six out of eight answered affirmatively." This example could be multiplied by other misuses of statistics, none of them the fault of either the pollsters or their methods but of the people who interpret the results.

f. The validity and reliability of public opinion polls depend greatly upon the clear wording of the issue under consideration. For this reason the statements are almost always pretested and reworded so that they will not be either ambiguous or slanted. This has been done with great skill by experienced American pollsters, especially when they ask questions about major national issues.

The polling method is not, of course, the only or the best way to study human behavior. Even with all its refinements in the hands of experts, it is still a clumsy research mechanism. Polls have been both extravagantly praised and thoroughly mistrusted. They are trying to measure what is not directly observable: the conceptual patterns of people. It is safe to say that when scientifically conducted they are a helpful adjunct to the more reliable and direct methods of research, such as participant observation, depth interviewing, and group tests of all kinds.

## 5. SOME POLITICAL PATTERNS

Political behavior has become institutionalized in the United States. Politics in our country is much more standardized and regularized than most foreign observers realize. We are often called a young nation, but our polical system is older than that of most contemporary countries. Furthermore, we have consistently been a country with only two major political parties. It is also true that the successful operation of political "machines" has become part of our national life. These three factors have added tradition and durability to the American political institution.

Certain political customs appear to be characteristic of American behavior patterns. The most curious of these is political apathy. In a country where education is compulsory, the literacy level high, democracy greatly valued, and suffrage almost universally available, there is relatively small participation of voters in elections. Apathy at the polls may be an expression of the freedom to vote or not to vote. No law compels Americans to vote, and there are probably many Americans who would not admit to a moral obligation to vote.

Voting behavior seems to follow several patterns, and the following statements are a rough summary of reliable research findings about them. The statements, however, describe rather than explain voting patterns.

**a.** People with higher education tend to vote more regularly than those with less schooling. Better-educated people often have greater interest in and knowledge of the issues involved in elections. The act of registering and voting is in itself not complex and requires no higher education. This is especially true in an increasing number of urban places where voting machines have been installed.

**b.** People with higher incomes vote more frequently than those with lower incomes. While the vote of a poor man has equal weight with that of a wealthy man, it appears that the latter has a greater economic stake in his country and a greater incentive to preserve it. It is true, of course, that the higher the income level the fewer voters there are and thus the numerical weight of lower-income votes is far greater. The middle class can at any time outvote both the rich and the poor.

**c.** More men vote than women. This is both proportionately and numerically true, even though there are more females than males of voting age. The traditional notion that politics is not a "woman's business" is to some extent still prevalent. In spite of the enfranchisement of women and their wider participation in all social activities, their interests are still for the most part nonpolitical.

**d.** Urban and suburban residents vote proportionately more than rural residents. Education and income partially account for this difference; also, campaigns are more intensely waged and voting places are more accessible in towns and cities. Political issues are more sharply drawn in the large centers of population, and a greater effort is made by the political parties to "get out the vote."

**e.** The majority of voters regularly support the same party in election after election. In national elections the Democratic party gets into power at one time and the Republican party at another time because there exists in America a relatively small number of voters who switch from one party to the other. These so-called independent voters are therefore an important minority category in the American population.

**f.** Party allegiance often "runs in families." A sort of tradition of party support and voting patterns exists in families and is handed down from father to son. As might be expected, husband and wife also tend to vote for the same person and party.

**g.** More than half the eligible voters do not exercise their franchise in state and local elections. It is only in national elections that the proportion of voters goes higher than 50 percent. The proportion of nonvoters remains extremely high in several southern states where many Negroes are discouraged from voting, where the population is largely rural, and the literacy rate and the level of education are low.

There are several other patterns of negative behavior that distinguish the American voting institution. Unlike the voters in many other countries, most American voters do not identify themselves with one major party because of their national background, religion, political philosophy, or economic status. Although politicians are aware of these variables and often make subtle appeals based on them, neither major party can claim the allegiance of voters on these grounds. It is probably true that in some localities Protestant businessmen and farmers vote for the Republican party and in other localities urban Catholic workers vote for the Democratic party; but this is by no means a nationwide phenomenon.

## Suggested Readings

Benedict, Ruth. *Patterns of Culture*. Baltimore: Penguin, 1934.

Goffman, Erving. *The Presentation of Self in Everyday Life*. Garden City: Doubleday, 1959.

Goodman, Paul. *Growing Up Absurd*. New York: Random House, 1960.

Kluckhohn, Clyde, *Mirror For Man*. New York: McGraw-Hill, 1948.

Riesman, David; Glazer, Nathan; and Denney, Reuel. *The Lonely Crowd*. Garden City: Doubleday, 1953.

Sumner, William Graham. *Folkways*. Boston: Ginn, 1906.

# 8
# Roles

THE MEANING OF A DRAMATIC ROLE THAT AN ACTOR performs in a play is familiar to everyone. The actor temporarily assumes the personality and behavior of a fictitious or historical character and enacts his part in the play as though he were the person depicted. The concept of the social role is analogous to that of the dramatic role. The main difference is that in the social role the individual plays himself. The social role is not fictitious or temporary; it has been learned in the process of socialization, enacted in the various groups in which the person participates, and "internalized" in the social personality of the individual.

We have seen that behavior patterns are the recurrent uniformities of social conduct, both overt and covert. When a number of inter-related behavior patterns are clustered around a social function, we call this combination a social role. For example, there are certain repeated patterns of behavior—actions and attitudes, duties and privileges—expected of each member of a family. In the performance of this behavior he or she is enacting the familial role. The social role is recognized and specified by the social need toward which it is directed and by the social group in which it is enacted.

We must not think that the person merely assumes a role for a while and then casts it off. Each person has many roles, but they are intertwined and deeply imbedded in his habitual ways of thinking and acting. The individual is simultaneously an actor and a member in the basic groups of the society; during the socialization process he tends to learn all the basic social roles simultaneously. Throughout his whole life he is expected to "play his part" as a member of society, and this he does in the enactment of his social roles.

212

## ROLE AND SOCIAL PERSONALITY

From the sociological point of view, the social personality is the sum of all the roles the individual plays. These roles are called *social* because they represent uniformities of conduct shared by many people. The role can be studied scientifically, analyzed in detail, and observed in operation because many people perform the same role in relatively the same way. The typical father role, or sales-clerk role, or teacher role, can be recognized among the people around us in society. If this were not true, social scientists could not study organized human relations, and the society could not function in any orderly or systematic way.

The social personality is in essence the total role-system through which the individual "deals" with society. Each person participates in numerous groups, and in each of these he plays his part or enacts his role. He does not invent the manner in which he will do this; he does it the way it is supposed to be done. A man may be the father of a family, a salesman in a business, a vestryman in a church, the lead-off man on a bowling team, a member of a parent-teacher association, a precinct worker in a local political party. He is the same person, but is playing institutionalized roles in the basic familial, economic, religious, recreational, educational, and political groups of his community.

It is important to note that although he is the same basic personality in whatever group he participates, he is expected to, and actually does, act somewhat differently in each group. It is obvious that a man does not behave in exactly the same way in a religious service at church and in a golf tournament at the country club. The situation is different, and the function of the group is different in each instance. Three elements combine—the situation, the function, and the group—to make the difference to which the individual must respond. In making his response to these elements, the person is performing his patterned social role.

In discussing the social person we indicated that we leave the analysis of the individual personality to the psychologist. We are not suggesting that social personality replaces individual personality. Each individual is in some sense unique, and the social history of two persons, even of so-called identical twins, can never be precisely identical. When we analyze social roles and the social personality, we are abstracting from concrete individuals that which is common to them, shared by them, and culturally patterned.

## ROLE AND STATUS

There is a confusion among students of society about the difference between role and status similar to the confusion that sometimes exists in the concepts of institution and group. The latter concept has been clarified by the distinction that the basic unit of the institution is the behavior pattern, while that of the group is the social person. The terms "institution" and "group" cannot be used interchangeably, and we must also carefully note that the terms "role" and "status" cannot be used interchangeably.

As we have seen, status refers to the position of a person, class, or category in the social structure. Social status is a construct, an evaluation, arrived at by combining and applying the criteria of social values current in the society. It tells us where in social space the person is in reference to other persons. The social role, on the other hand, tells us *what the person does*. It is a functional and dynamic concept concerning the social performance of the individual, not an evaluation that other people place upon him.

The distinction between role and status is clearer when we realize that the social role is one of the numerous criteria by which a person's social status is measured. Besides wealth, ancestry, sex, age, and the other criteria of status, the functional utility of the person to the society is also evaluated. This functional utility refers to what he does in his social roles. In a pragmatic, dynamic culture where people want to get things done efficiently, the kind of roles which the person performs may be the principal criterion upon which his social status is evaluated. A person of high social status may be expected to perform certain roles in certain ways, but this is not the same as saying his social status is his social role.

## ROLES AND RELATIONS

We have seen how social statuses are linked with one another in social stratification. The social status of any person is meaningful sociologically only when it is compared, or related, to the social status of other persons. Social status is interpreted in reference to the levels of superordination, coordination, and subordination on which people can be located. In comparison with other persons, an individual has higher, similar, or lower social standing, and in this sense we may say that the relationship is between statuses rather than between persons.

It must be obvious also that social roles do not stand alone. It is meaningless to speak of them except in relation to the roles of other people. The various social roles the individual plays are related to one another within his own personality. But these roles are linked also, separately and collectively, to those of other persons. This linkage with others shows that roles are complementary. People complement one another by mutual and reciprocal social relations. In this sense we can say that social relations exist between roles rather than between persons.

Ordinarily one thinks of social relations as relationships among persons or groups of persons. This is, of course, a common-sense interpretation of the experience of people. But if we analyze the social relation more thoroughly we see that social roles are the intermediary mechanism of social relations. It is in and through their social roles that people react to one another. Mother and daughter experience a continuing personal relationship, but it is through the role of the mother and the role of the daughter that this relationship is carried out. Each acts and thinks in patterned ways that are known, expected, and responded to by the other.

Occasionally a person experiences a conflict of roles, and this means that roles are sometimes not in a complementary relationship. The demands of a man's business role may be at odds with the expectations of his familial roles as husband and father. At another level there may be role conflict for the military chaplain whose theological training pulls him toward peace while his military training pulls him toward war. Examples may be multiplied because every culture contains differentiated institutional goals and every social personality contains multiple roles.

## CONTENT OF ROLES

The definition of social relations as the reciprocal relationship between social roles becomes clearer when we analyze the content of social roles. We have said that the patterns of behavior, centered upon a specific social function and directed toward a social goal, make up the content of the specific role. The performance of the rights and duties consonant with the function is the core of the role; for example, the performance of the sacramental rites is the core of the role of the parish priest. Not all of the behavior patterns associated with the clergyman's role involve this strict moral connotation. The time at which the priest recites his private prayers, or the manner in which he prepares his sermons, would not be equally important or equally enforced by social pressure.

The variation of patterns within the role is again an indication of the range of social behavior acceptable within the society. A mother who abandons her infant is guilty of an outrage against the values of the culture; she goes contrary to its mores and convictions and is condemned for failing in an essential duty of her role. The mother who loves, protects, feeds, teaches, disciplines, and in general takes care of her child is enacting her role in socially approved ways. But in the minor details of this performance much leeway is allowed.

The social role is made up of both overt and covert patterns of behavior. The physician is expected not only to act like a physician but also to think like and to have the attitudes, values, and knowledge of a physician. There is a certain range of individual choices and of degrees of conformity, but this elasticity of role is socially permitted only up to a point. The physician cannot behave toward his patient as he does toward his preschool daughter or his drinking companion. The patient and, for that matter, the general public expect the physician to enact his social role according to patterns that are fairly well known in society.

The content of any given social role is always related to that of other social roles. In the physician-patient relationship, the patient is expected to take certain attitudes and to respond in certain ways to the physician. If we analyze our own behavior in different groups and situations and in relation to various persons, we shall see that this is exactly what we do. One need merely examine the commonly repeated relationships, such as employer-employee, teacher-pupil, lawyer-client, minister-parishioner, parent-child, or the ordinary relations of friends and neighbors, to realize that the content of one role must be consonant with the content of the other.

## EXPECTED AND ACTUAL ROLES

We must not think of social roles as arbitrary, rigid, and automatic mechanisms of behavior that allow no choice of alternative patterns. Each social role is more or less generalized and standardized in any given culture. Certain kinds of behavior are expected in the roles of motherhood and fatherhood in every society, and the fact that most mothers and fathers conform most of the time to these expectations makes it possible for the sociologist to recognize and analyze the roles.

It is only when certain aspects of some roles are rigidly imposed, as in some courtroom procedures and religious rituals, in formalized etiquette and diplomatic protocol, that the social role becomes inelastic. The human element —the ability to choose otherwise and the likelihood of making a mistake—is always present. Even in the relatively unchanging and traditional cultures there is not a complete and absolute conformity by everyone to the expectations of all role behavior. There is always room for at least slight variations, and in a rapidly changing culture these variations may be considerable.

As people become socialized, they do not learn isolated, unconnected, and irregular ways of behaving. They learn more or less complete roles by observing and imitating others and by being corrected and counselled by them. From this point of view it is the total role that is expected of the individual rather than any particular pattern within the role. As roles are repeated in relatively similar ways by more and more people, the roles become established and are expected of individuals. As we have seen, the expectation and the actuality are not always completely and perfectly realized. Knowledge of how he is expected to pursue a role, however, is often as influential upon a person's behavior as is the observation of the actual role enacted by others.

Examples of this influence of expected behavior are numerous. The local politician who is elevated to the position of a federal judge tends also to elevate his patterns of behavior to those expected of one in his new position. The prejudiced person often tends to restrain his most violent attitudes when he is in the presence of well-educated, intelligent, and liberal people. The man who is expected to .tell lewd jokes to his drinking companions is also expected to refrain from this practice when he is in the presence of their wives, and he is usually able to shift his patterns of behavior to fit the circumstances.

## Social Sanctions on Roles

The term "expectation," used above, means something more than mere anticipation. Social roles must be fulfilled if the society is to continue as an operating system. People must play their part, they must enact their roles in approved ways. The need of the individual to fulfill a social function is accompanied by the pressure of the society to see that he does it. There are social sanctions for the enactment of the social role. The society approves of certain things and disapproves of other things in the many possible ways in which a role can be performed.

The strength of social sanctions varies. Not all social roles of the person or within the society are equally important or compulsory. Nor is each segment of the role-content as important as all others. The three elements by which one may distinguish the socially significant from the socially trivial in behavior patterns may also be applied to the social role itself. The significance of the social role depends on its universality, compulsiveness, and value to the society. These three elements will account for the social sanctions exerted upon any social role.

The society judges each social role on several levels of behavior and applies pressure and sanctions accordingly. Within each social role there is (*a*) *required behavior*, without which the role cannot be performed. For example, the role of the college student requires that he register for a sequence of courses, that he attend lectures, and that he submit to examinations. On another level, the role involves (*b*) *allowed behavior*, about which the society or group makes no hard-and-fast rules. The college student may choose among extracurricular activities, read more than the required books, or write letters to the editor of the campus newspaper. There is also (*c*) *prohibited behavior*, against which the society employs penalties or negative sanctions. For example, the student is not permitted to incite others to a campus riot, throw chairs out of a window, or shoot dice in the college chapel.

The degree to which the individual conforms to the requirements of the first level of behavior and avoids the last indicates the degree to which he is properly performing his social role. It also indicates the degree to which society approves the enactment of his social role and to which the social sanctions of approval or disapproval are placed upon him.

### THE FORMATION OF SOCIAL ROLES

We have seen how the "social role" is analogous to the "dramatic role." The latter role is the creation of the playwright. The dramatic actor imagines himself to be someone else and pretends to be performing the actions of the imagined person. The social role, on the other hand, is not the creation of the social scientist, nor is it an imaginary performance by the individual. It is the creation of the culture in the sense that persons have performed it over and over; and while the principal roles exist everywhere, their formation has been somewhat different in each major society.

The existence and functioning of the basic social roles are necessary conditions without which there could be no social life. Like culture itself, roles are inherently present in societies and do not depend for their origin and existence upon the attainment of a certain level of development by a people. Primitive, preliterate, simple societies could not exist if the people did not carry out their social roles. In this type of society the roles are fewer in number but more rigid in required performance than in an urban, complex, industrial society.

One needs no more than a casual knowledge of the world's different cultures to recognize that even the basic social roles are not enacted in identical ways everywhere. Roles are molded according to the demands of the particular culture and society in which they are enacted. For example, some of the economic needs of a primitive society can be met through the relatively simple role of barterers. In a complex commercial society this function is multiplied and specialized into the various economic roles of purchasing agent, discount clerk, salesman, advertising manager, copywriter, radio and television advertiser, and many others. The number, content, and kind of social roles existing in a society are the developed product of that society.

The varying influence of the major institutions in any culture helps to account for the emphasis placed on the different basic roles. In a society where the economic institution is predominant, great stress is placed on the occupational roles; the main values center upon them, and their behavior expectations are quite exacting. In another society where the familial institution is predominant, the roles within the family and the kinship groups become more refined and demanding. A still different direction and judgment will be given to the social roles in a society where the political or the religious institution is pivotal.

## ROLES AND THE INDIVIDUAL

Every person is born into an existing culture in which the social roles have already been institutionalized. Since these social roles are very numerous and since no person can possibly enact all the existing roles, society must provide some mechanism through which role and person are brought together. We have pointed out that people acquire social status through ascription and achievement. They do not acquire roles this way. Strictly speaking we cannot say that roles are ascribed or achieved. Status is the result of a judgment in the minds of people; role is what one does. A person may have high achievement within a role, but he does not achieve the role itself.

Confusion in the use of these concepts can be avoided if we distinguish between preparation *for* and achievement *in* a social role. The mere fact that the role of elementary-school teacher exists in a patterned way in our society makes it possible for an individual to prepare for this role. The person knows ahead of time the requirements for the role, what kinds of abilities, knowledges, and skills will best fit him or her for the role of teacher. Certainly, work and study go into the preparatory steps, but this is achievement within the role of student and not, strictly speaking, the achievement of the role of teacher.

A correct understanding of this relationship of the role to the individual requires a realization of their mutual influence. While a society may multiply the number and kinds of social roles, it is only in a limited sense that we can say the individual person creates even the partial content of the role. The social roles that function in any particular culture are a product of the experiences and interaction of many people over a long period of time. Thus individuals have influenced and helped to shape particular aspects of roles. The individual enters upon existing roles, but he must in a sense "internalize" these roles, and in so doing he varies somewhat from other people in the performance of the roles.

On the generalized level of abstraction necessary in scientific study, we must say that the social roles are ready-made, preexisting formulas of social behavior to which the individual accommodates himself. In a limited sense and in some aspects of the role there is mutual accommodation. There are two general ways through which this accommodation takes place, that is, through which the particular individual and the roles he will enact are brought together. The first is by assignment and the other is by assumption.

The assignment of the social roles means that the roles are given to the person from outside himself. Assignment is accomplished in two ways, depending upon the kind of social role under consideration. In some roles the assignment to the person is *automatic*. For example, certain familial roles like those of son, daughter, uncle, aunt, grandparent, and cousin do not depend upon the decision of the individual. This is true also of any aspect of a social role the individual has from birth, such as age, sex, race, and ethnic background. Assignment of roles can also be *deliberate,* as when a child is adopted, or a girl is sold into marriage, or when an adult person is appointed to the role of bank manager or elected to that of county sheriff.

A person acquires a role by assumption when he takes it on voluntarily, through his individual decision. For example, by the decision to marry, the contracting parties assume the roles of husband and wife. Similarly, roles are assumed when one decides to follow one occupation rather than another, to become a university student rather than to seek gainful employment, or to strive for membership or office in any number of groups.

The distinction between assignment and assumption must not be oversimplified. In the complex situations of everyday life, there are many instances in which the deliberate external assignment and the voluntary personal assumption of the social role go hand in hand. There is cooperation on the part of those assigning the role and on the part of the person assuming the role. For example, the person who is willing to assume the role of godparent does not do so unless the parents of the child have deliberately assigned this role to him.

## CLASSIFICATION OF ROLES

The social roles existing in a culture may be classified from many points of view. We have already seen that some roles are assigned and others are assumed, that some are simple and others complex. We may classify roles according to the degree of social value attached to them; some are held in low esteem and others are highly valued. Some have strict requirements, deep responsibility, and involve serious action, while others are relatively lax in their requirements.

Each person enacts at least as many social roles as there are groups in which he participates. These are the roles that gain the most attention from social scientists and are most readily recognized and understood from everyday experience. We have seen, however, that groups can be classified in many ways and that there is no completely satisfactory and all-inclusive typology of groups. The same difficulty faces us here, and we shall utilize the same typology of social roles that we employed in the discussion of social groups.

We found that there are certain major groups of people in every society, and that in and through these groups people are enabled to fulfill their social needs. Since the purpose of the social role is to function with other persons toward social goals and since each person participates in some way in all of the basic major groups, there exists a social role corresponding to each of these groups. Everyone at some time or another plays a social role in the familial, educational, economic, political, religious, and recreational groups.

This kind of classification involves a distinction between major social roles and subroles. For example, within the major educational role a person may perform the subrole of teacher, student, principal, dean; within the

political role, a person may enact the subrole of ordinary
voter and taxpayer, or may have some appointed or
elected function to perform. The complicated network
of social roles within any of the major groups in society
is, in fact, a related system of subroles. The person must
be in either an inferior, an equal, or a superior role in
relation to all the other roles; a man must enact the roles
of father, husband, brother, son, cousin, or brother-in-law
toward the other persons in the kinship system.

## KEY ROLE

We have said that each person has a key status that is
the principal norm by which society esteems or disesteems
him. Similarly, each person has a principal function and
becomes identified with one of the major groups in which
he plays out his main role. The identification of a key
social role is simply a recognition of the fact that every
individual is limited in time, talent, and opportunity, and
also of the fact that a certain degree of specialization of
function is necessary in every society.

Like a person's key status, his key role tends to be
measured against the pivotal institution in the culture.
If economic groups and institutions absorb the most time,
interest, and energy, and contain the highest values of
the society, the key role will be the economic role. Then
when it is asked about a person, "what does he do?" the
reference is to his occupational or economic role. It is
obvious, however, that not every person is gainfully employed, so that even in a society dominated by economic
concerns there are many people whose key role is noneconomic.

While the most highly esteemed role in any society
may be that through which a person performs his occupational function, the concrete situation may indicate other
key roles. The key role of the adult may be economic,
while that of his adolescent son or daughter is the educational role of student and that of his wife the familial role
of mother. The professional politician, the full-time religious functionary, and the star athlete or entertainer gain

their livelihood in the various major groups, and their key roles are considered political, religious, or recreational, rather than economic.

## The General Role

Although a person plays various roles in various groups and associations and also enacts a number of subroles, the social actor is a single person. Structurally and analytically, the sum of all his roles constitutes his social personality. This total social personality is a structure *in action* that performs many functions as a single individual. From this functional point of view, the person has a total, generalized role that is the combination of all the different roles we recognize when we think of the person as a whole human being.

This concept of the generalized role may be clarified by the example of the man who is said to "play an important role" in his community or society. We mean more than his contribution as a member of the political or civic structure. We mean his combined roles as husband and father, neighbor, voter, churchgoer, and businessman or professional.

The general role, then, is not the same as the key or major role. Just as the various statuses a person occupies combine in his station in life, so also the various roles he enacts, when viewed as a whole, combine in his generalized role. This concept represents his total function or functions in the society—what he contributes to the society and what the society has become accustomed to expect from him.

## Some Roles in the American Society

### 1. The City Policeman

In small, primitive, and relatively simple societies approved behavior tends to be enforced by tradition and customs. As a society becomes larger and more complex it develops a system of written laws and an organized way of enforcing the law. The police force may be called the servant of the public; the policeman is also called a

peace officer. He is supposed to maintain the peace of
the community by defending the law-abiding citizens
against the law-breaking citizens.

The role of the urban policeman in America has
become fairly well institutionalized. As in every occupation, competence in this role varies in quality from city
to city and among the members of the force within any
particular city. More than any other city employee, the
policeman is on public view; his behavior is observed by
many. People tend to form judgments on the basis of
these observations and these judgments range from approval to disapproval. It may be useful here to consider
some of the conditions under which the American urban
policeman attempts to enact his occupational role.

a. Much publicity is given to rising crime rates and to
violence in the city streets, with a resultant strong public
pressure to "restore law and order." This problem is particularly dramatic in the confrontation between police and
unruly mobs of people. The police are expected to prevent, or at least to control, such occurrences and if necessary to meet force with force. Sometimes they are accused
of using too much force and at other times too little.

b. Unlike the police in most large European cities, the
American policeman carries firearms and other lethal
weapons and is expected to be judicious in employing
them. Despite some widely publicized instances of police
brutality, systematic research has demonstrated that the
great majority of law officers are reluctant to use their
weapons except under extreme provocation.

c. In the day-to-day performance of his duties the police
officer has an extraordinary power of discretion and must
make immediate decisions: whether or not to arrest a
person, whether or not to interfere in a quarrel. This is
a reversal of most occupational decision-making. In other
occupational structures discretionary power is narrowest
at the lower job echelons and widest at the upper levels.
This fact places an unusual burden on the intelligence,
objectivity, and sense of responsibility of the ordinary
policeman.

**d.** It appears that the American policeman is not accorded the social status and personal respect that are enjoyed by law officers in some other large Western societies, and the policeman recognizes this when he complains that he has a "thankless job." He is in a public service occupation which generally commands a lower salary than positions in profit-making organizations. Other criteria of social status are also involved: relatively low standards of formal schooling and the social background from which men are recruited.

**e.** The peculiar willingness of many "respectable" citizens to patronize illegal activities also makes the policeman's role a difficult one to perform. It is obvious that gambling, prostitution, and other irregularities would not flourish if there were not large numbers of citizens who desire them. Politicians are sometimes in league with crime syndicates. The honest police officer is often frustrated in the presence of such acceptable illegalities.

**f.** A more recent frustration is the complaint by many policemen that the law is on the side of the criminal. This refers to the court decisions that are meant to protect the rights of all arrested persons, define the technical procedures under which arrests can be made, and specify the conditions under which charges can be made and convictions obtained. Police feel that they are hindered in the performance of their duty, and that this is part of the explanation for the rise in unlawful activities.

From the point of view of the total law-enforcement system the role of the police officer is only one in a network of interlocking human relations. He may feel formally responsible only to his superiors in the department, but in practice he is answerable also to court judges, the mayor and city council, as well as to the general public. Unlike members of a labor union, he can do little to improve working conditions by his affiliation with a policeman's voluntary association.

It is said that in the long run a city gets the kind of police department it deserves. If the majority of citizens are themselves law-abiding, and have respect for the

dignity of law enforcement officials, they are likely to be
influential in maintaining a competent police force. Where
the citizenry ignores or condones illegalities, and the
public officials cooperate in such practices, the role of the
ordinary policeman becomes almost impossible of successful achievement.

## 2. THE TRAVELING SALESMAN

The itinerant peddler is part of the folklore of the
American culture. From colonial times on he traveled
through the growing nation, bringing his wares to the
people, cajoling them into buying, gaining a reputation
as a charming man of the world and sometimes also as a
clever swindler. He played a personal economic role in
the distribution of goods in the days before mail-order
houses, department stores, supermarkets, and chain stores.

The function of the traveling salesman is still the distribution of merchandise, but he is seldom now the retail
outlet for goods. There are still house-to-house salesmen
in American cities, but the traveling salesman is now most
often a manufacturer's representative. He is a wholesale
merchant, the intermediary between the manufacturer
and the retailer. Changes in American urban and business
life have brought about changes in the social role of the
salesman. Following are some of the main components of
this role.

**a.** Most of the social relations of the traveling salesman
are in secondary associations. He strives to build up primary relations with his customers, his colleagues, and
the employees of the hotels where he stops. Most of these
people, however, remain outsiders to him, and he remains
an out-group person to them. This is one of the reasons
why the successful salesman tends to be friendly and
jovial, and to get on a first-name basis with customers and
acquaintances. He feels the social need to establish at
least the fiction of primary relations with strangers.

**b.** The traveling salesman spends most of his time away
from his own primary group—his family, neighborhood,
parish, and local clubs. We have seen that primary group
relationships are declining in America. The salesman is

the outstanding evidence of this trend. The circus performer and the migrant worker usually travel with their families, but the salesman travels alone. He lives in hotels and motels, eats in restaurants, and often whiles away his spare time in movies and bars.

**c.** The salesman is externally released from both the social support and the cultural pressures of his community. In a sense, this may be called "abnormal" living because most people maintain a large number of primary relations and because the whole society requires the functioning of primary groups. When he is moving outside these groups and relations, the salesman is not immediately and directly accountable for his social behavior. The known values of his intimates and friends, to which he tends to accommodate himself when he is at home, do not support him when he is on the road. This fact is the basis for the many shady jokes and stories told about the traveling salesman.

**d.** The successful traveling man must not only sell goods; he must also sell himself. Perhaps nowhere else in the world is the notion so widely prevalent as in America that "personality" is the most important factor in selling. In spite of the social and cultural handicaps mentioned, the salesman must appear to be a charming, friendly, witty, and intelligent person. He must appear to be convinced that his product is better than that of his competitors in order to sell this conviction to his customers.

**e.** The functioning social role of the traveling salesman calls for an adaptive personality. There are certain generalized behavior patterns running through all his relations with his employers, his customers, his competitors, and others. Nevertheless, the social situations into which he enters vary in different cities; he must be ready to adjust himself to them. His ability to adapt to these variations often means the difference between making and losing a sale.

The social function of the salesman's role must not be lost sight of in this descriptive list. In an industrial and commercial culture like ours, selling is the tremendously important link between mass production and mass consumption. The modern manufacturer cannot count on word automatically getting around that his goods are of high quality and low price. If he makes a better mouse trap, the world will beat a path to his door only if the salesman clears the way and points out the path.

The scientific methods of economic distribution require the cooperation of many persons besides the traveling salesman. Radio and television actors, announcers, and commentators have taken over much of the selling function. There are many other subroles performed in general distribution, but the traveling salesman remains the key person. His social role expresses the energy, drive, optimism, pragmatism, discipline, and expectations of the ideal type of what has come to be known as the American personality.

### 3. THE PROFESSIONAL ATHLETE

There is probably no other large society in the modern world in which the recreational institution involves and affects so many people as it does in the United States. The functioning of a major institution, and of the groups that enact its patterns, requires large numbers of people whose principal social role is bound up in it. While this is true of many others who are full-time agents in recreational activities, we are concerned here only with the professional athlete as a modern American phenomenon.

The professional athlete is not only a symbol of American affluence, a proof that Americans have the wealth to support their entertainers and the leisure to watch them in action. He represents also one of the high social values in our culture, that of competition as a good thing in itself. The competitive spirit, especially the idea of being "a good sport," carries over from the recreational field into business and politics, into education, and even into religion. The American is expected to be aggressive in everything he does but also to be a "good loser" when he fails. Following are some of the components of the social role of the professional American athlete.

a. It is obvious that certain physical qualifications are basic to the athletic role. These are strength, agility, endurance, and skill. All these abilities require specialized training since the demands differ from sport to sport, for example, from wrestling to tennis. It is sometimes said that courage or "heart" makes up for what is lacking in physical stamina, but this is highly questionable in the case of the full-time professional.

**b.** Athletic ability is an economic asset which is treated like a scarce commodity. The supply never seems to satisfy the demand. It is sold to the highest bidder, who is usually some kind of manager or enterpriser; and when the ultimate buyer, the public, no longer pays for the product, it is discarded. The athletes themselves recognize this fact, and they try to earn as much as they can while their abilities last.

**c.** As athletics becomes more complex and institutionalized, the athlete ceases to be an independent agent handling his own affairs. In some respects he has representation in players associations, but he has little to say about the time and place where he will perform; and even in the actual performance he follows the advice of trainers, coaches, team captains, and managers. In most other social roles, the higher the person rises, the more freedom of decision he has, but the opposite seems to be true of the star athlete. He is "valuable property" that must be handled with extreme care.

**d.** The social role of the athlete requires also exemplary patterns of behavior in relation to the general public. Athletes must be kept away from gamblers and gangsters, and the professional leagues employ special detectives to report on players when they are out of uniform. Sports writers usually support this image of exemplary propriety for the youth of the nation. Press agents extol the virtues of athletes and try to conceal all but the most blatant breaches of conduct. This public responsibility is a further indication that sports have a moral connotation among American cultural values.

**e.** The demands of the social role of the athlete vary according to different publics for which he performs. It is usually said that there is an unspecified "sports public," but this is an oversimplified generalization. Sports vary in their social status because they appeal to people at different levels of stratification. In a rough descending order of status the most popular American sports may be ranked as follows: tennis and golf, basketball and hockey, football and baseball, boxing, wrestling, and horse racing. The star tennis player plays for a different public than does the star wrestler.

**f.** Since sports are essentially competitive, the athlete must be on one side or the other and must have social relations with the other athletes. In team sports, like baseball or hockey, he must be courteous and fair to opponents on and off the playing field. Even in individual contests like boxing, where the objective is to make his opponent insensible, the pugilist is expected to act "like a gentleman." The rules of the game govern this conduct during the actual performance, and the mores of professional athletes govern it outside the contest.

The professional athlete must play the role of public figure in America, but he is not esteemed at the same high level by everyone. To his followers and supporters he is an idol who is asked to sign autographs, put on benefit performances, and receive the acclaim of a hero. To the supporters of his opponent he is a "bum" who can be freely insulted and jeered at by the paying customers.

It is part of the social conditioning of the professional athlete that he must learn to be a target of both praise and blame. In the long run his actual competence does not depend upon popularity or unpopularity. His role calls for an equilibrium which can withstand either; and this is probably the ultimate reason why he is able to succeed as a professional.

## 4. The Elementary-School Teacher

America is unique among modern societies in its faith in formal schooling and in its willingness to maintain and expand its formal educational facilities. State laws exist, and are usually enforced, that fix the age limits up to which every child must attend school. The general level of formal schooling is rising far above these compulsory limits. More and more people are receiving higher degrees, and there appears to be no end to the number of special fields of learning in which an individual can earn an academic degree.

At the base of this ever-growing educational structure are the elementary-school teachers. Unlike in most other Western countries, in America more than three-quarters of these teachers are females. At the present time the elementary teacher is in great demand. She is still earning a relatively low salary, and her social status is slowly rising. There are many stereotypes and caricatures of the teacher. The following list provides a partial description of her functioning social role.

a. The elementary-school teacher must often act as a parent surrogate. Especially in lower-class neighborhoods where there is not much cooperation between parent and teacher, the mother "turns over" her child to the teacher. She often holds the teacher responsible for the behavior of the child. In many instances, the teacher has to train the child in fundamental etiquette that she might normally expect him to learn at home.

b. The social role of the teacher includes patterns of leadership. As a matter of fact, she is the leader in all the classroom activities. The attempts to inspire leadership among the children and to instill in them notions of self-reliance and self-government still leave the teacher with the only adult and really superior role in the classroom. She originates, guides, alters, and directs the activities of the group under her control, assuming almost all the leadership functions.

c. The essence of the teacher's role, and that which gives it its name, is the function of instruction. The techniques that are used for imparting knowledge appear to be an almost inexhaustible area of research and experimentation in American teachers colleges and departments of education. Many visual and auditory aids to teaching have been put at the disposal of the elementary teacher, and sometimes these techniques appear to be emphasized more than the content of instruction.

d. From the point of view of the total society the most important function of the teacher's role is the transmission of the culture. Because of the plurality of subcultures and the respect for ethnic diversity in our society, the children are in general expected to absorb the basic elements of the American way of life. The teacher teaches not only reading, writing, and arithmetic but also the American culture itself. She can hardly avoid doing this as an American talking about American things in an American way. She socializes and Americanizes her pupils.

e. The teacher in many ways acts as an example of behavior for the children. Much of the formal education the child receives comes through observation and imitation of the teacher, who may be more impressive in her off-hand remarks and her ways of acting than she realizes. The child does not imitate the teacher as much as the parent, but many adults recall vividly the attitudes and mannerisms of their elementary-school teachers.

f. In American elementary schools the teacher often has to be an entertainer more than a disciplinarian. The theory is widely held that the child's interest must be aroused and that it is somehow psychologically inadvisable to force him to do anything. There is no doubt that this makes great demands on the adaptability of the teacher in enacting her role. For most adults it is easier to dictate procedures to youngsters than it is to arouse their voluntary interests.

The teacher's social role is more dynamic in American society than it is in most other contemporary societies. Its patterns are not so rigid because the experimentalism of our culture has entered into them. The turnover of teachers—since many young women teach for only a few years before marriage—has also prevented the role from becoming too formalized. The teacher must be adaptive because the body of her knowledge is constantly expanding, and the child is learning more and more from the various mass media of communication.

The elementary-school teacher is a pivotal person in the whole educational system, and the social role she plays is much more significant than most Americans realize. She represents the principal institutionalized channel through which our cultural heritage flows. She is an instrument for the maintenance and reproduction of our cultural values in each succeeding generation.

## 5. THE SCIENTIST

The American society is usually thought to have a secular culture in which the "explanation of the universe" has been taken out of the hands of the theologian and philosopher and placed in the hands of the scientist. Ours has been called an "engineering civilization" because the application of physical science has resulted in the significant control of nature. These results are tangible and measurable. They bring material comfort and social convenience to millions of Americans.

We are interested here in the social role of the person who makes these results possible, the scientist. The application of scientific knowledge is not the essence of science. The important point is the network of both conceptual and external patterns of behavior that explains the scientist himself. What kind of man is he? What are his ways of thought, his methods and procedures? It is possible to indicate some of the characteristics of the scientist that help to answer these questions.

a. The modern American scientist is a cooperative agent in research, not the lone wolf and queer genius of fiction. The importance of coordinating various aspects of a research project, of making cumulative and simultaneous advances, and of sharing and comparing results has been recognized. This does not mean that the individual scientist is less a genius because he cooperates with others. There is still room for the flashes of insight that accompany the greatest scientific discoveries.

b. The scientist is usually a man of disciplined diligence. He works long hours in a systematic procedure of investigation and verification. The demands of the scientific function eliminate the careless and self-indulgent person from the occupation. Exactitude and precision are characteristics of scientific research, and even the "small" error must be corrected by constant rechecking of the data.

c. The successful scientist is a man of dedicated faith in the value of knowledge. The common misconception that the scientist is completely "value free" is belied by the repeated statements of scientists that what they are doing is really worth doing. It is obvious that the scientist cannot know all the consequences his research will have when it is applied by others in the total society. His faith is a fundamental assumption, only partially demonstrated by society at large, that his findings can somehow contribute to the general and steady improvement of human life on earth.

**d.** Honesty is a conceptual pattern or virtue characterizing the American scientist. It is implied in the scientific way of life. The social pressure of fellow scientists and of the general public places heavy sanctions on scientific honesty. Any attempt to "force the data" in order to "prove" the desired results is ultimately detected, and the individual who does this pays with his reputation and his livelihood. Furthermore, the observed examples of this kind of dishonesty as practiced under totalitarian powers have made the scientist particularly wary of censorship and "thought control."

**e.** The role of the scientist is also marked by the scientific skepticism essential in the search for truth. The scientist does not question basic knowledge, or the validly tested uniformities of his field. The scientist is constantly working at the periphery of accepted knowledge, at the frontiers of the unknown, and his explorations require that he be tentative and open-minded.

The American treats the scientist with awe and respect; the term "scientific" is a value-loaded word in his vocabulary. The high social status of the scientist is sometimes transferred to areas in his life in which he has relatively little competence. In interviews with the press he is often expected to make pronouncements concerning public issues about which he knows very little. The published results have sometimes been ludicrous, as when the expert biologist gives his views of demography, the physicist answers theological questions, or the sociologist dabbles in medical questions.

In spite of these occasional aberrations, however, the scientist is playing an increasingly important public role in the United States. There appears to be a trend toward a broader concept of the utility of science for our society and culture. Prominent and expert scientists in the physical and social sciences are assuming responsibilities for spreading factual information about their studies. This spreading of knowledge is a function of the gradual process of sociocultural integration that occurs in every maturing nation.

## Suggested Readings

Gross, Neal; Mason, Ward; and MacEachern, Alexander. *Exploration in Role Analysis.* New York: Wiley, 1958.

Klapp, Orrin. *Heroes, Villains and Fools: The Changing American Character.* Englewood Cliffs: Prentice-Hall, 1962.

Miller, Daniel; and Swanson, Guy E. *The Changing American Parent.* New York: Wiley, 1958.

Preiss, Jack; and Ehrlich, Howard. *An Examination of Role Theory: The Case of the State Police.* Lincoln: University of Nebraska Press, 1967.

Rommetveit, Ragnar. *Social Norms and Roles.* New York: Humanities, 1968.

# 9
# Processes of Interaction

HUMAN BEINGS IN SOCIETY ARE INTERDEPENDENT AND interrelated. Reciprocal contact, communication, and interaction are so essential to both the individual and the the group that without them the person would perish and the group would cease to function. People and groups can be and are related to one another in multiple ways, and the total society can be viewed as a vast and complex network of social relations, that is, of ways in which interaction occurs.

A difficulty sometimes arises in the use of terms like "relations," "human relation," "social relation." Ordinarily one speaks of his relatives as persons to whom he is attached by virtue of birth, adoption, or marriage. The abstract term "relation" is sometimes personified, as when we talk about the members of our family as our "relations." The sociologist employs the term in its most generic meaning as the link, or bond, of interaction that exists among persons and groups. In this sense it is not limited to family or kinship relations, but includes all relations in factories, schools, churches, political parties, sports clubs, and every other kind of primary and secondary group and association.

Usually we think of social relations as personal relations, and it is true that two or more persons are always involved in them; but it is also true that there is interaction between and among groups. In order to analyze the large network of social relations in society it is necessary to make certain abstractions from the concrete human beings involved in them. When we do this we find that human persons and groups are related by the fact of status, role, and process. The first two of these we will review only briefly; the third forms the subject matter of this chapter.

**a.** Relation by status refers to the linkage of social positions we have already discussed in the chapter on social status and stratification. It is the relation of position or standing that individuals occupy in reference to one another. We have said that social status is meaningless if it cannot be referred to other statuses in subordinate, equal, or superior relations. This concept is applicable also to the relation of groups, categories, classes, and other pluralities to one another. The status relation, as the word implies, is a static concept. The kinetic or dynamic aspect is seen only when a person through social mobility changes from one status to another.

**b.** Relation by role refers to the functional, reciprocal interaction that occurs when people enact their complementary social roles together, a question that we have already discussed in the chapter on social roles. This relation involves the expectations of social thought and behavior of people as well as the actual external and observable performance of these role patterns. The role is the mechanism through which people carry on their mutual behavior; the roles of different persons meet and are related. These role relations are easily recognized in the mutual interaction of friend and friend, parents and children, salesman and customer, and in large numbers of other patterned mutual behavior situations.

**c.** Relation by process is a further analytical refinement, and on a level of abstraction different from that of the role relation. The social processes are a few basic, typable forms of social interaction that cross-cut all the numerous social roles people enact. The term "process" has been taken over into sociology from the general scientific vocabulary, and means a dynamic course, or repetitive series, of operations. In the mechanical analogy the process usually results in a product, an achieved objective, but in social science we cannot speak of a "product" of social processes. In sociological terminology, the basic social processes are cooperation, accommodation, assimilation, conflict, contravention, and competition.

The social process is more than the link between two statuses or roles. Two persons who cooperate with one another or fight with one another are carrying on a social process that is something more than their status relation or their role relation. Both the process relation and the role relation involve patterns of interaction—behavior by two or more persons that is performed together by both terms of the relationship—but the distinction between the two kinds of relations requires further analysis. The process transcends the role; the process of competition or contravention transcends the role of the businessman who engages in these processes.

## RELATIONS AND ROLES

We have seen that persons interact through the expression of their social roles, and that the social role is composed of patterns of behavior surrounding a social function. When people fulfill the patterns of behavior consonant with their roles, they do so in relation to other persons. Since roles are always reciprocal—the employer implies the employee, the child implies the parent—we may say that the actual performance of roles entails social relations. The social person and his roles function with, are related to, other social persons and their roles.

When father and son communicate in a social situation, the man is behaving like a father and the boy is behaving like a son. This example can be multiplied by all social situations in which two or more persons interact. Just as social status makes no sense except in reference to other social statuses, so also the social role does not stand alone. The intercommunication and interaction of people playing their social roles constitute the social relation. This type of social relation refers to all the identifiable, repetitive patterns of social interaction in which two or more persons engage in the performance of social functions.

From the point of view of sociological analysis there are three important elements which must be distinguished here: (*a*) the numerous *patterns* of social behavior the individual performs that are coordinated and interrelated; (*b*) the *social role* that is a cluster of behavior patterns around an identifiable social function; and (*c*) the *role relation*, a functional pattern of social interaction that brings together the active roles people perform. We cannot say that the content of the social relation is nothing more than the content of the social roles as enacted between persons. The social relation is the link that brings together the roles, not the combination of the roles as such.

## THE CONTENT OF PROCESSES

At the abstract level on which we must discuss this complex question of human relations, we recognize that there are certain repetitive ways of behaving that run through all the types of human association people can have. The association of father and son, employer and employee, governor and governed, may be conjunctive or disjunctive. The people involved in these pairs may love one another or they may be antagonistic to one another. The social process is not merely the static position one person holds in reference to another, or even the patterns of behavior that make up the role, but the ways in which these roles and persons reciprocally function.

The principal social processes are cooperation, accommodation, assimilation, conflict, contravention, and competition. These ways of behaving are patterned relations in every society. They are present to some degree everywhere, but the emphasis placed on one or the other of them is not the same everywhere. The characteristics of behavior patterns we have already discussed are also applicable to the description of social processes. They consist of both external and conceptual ways of behaving, frequently recurring in fairly similar ways, shared in by many people, and having some social significance. The content of the behavior pattern and of the social process can be analyzed "as though" it existed apart from other patterns and other roles.

The social process must always be analyzed as a way of behaving which involves a plurality. In other words, the content of the social process always includes the behavior *between* two or more people that is shared *simultaneously* by them. This important point—the distinction between the role relation and the social process—is clarified when we use an example. The pattern of competitive behavior between two brothers can be analyzed as a social process which is distinguishable from the fraternal relationship existing between them. The social role of brother contains many patterns of behavior that have developed in the culture. But the social process of competition is something more than—it is "added to"—the situation in which brothers enact their roles. Likewise, brothers in conflict still remain brothers, and the social process of conflict is not the enactment of the social role of brother.

## UNIVERSALITY OF SOCIAL PROCESSES

The major patterns of social relations, like most human behavior in society, are largely standardized and routinized. The functional processes of interaction of group with group and of individual with individual have been observed in every type of group in which people associate. These processes appear to be fundamental to the maintenance of society in the sense that there are regularized and sanctioned ways in which they are conducted.

The universal basic social relations are few. Some societies minimize one or more of these basic social processes, and other societies maximize them. A polar example is that of competition, which is highly emphasized in Western civilization and largely de-emphasized among the Orientals. Every society has developed standardized procedures through which accommodation and assimilation take place and through which even contravention and conflict occur. The cultural expression of these main forms of social relations differs broadly from one society to another, but they exist and are observable everywhere.

## CLASSIFICATION OF PROCESSES

The broadest general categories of social processes are

those that run in two opposite directions. The *conjunctive,* or associative, processes are the patterns of related inter-action through which persons are drawn together and be-come more integrated. The *disjunctive,* or dissociative, processes are those in which people are pushed farther apart and become less solidary. In some degree or other, the conjunctive processes are always expressive of the social virtues of justice and love, while the disjunctive processes are always expressive of the social vices of injus-tice and hatred. We use the terms "virtue" and "vice" not as moral habits but as patterned forms of social relations that include both external and conceptual patterns of be-havior.

We do not classify these basic forms of social processes as either covert attitudes or as overt interaction, because each kind of social process must be presumed to contain both the measurable expression and the indirectly observ-able attitude. The disjunctive processes may be called *negative* to the extent that they reflect injustice and hostil-ity among people, while the conjunctive relations may be called *positive* in the sense that they reflect mutual altru-ism and justice.

The three conjunctive positive social processes are cooperation, accommodation, and assimilation. Each of these is an identifiable form of social relation in which the participating persons achieve some objective considered beneficial or desirable to themselves. Insofar as conscious motivation enters into these relations, they are an expres-sion of the participants' self-interest, but in their actual operation they must also be considered of benefit to the total group or society. They help to perpetuate and main-tain the society as a going concern.

The three disjunctive negative social processes are con-flict, contravention, and competition. They too are social relations because they are ways of behaving in which two or more persons must participate. While the two parties may not always participate equally in the relationship, there is never a case in which one is active and the other is completely passive. These processes are called negative because the people involved in them attempt to prevent others from attaining an objective which is considered desirable. They are called dissociative because the participants are at odds with each other rather than in harmony.

## COOPERATION

Cooperation is that form of social process in which two or more persons or groups act jointly in the pursuit of a common objective. It is not only the most common form of social relation; it is also an essential and indispensable requirement for the maintenance and continuance of groups and societies. Cooperation is, of course, a reciprocal relation. It cannot be one-sided, although it is quite obvious that cooperation neither requires nor often contains an exactly equal amount of effort by each side of the relation. When we say that people act jointly, we mean that they are contributing effort together and more or less simultaneously for the achievement of an objective.

It is also often true that one party in the cooperative relation may achieve more of the desired goal than the other party. We are speaking here, however, of the processes, rather than the fruits, of the cooperative action. Much of the success of cooperation is hardly noticed by people in everyday life because the practice of cooperation runs through all the major concerns of society. People assume that cooperation is the normal thing in doing business, providing material necessities, raising children, running the government. When the normal cooperative relation breaks down, we are able to recognize more clearly its importance.

Cooperation is a social process that admits of kinds and degrees. It is, for example, much more intensive and continuous in primary groups than in secondary associations. The primary group assumes that its members will cooperate, while the secondary association often has to encourage and promote cooperation among its participants. The family appears to require and obtain more cooperation than do the other major groups of a society. The amount and kind of cooperation exercised in the educational, economic, political, religious, and recreational groups appear to depend upon the social and institutional values current in any particular culture.

The factors that account for cooperation are complex and numerous. The conscious desire for an objective may be ultimately reduced to self-interest, loyalty towards groups and their ideals, the fear of attack by an out-group, the basic structural need for mutual dependence; all these factors function in varying degrees toward the continuing process of cooperation. We shall deal later with solidarity and social integration, but briefly we may say here that cooperation is social solidarity in action, and the same factors are commonly described by sociologists as the factors of social integration, cohesion, harmony, and solidarity.

## ACCOMMODATION

While cooperation is an essential and positive social relation highly beneficial to a society, accommodation is a kind of minimum working arrangement that enables people to continue their activities even when they are not in complete agreement and harmony with each other. The community, the factory, the school—almost any group in the society—strives for cooperation but may have to settle for accommodation. In a complex society where the social person participates in various groups, he may find himself cooperating with one group and merely accommodating himself to another group. It is probably demonstrable that every large group has both levels of members, the cooperators and the accommodators.

Accommodation may be defined, therefore, as that form of social process in which two or more persons or groups interact in order to prevent, reduce, or eliminate conflict. Accommodation is also the necessary process that occurs after a conflict is over, in that the survivors learn to adjust and adapt themselves to each other. The purpose of accommodation, however, is not merely negative or preventive. It is a means of living peacefully, of coexisting with one another, which may eventually lead to positive cooperation. It also is essentially a two-sided relationship, in which both parties, whether individuals or groups or whole societies, are participants in inter-action. It is characterized by "give-and-take" in the sense that each side makes an alteration in its behavior patterns in order to accommodate the other.

There are many subtle shadings and degrees of the accommodative process, and these are fairly well recognized by any student of society. Mere toleration between persons or groups is the minimum amount of accommodation. Compromise goes further than this and is the process in which each side makes concessions to the other. Arbitration and conciliation are frequently used conscious forms of accommodation. There are also situations in which one party may be coerced by law, or threats, or physical force into accommodation with a stronger party. The consequence of international conflict has always been some form of accommodation between the victor and the vanquished.

ASSIMILATION

Assimilation is a social process through which two or more persons or groups accept and perform one another's patterns of behavior. We commonly talk about a person, or a minority category, being assimilated into a group or society, but here again this must not be interpreted as a one-sided process. It is a relation of interaction in which both parties behave reciprocally even though one may be much more affected than the other. Assimilation is not so much a result as a process, although the degree of assimilation achieved in any society is an index of its social and cultural integration.

The process of assimilation, a reciprocal relation, must be distinguished from socialization, which emphasizes the cultural effect upon the individual. It is true that every person must necessarily experience throughout his life the learning of behavior patterns. This is socialization, through which he constantly adapts himself to the culture and learns to behave as a member of society. It is a general long-term procedure emphasizing what the individual does and what the effects of culture are upon him.

Assimilation is a specific process best observed in populations made up of people of divergent ethnic backgrounds. Clearly discernible cultural traits exist, coming from societies in different parts of the world. The varying patterns of thinking and acting meet and mingle. The people involved in this process do more than exchange cultural characteristics. They tend to adapt, adjust, and finally assimilate these traits to themselves. In this process the people are also assimilated to one another so that they now share similar patterns of behavior in a way different from that which previously existed in each party of the·relationship. For example, the cultural mingling of Moors and Spaniards is still discernible in southern Spain.

The degree and amount of assimilation that occur among people in any society depend upon a number of factors. The process tends to be slowed down where there are rigid lines of class and caste, and where there is a reluctance or inability to share the highly valued cultural items. Differences in language, religion, education, and wealth are sometimes major obstacles to the process of assimilation. Ethnic minorities in Europe are historical examples of these hindrances to assimilation, like the Polish communities scattered throughout western Russia, and the long-established German minorities in Poland.

## CONFLICT

Conflict is that form of mutual interaction through which two or more persons or groups attempt to remove each other, either by annihilating the other party or rendering it ineffectual. The most elementary form of conflict is armed warfare, in which large groups of persons meet in combat with the intention of destroying one another. The focus of attention and action in the process of conflict is always the parties involved in the relationship, but there is always present some other stated objective or purpose for which the conflict is waged. Conflict is then interpreted as a means to an end. Deliberate conflict merely for its own sake is probably a rare occurrence even in so-called primitive societies.

People talk of conflict in many loose connotations and it is necessary to specify the term carefully. One hears of a conflict of ideas between the younger and older generation, of industrial conflict between management and labor, of a conflict of interests between political parties. Attempts to put a competitor out of business or to murder someone are sometimes called conflict. These meanings are not the same as the sociological concept with which we are dealing. As a social process conflict is never one-sided; it is a reciprocal human relation in which both parties participate.

There can be no doubt that the preliminaries to conflict include various forms of disagreeable behavior. These are shown by words, gestures or actions of insult, abhorrence, rivalry, or contempt, or by personal and physical attacks. Conflict often grows out of competition and contravention and, unless the parties engaged in it are totally destroyed, it must be followed by some form of accommodation. Modern prizefighting, the purpose of which is to render one's opponent insensible, fits the definition of conflict; but conflict also has the aspect of a competitive sport in which the combatants are vying for economic gain, a prize, or a championship.

## CONTRAVENTION

Contravention is a social process in which the opposing persons or groups try to prevent each other from attaining an objective, whether or not they want it for themselves. It is sometimes thought of as a polite and genteel form of conflict because it contains hostility and antagonism without direct, head-on attacks upon the opponents. It is necessarily a social relation because there are always two sides to the process, two terms of the relationship, which are not, however, always evenly matched.

Contravention often takes place alongside, and even within, the cooperative process. Two or more segments of a national parliament or congress that must ultimately find some form of general cooperation for the welfare of the country frequently engage in contravention. The political parties are indispensable to one another and must in many ways coordinate their actions, but in other ways they contravene one another. Contravention takes many forms and is expressed in delaying tactics, in frustrating, thwarting, and denouncing others, in spreading false rumors and conducting "smear" campaigns. The use of the stereotype, especially one that emphasizes the negative qualities of a person or category, is a most common instrument of contravention.

Contravention is not sociologically significant if it is carried on merely on a personal basis as, for example, when two neighbors spread idle gossip about each other. It is often carried on in an organized manner between large categories of the population, between different religious and racial groups, and in some ways as a continuing process of what is exaggeratedly called "class warfare." There are many evidences of contravention, from protest to backlash, between the majority and the various minorities in a society. All these examples are characterized by the efforts of each party to prevent the other from achieving an objective without either destroying the opponent or attaining the objective for oneself.

## COMPETITION

Competition is a process of interaction in which two or more persons or groups are striving to attain the same objective. In the processes of conflict and contravention, as we have seen, attention is focused primarily on the other party as such. When two parties compete both focus primarily on the objective that both want to achieve and only secondarily on each other. Persons and groups compete *for* an object, and the competition is always stronger when the desired object is in short supply and of high value.

Competition is ideally carried out in a peaceful manner and is more formally regularized than the other disjunctive processes. There are conscious as well as implicit "rules of the game" that are followed by the competing individuals and groups. Indeed, competition is often considered a kind of game, with possible high stakes, that must be played fairly; it is thought to be socially beneficial even though disaster may occasionally befall the weaker competitor, as when the small businessman fails to survive his large rival.

The extent and degree of competition increase in a dynamic, open class society in which opportunities are numerous, values are measurable, and achievement is applauded. In fact, the competitive process in such a society often comes to be valued almost as highly as the cooperative process. Generally people compete for those items which are criteria of social status in a society. These are more numerous, more available, and differently valued in some societies than others.

## COMPLEXITY OF SOCIAL PROCESSES

Even the brief description we have given of the various processes of interaction indicates that these types of human relations must not be oversimplified. 'Several further considerations must be made in order to relate these processes to the concrete social situations in which they are experienced.

First, it must be clear from what we have said that none of these processes is found, at least for any length of time, in a "pure" form. Conflict almost always has overtones of competition, since the opponents are usually striving for something more than the destruction of each other. Long-term conflict and competition almost always also involve contravention. There is a similar overlapping of the conjunctive processes of cooperation, accommodation, and assimilation. In spite of this complex interweaving of the various forms of interaction, they are by no means synonymous, and they must for purposes of clarity and understanding be analyzed separately.

Second, the fact that these social processes transcend the specific content of role behavior is sometimes confusing. We have given sufficient examples to demonstrate that the specific content of the social role must be distinguished from the generic processes of social interaction.

The college student may enact his education role in a competitive manner, or he may be going through an accommodative process, but he still continues to perform the behavior patterns of his student role. A man may be in conflict with his brother-in-law and very cooperative with the fellow members of his church, but through it all he is still performing distinguishable familial and religious roles.

Third, the concrete operation of social processes sometimes appears complicated because the persons and groups involved may be performing two apparently contradictory types of interaction at the same time. The problem is clarified if we note the object involved in the social process. For example, two brothers may be competing for the love of the same girl, but at the same time be successfully cooperating in a business venture. Two political parties may be contravening each other on the poverty program or on questions of social welfare, but they may also be in agreement on a policy in foreign affairs.

Finally, the influence of the culture is an important factor in the ways in which these major forms of interaction operate in any society. The significant social values of the people help to determine, for example, whether competition is emphasized more than cooperation, or to what extent a racial or ethnic minority, or the lower social class, is allowed to participate in the social processes. The culture determines the rules and limits of the various processes, and also the value of the objects over which the interaction occurs. A Bushman, for example, may understand competition and even conflict over food and hunting rights, but not over oil fields, gold mines and uranium deposits. It is the cultural values that make the differences here.

## Conceptual Matrix of Social Processes

We have seen that the contents of social relations are both overt and covert patterns of behavior. In other words, when we study cooperation or conflict, we study not merely the external manifestations of behavior that identify the form of interaction but also the internal attitudes, ideas, judgments, and biases connected with it. Competition is a state of mind shared by many people as well as a pattern of behavior externalized in observable interaction. The same can be said of the analysis of the other processes: accommodation, cooperation, assimilation, conflict, and contravention.

There exist also in every society more generalized conceptual patterns of behavior that act as a kind of matrix for the forms of conjunctive and disjunctive interaction we have discussed above. The principal patterns for the conjunctive process are equity, justice, and love. These too are social relations because they involve reciprocal conceptual behavior and are not merely personal virtues or good habits that exist in the mind of the individual member of society. In fact, they cannot be realistically conceived except as a pattern of behavior between two or more persons who are equitable, just, and charitable to each other.

a. Justice is a pattern of interaction, a social process, in which the related parties perform obligations due each other. The relation of justice is a formal or informal contractual pattern in which the rights of one person or group are met by the obligations of the other person or group. The concept of justice and the actual expression of the social process of justice are found in every society, even though the manner in which they operate differs vastly from one society to another.

At this point we recall that the mores are the most compulsive patterns of behavior in any society. This means that the obligation to perform them, and to allow and encourage their performance in others, exists on the moral level of what the people in the society consider right and wrong. When a person deliberately violates the mores, he is jeopardizing the common welfare, he is "doing wrong" against the other people, and he is acting in an unjust manner. Society, in other words, claims the right to expect conformity to its most important behavioral patterns; persons and groups who thus conform are enacting the social process of justice.

**b.** Equity is a form of interaction that is expected in those areas in which behavior patterns are not morally defined or strictly enforceable. People who do what "common decency" expects, rather than what the strict letter of the law and the demands of formal social sanctions require, are carrying on equitable social relations. This is the kind of interaction that arises out of the social experience of what is the proper and fitting thing to do. Sometimes the equitable relation occurs in situations that are not exact duplicates of previous situations, like accidents or natural disasters.

More frequently, however, the equitable relation is recognizable in the vast areas of folkways and usages when these patterns are performed between and among people. Here again we recognize people dealing with one another under the aspect of general social goals and the common welfare, even though the equitable interaction does not consciously contain these objectives. The smooth flow of ordinary daily social relations, contact, and communication is generally made possible by equity rather than by justice.

**c.** Social love is a broad, general process in which the interacting parties wish and do that which is beneficial for each other. We are here talking about neither romantic nor conjugal love, which are narrow and limited forms of personal interaction. Social scientists often use the term "altruism" to signify the process of social love, which implies a degree of voluntary concern and service for others that goes far beyond either justice or equity. It is in a sense the most fundamental social relation, more basic than any other; without it social life would be intolerable if not unthinkable.

Social love does not operate under formal social pressure and it does not entail strict obligations enforceable by organized society. It is exemplified in many forms, and all the valued social virtues like kindliness, neighborliness, generosity, and goodwill, are manifestations of social love. This kind of reciprocal relation is the antidote of egoism, selfishness, ethnocentrism, and hatred, and is obviously exhibited in various degrees by every person in at least some of the social roles he enacts.

It must be remembered that we are considering these processes of justice, equity, and love from the sociological, not from the psychological and individualistic point of view. It may be important for the psychologist to know how they are developed by, or how they affect, individual personal behavior. In the present context we analyze them as social relations between and among persons and groups. It is clear that these three processes underlie the positive and associative relations of cooperation, accommodation, and assimilation. When they are deeply imbedded in the culture they tend to restrain and temper the negative aspects of the disjunctive processes of conflict, contravention, and competition.

## American Social Processes

### 1. THE VALUE OF COMPETITION

Americans for the most part seem to assume that competition is a good thing, that it is the "life of trade," that this social process contains many positive values. A comparison with some other societies reveals that there are "hard losers" everywhere but the preferable pattern in this country is to try to lose gracefully. Election campaigns are competitive, but the losing politician does not flee the country in fear of his successful rival. Riots do not ordinarily occur at the end of athletic matches; beauty pageants do not break up with the contestants clawing each other. Despite exceptions, it can be said generally that fair play and acceptance of the rules of the game have become traditional cultural patterns.

There is often a fine line of distinction between competition and conflict; and Americans usually define competition as a substitute for conflict rather than a prelude to conflict. When the child is encouraged to be self-dependent and aggressive, he is not being told to defeat others but to improve himself. He must be courteously competitive, and if he overreacts temperamentally in either winning or losing he is scolded for not being a "good sport." The following listing suggests that the process of competition is encouraged and valued by Americans in all the major fields of social behavior.

**a.** Economic competition is to be expected in a culture that applauds initiative and freedom, makes employment opportunities available, and emphasizes the material criteria of success. Business competition is not free and unfettered; it is more and more regulated with the intention that everybody gets a fair chance to compete. Antitrust laws and antimonopoly suits have become part of our cultural tradition; and while regulations never work perfectly they do tend to preserve both the spirit and the form of economic competition.

**b.** The notion of competition among young people in the educational institution is not an original American invention, but it has been extended to a larger proportion of educands here than elsewhere. In an effort to decrease the frustrations of unsuccessful competitors some educators have proposed the removal of competitive tests and scorings. In a sense, this attempt goes against the culture. As long as competition is considered a cultural value in itself, and as long as the system of grades and credits is employed as a measure of advancement right up through postgraduate studies, American youth will engage in educational competition and be affected by it.

**c.** In the recreational institution competition is said to be the "essence" of sports. Even the modified mayhem which characterizes professional boxing, wrestling, and football is applauded as the typical expression of the American competitive spirit. The "dirty" contestant who breaks the rules is penalized by the officials and often scorned by the audience. Athletics are considered a very healthy activity with moral and psychological overtones: they provide an outlet for youthful aggressiveness; they keep the young person out of trouble. Sports competition is supposed to substitute for and to help avoid conflict with others.

**d.** The familial groups in any society must necessarily be characterized by the basic process of cooperation among the members. Nevertheless, there are peculiar competitive aspects in the American system, especially in the premarital experiences of youth. The dating customs, and particularly the method of evaluating dates, involve a process of competition. Every college campus is the scene of competition among girls for dates with popular young men, and vice versa; and the prized objective is most often not marriage but the exchange of tokens of personal attachment. In a sense, this competition too is a game, and the person who loses the contest has to be a good sport.

**e.** Competition in the political arena is a recurrent social phenomenon in the American society. This is not only competition between individuals who are vying for office but also between organized groups of people who are supporting the respective competing candidates. Except in rare instances in minor elections, the candidate who does not have an organization to support him cannot hope to compete successfully for public office. In order to keep elections fair, laws have been evolved to control campaign spending.

**f.** Among religious bodies the American society has gradually developed a system in which conflict has been replaced by competition. Religious denominations are numerous, and none of them contains more than a minority of the population. The result is that no one, with the exception of a few full-time church functionaries, thinks about "defeating" other religious groups or of "putting them out of business." While the ecumenical movement promotes cooperation, there is still a typically American competition for souls, for increased prestige, and for the prize of bigness.

These examples indicate that competition enters in some form or other into all the major areas of American social life. Both as a conceptual pattern and as a pattern of external behavior it is an extremely important sociological element. It would be naive to suggest that the processes of conflict and contravention are of no importance, but it is a fact that their effects have been minimized by an emphasis on competition. What appears to be unique in the American culture is the evaluation of competition as a positive, associative form of social process instead of a negative, disassociative relation, as it seems to be considered in many other cultures.

## 2. AMERICAN TEAMWORK

Americans are fond of boasting that cooperation is the most effective form of human relation. The primary proof of this assertion is the organized, coordinated, cooperative system of mass production and mass distribution that has made available to the people an abundance of commodities and services. The belief that *anything* can be done through teamwork pervades the American culture. "Let's all work together" is a slogan heard frequently everywhere in the country.

An analysis of the way social cooperation actually works requires some sober reflection and tends to temper boastful enthusiasm. Large-scale cooperation is thought of as the means for solving large-scale social problems. The American approach seems to be expressed thus: "Here's a big problem; let's get together and solve it." But still there remain tremendous unsolved social problems in the United States. Even if we grant that these problems *can* be solved by teamwork, what are the underlying conditions that assist or hinder cooperation?

In general it may be said that people will voluntarily cooperate under three conditions: first, if there is concrete action to be taken; second, if the responsibility for performing the action can be fixed; and, finally, if the people agree that the action is worth performing. When there is consensus on these three points, Americans tend to cooperate willingly and successfully. Let us demonstrate this generalization with several examples.

a. Americans usually cooperate readily, generously, and effectively when faced with a disaster. They give help to victims of fires, explosions, floods, and epidemics. People cooperate in the organization of relief. They usually feel they should do something concrete—donate money and supplies or give immediate physical aid. The Red Cross is usually the coordinating agency for this relief; when there is a major disaster, help comes from all over the nation as well as from the communities near the disaster scene.

The teamwork of Americans during the two world wars is the major example of the efficient handling of a disaster problem. Social cooperation reached a peak then and was more widespread and more effective than any attempts at organized peacetime cooperation. This fact stands out in dramatic contrast to the draft riots of the Civil War and to the widespread protests, peace marches, strikes, and demonstrations that accompanied the war in Vietnam. In the latter instance it may be said that most Americans became war weary, but the much more important factor was the lack of conviction that the war effort was worthwhile. More and more people felt that the war in Vietnam did not "make sense," that it was irrational and immoral as well as unsuccessful, and did not deserve popular support. One cannot expect typical American teamwork in a situation of this kind.

**b.** American society exhibits also an area of ambiguous social problems where there is a general lack of cooperation and where often the initial teamwork breaks down. This includes a general feeling that "something is wrong" and also that "somebody ought to do something," but there is no real consensus about the seriousness of the problem and no exact way of fixing the responsibility for cooperation on definite people. In such a situation people often do not know what to do and leave the solution to others.

Most of these problems skirt delicately around moral issues and values. Juvenile delinquency in the urban schools and streets, the spread of pornographic and lascivious material in books and magazines, the known existence of commercialized vice of all kinds, police brutality and corruption in some places, organized interstate rackets—all these are examples of prevailing social problems that require social cooperation for their solution. Here and there effective but usually temporary "cleanups" have occurred, but in general these problems suggest that everybody's responsibility is nobody's responsibility.

c. A third type of social problem exists in which there has been only partial cooperation. Here one finds a consensus about the values involved but much disagreement about what is to be done and who is to do it. Americans seem to agree that every family is entitled to a decent home, that every person should have adequate health care, that workers should receive sufficient income, that better highways are required, that relations between the races should be improved.

Many people fail to cooperate in the solution of these problems; in fact, there are instances of organized teamwork that contravenes the current attempts to solve the problems. A certain amount of improvement has been achieved, but effective opposition has often been based on the argument that the method of procedure is in some way "un-American." In other words, in such instances people are not always in agreement on the values involved in the process of cooperation.

American teamwork, or social cooperation, is particularly interesting when we appreciate the high value Americans place on the competitive process. There is in fact no contradiction in the simultaneous existence of cooperation and competition as important processes within the same culture. An unusual characteristic of American culture is the apparent belief that competition itself gets things done as efficiently as cooperation. The feeling is that competition stimulates social action and that cooperation within the group results from competition with other groups.

## 3. THE AMERICANIZATION PROCESS

The "melting pot" is a popular figure of speech for what is more precisely termed the process of Americanizing people from all over the world. This assimilation is widely discussed in our country, and the large number of immigrants who have come to the United States has made the study of assimilation an important project for American sociologists.

Many Americans assume that assimilation has been a one-way process entirely; that America has "given," and the immigrant has "taken." We must remember, however, that assimilation is essentially a social relation, a form of reciprocal communication, and that both terms of the process are involved in mutual behavior. It is perhaps a valuable lesson in the prevention of ethnocentrism to analyze briefly some of the contributions made *to* our culture by foreign cultures.

**a.** The basic concepts of democracy, that is, of liberty and equality, come out of the philosophy of the enlightenment in eighteenth-century Europe and have their origins still earlier in the social philosophers of Western civilization. The legal system that surrounds and protects the application of democracy is largely a cultural debt to England.

**b.** The central religious ideas of the Judeo-Christian religion are also a European importation. Although the actual practice of American religion has taken numerous and sometimes bizarre forms, the underlying beliefs in divine providence, the redemption from sin, the brotherhood of all men under God have been widespread influences in the social relations of Americans. During the years of highest immigration, clergy of all faiths accompanied their countrymen to the United States, helped them to preserve their religious traditions, and often impressed their own ethnic traits upon the people they served.

**c.** The most obviously borrowed cultural pattern Americans have assimilated from foreigners is the English language. The changing pronunciation, the abandoning of old words, and the coining of new terms have brought numerous accidental variations in the use of the "mother tongue"; but our language is still basically an importation from England, and changes are frequently imported from other countries.

**d.** Little of the food we enjoy is originally or typically American. Every large city is dotted with restaurants offering the food specialties of different nationalities: Armenian, Chinese, French, Italian, Mexican, and many others. Even the eating utensils we use are of foreign origin. An interesting aspect of assimilation in these restaurants is that the "foreign" eating places are owned, operated, and patronized mainly by Americans.

**e.** Most of our clothing styles are of foreign origin and, until the invention of synthetics, so were most of our materials. Clothing fashions—especially for women—are notoriously changeable but it is difficult to find an "original" American creation that is not in some way imitative of foreign styles. Even the "natural" difference between male and female clothing, which makes the appearance of Americans so different from that of Asiatics and which is now also in a state of flux, is in reality an imitation of European customs.

**f.** The architecture of American public and semipublic buildings imitates styles from ancient Greece and Rome and from medieval Europe. Even the newer, so-called "functional" designs, employing steel, glass, and concrete, have their origins outside the United States in, for example, the *Bauhaus* group in Germany. Our architects probably agree, however, that the skyscraper is a distinctively American invention.

This is a meager list of innumerable cultural items, physical objects, and conceptual and behavior patterns that our people have Americanized through the process of assimilation. Many aspects of our school system, our religious practices, and our family customs have their roots in the non-American worlds. We must realize, however, that because of the time perspective and the relations we now have with foreigners, the assimilation process is slowing down. America is developing its own cultural characteristics.

The further we are removed in time from the large flood of immigrants, the less significant becomes the original impact of assimilation. This is as applicable to the native American as it is to the immigrant himself. Also the immigrants of recent decades have had better education and less need to be accepted and assimilated; some are intellectuals, and are of higher social status than those who came at the beginning of the century. It should be noted that .there is now a kind of reverse procedure of cultural exporting from the United States. The American style of life, which is sometimes derided as "coca-colization," is invading other cultures while foreign contributions to the American culture seem to be lessening.

### 4. EXAMPLES OF CONTRAVENTION

In the development of the American culture there has been a peculiar emphasis on two negative social processes. There has been an encouragement of fair competition on the one hand and an attempt to lessen conflict on the other. Little attention has been paid, except by the social scientists, to the process of contravention, which may be called an intermediary form of opposition. Yet this process is actually widespread.

Contravention is a recognizable social process, but it appears to be misinterpreted because it is often employed as a substitute to avoid conflict or as an aid to better one's chances in competition. People contravene (oppose the goals of) one another because they are competitors who are unwilling to become outright enemies. Contravention occurs in all types of human relations, institutionalized situations, and social groups.

The following are examples of contravention commonplace in American life that are recognizably distinct from the social processes of conflict and competition.

a. Legislators and lawyers are adept in the use of contravention techniques. Opponents in Congress are hindered by the tabling of motions or by the burying of resolutions in various committees. Lawyers in the courtroom sometimes use stalling tactics in favor of their clients. Insurance companies are sometimes reluctant to settle large cases, and they use various legal court procedures and administrative practices for hindering the success of claimants.

b. Contravention has frequently been used to prevent members of minorities from voting or holding office or from enjoying other civil rights. Southern politicians have employed various kinds of delaying tactics in order to prevent racial desegregation of public facilities and other changes promised by the civil-rights act. In some instances Negroes who became active in the civil-rights movement are denied banking facilities and credit in business places. There are numerous other tricks of contravention in this area.

c. Contravention has been a frequent instrument on both sides of the labor-management relation. The employment of labor spies and of yellow-dog contracts to prevent union organization seems to have abated, but the more subtle form of welfare paternalism in some companies still discourages unionism. The slowdown on the assembly line and the technique of "reporting sick" in other forms of employment are examples of contravention on the part of employees.

d. In the business world there are many ways of contravening one's competitor, and this is seen especially in the advertising of products and services. Everyone knows the comparative advertising campaigns conducted in the car-rental business, in the Volkswagen approach to the American auto market, in the extravagant claims made for one cigarette over other brands, for one toothpaste, mouthwash, or deodorant, as being better than all others.

e. The striving for a higher class-status is contravened in many subtle ways, usually by women. Those who can control the invitations issued for dinner parties, balls, and similar leisure-time activities may see that certain people do not receive one. Some people are kept from membership in clubs and from attendance at exclusive schools not necessarily by formal rules but by deliberate and informal hindering processes.

Contravention is common in the ordinary, everyday life of people in our society. The differences of opinion, the arguments between the older and the younger generations, are all indications of this social process. The "battle of the sexes" is essentially contravention rather than conflict and is seen in derogatory remarks made by men or women against the other sex; in ways of frustrating the ambitions of women in careers that men call their own; and in the negative gossip of some older single women against men in general.

This process is at work also among the many minority categories of the American population. These people's strivings for higher social status, for economic gains, and for political participation are often thwarted by others. The small farmer and businessman, the immigrant and ethnic groups, the domestic and migrant workers, and many others experience contravention in many ways. Some of the competition among the major religious bodies in our country is aided by subtle forms of propaganda, stereotyping, and name-calling that may be called contravention.

The most notable national example of contravention in recent years has occurred in the investigation of subversives. Many honorable persons who were once connected with Communist groups have been seriously thwarted in their careers and other pursuits because they are considered to be presently guilty of previous association. These people are denied certain kinds of employment and the accompanying status because others tend to generalize and label them "subversive." The accused individuals are not destroyed; destruction would be the outcome of conflict.

## 5. MINIMIZING CONFLICT IN AMERICA

While the American population is gradually becoming more integrated by the assimilation process, we must remember that there are still many diversities among our people. Social dissent has been common in our history and it has sometimes erupted in social conflict. Sectional, religious, racial, and ethnic differences have at times exploded in violent riots, which were intended to publicize and remedy patterned abuses of social justice.

In recent years many factors have been at work to alleviate and to prevent these older conflicts, but meanwhile new kinds of dissension have arisen. Impatience with the slow pace of social progress has led to a distrust in rational discourse, legal procedures, and social reform as means to settle conflicts. There has been impatience too with the tactics of "nonviolent" civil disobedience and a turn to direct action for immediate response to non-negotiable demands.

These tactics, inspired often by college students and ex-students who occupy campus buildings, defy the police and law courts, and encourage street riots, constitute a challenge to the normal patterns of "law and order." Conflict itself involves the use of force on both sides. The traditional American ideology has been rational, but often slow, in the attempt to minimize conflict and promote social justice.

It may be helpful to list some of the forces presently at work in the attempt to remove conflict and to encourage cooperation among the divergent elements of the population.

a. College courses in social science have presented an analysis of the factors of intergroup conflict. These courses provide, at least by inference, some of the social possibilities of programs for avoiding conflict. These academic courses reach only the young college students in our society, and only a limited number of these. Nevertheless, if it is true that college graduates will have in later years an increasing influence upon social relations, these courses are of great value.

b. Intergroup programs specifically designed for the alleviation of conflict and the promotion of cooperation are increasing. These programs take the form of workshops that may meet for several weeks during the summer, of annual conferences for experts in the field, and of various kinds of meetings sponsored throughout the year. The annual celebration of Brotherhood Week provides an opportunity for concentrated attention by Americans upon the techniques of social cooperation.

c. Various mechanisms have been devised for the reduction of industrial conflict. The widespread use of collective bargaining, the facilities of the National Labor Relations Board, and the techniques of arbitration and conciliation have all helped to bring about relative order and peace in labor-management relations. This is an area in which there was actual conflict and bloodshed during the 1930s.

In some sections of the country these mechanisms are still opposed, but large-scale industry has accepted and often even promoted their use.

d. A number of effective organizations and movements have been at work to reduce tension and remove conflict in race relations. In spite of the understandable impatience of militant Black groups, and of the so-called conservative "backlash" that uses the slogan of "law and order," there has been long-term progress in this field of human relations. Besides organizations professionally dedicated to this work, there are large numbers of interracial committees working toward this end in religious, political, and civic affairs, in military and veterans' organizations, in women's clubs, labor unions, and other associations.

e. Efforts are made also to remove religious conflict, not only in national organizations of Christians and Jews and in federated Protestant churches, but also within most of the major religious bodies. The latter groups take various forms of social action through which they are indoctrinating their own members in the importance of social virtues. The theological differences still remain in the various religious bodies, but ecumenism has now become popular and there is a continuing stress on cooperation and unity on nonreligious levels.

One of the most encouraging aspects of all these efforts to reduce conflict lies in the fact that they are deliberate and rational. Most of the people active in them repudiate the notion that "things will somehow work out by themselves" or that "time will cure the problems." The leading and most influential persons in large communities and large organizations appear to be convinced that internal conflict can be consciously avoided. The techniques of cooperation are constantly being refined, and intelligent appraisals of them continue to be made.

The population of the United States provides a laboratory for experimentation in these programs. The assumption that every society, no matter how advanced, always contains the potential of social conflict beneath the surface has been neither proved nor disproved. This potential appears to be reduced when the major divergences are reduced; but the American people seem to be intent upon demonstrating that conflict can be minimized even while important differences remain among the population.

## Suggested Readings

Abrahamson, Mark. *Interpersonal Accommodation.* Princeton: Van Nostrand, 1966.

Coser, Lewis. *Continuities in the Study of Social Conflict.* New York: Free Press, 1967.

Dahrendorf, Ralf. *Class and Class Conflict in Industrial Society.* Stanford: Stanford University Press, 1959.

Gordon, Milton. *Assimilation in American Life.* New York: Oxford, 1964.

Sherif, Muzafer. *Social Interaction: Process and Products.* Chicago: Aldine, 1968.

# 10
# Institutions

LIKE SEVERAL OTHER TERMS THAT HAVE A TECHNICAL, scientific meaning in sociology, the word "institution" is often used in a nonsociological sense. One hears that some eccentric person in the neighborhood has become an institution, or that an orphanage is an institution for the care of children, or that Little League baseball is a community institution. It is true that these usages are correct in the informal context in which they are employed, but they are not correct according to the strictly scientific definition of the term.

DEFINITION OF INSTITUTION

Sociologically speaking, an institution is not a person or a group. It is part of the culture, a patterned segment of the way of life of a people. As we have seen, overt and covert patterns of behavior build up into social roles that persons enact and into various kinds of social relations between and among persons; chief among these relations are the social processes. Social relations and social roles form the major elements of the institution. An institution is a configuration or combination of behavior patterns shared by a plurality and focused upon the satisfaction of some basic group-need.

The definition of the institution may be better understood when we list and describe its characteristics. The cultural institution must contain the following essential elements.

a. Although we do not personify institutions, we say that they are purposive in the sense that each has as its objective or goal the satisfaction of social needs. They are the major ways of behavior through which people in association with one another get things done.

b. They are relatively permanent in their content. The patterns, roles, and relations that people enact in a particular culture become traditional and enduring. Like any man-made object, they are subject to change, but institutional change is relatively slow.

**c.** The institution is structured, or organized, or coordinated. The components tend to hang together and reinforce one another. This follows from the fact that social roles and social relations are in themselves structured combinations of behavior patterns.

**d.** Each institution is a unified structure in the sense that it operates as a unit even though it is interdependent with other institutions. No institution can be completely separated from other institutions in the culture, but each does function as an identifiable series of behavior patterns.

**e.** The institution is necessarily value-laden because its repeated uniformities of behavior became normative codes of conduct, some of them written into rules and laws but most of them subconsciously exerting social pressure on the people.

From these characteristics we may form the following more complete definition. An institution is a relatively permanent structure of social patterns, roles, and relations that people enact in certain sanctioned and unified ways for the purpose of satisfying basic social needs.

### Institution and Group

The terms "group" and 'institution" are often confused. It is well to emphasize again that these terms are not synonymous. The concepts they represent are distinguishable, and the objects they conceptualize are quite different in the real order of existence. The concept of institution is, of course, an abstraction, but the institution itself is as real as, and far more significant than, any material object of culture.

In the strict technical definition an institution is not a group of people. We have seen the importance of distinguishing betwen persons and the behavior patterns they perform. What the person does or people do is distinguishable from what the group is. Patterns of behavior, processes, and roles are institutionalized, but persons and groups are not. The group is a plurality of persons who enact institutions. The college is essentially a group of people who are following an orderly system of behavior called the educational institution. Similarly, the political institution is not made up of politicians, but of the kinds of behavior that have come to be called political.

The internal attitudes and the external customs of a group of people are focused upon the collective satisfaction of basic social needs. The mores, folkways, and usages are institutionalized ways of doing things together. They are not merely random and haphazard bits of human conduct. They are channeled toward recognized and valued goals. The people link them together in the performance of their roles and processes, and all of these taken together are an institution.

## THE FUNCTIONS OF INSTITUTIONS

What does the institution "do" for people in their group life? In order to answer this question clearly we must make certain preliminary remarks. First, the objective, purpose, or goal of an institution is the same as that of a group. Economic, religious, and political groups strive for economic, religious, and political ends, which are institutionalized in the culture. Second, the functions performed by the group are the conceptual and external activities performed in patterned ways by the people. They are what people actually do in their social roles and relations, and they constitute the main content of the institution. Third, besides these specific institutionalized objectives and these patterned activities of the people, there are certain generalized functions that all institutions perform for the people in society.

It is only these generalized functions of institutions that we discuss here. These again may be classified from two points of view. If we scrutinize these institutional functions in relation to their effects, or influence, upon individual persons and upon groups, we note that some of them may be termed *positive* and some *negative*. Let us look first at the positive functions of institutions which bring about a higher level of integration and coordination in groups.

**a.** Institutions simplify social behavior for people. The ways of thinking and acting have become largely regularized and prearranged for the individual before he enters the society. He does not have to stop and learn or invent his own way of doing things, because the institutions to which he has become accustomed during the socialization process provide a way for him. We have seen that much social behavior is nonrational and almost automatic for the individual; this happens because the behavior has been institutionalized.

**b.** As an extension of this function, the institutions also provide ready-made forms of social relations and social roles for the individual. The principal roles and relations are not "invented" by individuals even though these roles and relations are human products. In most instances the person knows ahead of time what behavior is expected of him in relations with other persons and in the enactment of roles. The institutions provide preexisting roles in which the individual can develop his own special abilities and wishes. Since he knows or can find out what is expected and what actually occurs in the role of business executive, lawyer, husband, baseball player, and so forth, he is able to fit himself for the performance of the role. This means in essence that the role has been institutionalized.

**c.** Institutions act also as an agency of coordination and stability for the total culture. The striving for consistency is a logical tendency in human society and is aided by institutions that stabilize and harmonize the behavior of the people. Ways of thinking and behaving that are institutionalized "make sense" to people. They provide a means of security because they become the normal and proper ways of which the great majority of people approve. While segments of an institution may change in a dynamic culture, the major institutions continue on in a stable and enduring manner.

**d.** Closely allied with the function of stability is the fact that institutions tend to control behavior. The institutions contain the systematic expectations of the society. Because institutions exist, the individual person knows how he should act and think among other persons. Group behavior is often subconsciously fixed through constant repetition, and when there is need for planning the group can easily ascertain from its institutions the normal modes of procedure. Individuals and groups find it easier to conform than to deviate from institutions. Social pressure is maintained even on the prospective deviant groups by the mere existence of institutions.

Besides these positive functions of institutions, there are also some *negative* aspects to be taken into consideration. Since no culture operates in all its segments to the optimum benefit of all the people, it is to be expected that certain difficulties arise through the functioning of institutions.

a. In general, the major negative function of institutions is the way in which they sometimes obstruct social progress. Because institutions conserve and stabilize social behavior, they tend to be rigid and to discourage change. This conservatism has a twofold function. The institutions sometimes conserve patterns of behavior even when the values represented by this behavior have become outmoded. On the other hand, they sometimes conserve the social values that are quite inconsistent with the external behavior of the majority of the people. This resistance to change is implicit in the notion of the institution as the "cake of custom" or in the notion that it rules with the "dead hand of the past."

b. Similarly, institutions sometimes serve to frustrate the social personality of individuals. People who do not fit into the culture and who try to resist the control of its institutions are considered odd. They may be misfits because they are unwilling to allow the institutions to hold them down too rigidly. These people often become deviants of one kind or another, attempting reform movements, committing criminal and delinquent behavior, or acting in ways that others consider culturally abnormal. Absolute individual freedom does not exist in any society, but personal frustrations readily occur where individualism is a high ideal but at the same time institutions force people to conform.

**c.** Another negative function is the diffusion of social responsibility. Customary ways of behaving that are completely out of date, that harm some individuals and groups, and that require reform are sometimes permitted to continue because no one takes the responsibility for changing them. This diffusion of responsibility is evident when people complain about "the system" or when they justify their behavior on the grounds of established custom. An institution may work injustice upon people, but the fact that it is long established gives it a sanction. In some instances, people who are fearful of change are also willing to accept the discomforts and inconveniences of established routine.

## UNIVERSALITY AND VARIABILITY OF INSTITUTIONS

We have seen that patterns, roles, and relations, which are the ingredients of institutions, exist in every society. It is likewise true that they are everywhere systematically arranged into institutions. Not only is social behavior always institutionalized, but the major institutions are necessarily present everywhere. The basic universal social needs are satisfied in some culturally approved, systematic way in every society. These basic institutions—familial, educational, economic, political, religious, and recreational—are so essential to a culture that without them social life would be unthinkable.

Anthropologists have never discovered a primitive, contemporary, or historical society in which these basic institutions did not exist. This fact obviously argues to the fundamental necessity for these institutions. But anthropologists have also found a tremendous variety in the way these institutions satisfy minimum basic needs. Anyone who has a smattering of knowledge concerning people outside his own culture recognizes that family customs, religious mores, recreational trends, and the other institutionalized patterns differ considerably. The ways of conducting educational, economic, and political affairs show great variation from culture to culture.

This combination of universality and variability should not be puzzling to one who recognizes the plasticity and potentiality in social behavior. As we have seen throughout the study of sociology, people are in some ways everywhere similar and in some ways everywhere dissimilar. We must recognize first, that human beings have demonstrated great ingenuity and adaptability in satisfying their social needs. Secondly, a certain degree of choice and decision is involved in the selection of alternative ways of doing things, and only people can make such choices. Finally, the geographical environment in which people live differs widely and has a certain degree of influence on the ways in which they develop their social behavior.

## CLASSIFICATION OF INSTITUTIONS

We have seen that there are many ways of classifying social groups because there are many points of view from which groups can be studied. Similarly, institutions lend themselves to classification from different points of view. Some institutions are strongly compulsive, others place little obligation on people; some are as wide as the society in their application, others are relatively local; some involve high social values, others deal in a lower order of values.

For purposes of clarity, the most fruitful general classification of institutions is the twofold division into *major* and *subsidiary* institutions. This distinction is made on the basis of three characteristics: universality, necessity, and importance. The major basic institutions are those that have the largest number of people participating, that are essential to the society, and that are considered most important for the individual and the common welfare. These are the familial, educational, economic, political, religious, and recreational institutions.

The subsidiary institutions do not have these characteristics. They are the numerous, minor, and variable institutions that are contained within the major institutions. Every subsidiary institution can be classified under one of the major institutions, although in the concrete life-situation it may partake of the aspects of several major institutions.

The following is a brief description of the major institutions, with some indications of the subsidiary ones that are found within them. We must recall here that patterns, roles, and relations are contained within the institutions and that these are the instrumentalities social persons use in the conduct of social life.

a. The familial institution is the system that regulates, stabilizes, and standardizes sexual relations and the reproduction of children. Its most widespread form is the monogamous union of male and female living together with their children in a household. The subinstitutions of courtship, marriage, child care, in-law relations, and many others are contained under this main institution.

b. The educational institution is basically the systematized process of socialization occurring informally in the home and in the general cultural environment, and formally in the complex educational arrangements of the society. Within the framework of this institution are the subsidiary arrangements for grading and testing, graduation and degrees, homework and the honor system.

c. The economic institution is the configuration of patterned social behavior through which material goods and services are provided for the society. It involves fundamentally the production, distribution, exchange, and consumption of commodities. There are many subsidiary institutions like credit and banking, bookkeeping, advertising, collective bargaining, and seniority systems.

d. The political institution functions primarily to satisfy the need for general administration and public order in society. There are many subinstitutions within it such as the legal, police, and military systems, the forms of appointment and election to public office, and diplomatic relations with foreign countries.

e. The religious institution satisfies man's basic social need for a relationship with God. It is expressed in creeds and in forms of worship people perform together. It always includes moral and ethical systems indicating the rightness or wrongness of both external and conceptual patterns of behavior. Subsidiary institutions are lay-clerical relationships, systems of prayer, and arrangements for divine services. Practices of magic and superstition are in some places institutionalized by religious groups.

f. The recreational institution fulfills the social need for physical and mental relaxation. It includes numerous subsidiary institutions such as games, sports, and dancing as well as the aesthetic systems of art, music, painting, and drama.

### NETWORK OF INSTITUTIONS

The coordinated network of interdependently functioning major institutions is vital to the continuance of culture and society. No institution can exist by itself; each influences in varying degrees all the others and is in turn influenced by them. The whole configuration of major and subsidiary institutions is articulated through the social relations and roles enacted by persons and groups.

The interdependence of institutions is demonstrated in many ways, especially in large, complex, and industrialized societies. For example, impairment of the orderly functioning of the economic institutions would have grave effects upon all the other institutions. The clearest historical example of this is a major economic depression that brings about changes in the ways in which people live out their other institutionalized roles. Major changes in the patterns of family living, or in the political institution, seriously affect the other institutions.

This very interdependence sometimes makes it difficult to assign every subinstitution clearly to one of the major institutions. Since man is a total personality, his behavior patterns overlap the institutions. Furthermore, although there are many inconsistencies, the institutions cooperate and dovetail with one another. For example, some forms of athletic sports are subsidiary institutions that may be considered both recreational and economic but are also performed within the framework of subsidiary educational and religious groups.

There are many other examples of this complexity, all indicating that no social group can purely and exclusively perform the patterns of only one institution. A religious group, identified by the fact that it pursues primarily the function of the religious institution, also performs other institutionalized functions—educating children, providing recreation, and raising and spending money. Similarly the state does not necessarily "invade" the rights of individuals and groups when it promotes the welfare of familial, economic, educational, and other institutions. This is simply an example of the basic fact that no person or group can be purely and exclusively political.

In spite of the fact that the different institutions are interwoven in the web of culture and are necessarily interdependent, they are not always in harmony with one another. There are instances of institutionalized patterns working at cross-purposes or at least being to some degree inconsistent. An easy example of this inconsistency is seen in the economic and religious institutions. If a prime motive of the economic institution is the pursuit of profit and if that of the religious institution is selfless service to God and humanity, there is an incongruity for the person who is endeavoring to fulfill the expected roles in both institutions.

While it is true that the social person may choose from many alternative patterns within any given institution, he tends to follow those that are most standardized and approved. The man who is by all norms an exemplary husband and father may also be persuaded that it is "good business" to extract exorbitant rents from slum tenants. The church warden who attends religious services on Sunday morning may also take his out-of-town guests to a lewd performance at a nightclub on Sunday evening. These internal inconsistencies of role behavior are not always recognized by individuals because the external inconsistencies of institutions have come to be taken for granted as approved and expected modes of behavior.

## INSTITUTIONS AND SOCIAL SANCTIONS

We have seen that persons can be ranked according to higher or lower status and that roles are differently esteemed in society; some persons and some behaviors are approved and others are disapproved. From this it follows —and it is also an empirically demonstrable fact—that in any culture the institutions are ranked in order. The major institutions are more important than the subsidiary institutions.

The *pivotal* institution, however, is most important of all. We have seen that among the numerous social roles the person enacts there is his key role, which is recognized by other people as being the most important and influential. The pivotal institution is to the culture what the key role is to the individual. Historical examples of pivotal institutions are numerous. The old Roman culture was dominated at one period by the political, the Chinese by the familial, the Indian by the religious, and the American by the economic institution.

The rise of the pivotal institution to its place of prominence must obviously have the positive sanction of the people in the society. This means that the values expressed, the functions performed, and the roles enacted in that institution must have the general approval of the people. The person therefore "sacrifices" certain aspects of his roles in the other institutions because of the expectations and demands of the pivotal institution. This is further evidence of the interdependence of the major institutions; when the people center so much attention upon the pivotal institution, any serious disturbance of this institution has far-reaching consequences throughout the culture.

Despite the high esteem in which the pivotal and other major institutions are held, there continue to exist in every culture certain subsidiary institutions that are sanctioned with penalties. For example, patterns of criminal behavior develop mainly as a subsidiary economic institution even though crime is negatively sanctioned. Gambling is a recreational institution that is widely disapproved. Ticket-fixing and police brutality are institutionalized in some places despite the general disapproval of this kind of behavior. The study of the extent to which these forms of behavior become social problems must be taken up elsewhere.

## INSTITUTIONAL SYSTEM AS A TOTAL CULTURE

The major institutions are conceptualized as a complete and continuous network in which both the totality and all its segments are a functioning system. This we call the culture of a society. In order to visualize this total institutional system more clearly, it may be helpful to note the following.

**a.** Once the pivotal institution is recognized, the position of the remaining major institutions can be conceptualized as clustering around it. Within each of these may be placed the subsidiary institutions, some of which are closely integrated and others of which are incidental or even partially inconsistent with the major institution.

**b.** The major institutions can be identified by the objectives they are pursuing, but their relative position of importance in any culture can be judged by other criteria. Thus, the "power position" of a major institution can be judged by the degree of control and dominance it exerts over other institutions, the extent to which it "invades" other institutions, and the strength of its affiliation with them.

**c.** Since patterns, roles, and relations are institutionalized around certain central objectives, they can be studied from the point of view of the person in action. The position and importance of any given institution can be evaluated according to the degree of interest and the amount of time and energy people have for it.

**d.** Social values are involved in all institutions, and one may say that the position of any institution depends largely upon these values. This again requires a knowledge of the persons who perform institutionalized behavior. If the persons of high social status in any society gain this prestige through the economic rather than through the religious institution, this reflects the importance of both the economic values and the economic institution.

It is important to remember that the institutional system operates for and through people. It can never be conceptualized as either internally or externally static, because it grows and changes through actual human be-

havior. Sometimes a minor institution stays on in a culture after it has ceased to be useful. Sometimes institutional changes are induced through legislation and other
deliberate efforts. At any rate, institutions do not exist
unless they are used by associations of people, and the
fact is that institutions need people as much as people
need institutions.

## Aspects of American Institutions
### 1. THE PIVOTAL INSTITUTION

A key to the understanding of any culture is a knowledge of its dominant major institution. It has been said
that the American society has a "businessman's culture,"
and more recently that a kind of "military-industrial complex" operates for the benefit of business profits, so that
what has made America great is nothing more than its
system of economic free enterprise. Statements of this
kind are, of course, crude exaggerations made by the
misinformed, the chauvinistic, and perhaps the disgrun-
tled. A quick judgment about a whole culture is easy, but
it is also usually erroneous, especially if it is the result of
ethnocentrism.

Nevertheless, it is true that a total culture is colored
by its dominant institution and that in the American
society all the major institutions are influenced by the
economic institution. Americans usually think that this
is logical and "natural," since preparing for one's lifework,
making a living, providing for a family, getting ahead,
getting a raise and a promotion are all extremely important things. Not every society, however, considers these
matters to be so important as we do. Furthermore, while
we may believe that the religious institution is on a higher
plane of values than the economic, or that economic activities are basically merely a means for better familial
and recreational life, objective analysis shows that in our
culture these institutions are also greatly influenced by
the economic.

The following items give a brief indication of the ways
in which economic patterns and values have invaded and
influenced the behavior of Americans in other institutions.

**a.** In the educational system in America a great deal of lip service is paid to the importance of the humanities —literature and the other "cultural" subjects—particularly on the college level. The fact is, however, that the overwhelming majority of male students and a good many female students concentrate on "useful" subjects. They know that graduates with specialized training get the better jobs sooner, and their parents know it too.

**b.** The peculiar American pattern of religious institutions, in which each church has to fend financially for itself, has put a strong emphasis upon economic activities. The pastor who is a good businessman, gets contributions, pays the debts, and maintains a large number of buildings is the man who receives wide approval. The United States is probably the only country in which a life of Christ which depicted him as a successful businessman could be a best seller. The biblical parable of the talents is often interpreted to mean that a man is morally obligated to use his abilities for economic and material advancement.

**c.** The commercialization of recreational activities shows how economic patterns have invaded this institution. Other societies have rewarded their athletic heroes with ivy crowns and feasts and medals, but in our society they are mainly professional heroes who expect and receive high financial rewards. The stage is not subsidized by the community; it has to be a profitable enterprise or it ceases to function. The same can be said of other media of entertainment and of many other leisure-time activities.

**d.** The political institution has been affected by the fact that government has become "big business." Although there is no political compulsion that forces the government to show profit or balance the budget, there have been frequent demands that we should have a businessman in the White House. Lack of success or experience in business has been used as a campaign argument against presidential candidates. The fiscal policies of the government, the direction of federal banks, the raising and spending of tax money, and the problem of controlling inflation and preventing depression are all examples of economic patterns entering the political institution.

e. In the familial institution economic demands have altered patterns, roles, and relations of Americans. The amount of time a man can spend with his family, the type and amount of commodities the family consumes, the employment of women outside the home, and the movement into cities and suburbs are all examples of the way in which the economic factor invades the home. The gainful occupational function has limited, if it has not replaced, family and ancestry as the most powerful of the criteria of social status. Economic values have added steady pressure to the rising material standards of family living.

In a brief description of this kind we must be careful not to fall into the fallacy of single causality. It would be an error to assume that all the institutional problems which face Americans are fundamentally economic and that, if the economy can be straightened out, all will be well in our society. We have sufficiently illustrated multiple causality and institutional interdependence to show that all the institutions are fundamentally important. To point out that the economic institution is the pivotal institution is not to say this institution is the total culture.

## 2. THE CHANGING MARRIAGE INSTITUTION

The European who visits the United States is often fascinated by the institutionalized aspects of American marriage and family life. The visiting Oriental is often shocked by them. The reaction of these foreigners indicates that the American marriage institution is quite different from that found in some other cultures. It also indicates that ethnocentrism—judging a strange culture on the basis of one's own cultural values—is universally exercised.

The familial institution is an integral segment of the American culture. Because we have been so thoroughly saturated with our own culture, Americans find it difficult to stand off and view this institution objectively. We often fail to realize that many "family problems" are a logical part, and perhaps a necessary consequence, of the marriage institution. In our dynamic culture this institution has changed considerably from the forms which it took in early America and even from its original European model. Following are some of the more significant conceptual and external patterns of behavior that highlight change in this institution.

**a.** The sacramental character of marriage has been almost completely ignored in many American families. The notion that marriage implies a sacred promise to God, as well as to one another, has often been overlooked even among couples who practice a religion in which this notion nominally prevails. A church is the most popular place for a wedding, but the inner significance of a devine promise, mandate, and relationship is frequently ignored.

**b.** The marriage contract and the subsequent bond upon which family unity is built are said to be things of the heart. The emphasis upon romantic love as the essential foundation of family life has been so thorough among Americans that we are shocked at the notion of a marriage of convenience, of marriage brokers, or of marriage for reasons of financial and social status. In many instances the marriage contract lasts only as long as the heart is in it, and the most desperate requirement of the married couple is that they "stay in love." Unlike a financial contract or a political commitment, the marriage promise in this contract allows for a change of heart and mind.

**c.** The contractual aspect of the husband-wife relation is reflected in the concept of an equal partnership in marriage, not one in which the husband is seen as a kind of senior member and the wife as managerial assistant. This was seen as a pragmatic American arrangement even before the Women's Liberation Movement gave it added impetus and support. While the concept of duty is involved in all contractual arrangements, there is a notable emphasis here on the equal and independent rights of the two individuals. Again, the focus is upon the personal happiness which every American marriage is supposed to bring to the partners.

**d.** Since each family is expected to make its own way, dowries and family fortunes do not supply the financial foundations for marriage. Inheritance taxes have decreased the latter and custom has banished the former. The newly married American couple receives many gifts and household appliances, but these are a kind of loan that has to be paid back when other friends and relatives marry. The family's necessity to fend for itself, together with the social pressure for higher standards of living, places a great strain upon human relations within the family.

**e.** The discontinuity of generations, and therefore the loosening of traditional kinship ties, is evident in the separate households that newly married couples establish. This separation from the parental home, the result of job and territorial mobility and upward social striving, is more than a spatial removal from the old homestead; it is also an aspect of the decline of primary group relationships. The young couple loses the cultural support of the kinship group, has to develop new social relations that are not kin-based, and must depend more heavily upon the husband-wife relationship. They also lose the social benefit of stability that accompanies attachment to a territorial community.

**f.** In the light of the above it should not be surprising that serial marriages have been widely accepted among our marriage patterns. The lack of traditional stabilizers has not made us lose faith in marriage. On the contrary, more Americans marry, and marry younger, than people in any other Western country. But the American has a moral scruple about taking more than one spouse at a time, and the pattern of keeping a mistress or of having a lover is a violation of the general code of marital standards. There is no cultural compulsion for this kind of conduct since divorce and remarriage are so easily arranged and so widely accepted.

**g.** The extent of child-spacing and the effect it may have on the marriage pair have not been sufficiently studied to warrant extended comment. The relatively high birth rate during the decade following the Second World War has declined, and the average family size is smaller than it was two generations ago. The movement for planned parenthood has introduced pragmatic rationalism to the marriage relation, not only on spacing and limiting the number of offspring, but in promoting research to increase the fertility of childless couples.

The list of institutionalized patterns in American marriage must not lead to the negative conclusion that Americans despair of its basic and successful social functioning. In no other society has this institution been so thoroughly studied; nowhere else are there so many marriage counsellors and clinics, so many statistics gathered and books written on this subject or so many lectures and academic courses devoted to it.

It should be noted also that the patterns described above are integrally related to the total American culture. They reflect the patterns of other institutions, are logically interwoven with them, and are behavioral expectations in the kind of culture we have. Indeed, it would be surprising, in view of the major institutions and of the total culture, if the marriage institution did not have these characteristics in our society.

### 3. Aspects of the Political Institution

Americans boast of the great advantage of political freedom, of the high ideals of democracy, and of a political institution that has endured while many others have collapsed. Often however, the same Americans decry politics as a "dirty game," complain about "cheap" politicians, and call for a reform to "clean up the mess." There is, of course, a vast difference between the idealized version of the American political institution and the practical everyday patterns of political behavior. A realistic appraisal of the ways in which our institutions function relieves us of either pessimism or idealism.

There are certain patterns within the American political institution that appear to be characteristic of our culture. They are present to some degree in the political institutions of other societies, but they do not play as important a role there as in our own. These patterns, which are typically American only in the sense that they are in widespread use here, help us to understand the operation of the total institution of politics.

**a.** The spoils system is not an American invention, but it is worthy of note because many Americans resent it and many foreigners are surprised to find it here. In essence it means that the winning party in an election assumes the right to assign jobs and patronage to those who have helped to win the victory. No one questions the president's right to select his own cabinet and other officials, since he obviously requires cooperative assistance of his own choosing. There are many other jobs, however, directly or indirectly political, that the winning party, from the top federal level to the small-town and county level, has the right to assign. The civil service system has gradually and persistently decreased this practice, but the spoils system still flourishes.

**b.** In general, upper-class persons are unwilling to serve in the political system. Although they will take top-level jobs in the diplomatic service and in Washington, most of these people prefer to be served rather than to serve. The political apathy of the masses in America is matched and reflected by the apathy of people of high social status. This is partly because of two cultural phenomena: first, the belief that one somehow "soils" his hands by mixing with politicians; and, second, the fact that the political institution is not the dominant institution of our culture.

**c.** Closely allied to this pattern is the low esteem accorded political servants. Even in those cases where the political office itself holds high prestige—as the presidency, cabinet membership, ambassadorships, and to some extent congressional and gubernatorial posts—the incumbents of the office are often criticized for being "merely politicians." It appears to be the right of people in a democracy to excoriate and calumniate their public servants. Even though successful politicians are always surrounded by groups of loyal and devoted followers, they are always subject to vilification by still larger numbers of people. This conceptual pattern of low esteem appears to be bound up with our political institution.

**d.** It appears that the successful politician is often obliged to pose as the defender of the people, a homespun man who shares the interests of the people. This pose has deep moral implications because it often means that political expediency, that is, giving the people what they want, takes precedence over political statesmanship, that is, acting on the basis of social and moral principles. The pattern requires the politician to identify those dangers from which he is defending the people: the international bankers, the munition manufacturers, the labor racketeers, the ruthless employers, and, especially of late, the "subversives." All of these opponents are pictured as dangers to our American way of life.

**e.** The United States is remarkable for the fact that it contains a relatively diversified population and at the same time does not have a multiplicity of strong political splinter parties. A third-party presidential candidate has no practical expectation of election. On the national level the political philosophy of the two major parties is often indistinguishable, although within both parties there is considerable dissension between right and left elements. The American politician who wants to serve the majority of people and to win the next election cannot afford to be a proponent of either the extreme right or the extreme left. It is true that the political mood of the people exhibits gradual changes, but the American political institution lacks effective radical and revolutionary elements.

Many other patterns of thinking and acting exist within the American political institution. Those we have discussed tend to be informally institutionalized yet extremely effective patterns. The sociological study of the actually functioning institution requires a knowledge beyond the formal and idealized norms and regulations of the institution. If we are interested in the manner in which an institution actually works, rather than merely in how it ought to work, this kind of insight is necessary.

We must repeat that the American political institution "fits into" the total American culture. Much of what goes on within it can be objectively understood only when interinstitutional relationships are recognized. Even though there are certain inconsistencies, especially in institutional values, the major American institutions have reciprocal influence.

## 4. INCREASING INSTITUTIONALIZATION

It is commonly observed in sociological literature that America is shifting from the communal to the associational type of society. Secondary groups are more emphasized; more groups with specialized functions are arising; and casual contacts are replacing primary relations. In general our society is becoming more and more adaptive, stratified, multiple-functioning, loosely-structured, and rapidly changing.

A necessary concomitant of this kind of social development is the increase of institutionalization. The components of the institution—behavior patterns, social roles and relations—are becoming more specialized, formalized, and regularized. In spite of our insistence upon the importance of freedom and self-direction, we Americans are being more and more forced into formal routines of behavior. Increasing institutionalization is part of the personal price we pay for the advantages of a highly-developed, complex, industrialized society.

Following are some of the indications and examples of this process of institutionalization in our culture.

**a.** The red tape in the social system is irksome to many Americans when they fill out job applications or tax forms, register for school, or apply for public welfare assistance. They find that "everything has to be in triplicate." There are so many steps to be taken, so many individuals to consult, that people become exasperated. The number of formal requirements is increasing; more records are being kept; and behavior is often regulated on the basis of records and requirements.

**b.** The underlying motive for institutionalization appears to be the American drive for efficiency. The required actions are often time-wasting and inefficient from the point of view of the individual, but the focus is on the efficiency of the larger association, the total institution and system. To get things done in a rational and orderly way requires that large numbers of people perform the same act in the same way. There is probably a point of "diminishing returns" at which the devices of efficiency become cumbersome and wasteful, but it is not easily recognized if the patterns have become highly formal.

**c.** Institutionalization is seen also in the rigid routine of roles. As performance becomes more specialized, particularly in gainful occupations, the component patterns of the role become more automatic. There are many jobs, even relatively high in the occupational structure, where originality and ingenuity are discouraged. The crude statement of the employer that "we don't pay you to think" is not really replaced by the encouragement of an employees' suggestion box. The most valuable suggestion is one that can increase efficiency; if it is accepted, it will usually further routinize the occupational role.

**d.** The multiplication of roles within any major institution and group logically accompanies the specialization of functions. The discovery in industry that total productivity could be increased when each operation was reduced to its smallest, repetitive, unit-acts has been carried over into the political and educational systems and in some degree to the other institutions. The consequence of the simplified role is the multiplication of roles. This is not essentially a matter of "making jobs" for the sake of keeping everybody busy but of getting the total operation completed more efficiently.

**e.** Bureaucracy has increased along with institutionalization in the major groups of American society. To organize social behavior effectively, so that people's roles and relations function efficiently, has been the objective of ever larger and more numerous bureaus, boards, panels, and committees in government, business, churches, schools, and other groups. Not only is this an attempt to decrease the complexity of administration at the higher levels, it also contributes to justice and equity through the universalistic handling of problems. This seems arbitrary, and often causes inconvenience to people who seek a particular treatment of their own case.

**f.** Institutionalization always occurs with the increase of the importance of secondary associations. The primary relations are informal, intimate, and adaptive. The individual in the primary groups may be a relatively rigid and traditional personality, but his patterns and roles can be adapted to him. In secondary associations, by contrast, the patterns, roles, and relations must be formal, mandatory, and fairly rigid, and the individual must learn to adapt himself to them. It may be said that these larger groups are operated and regulated by institutional forms rather than by the personalities that constitute them.

Finally, it must be pointed out that every society is in some degree institutionalized. All people must necessarily use behavior patterns, and all groups must use institutions. When we say that American society is becoming more institutionalized, we mean that the institutions are becoming increasingly important, more formal and rigorous, and are affecting more people in many more ways than ever before. In this kind of society the universal fact that we are "creatures of our culture" takes on new meaning.

## 5. INSTITUTIONAL INCONSISTENCIES

We have said that in general the term "institution" implies a related network of social behavior integrated around social needs. But at the same time there are also inconsistencies and lack of integration within institutions. The fact is that no culture is entirely integrated; no culture has all its components in consistent coordination with one another. There are parallel lines of social behavior in minor or subsidiary institutions that appear to be inconsistent with one another.

In the American culture there are numerous irrelevancies that are cultural residues rather than outright inconsistencies. For example, the wearing of ties by men, the buttons on a man's coat-sleeve, the construction of open fireplaces in apartments that are centrally heated, the use of candlesticks, and many other patterns are now ornamental rather than functional. These are residual from earlier stages of the American culture, and though they exemplify the endurance of traditional usage, they cannot be considered examples of major inconsistencies.

Institutionalized ways of behaving can never be totally inconsistent or in total conflict with the culture. Even among the major examples of institutional inconsistencies in the American culture there are some elements that are consistent with some other elements. A conclusion about the inconsistency of an institution depends upon the vantage point from which it is viewed and upon the other institutions to which it is compared and related. Let us illustrate this fact with several well-known and widespread instances.

**a.** Institutionalized bribery is relatively common in many areas of American public life. Some of it is "polite" and just within the law, but much of it completely and directly violates the law, to say nothing of the ideals of public honesty. The word "graft" is colloquial in the United States, and it is defined as the "illegitimate receipt of money through and by official service." Here is a practice that has become smoothly patterned; it has become institutionalized, and it may well be called inconsistent.

From another point of view, however, it is highly consistent. It is possible only because there are large segments of our population that demand the kind of services obtained through bribery and graft. The outstanding example of such services in our recent history was the bootlegging of illegal liquor during the Prohibition period. Other current examples in some places are: houses of prostitution, of gambling and lewd performances, the traffic in narcotics and other illegal commodities, the maintenance of buildings that are fire hazards, and the suppression of organized labor.

**b.** Nationally, the divorce system has been termed a "legal jungle" because of its internal inconsistencies. The causes for divorce and the requirements of legal procedure differ from state to state; but still more confusing is the fact that the majority of divorces are based on collusion between the interested parties, a practice that is strictly illegal in all divorce courts. And, of course, divorce is inconsistent with the traditional institution of permanent and monogamous marriage.

On the other hand, the divorce system is consistent with a number of strongly entrenched and often misinterpreted American behavior patterns. It conforms to the widely accepted notion that marriage is primarily an instrument for the happiness of the partners and to the emphasis on personal freedom and equal rights. Even the subsidiary patterns of allowing the wife to file for divorce and of favoring her in the divorce settlement indicate an aspect of chivalry that has survived.

c. Institutionalized racial discrimination is a major inconsistency in the American culture. The racial pattern has been termed the great contemporary American dilemma because it is patently at odds with the stated values of democracy and Christianity.

Nevertheless, it conforms with the long-term Anglo-Saxon attitude of superiority toward the colored peoples of the world. It is an instrument also for maintaining social class and caste by many whites who do not possess enough of the other criteria of social status. By attempting to treat Negroes like immigrants, it continues America's century-old tradition of utilizing and exploiting the newest and lowest stratum of society. Even local autonomy and state's rights have been invoked in some areas to justify the pattern of racial discrimination.

From the point of view of ultimate cultural values of the American people it is probably true to say that much of the explanation for institutional inconsistencies is a mere rationalization. Often false reasons, self-interest, and values of a lower order are employed to justify inconsistent social behavior. Rationalization, however, does not lessen the social reality. It does not make it less a social fact that the inconsistencies actually exist.

## Suggested Readings

Feibleman, James K. *The Institutions of Society*. London: Allen and Unwin, 1956.

Hertzler, J. O. *American Social Institutions.* Boston: Allyn and Bacon, 1961.

Hiller, E. T. *Social Relations and Structures.* New York: Harper and Row, 1947.

Hoffsomer, H. *The Sociology of American Life.* Englewood Cliffs: Prentice-Hall, 1958.

Presthus, Robert. *The Organizational Society.* New York: Knopf, 1962.

# 11
# Culture

CULTURE IS ANOTHER STRICTLY TECHNICAL TERM IN social science that is widely used in various nontechnical meanings. We sometimes hear that a cultured person is one who has refinement and good manners, who recognizes and enjoys the aesthetic and better things of life. In this restricted meaning, culture can be possessed only by the relatively few persons who have the leisure, wealth, competence, and interest to indulge in and "cultivate" these patterns of refinement.

The sociological fact is that every normal person in a society is cultured. As we have seen, every person goes through the socialization process. From infancy he begins to learn to accommodate himself to the patterns of behavior that are socially acceptable and to recognize those that are not acceptable. He gets training in the pursuit of social roles; he is always in the midst of social relations. As a participant in groups and in the total society, everyone must necessarily be a cultured person. The scientific definition of culture cannot be applied only to the fortunate few in the upper strata of society.

## CULTURE IS THE HUMAN PRODUCT

Culture is man-made, and speaking broadly one can say that everything man makes is part of the culture. Man is by nature a social animal, productive and creative, and the total sociocultural system is man's production. In this sense we can say that all of group life and all of society are cultural products. They have been cultivated through long generations of man's history. For purposes of analysis, however, we ought to make a clear distinction between culture and society by saying that culture is something that society makes and uses.

From this point of view, then, culture is not the group or the society. It would be confusing to use these terms interchangeably because we would miss the whole distinction between people and their patterns of behavior. People in group life have a behavioral system; they make use of institutions; they possess a culture. It is true that man is both the creator and the creature of the society in which he lives. But one should not identify the possessor with the thing possessed. We could not proceed intelligently with our analysis if we did not treat culture separately from society.

If culture includes all the products of man it ought to include also his artifacts, all the things he has made for whatever purpose. Up to this point in our study we have carefully avoided the inclusion of material items as components or segments of culture. The logic of definition requires that only similar things be placed in the same category. If behavior patterns are the irreducible components of culture, and if these combine into roles, relations and institutions, it would be illogical to include among them items like footballs, refrigerators, prayer books and spacecraft.

It should not be assumed, however, that the "mere" materiality of these culturally produced items renders them sociologically unimportant. They are indeed bound up with the lives and survival of persons and groups and they deserve careful consideration in the scientific study of society. We can pause here only to point out several reasons why the student should have some knowledge of these material culture items.

Perhaps the prime reason for studying material culture products is that they are meaningful *symbols* of human behavior in the sense that the culture can be interpreted from the kinds of objects used and valued in the society. Secondly, they may be called *vehicles* of the culture that carry much of the physical load of the social functions. Thirdly, they are *instruments* that the people use in enacting their behavioral patterns. Finally, they are the *products* of the people in the society who invented and fashioned them as a response to their social needs.

The technological skills that are associated with the making and using of material culture items are in themselves part of the culture. The objects themselves vary tremendously from one society to another, and they tell us much about the people who fashion and use them. An igloo differs from a city apartment-hotel, a stone cathedral from a small country church, a bulldozer from a rake, but all these are similar in the fact that they are the products and the expression of the culture. These things constitute a man-made artificial environment that intervenes between people and the natural environment and tremendously affects the patterns of living. In the study of prehistoric cultures these extant objects are the only evidence from which the culture can be "reconstructed."

Besides the distinction we have made between culture and society and between the behavioral and material items of the culture, we ought to mention the obvious exclusion of animal behavior. The sociologist is directly concerned only with the patterned regularities of human conduct and not with those of subhuman animals. Instinctual regularities of so-called gregarious behavior in animals, whether wild or domesticated and trained, do not serve as a model or preview of human behavior patterns. Culture exists nowhere except among human beings. The ability of even highly trained animals to perform a repetitive pattern of tricks may be proof of the trainer's human skills but is at best a caricature of man's behavior.

## DEFINITION OF CULTURE

A hundred years ago E. B. Tylor, an Englishman, defined culture as "that complex whole which includes knowledge, belief, art, morals, law, custom, and any other capabilities and habits acquired by man as a member of society." His studies dealt mainly with primitive peoples, and his definition of culture was obviously not synonymous with civilization. Culture exists wherever people are, so that in precise scientific language one speaks of primitive cultures and civilized cultures, the latter being more complex and developed than the former. There is an arbitrary line that divides one from the other, and it is often difficult to determine the basis upon which this line is drawn.

The word "civilized" is derived from the Latin *civitas* and *civis*, meaning town and town-dweller, and it implies a people who are sedentary, literate, and complex in their behavior. In a civilized, as compared to a precivilized, society the people live in large, permanent aggregates and associations rather than in small nomadic tribes. They have a written language for recording their history that is of great educational value. They develop a diversification of functions and specialization of labor. Their behavior is more formally institutionalized and their whole culture is more complex than that of precivilized people.

It is clear that culture and civilization are not synonymous terms. All persons and every people have culture at different stages of development. When we make a distinction between precivilized and civilized cultures we must realize that these characteristics of structure and function are a matter of degree. If we were to emphasize scientific, technological advances as the measure of civilization, we could probably place all cultures on a continuum from the least to the most civilized, from the most primitive to the most sophisticated.

In the broadest sense we say that culture includes all the capabilities and customs acquired by human beings in association with their fellow human beings. The smallest and irreducible basic component of the culture is the recurrent pattern of social behavior. We have seen that these patterns combine into various social roles and into forms of interaction, or human relations or social processes. These again are the components of the numerous institutions, major and subsidiary, that are present in every culture. We may say that the largest segment of the culture is the institution and the smallest segment is the behavior pattern.

Briefly, culture is the total configuration of institutions that the people in a society share in common. The term "configuration" refers to the web, matrix, or network in which the related and coordinated institutions function as a whole system. The people share this cultural system, but not in the sense that every individual and group participates equally or does everything in exactly the same way. There are some social roles that cannot be enacted by some persons. There are some institutions that demand much more participation than others.

## CULTURAL HERITAGE AND ENVIRONMENT

From the point of view of persons and groups it is essential that the total culture be conceptualized as both hereditary and environmental. We are born into a culture and we are surrounded by it, that is, we are immersed in it from the time we are born. This is important because culture is both taught and learned, and it is acquired by the individual from his elders and his contemporaries. The socialization process is the channel through which the individual becomes assimilated to the culture of his society.

When we say that the culture is hereditary, we mean that the institutionalized ways of behavior are symbolically transmitted from one generation to another. The particular institutions are built up by the accretion of many persons' experiences over a long period of time. Individuals come and go, but culture persists; it must be handed down in some form or other. The cultural heritage has nothing to do with physical generation or biological transmission, through which the individual receives only the potential capacity to absorb the culture and to become a cultured person. The newborn child is already a human and social person at birth but he becomes a cultured person through association with others.

The culture endures but the individual human being comes into it and eventually goes out of it. The sum of the institutionalized behavior patterns in any society forms the cultural heritage into which the newborn infant enters and which the individual leaves behind him when he dies. When we say that some ancient culture has entirely disappeared we mean either that the whole people using it was wiped out or that it gradually merged into some other major culture. Any particular culture exists only in and through human beings, but no particular human being is essential to the culture. Because the culture preexisted any individual person, and endures longer than he does, it is possible to speak of culture, of patterns, and of institutions as though they exist independently of persons.

It is only by conceptual abstraction that we can distinguish the environmental from the hereditary aspect of culture, but it seems analytically necessary to do this. When we say that the culture is also environmental we mean that it "surrounds" the person all during his lifetime. He lives in a society in which the culture already exists. The culture that each generation inherits from its ancestors is the one that each individual has to learn to live with. It is obvious, but extremely significant, that a Mexican grows up to be a Mexican and that a Greek grows up to be a Greek. This is the cultural environment in which he lives and develops and which he leaves behind him when he dies.

It is not a contradiction to remark that while people are the only and ultimate creators of the culture, they are also in large measure the creatures of their culture. A person may escape society for a while, but he can never escape culture. The cultural environment is probably the strongest single influence upon the social behavior of the great majority of people. Even in isolation, where the person tries temporarily to "get away from it all," he thinks and acts according to the patterns of behavior to which he has become accustomed. The institutions of his culture have formed his social personality and have fashioned the social roles he enacts as well as the values he accepts.

The pervading influence of the native cultural environment is seen most dramatically in those who visit or immigrate to a society with a culture different from their own. The language barrier itself is a large obstacle to understanding the foreign culture. Language is a behavior pattern so deeply embedded that little native children can speak their own, while the adult foreigner can only struggle with the same language. Not only the language but the customs of the people are strange. The ways of thinking and doing things, the social values and forms of relationships, are difficult to comprehend and to accept. It is easy to make a mistake about proper behavior and to offend against etiquette. Whole generations of immigrants have remained culturally marginal to the end of their lives. A foreigner seldom if ever "goes native" by losing all traces of the culture in which he was originally socialized.

The total culture—hereditary and environmental—necessarily contains the basic major institutions: familial, educational, economic, political, religious, and recreational. Since every total society must have the major groups who associate for the satisfaction of these basic social needs, these groups necessarily use institutionalized ways of behavior. The subculture—in its broadest sense a large variation within the major culture—also contains these basic institutions.

## DESIGN FOR LIVING

We have pointed out that behavior patterns are also normative; they become the models, or designs, or blueprints, according to which people are expected to act, to which they tend to conform. The same can be said of social roles, relations, and institutions. Since the culture is the sum of all these phenomena, the culture can be called the "grand design" for living. It can be abstracted from the concrete behavior of everyday life, and studied in rough analogy to the architect's blueprint for a building. The blueprint is not the building, but it is a design by which one can understand the building—especially after it has been constructed.

Without reifying or personalizing the culture we can say that it exists in order to systematize the satisfaction of the social needs of people: the means for this satisfaction are the various major and subsidiary institutions that constitute the culture. We note that these several basic needs are met with institutionalized ways of behaving. We have already noted the generalized functions of the institution: simplifying behavior, providing roles and relations, and exerting social control. Each of the institutions has its specialized objectives, but the culture as a whole performs functions beyond these objectives.

**a.** The first function of a culture, the main thing that it "does," is to provide a blueprint or design for living in any given society. It systematizes the social behavior of large numbers of people so that it is not necessary for each of them to build his own culture. Because of culture the people participating in the society do not have to relearn constantly or to invent ways of doing things. The culture "makes sense" out of all the various segments of social behavior by coordinating and relating them in a whole system.

**b.** The culture brings together, contains, and interprets the values of a society so that people recognize and appreciate what is worthwhile. It is through the culture that people discover the meaning and purpose of both social and individual living. People sometimes become so attached to the values current in their own society that they become ethnocentric and deride the values of other cultures. This exaggerated sense of cultural loyalty lacks objectivity but it underscores the fact that the culture does provide a strong value-orientation for people.

**c.** From another point of view we may note that the culture is itself a basis for social solidarity. Individuals are not only devoted to their own cultural traditions, they also tend to be loyal to others who share those traditions. Patriotism, or an objective love of one's own country, is in effect a deep-seated appreciation of its cultural characteristics. The definition of culture includes the essential notion that the people of a society function together for the attainment of worthwhile common objectives. This cooperative effort both contributes to and follows from social solidarity. Wherever the culture begins to disintegrate there is a weakening of both social solidarity and cooperation.

**d.** From a comparative point of view the culture serves as a "trademark" that distinguishes one society from another. It is the culture that makes the difference between

the Portuguese and the Polish, between the English and
French Canadians, between the Algerians and the South
Africans. Culture characterizes a people more meaningfully and more scientifically than the color of their skin
or any other physiological marking. It provides for the
student of society a measuring rod for discerning the differences among peoples that is more realistic than territorial and political boundaries.

e. Finally, and most important for human beings, the culture of any society is the dominant factor in establishing
and molding the social personality. While there is a variety of unique differences from person to person, as well
as a wide range of behavior patterns from group to group,
there is also a kind of cultural stamp upon the personality
that no one can escape. Obviously the self-directing individual has the ability to choose and adapt, and no two
individuals can ever be completely identical; nevertheless
the social personality is by and large the product of the
culture. This is what makes it possible to speak of the
"typical" Egyptian or Welshman or Mexican.

An analysis of these functions will readily indicate the
tremendous importance of culture not only for the individuals and groups within the society but also for the
relations of one society to another. It can be said that a
society is what its culture makes it, even though the ob-
verse is also true: a culture is what the society makes it.
Culture and society are inextricably bound up with one
another; and people and cultural patterns are constantly
influencing each other. Mutual adaptation is a never-
ending process wherever there is group life.

CULTURE AS IDEOLOGY

If it is the culture that makes the difference between
one society and another, we ought to look at this differ-
entiating aspect in more detail. What is it within the culture that gives the special stamp, or "trademark," or characteristic to the people of one society as compared to
other societies? Men in Russia embrace and kiss each other
in public; men in the United States would not do this.

June is the popular month for weddings in the United States; in Chile it is December. German parents are much less permissive with their children than áre American parents.

Selected culture patterns of this kind can be collected, counted, and analyzed in an almost inexhaustible litany of cultural differences and still leave the central question unanswered. Sorokin called the sum of all these patterns the behavioral culture and maintained that their meaning must be found in the ideological culture. This means that a society can be identified by its "culture mentality" and that it can be placed somewhere on a continuum from a sensate culture (materialistic, secular, empirical) to an ideational culture (transcendental, sacred, spiritual). Each culture is then identified by its system of meanings, its core of values, ideology, or ethos (a term introduced into the sociological vocabulary by Sumner).

From this point of view it is the ethos that gives the society its special character. This notion can best be understood by recalling what we have said in the chapter on social and cultural values. The combined set of ultimate values—the beliefs and ideals that people cling to and live for, that are worth preserving and defending—this is the ideological level of the culture. All the peculiar and observable behavioral customs of a people begin to make sense to the social scientist to the extent that they are consistent with the ethos. The more important the behavior pattern in the minds of people the more likely it is to conform to the basic values.

A less abstract approach to the ethos may be demonstrated by what we have said in the chapter on institutions. We indicated there that a culture can be specified, that is, differentiated from other cultures by its pivotal institution. There are cultures that can be classified as commercial or industrial because the economic institution tends to dominate much of the group life and values of the society. Other cultures have been characterized by their familial institution, as prewar China; or by their political institution, as ancient Rome; or by their religious institution, as medieval Europe. An understanding of the dominant or pivotal institution provides a helpful insight into the values and patterns of the society and gives meaning to the larger interpretation of the culture.

This institutional analysis helps to explain why the ideological culture, or the ethos, of one society differs from that of other societies. For example, in the United States the demands of the economic institution, of business, gainful occupation, making a living, have a direct influence on family life, on the educational system, on political organization, recreational patterns, and even on religious activities. Since the major components of the culture constitute the total institutional system, we know that the pivotal institution influences not only the other institutions but also the cultural ideology, or ethos. Any attempt to explain why the values of the economic institution are dominant, rather than those of the family, or of religion, would take us beyond our present discussion.

## CULTURE CHANGE

While it is possible to delve historically into the origin of this or that cultural pattern, the origin of culture as a whole is simultaneous with the origin of society. Culture is the necessary concomitant of society and has existed wherever human beings have lived in group life. Nevertheless, cultures vary greatly from one society to another, from one period of time to another, and to a lesser degree a culture may vary internally from one institution to another.

Why and how do adaptations occur in a culture? We have seen that although behavior patterns demonstrate a certain regularity and order, they are also functional, dynamic, and kinetic. A total culture is always in movement, both in relation to its internal components and in comparison with other cultures. For a dramatic example of this comparison, one need merely look at the dynamic, developing culture of Israel and note how it differs from the older culture of the surrounding Arabic world. Many factors are at work in the differentiation of cultures, from the geographical environment to a people's ingenuity in finding and choosing among a variety of alternative ways of acting and thinking.

Because there are multiple factors of change, there is no single complete and all-embracing explanation for cultural adaptation. Yet in general terms we may speak of the two broad processes of diffusion and convergence and at the same time realize that these tend to overlap in the historical development of a culture. Diffusion means nothing more than that behavior patterns are communicated from one culture to another. Some are accepted; others are rejected. The diffusion of a behavior pattern from one culture to another requires contact and communication between the people of different societies.

It is no accident of history that culture changed and developed most rapidly in those areas of the world where peoples could meet one another. Primitive cultures remain primitive in isolated places, deep in the jungles, high on mountain ranges, in deserts that are difficult of access. African societies existed at various stages of cultural development before the continent was "opened" to Europeans. Since that time there has been an almost explosive diffusion of cultural phenomena back and forth between the African and European continents.

The diffusion of culture tends to be piecemeal, while the convergence of two or more cultures leads to a kind of all-pervasive change into a "new" and different culture. There are many historical examples of convergence: the expansion of the early Roman culture into the northern tribes; the Norman invasion of England; the fusion of the Moorish and Spanish cultures. In the Americas the clearest example is the Mexican culture that has evolved from a combination of Indian and Spanish cultural features.

The major cultures of the world continue to develop through diffusion and convergence, which are the most important explanations of cultural adaptation. The physical intermingling of people from different backgrounds has increased tremendously because of both forced and voluntary migration. People transport with themselves the behavior patterns from their original culture. More important than physical intermingling, however, is the rapid communication of ideas, experience, and knowledge from one culture to another. Cultural exchange is now instantaneous through the media of radio and television.

Besides these cross-cultural aspects of change there are also adaptations internal to a culture. Even in the most dynamic cultures some segments seem to move more rapidly, and some more slowly, than others. This concept of differential adaptation was analyzed by William Ogburn in his theory of the "culture lag." An understanding of this concept requires some knowledge of both social change and social values. There must be a value norm according to which the lag can be determined; this constitutes the central difficulty in the measurement of culture lag.

How can we tell which institution in the culture is leading and which is lagging? It is impossible to have complete stagnancy, security, and predictability of institutional behavior, and it is apparently also impossible to have the same rate of change in the same direction by all the people in all major groups. The same person may be judged quite "progressive" when he enacts his role in the economic or recreational institutions, and yet be quite "backward" in his political or religious behavior.

An adequate concept of the culture lag almost necessarily involves value judgments. The concept usually indicates a negative aspect of social behavior. If one can decide what constitutes social progress in any given culture, he may be able to judge which institution is lagging behind the others. On the other hand, if mere change, or rapidity of change, is used as a norm, the negative connotation of the culture lag is lessened. For example, in most Western countries, very rapid change has occurred in the development of technological, industrial, and mechanical techniques. This means that the economic institution has been the fastest moving one in the culture and that the varying "space" between it and the other institutions constitutes the culture lag.

## Distinctive Features of American Culture

### 1. SOME AMERICAN CULTURE LAGS

The theory of the culture lag has been criticized mainly because of the difficulty of deciding upon the norms according to which the lag is measured. If a person declares that American material patterns of economic production are far ahead of nonmaterial patterns (ideas, attitudes, and values), he could find many examples to prove this culture lag. He could also demonstrate with his many examples that many of our ideas are far ahead of our practices and that some material patterns lag behind the non-material.

Americans tend to use one institution, the economic, as the norm by which to measure the progress of our other institutions. The success that Americans have had in the production and distribution of goods and services has been so spectacular that it draws wide attention both here and abroad. Furthermore, this kind of success can easily be enumerated, measured, and compared by means of scales and graphs. The familial, educational, political, and religious institutions should not, however, be underrated simply because they have not adapted themselves in the same way or have "lagged behind" the pace of the economic institution.

To understand the culture lags in America, it would be fruitful to select other norms of evaluation and measurement. Instead of comparing the material with the non-material patterns or the economic with the other institutions, we may use as a norm the current knowledge and resources at the disposal of American people for the improvement of their institutions. There are institutions in which we have the "know-how" and the physical equipment to make improvements and progress but have not done so. In determining culture lag, actual improvements should be measured against realistic potential ones, that is, those that could be made with the knowledge and resources now at hand.

Following are some of the striking examples of American culture lag in areas where the potential and the actual have not been brought together.

**a.** A significant proportion of American families are living in inadequate housing. The mass production of housing has not achieved and probably cannot achieve the refinement of techniques employed on the assembly line for the production of movable units. Our national wealth, however, is more than sufficient to provide decent housing for everyone, and our experience in public and low-income housing has been extensive enough to build the needed dwelling units without delay. This is an example of cultural lag because we have both the material and the knowledge to fill the gap.

**b.** There are people in the United States who suffer from hunger, whose diet is insufficient and improper. Whatever the immediate personal and social reasons why individuals and families suffer from malnutrition and inadequate food, the fact is that we Americans possess superabundant food resources and the knowledge of ways to distribute this food. The fact that numbers of Americans are not well-fed, that we actually do not bring surplus food and hungry people together, is an elementary example of cultural lag.

**c.** Another lag in our culture is seen in the lack of medical care for many Americans. Medical science has made tremendous advances in our times, and the country is wealthy enough to provide all the physical instruments of healing for all the people. Every year Americans experience many curable sicknesses, and needless deaths occur, because medical science is not made available to those who need it. While death is inevitable for every individual and some diseases are still incurable, the lag between the potential and the actual in medical care is tremendous.

**d.** Although the United States boasts of an extensive public school system which is meant to provide free education for everyone, there are still many places and many people to whom it does not extend. This country certainly has the resources to provide an adequate education for every individual. The culture lag is especially noticeable in the poor school opportunities in the very places where they are needed most, like the inner city areas. The newest schools with the best teachers exist in places where the educational level of the people is already high.

**e.** Perhaps the greatest culture lag, the one that helps to explain the above examples, is the disparity of income among our people. The United States has the wealth to provide and guarantee an adequate income for every family in the country. Opposition to such an arrangement indicates a large culture gap in the value system of our society between the principles of individual effort and the principles of social welfare.

Many Americans do not have equal access to recreational and educational facilities. Others receive unequal treatment from the police and the courts. Still others find themselves thwarted in their political and religious aspirations. In many instances these situations may be due to personal imcompetence and irresponsibility. They must, however, also be termed examples of cultural lag, even though they are often pointed out as the "price one pays" or the "risk one assumes" in living in our dynamic, progressive, and adaptive culture.

Pointing out the lag between the potential and the actual does not indicate the reasons why these lags persist in our society. It is likely that the causes lie deeply rooted in certain traditional American cultural values like free enterprise, private property, the profit system, inviolability of the home and family, or in characteristics like the political inertia of the masses. Most of these are part of the philosophy of individualism, which is itself an enduring pattern of our culture.

## 2. Afro-American Culture

It is commonly observed in social science that distinctive cultures develop when a large plurality of people is sufficiently separated from other organized people. An isolated society that has little contact and communication with other societies tends to maintain traditional and slow-moving patterns of behavior. We have seen, however, that distinctive cultures develop also by diffusion and by convergence with other cultures.

The case of the Negro American presents a sociological paradox: the white racist who could not enforce physical isolation on the Negro wants him to be culturally segregated, to have his own foreign, African, self-developed, nonwhite culture. Until recently the great majority of Negro Americans have resisted this attempt at cultural segregation and have insisted upon the right of full assimilation and acceptance as acculturated Americans. This movement persists, but it has been met by a relatively recent countermovement in favor of an Afro-American culture.

Students and young intellectuals, especially those who like to style themselves radicals, are promoting this Afro-American culture. What are the explanations for this trend? Does a genuine Afro-American culture exist in the United States?

a. When the slave trade began, many separate societies and cultures with different languages existed on the African continent. When brought to North America the African was deliberately separated from members of his own tribe precisely in order to prevent social and cultural unity among the slaves. This meant that he was a cultural isolate who came into an alien culture and met only with strangers. Cultural shock was intensified for him in a way that the loneliest white European never experienced.

b. From the point of view of the Black slave population this isolation meant that no single African culture, or subculture, was able to take root among them. If the Africans could have migrated as a cohesive social group or could have joined with others who shared their language and customs after they arrived, as the white European immigrants often did, there would have been a probability of a separate and distinct culture of African origin.

c. The historical fact is that African culture died in America, and the Negroes became acculturated Americans, long before the mass immigration of white Europeans in the second half of the nineteenth century. Although there were many free Negroes in America,

neither they nor the slaves were ever completely independent of the dominant white culture. In the latter
part of the last century it was thought that "equal segregation" would develop a distinctive Negro society and
culture, but this development did not come to pass.

**d.** What is now described as Afro-American culture is
a novel, contrived, and deliberate importation of some
of the more visible and superficial culture patterns like
types of clothing and hair styles. All the major institutions remain culturally American. Family life and religious practices of a small minority have been influenced
by the Black Muslim cult, which is itself a recent spurious
importation from the Arabic countries. Sociologically,
Afro-American culture must be seen as an artificial and
ingenuous invention.

**e.** This invention appears to be a deliberate attempt to
reconstruct a cultural tradition. Unlike the Garvey movement, it does not include a back-to-Africa plan anymore
than Irish-Americans promote a back-to-Ireland move,
or Polish-Americans plan a back-to-Poland program. But
like Marcus Garvey, the new Afro-Americans want to
establish the dignity of their preslavery African origins.
The "hyphenated" white immigrant wanted to become
American, but he also preserved some nostalgia and pride
for his native land.

**f.** There are some social scientists who call this movement a "search for identity." In the continuing pattern
of racial inequality the Negro American is still identified
by many whites as a second-class citizen. He seeks a
social status and identity that can be measured, not by
Caucasian values but by African values. In a vague sense,
this is a kind of national identity inspired by the wave
of nationalism that has swept the African countries since
the end of European colonialism.

It must be remembered that all cultures are man-made
but that they tend to develop by accretion over generations. The deliberate invention of the Afro-American culture is immediate and purposive. Few Negro Americans
will embrace African religion, and fewer will learn to
speak Swahili. But the Afro-American culture will be

bolstered by the study of Negro history, by an appreciation of African cultural developments, but especially by the self-confidence and dignity with which the great majority of Negro Americans will continue to insist upon their status as fully accepted and respected American citizens.

### 3. THE CHANGING RURAL CULTURE

The United States is one of the least rural nations, but it is also one of the most successful agricultural nations in the world. Each decennial census shows a decreasing proportion of our population actually living on farms and being gainfully employed workers on farms. At the same time we have a tremendous surplus of agricultural products, billions of dollars worth of extra foodstuffs, that we cannot possibly consume. The trend continues in opposite directions: a decreasing number of farmers and an increasing quantity of agricultural products.

This is a situation unique in the world's history. Mankind has been predominantly rural and agricultural for as far back in time as we can trace human history. Most human experience has been enacted in rural society with a rural culture; and this has been true until recently in the Western world and even in the United States. Rural traditions run deep in our culture.

The current transitional phase of American rural culture is characterized by a number of elements that have not previously appeared in the same combinations. There were periods of time, and there were societies, in which a relatively clear distinction could be made between the urban and rural culture. Not only did the institutional functions differ in the two areas of the same society, but the urban and rural people were physically and socially separated from one another. In the present American society the two have been brought into contact through the media of transportation and communication.

Following are the most significant changes that have come to the rural areas. Taken in combination, they represent an important trend in the cultural patterns of the American farm population.

a. Urbanism has invaded the rural way of life. Generally, this means that the city has been brought to the country. We think of urbanization as the process of migration from the rural to the urban areas or as a concentration of many people in a limited territory. There has been much rural migration, but the farm and the ranch have become mechanized, and the rural people have more and more accepted urban patterns of behavior. Physical isolation in which distinctive cultural patterns may develop and endure loses its cultural influence as radio and television programs and newspapers from the city reach the farm.

b. The most spectacular alteration in the American rural culture appears to be that of the familial institution. The farm is changing from a family enterprise, in which each member makes a valuable economic contribution, to a large business operation, in which skilled labor and expensive machinery do the work. The functions, roles, and relations that traditionally characterized the farm family have had to take new directions and new forms. There is more leisure for the mother to pursue noneconomic functions and for the children to obtain a greater amount of schooling. The rural home is no longer the center for recreational, educational, or religious functions.

c. The primary relationships in the old rural neighborhoods are declining. Although the farmer has always been conservative and individualistic, there is no longer the need for the kind of cooperation that once existed. This cooperation took the form of economic help in gathering the harvest, in borrowing and lending implements, and in building barns and fences. Congeniality patterns of the past, like all-day visiting, church dinners and festivals, and barn dances, have largely gone out of fashion. Rural people range farther afield for their recreation even while they have become more self-sufficient in their economic activities.

d. Economic relations with the city have multiplied as the mutual dependence of city and farm has increased. Obviously, urban people have always depended upon agriculture to supply their food. The financial dependence of the farmer upon the city centers has now become greater than ever. Gasoline and oil, fertilizers and tools, field machinery, and barn equipment cannot be obtained through barter. The cost of the farmer's operation and the price he receives for his products are governed largely by factors outside his control.

e. The development of numerous secondary associations has broadened the cultural milieu of rural people. Participation in these larger groups has had a great increase. More young people participate in organizations like the 4-H Clubs and Future Farmers of America and more adults in cooperatives, marketing associations, and various programs sponsored by county and state farm bureaus. The growth of secondary groups in the rural areas has followed at a slower pace the pattern of larger, formalized groups in the cities.

f. The political institutions of the rural culture have been altered by the farmers' new relations to federal and state governments. Price supports, crop control, import taxes, and credit restrictions cannot be handled by the local government. The farmers' political needs go far beyond the local township or county and include national and even international issues. Since he is also part of this total complex society, the farmer has necessarily had to widen his horizon, ·and this is simply another way of saying that the rural American culture has decreased the difference between itself and the more typical urban culture.

This list of items must not be interpreted as describing a universal change applicable in all rural areas in the United States. There has been an unevenness in rate and kind of change in different parts of the country. The most widespread change has been from the small family-farms to so-called factory farms. The latter have been most often gigantic operations existing in all the farm states and owned by food-processing corporations. Unorganized migrant labor has been introduced in some of these places; and social conditions exist that were unknown on the traditional, conservative family farm.

4. THE SOUTHEASTERN REGIONAL CULTURE

The region known as the Old South, comprising the eleven southeastern states, has been both romanticized and vilified. Equal misrepresentation has been made in the name of realism and in the name of poetry. To most Americans, the southeastern region is a culture area distinct from the rest of the country. The people act differently; they speak with a drawl; they move more slowly than other Americans. They have traditions of hospitality and gracious living; they even have food patterns and religious practices peculiar to the region.

Society and culture are changing very rapidly in the Southeast. Mechanization of the farms has pushed people into the local towns, into midwestern and northeastern cities, and into the Southwest and the far West. The growth of cities and the increase of industry have quickened the pace of living. Facilities for health and education are improving. Patterns of political behavior are shifting. Even the traditional relations between upper and lower class, between Negro and white, are changing gradually.

Although this transition is relatively rapid at the present time as compared with a generation ago, it is still possible to capture the main elements that gave the Old South a distinctive subculture within the total American culture. The rest of our society is also changing, and in many ways more rapidly; but in spite of this fact the southeastern culture is tending to merge with the total culture. It is in this sense becoming more American. Traditional cultural differences will endure, but they are fading in importance. Contemporary southeasterners do not take them as seriously as their grandfathers once did.

One of the most significant facts, which is frequently overlooked, is that the Old South has become the New Southeast. For a long time it has been unrealistic to maintain the fiction that the United States is divided into only two sections, the North and the South, although this regional view still persists among the older people in the Southeast. The United States has expanded tremen-

dously in area and population since the Civil War, so
that a double process of shrinkage and of Americanization
has been going on in the southeastern region.

Following are some of the main factors that help to
account for the residual regional differences of culture
in the southeastern states.

a. The composition of the population gives one of the
main clues why this subculture differs from the total
American culture. The immigrant stock, both white and
black, has a longer continuing history than that of the
other parts of the country. The Old South was practically
untouched by the successive waves of European migration
from the 1840s until the First World War. While these
immigrant peoples were spreading across the northern
states, the Southerners continued to reproduce themselves
and in later decades were able actually to "export" persons to other parts of the country.

b. It must be noted that this lack of immigrant stimulus
was an important factor in maintaining regional cultural
forms. Foreigners did not come to America merely as
physical entities. They brought with them cultural patterns, ideas, attitudes, and values, which fused with the
dynamic and receptive total culture. Most of this cultural
influence bypassed the Southern people. The Southeast,
therefore, became "Americanized" more slowly than the
rest of the country, and there is still today a residual
ethnocentrism and even resentment against "foreign"
ideas. The traditional, conservative ethos of the region
was formulated over this long period of time.

c. Much can also be made of the fact that this region
has been mainly agricultural and rural. Patterns and institutions change more slowly in the rural environments;
and the type of farming adopted also helped to slow
down change. The South was not a land of numerous, independent, vigorous farmers who managed their own
small holdings. The dominant agricultural pattern was
that of the large plantation, concentrating on single
money-crops and paying minimum attention to conservation of natural resources.

**d.** The plantation system was also a system of human relations, and it is in this area that a great hindrance to cultural development existed. The fact that the middle class was practically nonexistent marked off the Old South as being nontypical in middle-class America. The mass of Black workers, both during and after slavery, and the attitudes the dominant whites took toward them, constituted a distinctive non-American feature of Southern culture. Freedom of movement, of work and opportunity, of upward mobility is a basic ingredient of the American culture, and formalized restrictions hampered this freedom everywhere in this regional culture.
**e.** The segregation system, the studied practice of keeping the masses, especially the Blacks, on the lowest rung of the social structure, has affected all the major institutions of the Southeast. It has affected the family by a peculiar combination of strict marriage prohibitions, illegitimacy, and loose sex relations. It has accounted for the low rate of literacy and the inadequate educational system. It helps to explain the religious practices arising from literal fundamentalism. It affected the antilabor attitudes of both big business and professional persons and helped to maintain an archaic political philosophy.

It is no oversimplification to point to these elements—the composition of the population, the type of agricultural system, and the structure of segregation—as the principal factors in the development and maintenance of the Old South's subculture. The extent to which these elements have differed from the general patterns of the American culture, and the extent to which they are now changing, mark the progress of the Americanization of the southeastern region. There will probably remain an identifiable regional subculture as long as minor institutional patterns endure. Rapid change, however, is now occurring in the major factors mentioned above; and this necessarily implies the emergence of behavior patterns in the New Southeast that more closely resemble those of the total American culture.

## 5. THE AMERICAN INDIAN CULTURE

One of the less pleasant accusations made against the United States is that it is a racist society. This accusation is usually focused on the unequal treatment of Negro Americans, who constitute the largest racial minority in the country. It also refers to the legal exclusion of immigrant Asiatics and to the specific treatment of Japanese-Americans during the Second World War. The case of the American Indians is also a case of racism that is largely kept out of public view because the Indians have been isolated on reservations.

It seems significant that no other racial minority has come under the jurisdiction of a specially organized government bureau, as is the case with the federal Bureau of Indian Affairs. This suggests that the Indians are wards of the government, cultural orphans who are at one time encouraged to assimilate themselves to the American cultural family and at another time encouraged to maintain their cultural independence outside the larger American system.

Unlike the artificial and largely spurious Afro-American culture, the Indian culture is authentic, traditional, and indigenous to its native land. It exemplifies characteristics that allow it to be discussed separately from the white man's culture.

a. The Indian population is growing and its culture will not die for lack of Indians to carry it on. Over the generations the culture has expanded to include "outside" elements that were not available to the aboriginal people. Many American Indians speak English; many have accepted the Christian religion. They make use of many of the tools, vehicles, and artifacts introduced from outside. The pressure of the white population and the carving out of "reserved" territories have forced the Indians into a relatively stable and non-nomadic existence.

b. There are many Indian cultures, marked by diverse languages and traditions. The Navajos differ from the Sioux; the Cherokee of North Carolina have a culture different from that of the Nez Perces of Idaho. This cultural diversity is not as wide as it was before the coming of the white man, but it is still so persistent that many Indians prefer to be identified by the name of their tribe rather than simply as Indians. This relative autonomy may partially explain why there has not been a united movement for civil rights among American Indians and why they have not constituted a strong political pressure group. It was not till 1948 that they were guaranteed the right to vote.

c. One of the tribal characteristics that sets most American Indians apart from most American whites is an emphasis on the kinship system. Instead of the typical urban American conjugal family of parents and children, the Indians prefer to maintain the broader relations of the extended consanguine family. This means that the primary group with its personal loyalties and close relationships acts as a strong bond of social solidarity. This also explains the reluctance of many Indians to face the alienation and loneliness of urban white America.

d. This rough description of a familistic culture, as distinct from a contractual culture, includes other common characteristics. The whole process of socialization and of conformity to the behavioral norms tends to be reinforced by tribal custom more than by a detailed legal system. Honesty and loyalty depend more on traditional norms of acceptable behavior than on the strong arms of law enforcement officers. If this were not the case the American Indian culture could not have survived as a distinct system.

e. Status differences, as measured by the possession of valued cultural items, exist among American Indians as among all peoples, but such resources are not as available as they are in the competitive white society. For example, the accumulation of wealth, one of the principal criteria of social status, has been neither encouraged nor widely available for the great majority of American Indian tribes. The fact that there are some "oil-rich" Indians, and that some families encourage college education for their sons does not gainsay the fact of large-scale poverty among American Indians.

In broadest outline the cultural features of American Indian life reflect what the social scientists usually call the communal type of society as contrasted with the associational type. The resistance of the Indians to cultural absorption into the larger white society has been matched by the general racist policy of whites that excluded Indians since colonial times. There have been cross-cultural exchanges, as there have been interracial marriages, but there remains a clear-cut distinction between the cultural life of American Indians and that of American whites.

## Suggested Readings

Arensberg, Conrad, and Kimball, Solon. *Culture and Community*. New York: Harcourt, Brace, 1965.

Barnouw, Victor. *Culture and Personality*. Homewood: Dorsey, 1968.

Honigman, John. *The World of Man*. New York: Harper, 1959.

Mead, Margaret. *Continuities in Cultural Evolution*. New Haven: Yale University Press, 1964.

Sorokin, Pitirim. *Social and Cultural Dynamics*. Boston: Porter Sargent, 1957.

# III
# Culture and Society

The previous sections have given us a conceptual framework and some scientific insights into the parallel analysis of persons and society, of patterns and culture. In this section these two separate lines of analysis are brought together in the study of various sociocultural phenomena.

The essential study of the meaning of group life and cultural habits is done through an analysis of values (chapter 12). People are both the subjects and agents of mobility (chapter 13) and all sociocultural phenomena undergo change (chapter 14) and are influenced by various forms of control (chapter 15). The norms and values of people are sometimes violated by deviation (chapter 16), but there exists also a necessary degree of sociocultural integration (chapter 17).

# 12
# Values

PERHAPS NO OTHER SUBJECT HAS CAUSED SO MUCH controversy among sociologists as the study of values. Their attempt to act as "value-free" scientists has sometimes led to the suggestion that they believe social values have no reality, cannot be studied without the involvement of one's personal values, or are purely psychological and ethical phenomena outside the orbit of social science. At the present time, however, it is generally agreed among sociologists that values are important *social facts* and that they can be submitted to scientific study and analysis.

## DEFINITION OF VALUE

The use of a descriptive definition instead of a strict logical definition has caused confusion in the discussion of social values. Descriptively we may say that everything that is useful, desirable, or admirable to the person and group "has a value." Must we say, therefore, that the thing itself is not a value, but that it merely contains a value? For example, is education itself a social value, or does its value lie in the capacity it has for satisfying certain basic social needs? The fact is of course that the importance an object has transfers to the object itself, so that education is not only socially valuable, it is a social value. The sociologist finds his data among people in society, and he finds that in the minds of people a certain "worth" is attached to education.

We have, then, three elements that must be considered in the discussion of social values: ( *a* ) the object itself which is a value, ( *b* ) the capacity of the object to satisfy social needs, and ( *c* ) the appreciation of the people for this object and for its capacity to give satisfaction. We may recall here that the same object can be given different definitions according to the different aspects from which it is viewed. We have seen that repeated uniformities of

323

behavior can also be viewed as norms, or models, of behavior. Similarly, we may say that certain "worthwhile" objects, as judged by the people in a society, are both social values *and* the criteria of social values.

Sociologically, values may be defined as those criteria according to which the group or society judges the importance of persons, patterns, goals, and other sociocultural objects. We are not directly concerned here with either the intrinsic worth of these things or with the specific personal valuation made of them by any particular individual.

## CRITERIA OF VALUATION

Values, therefore, are the criteria that give meaning and significance to the total culture and society. More fully described, the values of concern to the social scientist have the following characteristics. They are *shared;* they are agreed upon by a plurality of people and do not depend upon the judgment of any particular individual. They are *taken seriously;* people connect these values with the preservation of the common welfare and the satisfaction of social needs. Values involve *emotions;* people are moved to make sacrifices, even to fight and die for the highest values. Finally, since values require consensus or agreement among many people, they may be conceptually *abstracted* from the various valued items.

We have already seen that every society employs criteria by which it determines the social status of persons and by which it places pluralities of persons on a higher or lower rank of appreciation. These criteria are called the determinants of social status and class. The people consider the following more or less objectively measurable determinants to be worthwhile: family and ancestry, wealth, functional utility, education, religion, and biological characteristics.

When we inquire about the social status of an individual we are really asking about his social value as measured by these criteria—the objective esteem or disesteem, approval or disapproval, attached to him. The manner in which people evaluate one another and the kind of cultural object they hold in high or low esteem are of great basic importance to the functioning of society. Value judgment, or social evaluation, necessarily implies a comparison of what is better or worse, higher or lower, in esteem and approval. These judgments are, of course, sometimes false, as in the case of extreme ethnocentrism.

## THE SOURCE OF VALUES

It is an oversimplification to say that values are important because people are important. It is true that values have no scientific meaning for the sociologist except insofar as they are connected with human beings. The social person and his behavior patterns are the starting point of study for sociology. What makes some people (and their behavior) more important and more highly valued than others? Why do all social and cultural phenomena have value only because they are related to human beings? We are seeking here the answers to these questions in the sources of values, and these sources may be analyzed on two levels.

We have already seen that social status, that is, the evaluation of the person by others, comes *extrinsically* to the individual by ascription and achievement. The social consensus of high or low status is based on the individual's possession of those items that are highly valued in the culture. They are circumstances and conditions the value of which the individual cannot control. Stated briefly, this means that the source of values is external to the social person.

Social esteem comes to the person of good family, not because of the person himself, but because good family is a criterion of high value in his society. The merit is, as it were, transferred to him from outside himself. Similarly the high value of the wealth he possesses and the religion he practices is transferred to him. The social esteem attached to his functional role, to the type of education he has, and even to some extent to the physical qualities he possesses, has its source in his cultural environment. All these valued items are part of the culture content surrounding the individual.

On another level of abstraction, however, there is also a source of values *intrinsic* to the social person. The human dignity of the individual entitles him to respect. The mere fact that he is a person accountable for his behavior, praiseworthy for his good deeds and reprehensible for his evil deeds, is a basis for social evaluation. The moral right to personal inviolability is centered on the fact of humanity itself. This inviolability, responsibility, and dignity are not originated by the society and then handed over to the individual.

The fact that society recognizes and appreciates this inner source of evaluation is historically demonstrated by the exceptions taken to it. When men have enslaved other men, degraded their dignity, or shamefully exploited them, they have justified their actions by the argument that the victims were somewhat less than human. The abused race or category of people had to be considered as a lower order of being, without human rights and dignity, irresponsible and violable, in order to justify their enslavement. The attempt had to be made to remove the inner source of evaluation because societies everywhere have recognized the validity of these inner values.

## VALUES AND BEHAVIOR PATTERNS

The meaningful study of patterns of behavior, both overt and covert, requires an understanding of the values current in a society. These patterns do not have equal importance; mores are more compulsive than mere usages. One of the reasons we often cannot understand the behavior patterns in foreign cultures is because we do not know and understand the values of the culture. The behavior that seems insignificant or absurd to us in a primitive culture may have great importance and value to the persons who perform it. Similarly, a lack of conformity to the patterns in one's own society often implies a lack of knowledge of the important social values.

It is the high value attached to monotheism, patriotism, and monogamy that places the central patterns of religious, civic, and marital behavior among the mores.

The philosopher may point out that God is essentially of higher value than human beings and that man is essentially more valuable than inanimate objects. The social scientist, however, operates in the extrinsic order, and it is through a knowledge of social values that he comes to judge whether a behavior pattern is trivial or essential to the people in the society. Behavior patterns that have the highest social value are also accompanied by the widest conformity and the strongest social pressure to conform.

## VALUES AND SOCIAL ROLES

We could not speak of the values attached to behavior patterns were it not for the persons who perform these patterns. Values exist only because there are persons worthy of evaluation and competent to evaluate other persons and things. Just as the person-in-action is the irreducible component of society, so also is he the ultimate focus of values. The principal mechanism through which people express and symbolize values is the social role.

We have seen that patterns of behavior combine into social roles through which people function toward desired social goals. The patterns that constitute the role are variously evaluated on a continuum from the most to the least important. The college student knows that the existing series of behavior expectations within his own educational role is not of uniform social value. Studying for an examination is of greater value than attendance at a fraternity meeting. Writing a term paper is more important than having lunch in the college cafeteria. The person is expected to know the varying degrees of value attached to the different patterns within his role and to concentrate on the more important ones.

In the total society the multiple social roles of the person also differ in value. This again depends upon the dominant institution of the culture and to some extent also on the age, sex, and other circumstances of the individual. While it is true that the economic, the familial, or the religious role may have the highest social value in any particular culture, it is also true that any given individual may have a differing dominant role. For the wife and mother, the familial role has the highest social value in any culture. A bishop is expected to place his religious role above his economic, political, or any other role. Society, in other words, invests social roles with degrees of social value, and the behavior patterns of individuals must be in accord with these values.

## VALUES AS BEHAVIOR SANCTIONS

We have said that wide conformity, social values, and social pressure are objective indexes by which we can determine mores, folkways, and usages among the behavior patterns. Ultimately, however, the social value attached to a set of behavior patterns exerts strong pressure on people so that they conform to the value. This means that social values act as norms or standards of behavior patterns. When society in general approves or disapproves a certain course of conduct, it is in effect saying that the behavior in question is right or wrong, correct or incorrect.

Social sanctions—the rewards and penalties society visits on the person because of his behavior—are intimately bound up with the ways in which the people evaluate their behavior. The hero and the public servant are honored and rewarded; the criminal and the racketeer are despised and punished. In both cases, however, the strength of the sanction is usually commensurate with the value attached to the behavior. For example, the penalties attached to the various types of criminal behavior are graded from light to severe on the basis of the way in which the people grade the behavior itself. Capital punishment or life imprisonment is the sanction on first-degree murder, while a small fine is the sanction for a parking violation.

The system of rewards and punishments employed by a society has its ultimate basis in the value system. If there were no values in a society, and if these values were not known to differ in degree of importance, the society would lose its strongest instrument of social control. Although the system of values is the result of the accumulated wisdom of human experience, these values have a direct effect on contemporary human experience. They determine what is required of people and what is forbidden, what is praised and rewarded, and what is censured and punished.

## VALUES AND SOCIAL PROCESSES

We have seen that people in society are related to one another most significantly through the reciprocal performance of their social roles. This relationship of person-to-person and of group-to-group is largely regulated and controlled by the values of the society. The whole network of status relations, superordinate, coordinate, and subordinate, could not operate if the people did not recognize and agree upon a body of social values. For example, the relationship between parent and child can be analyzed not only from the behavior of the roles themselves but also from an evaluation of the relationship itself.

The generic social relations, or social processes, in organized society are patterned according to relatively few basic types, some of them conjunctive and others disjunctive. Social values are involved in the actual functioning of these relations. The processes of cooperation, accommodation, and assimilation are usually highly valued because they promote harmony, good order, and social peace. The reasons why people cooperate, the functions they perform, and the cooperating participants themselves are all measured by the criteria of higher social values.

The disjunctive processes are usually ranked lower in the scale of values, but the actual participation in these negative relations is often motivated and justified by higher social values. For example, the process of conflict as such is usually abhorred by the people in the society, but when the process is invested with other criteria like patriotism, heroism, justice, protection of the home, or personal and national honor it becomes highly valued. Under similar conditions and with similar motivation, the process of contravention is also raised to a higher rank of evaluation. In some cultures, the process of competition, through ordinarily a negative relationship, is often praised and encouraged on the assumption that it has a value "in itself."

This discussion of social processes indicates that social values are not merely norms of behavior but are also often used as a basis of motivation of behavior. If certain criteria of approval and disapproval exist in a culture, it is logical that people appeal to them as a justification for their own behavior. Nowhere is this seen so clearly as in the network of social relations. It is a fundamental need of the normal person that he have social status—that he be thought well of by others, even that he think well of himself. The individual cannot successfully deal with others if he does not conform to the expected and approved ways of behaving, and this is another way of saying that he conforms to a system of social relations because they are invested with social values.

## CLASSIFICATION OF VALUES

Social values are closely related to patterns of behavior, social roles, and social processes, as well as to the whole stratification system of a society. Any one of these social phenomena could serve as a starting point for the classification of values. For our own analytical purposes, however, we will employ three bases of classification: the social personality, the society, and the culture. Although we are thus classifying values from three points of view, we must remember that the values discussed combine and overlap in all three.

a. The degree of compulsiveness provides a continuum on which social values may be conceptually arranged, that is, arranged according to the degree by which they affect the social personality. At one extreme are the morally strongest, internalized values the person accepts as a matter of conscience. The violation of these values would create in the normal person feelings of guilt and shame. He feels compelled in conscience to comply with these values, and the society makes intense efforts to assure compliance. At this pole are the most rigid commandments, and no matter how they are worded the values imply both "thou shalt not" and "thou shalt." For example, the positive values of monotheism, patriotism, and monogamy imply the negative criteria of polytheism, treason, and bigamy.

The social values that imply the highest moral and ethical compulsion tend to be the moral core of the individual's own personal ethics. From this high point the continuum shades off to the less important and less compulsive values. This does not mean that there is always less conformity to these lower values by the members of the society, but people often conform to them from convenience and habit rather than from an intense conviction of their worth. There are obviously many patterns that are less compulsive because they are clothed in lesser values. For example, conventional forms of etiquette, norms of convenience and efficiency, and matters of aesthetic taste can be violated without the feeling of guilt and without serious social reprisals. At this end of the continuum of values, the moral quality of the behavior is not emphasized.

b. Social values may also be arranged on a continuum of associative functioning, as we have seen in speaking of the social processes. Some social values are more important than others in getting things done in society and in achieving cooperative efforts among persons and groups. These highest values indicate what is desirable and even essential for the continuance of society and for the common welfare. In this area the social relations of justice and love are most operative, and also there is a balance and a relationship between high values like personal freedom and social authority. Whatever contributes to cooperation, accommodation, and assimilation may be said to be of associative value.

At the other pole of this continuum are the negative or antisocial values. They constitute an area of value conflict and emphasize the confusion between personal and social obligations. It cannot always be said that what is good for the society is good for the individual and vice versa. Values that are negative and dissociative from the point of view of the total society may be highly esteemed by an individual person, an interest group, or a pressure group. Nevertheless, any value, whether it is racial superiority, business loyalty, or religious beliefs, which promotes the negative social processes must be termed a disjunctive value.

c. Values may be classified most meaningfully according to their institutional function in the culture. This classification agrees with the common usage of terms; we frequently identify separately values that are religious, political, economic, and so forth. Here we do not speak of a continuum from higher to lower, compulsive to permissive, positive to negative, although within the major institutions each of these sets of gradations can be recognized. The systematic analysis of social values in a culture reveals that there is a set of values employed in each of the major institutions. People who perform their functions in a corresponding major social group such as the family recognize that there are certain major values to which they must adhere in their family life. The political and economic groups are also governed by distinctive social values. There are also important values in operation in the religious, educational, and recreational groups of any society.

In this sense it may be said that social values, like patterns, roles, and relations become "institutionalized." Values attached to certain cultural behavior for a long time simplify and ease the functioning of the institution. They become closely identified not only with the behavior itself but with the behavior in this or that institution. The longer the value and the behavior endure together and the more closely they are identified, the more likely it is that the combination will be institutionalized. That is why in traditional, slowly changing societies there is a tendency to say that there is only one way to bring up children, to plant crops, to practice religion. The institutional value has merged with and reinforces the accepted institutional pattern.

## FUNCTIONS OF VALUES

It is fairly clear from the definition of the term what the purposes of values are in a culture. We have seen that values are conceptually recognized, emotionally charged, shared in common, taken seriously, and that they act as norms of judgment. It is also clear that values as such are not goals or objectives of social action and thought. They are not the things sought, but they are what gives the sought-after things importance. People use them as norms and criteria that point the way to goals and objectives.

In more detail we may indicate that the mere presence of social values brings about certain social consequences. The actual pursuits of these social results may be termed the general functions of social values.

**a.** Values provide a ready-made means for judging the social worth of persons and pluralities. They make possible the whole system of stratification that exists in every society. They help the individual himself to know "where he stands" in the eyes of his fellowmen.

**b.** Values focus the attention of people upon material cultural items that are considered desirable, useful, and essential. The item so valued may not always be "best" for the individual or group, but the fact that it is a socially valued object makes it worth striving for.

**c.** The ideal ways of thinking and behaving in any society are indicated by the values. They form a kind of blueprint of socially acceptable behavior so that people can almost always discern the "best" ways of acting and thinking.

**d.** Values are guideposts for people in their choice and fulfillment of social roles. They create interest and provide encouragement so that people realize that the demands and expectations of the various roles are functioning toward worthwhile objectives.

**e.** Values act as a means of social control and social pressure. They influence people to conform to the mores, encourage them to do the "right" things, and give them a feeling of merited esteem. On the other hand, they act as restraints against disapproved behavior, indicate certain prohibited patterns, and make intelligible the feelings of shame and guilt coming from social transgressions.

f. Values function as a means of solidarity. It is an axiom among social scientists that groups cluster around and are united by common shared values of a high order. People are attracted to others who cherish the same values; but it may be said that common values are among the most important of the factors that create and maintain social solidarity.

## CONFLICT OF VALUES

Although the general values that are widely accepted in a culture have an integrating effect on the people, social problems may in some instances develop from social values. These problems arise primarily in two instances: first, when there is a discrepancy between the expressed values of the culture and the actual behavior of the people; and second, when the values of the various subgroups in the society are in conflict.

a. A social problem may be roughly defined as the disparity between the level of social values and the level of social behavior. If the people did not have high values, strong beliefs, and expressed ideals, there would be no norms against which behavior patterns could be measured. If there were no high values attached to persons and property, there would be no sanctions on their violation, and there would be no crime problem in society. Similarly, substandard housing, sexual promiscuity, racial discrimination, child labor, and all other social problems could not be defined unless there were value norms against which this kind of behavior could be judged.

The ranking of social values becomes important in this respect. As it achieves successive subsidiary goals, the progressive society constantly revises and raises its standards. Social values are not absolutes, but they are always out of reach of the people. The gap between behavior and values can never be entirely closed. The fact that human beings in the aggregate aspire to more than they can achieve means that there will always be social problems, and in this sense social values "cause" social problems.

**b.** Even though a culture is meaningfully integrated by the general consensus concerning the highest values, there are many instances within a society in which one set of values is in conflict with another. We have already discussed this aspect of institutional inconsistency. Conflict occurs when the values of the familial institution, for example, are not congruous with those of the economic institution, or when the values represented in the educational role are inconsistent with those of the home. The values of the church sometimes clash with those of the state or of the business world.

This clash of values is most apparent in a pluralistic society in which large numbers of diverse groups are striving to bolster the loyalty of their members and to make their influence felt in the larger society. The interest groups and the pressure groups are value groups. In a democratic society, the right to maintain and to express diverse values is protected, and there are usually mechanisms through which compromise of values is possible. Nevertheless, most of the major social problems can be stated in terms of the clash of values.

This value diversity necessarily has an effect on the social personality. In an industrialized, urban society few people can spend their whole lives isolated in groups that have congenial values. Contact with other groups and experience in other social situations highlight the contrast of social values and norms of behavior. Institutional inconsistency, the value expression of social problems, is translated into role inconsistency, the value expression of personal problems. The adaptive personality is most often able to override this difficulty, but for others it causes frequent and painful self-compromise.

## ULTIMATE VALUES

The social scientist does not study immutable and absolute values. Insofar as these exist, they are analyzed by philosophers, theologians, and students of ethics. Mutability is an essential characteristic in all societies and cultures. Change is also characteristic on the level of social values, which are nowhere completely fixed, rigid, and immutable criteria of behavior. The fact that value systems differ from one culture to another, from one time to another within the same culture, and even from one region and class to others within the same society, demonstrates the flexibility and mutability of values. This means of course that the criteria of judgment for what is good or bad, right or wrong, correct or incorrect vary considerably in the minds of men.

In the light of this universal mutability and variation of social values, it is obvious that the term "ultimate values" must be used with scientific caution. Nevertheless, this concept has been formulated and used by social scientists in a relative or "semi-ultimate" sense.

It can be demonstrated that the people in any particular society accord general consensus to a core of important social values. These are the ultimates for this society, the relatively few basic values against which the people measure their behavior and which characterize a culture and differentiate it from other cultures. These core values are seen most easily within the institutional framework, each major institution containing one or more of the most important social values. The ultimate social value may be the expression of affection in family life, democratic procedures in the political system, monotheism in the religious institution, and other similar basic principles.

The concept of ultimate values may refer also to the minimum consensus found in all societies concerning the fixed "principles" of behavior. Although they vary in their interpretation and application of these ultimate social values, all societies everywhere put prohibitive sanctions on incest, murder, blasphemy, and stealing. All societies place a high value on fidelity, friendship, love, and justice. This is another way of saying that the psychic unity of mankind is exhibited not only in basically similar human intellects and wills but also in a similar minimum social conscience.

## Aspects of the American Value System

### 1. AMERICAN MATERIALISM

It appears to be almost inevitable that a society's values become most important in that area of behavior in which the society has been most successful. The American society has had its most dramatic success in its mastery over the physical environment. Americans have dealt with matter in a skillful and ingenious way that has probably never been surpassed in the history of humanity. This success in handling and mastering matter has resulted in a tendency to use material criteria even in the judgment of spiritual and humanistic achievements.

Materialism is a question of degree, and the statement that American culture emphasizes materialistic values must not be interpreted to mean that it contains no spiritual values or that spiritual values are completely irrelevant. We are speaking here of a tendency to, and an emphasis on, quantitative measurement. The emphasized norms of judgment in the American culture are the characteristics of matter: size, numbers, frequency, and speed. The sensate qualities of matter are emphasized when it is said that a product looks, feels, and tastes "better," that it gives more comfort, pleasure, and convenience.

Foreign observers have sometimes made the exaggerated statement that in the American society most behavior has been reduced to a "question of dollars and cents." They are misled because in America some values have been expressed in pecuniary terms. Many Americans feel that the most successful father is the one who "best provides" for his family, and this provision is measured by the amount of money he brings home to his family. Movie fans watch expectantly for the yearly announcement of earnings by their favorite actors and actresses to find out who have been the "best" entertainers.

It is commonly assumed that the most successful clergyman is the one who draws the largest audience to his pulpit or to his radio or television program. The pastor or minister who runs his congregation in a "businesslike way" and who has paid off the debt on a church building is highly praised. Similar criteria are often employed in evaluating the function of college and university presidents, who tend to move off the academic level and into the ranks of business managers. The mayor, governor, or president who is seeking reelection spends much of his campaign convincing the people of his fine record in financial and material achievement and improvements.

All these roles are also measured by nonmaterial and nonpecuniary criteria. The political functionary, the educator, the clergyman, the entertainer, and the parent are also appraised according to the major values current in their corresponding major institution. This is to be logically expected, and probably occurs in all societies. Thus it is not true that the institutional values have been converted into, or absorbed by, financial and quantitative norms of measurement. What has happened is an invasion of the major institution by a set of values that apply properly in the economic institution.

In a materialistic culture like ours there exists also the vague assumption that spiritual and humanistic gains almost automatically flow from material success. There is, of course, the demonstrable fact that cultural values often suffer when people fall below a minimum standard of material living. Peace of mind, cultural interests, and normal social relations require something more than material subsistence. This, however, is quite different from the notion that the more material success a person has the happier he will be, or the notion that all social problems will disappear if poverty is abolished, or the notion that material success is an index of divine blessing.

The vigorous young American culture stands in contrast to traditional, slow-changing cultures. We emphasize objects that are the "biggest and the best"; they emphasize those that are the "oldest and the best." We logically stress those matters in which we have achieved the most success; the longest bridge, the widest highway, the tallest building, the fastest jet plane—all quantitative measurements. It is characteristic of the American society to look forward to the near future when it can surpass even these superlatives.

It would be a great error to conclude that the American culture is pervadingly materialistic simply because Americans find measurable symbols the handiest way of expressing the numerous nonmaterial functions and values. Because the father's job and salary are used as an index of his affection for his family, this does not mean that paternal affection is weak or absent. Because material symbols are employed to measure success in religious, economic, and political institutions, this does not mean that religious motivation, business loyalty, or concern for the common welfare has decreased in these institutions. Materialism has not supplanted nonmaterial pursuits and functions. Indeed it can probably be demonstrated that the pragmatic, down-to-earth use of measuring techniques has been an incentive to further and better effort on the level of nonmaterial activities.

## 2. INCREASING CONCERN FOR HUMANITARIAN VALUES

The term "materialistic culture" is a relative term, and in the American society material achievement is not generally considered an end in itself. To lust after wealth for its own sake is characteristic of the miser but not of Americans in general. Wealth is considered a means to use in producing or consuming more commodities and services. No American is willing to admit that he is accumulating wealth as an end in itself. Even if he is doing this, he rationalizes his conduct with more worthy explanations.

The father of the family may spend his time and energy in business activities, and he explains that he is doing this for his wife and family. The college president who pursues the alumni for contributions and seeks to build up the endowment fund explains that higher education is now a costly business. These examples indicate that while material achievements come to be used as a norm of success they are also used as a means for fulfillment of higher goals. There is nothing inherently illogical or incompatible in this combination.

It is in the light of this fact that the American culture demonstrates a concern for both material success and humanitarian values. One may say that these concerns

are increasing along parallel lines, and there may be a
kind of mutual causality between the two. As we realize
more and more the tremendous potential of our natural
resources in terms of material benefits to the masses of
people, we tend to realize also the importance of promoting and extending the higher values.

Following are a few of the more obvious examples of
persons and categories who are promoting, participating
in, and benefiting from the increasing humanitarian character of the American social conscience.

**a.** The developing concern for humanitarian values may
be seen in the extension of the rights, privileges and potentialities of American culture to more categories of
Americans. It was an almost inevitable cultural trend
that women should win the right to political suffrage as
well as to push vigorously for equal rights in business,
education, and religion. There is still considerable opposition to the achievment of equality across sex lines but the
movement for women's rights continues to gain strength.

**b.** Another example is that of the child-labor laws, to
which there was also a certain amount of opposition. They
were made to protect children against exploitation, and
although they are sometimes still violated, the general
principle that society must protect children is now accepted in the American culture. The right of labor to
organize and to bargain collectively is now written into
our laws. The promotion of fair employment practices
that attempt to remove discrimination against minority
peoples was first accepted in a few states and eventually
spread to the entire nation by act of Congress.

**c.** The concerted efforts to protect religious and racial
minorities in the American society are symptomatic of this
growing concern for humanitarian values. This protection
has been pursued more vigorously than ever during the
past decade. There are still racial and religious bigots in
America and there probably always will be, but the trend
toward the removal of external abuses and discrimination
is unquestionable. The conscience of the society continues
to be challenged by vigorous minority groups who are in-

sisting that the humane values of the American culture be respected in practice.

**d.** People who are handicapped in various ways are also receiving more attention in the numerous programs of social and humanitarian welfare. Polio victims, children with speech and hearing defects, illegitimate and orphaned children, dependent mothers, the aged, the unemployed, and many others represent categories of persons who cannot solve their problems unaided. The sporadic philanthropy and voluntary charity of the past are being supplemented by efficient and organized campaigns for funds, as well as by the official commitment of funds and services by local, state, and federal government.

An interesting aspect of the practical application of humanitarian values is the kind of opposition it almost always meets. Before the change is made the people generally give lip service to the ideal but object to the particular practice proposed. After the change is made the people learn to accommodate themselves to both the ideal and the practice. Hardly anyone argues now against women voting, or against the laws protecting children from exploitation, or against medicare and social security, but each of these improvements was gained over large opposition.

The opposition is invariably and curiously based on the argument that the extension of rights to others is an invasion of private rights. There is merit in this argument only insofar as the formal obligations of the individual increase when he must observe the rights of others. Rights and obligations are correlative, and it is to the credit of the American people that this fact is more and more accepted in the social conscience. There is nothing inevitable or absolute about this cultural trend, and its social causes and conditions are numerous, but it is a demonstrable fact of contemporary American society.

## 3. ULTIMATE CORE OF AMERICAN VALUES

The American society contains so many diverse groups and categories, and the American culture contains so many diverse value orientations, that at first glance it would appear impossible to find a core of values on which all Americans agree. Nevertheless, there are certain ideas and beliefs that are widely manifested in external patterns of behavior. If we abstract from these, we find that which is considered important by the majority of our people. This is the value system.

In spite of the differences in religion, race, ethnic background, economic status, and regional subcultures, most Americans would subscribe to these values. This is what we mean by an "ultimate core" of values, a series of major themes running through the culture. In combination, they are typically American, although each will be found to some degree in other cultures also. They are ultimate, not in any absolute sense, but in the sense that they are the highest common denominators of what the people hold in high esteem.

a. The value of a rational approach to life is almost universally accepted among Americans. This is seen in the constant endeavor to reexamine concepts and practices of the social system and to seek more reasonable, time-saving, and effort-saving ways of doing things. We have been called an engineering civilization, intent on applying science to the control of nature and to the solution of all problems. There is still, of course, much folklore and superstition and many irrationalities and inconsistencies in our culture, but the dominant approach is a scientific one.

b. Closely allied to the rational approach is an emphasis on the value of progress. A belief in the perfectibility of society, culture, and personality has been a kind of driving force in our history. Americans have faith in the future, not as the simple evolutionary passage of time, but as a period in which human effort can be successfully applied to the solution of problems. The important aspect here is the American state of mind, willing to accept change and experimentation; it is a kind of national attitude that change induced by intelligent effort is bound to be good.

c. The value of individual success is greatly stressed as an accompaniment of the rational approach to progress. We have seen that success is often measured by material and pecuniary rewards, but this does not mean that success is valued only when it is achieved through business and economic efforts. The so-called self-made man or woman may be a physician, an athlete, or a beauty queen as well as a biochemist or a physicist. For the most part success is valued as a result of achievement, but there is also a wide acknowledgement that the "breaks" play a part on the road to success.

**d.** A high value is placed upon work in the American culture. One of the principal criteria of a man's worth is "what he does," that is, his functional utility to society. The drive to work has in the past amounted almost to a compulsion among Americans. With the national increase in material comfort, success, and leisure this compulsive aspect of work has lessened somewhat in the individual, but there is still a general emphasis on activity, on "getting things done." The foreign observer is always struck with the hustle and bustle of American cities.

**e.** One of the few traditions of the relatively young American culture is its emphasis on the value of freedom for the individual. The recognition of the intrinsic qualities of man—his moral responsibility, his inviolability, and his dignity as a creature of God has been typical of our value system. Freedom no longer means merely a release from political restraints and economic coercion. Freedom for both the individual and the society is almost universally accepted as a value among Americans even though it is sometimes violated.

Many other facets of American social behavior also give a clue to our core of ultimate values, but most of them appear to be correlated with those we have already mentioned. The curious combination and balance of the two central values of materialism and humanitarianism indicate the American faith in both physical and social perfectibility. They show also the intention of a free society to work hard, successfully, and scientifically to achieve progress.

## 4. VALUE IDEOLOGIES

While it is possible to talk in general and often vague

terms about the American value ideology, it is also necessary to realize that a pluralistic culture like ours reflects
various ideologies. The contrasting subsystems of values
are sometimes interpreted as class differences (proletariat
versus bourgeois) or racial differences (white versus
Black) or religious differences (Christian versus Moslem).
There is no doubt that values, or the strength of value adherence, are differently emphasized according to one's
position in status, racial, and religious categories.

Cutting across all these subsystems of values, however,
is another broad division of ideologies. This used to be
a rough distinction between traditionalists and conservatives on one side, with the liberals and progressives on
the other side. A third ideology, that of radicalism, has
had relatively few supporters although it has sporadically
been suspect of potential danger to the American way of
life. A new wave of interest in radicalism arose in the late
1960s, promoted not by the working class, as may be
expected in a capitalistic society, but by student groups
of largely bourgeois background.

Let us examine some aspects of these three ideologies—
conservative, liberal, and radical.

a. In a rapidly changing sociocultural system these three
ideologies appear to have differing interpretations of social
change. Conservatives are reluctant to allow any changes,
except in some instances change back to earlier traditions.
Liberals feel that every change should be made on a basis
of rational discourse and popular consensus. Radicals promote immediate change, forcibly if necessary, but by
whatever means may prove effective.

b. Obviously, the proponents of all three ideologies place
a great value on the morality of their position. There is
a curious similarity between conservatives and radicals
in that they both tend to be moral absolutists. It is no
accident that both conservatives and radicals tend to ex-
communicate people who do not hold strictly the respective basic ideology; they do not allow revisionists within
the ranks, and they cannot tolerate outside opponents.
The liberal ideology is morally relative and logically tolerant. Ideally, its proponents insist on the moral right of

both liberals and antiliberals to hold different value positions.

**c.** Any value ideology intending to win support among the American people must contain a clear concept of individual freedom. The conservative philosophy is in many ways peculiarly like the "rugged individualism" that was much advertised at the turn of the century and which usually meant that those who enjoyed power also enjoyed freedom. The radical position sees individual freedom restrained by the large demands of the society. In the name of ultimate freedom for all it requires immediate obedience of all members of society. The liberal ideology appears to allow the greatest latitude and is in the ambivalent position of protecting the liberty of both conservatives and radicals.

**d.** Value ideologies differ also in their views of social structure. The conservatives place emphasis on stability and permanence of structure; they seem to think that the organizational program of the Founding Fathers was perpetually valid and not to be tampered with. The radicals are impatient with all structures. They cry for destruction, rather than reconstruction, of the establishment, the institution, the system. The liberal ideology calls for planning and social engineering, assuming generally that all social structures are reformable and flexible.

**e.** The evaluation of the human being, the social person, must be a basic ingredient of any large social ideology, and we assume that the whole sociocultural system is instrumental for the benefit of mankind. Both the conservatives and the radicals seem to look with suspicion on the ordinary citizen as a weak person who needs constant guidance and restraints. The common man is not to be trusted for either intelligence or good will. Here again the liberal ideology has a different point of view, placing great faith in the so-called common sense of the people, assuming in some vague way that the great majority of citizens are dependable, intelligent, and competent.

These are admittedly rough comparisons of the general values contained in the conservative, radical, and liberal ideologies. Any attempt to present a brief digest of these broad value systems is open to the criticism of oversimplification. Objections can be raised at any point because there is often disagreement among the spokesmen within each of the three systems, and this is itself characteristic of the open quality of American values.

## 5. SOCIAL PROBLEMS

It appears to be the nature of American society that it constantly creates social problems. This statement may discourage those who feel that social science should be a tool for the alleviation of social problems. But, given the characteristics of American values, it is logical to assume that our social problems will never completely disappear. In a sense it is also the lesson of history that problems are inevitable concomitants of society.

This is, of course, a matter of degree. A relatively static culture may strive for and achieve a kind of permanent good order in which there are few major disturbances. Primitives tend to accept the facts of social life in a way that is impossible for contemporary Americans. One of the dominant notes of our culture is a belief in perfectibility and in the necessity for attempting to achieve it. A dynamic society whose sights are always being raised must inevitably continue to have social problems.

a. The rising level of education in the United States has contributed to the recognition of social problems. This recognition is a specific part of the curriculum in the expanding area of social science. In this kind of culture the inquiring mind projects into the future. Data are available in more abundant detail, and no area of dislocation and disorganization has been left unexplored. Americans now know more about social facts than ever before. While it is true that social science adheres to the discovery, analysis, and discussion of social facts, the student of social science, as an interested citizen, also dwells almost necessarily upon the social possibilities for the future.

Education in increasing amounts helps to make Americans dissatisfied with present conditions. It not only recognizes social problems but in this sense it tends to "create" them. Large numbers of educated persons seek for themselves a greater participation in American values, but they also promote those values for the whole society. It is no accident that the American intellectual has larger dreams of a better society than the proletarian social reformer could ever envision.

**b.** Technological progress has been another large factor in the area of sociological problems. This refers principally to scientific inventions, the creation of material things, and the constant drive to make better things in better ways. But technology also affects and is applicable to social organization. The need to readjust oneself, not once but often, to the changing demands of invention and production prevents the achievement of a permanently stabilized social order. It holds out a challenge to our society to reestablish the balance between our technical possibilities and our real patterns of behavior.

**c.** Rising material standards of living have also held out to the American people new notions of what "ought to be" and what "can be." This is partly the result of the characteristic American mastery of physical nature and the basic fact that our country is endowed with tremendous natural resources. Many factors, however, besides nature and technology have contributed to the constant rise in living standards. The channels of communication have made known the possibilities, and an excellent transportation system has brought them to remote places.

In combination, these three factors—education, technology, and material standards—have been aimed at the satisfaction of the social and cultural needs of the American people. In the very act of improving social conditions there has been a refinement and elevation of the criteria by which social conditions are measured. These criteria are values. The gap between social values and social conditions, which gives meaning to the concept of social problems, has not been closed. Both levels have been raised and the social problems remain.

The discrepancy between social values and social conditions is the difference between "what ought to be" and "what is." The sociologist studies both as social facts, and notes that their relationship constantly moves to a higher

level. As things improve we aspire for more. Standards
of living our grandfathers tried to attain have been
reached and surpassed. Their values have been transmitted to us, but we have raised them to higher levels.
Our dynamic social philosophy apparently demands that
the distance between values and conditions never be
bridged.

## Suggested Readings

Jacob, Philip E. *Changing Values in College.* New York:
Harper & Row, 1957.

Kohn, Melvin L. *Class, Occupations and Values.* Homewood: Dorsey, 1969.

Lynd, Robert S. *Knowledge for What?* Princeton: Princeton University Press, 1939.

Morris, Charles. *Varieties of Human Value.* Chicago:
University of Chicago Press, 1956.

Perry, R. B. *Realms of Value: A Critique of Civilization.*
Cambridge: Harvard University Press, 1954.

Scott, William. *Values and Organizations.* Chicago: Rand
McNally, 1965.

# 13
# Mobility

MOBILITY IS A SOCIAL PHENOMENON GAINING MORE and more attention from both scientific and lay observers in the modern world. In its most general interpretation, mobility refers to any movement or migration of people in time, in physical space, or in a social structure. The term is not used by social scientists to refer to a social movement, which is defined as a concerted, continuous, organized agitation of a group with a program directed toward social goals. A mass movement, or a movement for social reform, is not included under the heading of either physical or social mobility.

Obviously all mobility must occur in time and place, but there is a difference between physical and social mobility. The latter refers to a change of social status by a person or group. We have already discussed status and stratification, and we are aware that positions in the social structure are higher or lower in relation to one another. Movement upward or downward among these social positions is called social mobility.

Physical mobility is usually called migration. It is the movement of people from one geographical spot to another, and it is a phenomenon of increasing frequency in modern society. It includes forced relocation of large groups of people, eviction and dispossession of unwanted people, voluntary permanent migration from one country to another or from one region to another within the same country, as well as local residential change. Travel for business or pleasure, shopping trips, daily commuting to office or factory—these constitute physical movement from place to place, but are not studied either as migration or as mobility.

## TYPES OF GEOGRAPHICAL MIGRATION

History is filled with accounts of the migrations of peoples. These have been of two general kinds, voluntary and forced. The voluntary movement of people from one geographical area to another is determined by numerous factors; since it is a free movement, its effects upon the persons involved are quite different from those of forced migration. This latter type of movement takes several forms: the expulsion of unwanted people, the herding of people into reservations and concentration camps, the transportation of enslaved individuals and groups.

Geographical mobility always implies movement over a physical distance and is often from one country to another. Internal mobility, that is, movement within the territorial boundaries of a nation, is also of great sociological significance. There are few nomadic peoples, such as herdsmen and hunters, in the modern world, but most large countries include groups of migratory workers, journeymen, peddlers, gypsies, circus people, farm harvesters, and so forth. These are permanent itinerants who have no fixed domicile and who move mainly for economic reasons.

In large industrial societies there is an almost continuous movement of people out of the rural areas into towns and cities. This voluntary one-directional mobility is selective. Women tend to move to commercial cities and men to centers of heavy industry, and most of those who move are young adults. International migrants have most often been individuals while internal migrants tend to move as whole families. There are, however, many exceptions to both these statements. There appears to be no convincing evidence that the energetic (or conversely the shiftless and unsuccessful) migrate more than other people.

## REASONS FOR VOLUNTARY MIGRATION

The reasons why people move from one country or region to another are numerous and complex. Traditionally, the economic factor has been a major influence, whether one speaks of nomads seeking better food supplies, workers looking for better jobs, or families trying to improve their material standard of living. The decreasing need for agricultural workers tends to push people out of rural areas, while increasing industrialization pulls them toward opportunities in large population centers and the desire for better living-conditions attracts them to the suburbs.

Many noneconomic factors also motivate mobility. People have migrated to escape political oppression and racial discrimination; they have migrated in search of a place where they could enjoy religious liberty. Families sometimes change their residence to take advantage of better educational facilities for their children, or to be closer to congenial friends and relatives. Migrants often follow a pattern in moving to those places where their previous neighbors and acquaintances now live.

### EFFECTS OF MIGRATION

The migration of people from one place to another has various effects upon the migrants themselves and on the groups and structures into which they move. Historically, the most significant result of migration has been the diffusion of culture. It has meant contact and communication between peoples who had been culturally and geographically isolated. Patterns of behavior have been exchanged, new ideas have been combined, and culture has been enriched and expanded. This does not mean that the mingling of people has always been a peaceful process or that it produced immediate social progress.

Cultural diffusion and convergence occur when people migrate, intermarry, and interbreed. Racial stock that has been preserved through centuries of isolation is mingled with other racial strains as a result of geographical mobility. The notion of a "pure race" in large contemporary societies has been discarded by social scientists. Biological mixtures have always resulted through migration, whether this was invasion and conquest, peaceful wandering, or deliberate colonization. In the most mobile of the large societies, ethnic strains become entangled and cannot be traced back more than a few generations.

The effect of internal migration in large modern societies has been urbanization of the culture. Urban ways of thinking and acting, urban social relations and structures, and increasing secondary associations reach more and more of the population as people crowd into the cities. City families are smaller and the urban birthrate is lower than that of rural areas. The sex ratio tends to decrease, that is, there are fewer males than females, as the population becomes more urbanized. Medical, educational, and recreational facilities become more available for the people.

The effect of migration on the individual varies according to social situations. The migrant does not always find himself a complete stranger in his new environment. He usually moves into localities in which his "own kind" are already living. For this reason, urban neighborhoods can often be identified by the ethnic, religious, or other similarities of the people in them. Even in the most open society two or more generations are required before the migrants are assimilated into the general population. In the early stages of this assimilative process the migrant is often a marginal person but not a total stranger to either his previous or his present environment.

## TYPES OF SOCIAL MOBILITY

Geographical mobility is movement in physical space while social mobility is movement of people from one social position or stratum to another. We have previously seen that every group or society has a social structure in which persons and positions are at different levels of stratification. Conceptually, the parts of the structure are both coordinated and distant from one another, and social mobility may be defined as any shifting of position within the structure.

From the point of view of direction of change in position, social mobility is classified as horizontal or vertical. Horizontal mobility means movement back and forth on the same social level from one similar social group or situation to another. Theoretically, people of the same social class have access to one another because they share roughly in the same degree the same criteria of status. Concretely, however, especially in large population concentrations, various "social sets" on the same plane do not always have social relations with one another. The permanent movement of an individual from one set to another is horizontal social movement.

This horizontal mobility is significant to the persons immediately involved in the movement because they have changed the set of people with whom they associate. The manner in which the social personality adapts itself to new people is not difficult or demanding if the persons involved are really in the same social class. One sees this smooth transition frequently in the marriage of people whose families, though strangers to each other, are in the same social class. Since there are often fine shadings of distinction among subclasses in the same general stratum, this change may also often involve a certain degree of vertical mobility.

Vertical mobility is a more widely discussed and more significant type of movement than horizontal mobility. It is defined as the movement of people from one social status to another, from one class to another. The factors and conditions for vertical mobility are more numerous and complex than those involved in the relatively simple movement along the same social plane. Obviously, vertical social mobility can be either upward or downward. The person may shift to a higher status, or he may slip to a lower status, and the difference between the two can be deeply significant to the individual.

ROLE MOBLIITY

The social personality is defined as the sum of all the social roles an individual enacts. Since the individual is the social person in action, and since people usually perform one function at a time, there is necessarily a shifting from role to role. This is what we mean by role mobility. If we observe the individual in action, we find that this type of mobility may be analyzed on three levels.

a. Every person enacts multiple roles even while he remains a total integrated personality. Each different group in which he participates calls for the enactment of a different role. In the course of a day the husband and father shifts from these familial roles to his economic and recreational roles, perhaps also to his political and religious roles, and then back again to his familial roles. Through constant repetition as well as through knowledge and interest in the various functions and goals of the different groups the individual usually makes these transitions smoothly and consistently. This kind of role mobility is so commonplace that it is not noticed until a person breaks down or becomes frustrated by conflicting demands of the different roles.

**b.** A second observable type of role mobility is the normal successive assumption of new roles. During the course of lifelong socialization the individual person develops gradually from role to role. In early childhood he first learns familial and recreational roles, then the formal patterns of the educational and religious roles, and somewhat latter undertakes the obligations of the economic and political roles. He assumes new roles again when he marries and becomes a parent. Obviously this assumption of new roles does not mean the abandonment of previously learned roles. The social personality, as we have seen, contains many roles and the point we make here is that the principal social roles are assumed, or learned, successively and not simultaneously.

**c.** A third kind of shifting of roles is that of occupational mobility, characteristic of the large, modern, urban and industrial society. Sociologists have commented most upon the vertical aspect within the economic structure: upward mobility by promotion from job to job, or downward mobility by demotion. With the specialization of functions there are refinements of strata within both the blue-collar and white-collar categories. Since the occupational role is frequently the key role for the individual, and the main criterion upon which his family's social status depends, it is given attention as an instrument of general upward social mobility. The person who starts as an office boy and works his way up to the presidency of a company is the old-fashioned American example of occupational success.

Occupational mobility is often also relatively horizontal, a shifting from one kind of job to another. The high-school teacher gets a job as insurance salesman. The factory laborer becomes a taxicab driver. The medical technician gives up her position to become a private secretary. People in the learned professions, however, do not often shift to another profession, although there are some cases of movement into a second career. When we say that an industrial society develops and requires a mobile labor force, we are speaking not only of the ability to migrate from one place to another, but also of this willingness to shift to different types of lower-echelon employment. Perhaps no society has exemplified this kind of role mobility as much as the American society has in its occupational system.

## CIRCULATION OF THE ELITE

Since mobility goes in two directions, people from the upper classes descend socially while people from the lower classes move upward. This is an oversimplification if it is applied to the social mobility of an individual person within his own lifetime. The mere fact that family background is one of the criteria of social status seems to demand more than one generation as a time span in which an extreme change can occur. This is true even in an open-class society and is logically more the case in traditional, rigidly stratified societies.

It is sometimes asserted that an open-class society with much upward mobility disintegrates relatively quickly. According to this hypothesis, the "best" people fail to reproduce themselves, lose their social vigor, and become degenerate and disorganized, so that they and their progeny "disappear," or slip from their high status. Into their places move people from the lower classes, people who are not endowed with noble character, social awareness, and leadership qualities. Behind the hypothesis are certain biological assumptions about the inheritance of innate abilities, as well as psychological simplifications concerning the lower mentality of the masses.

This theory is not only unpopular in modern democratic societies, but it appears to have been disproved by the experiences of countries like Canada and the United

States. The children and grandchildren of uneducated, lower class, white immigrants have moved into the middle and upper classes without any apparent detriment to or "degeneration" of the society. Biological and psychological testings have dispelled the old-fashioned notion that class or race accounts for innate tendencies toward intelligence or morality. Social scientists generally agree that the concept of the "elite" is a culture-bound concept, varying in meaning from one people to another.

It must be pointed out that social mobility is not a continuous uninterrupted movement but one that proceeds by stages. It is somewhat analogous to the physical movement of people from farm to small town to large city to suburbs. It requires time, even in a relatively dynamic society; and upward mobility tends to be that of families rather than of individuals. Furthermore, the great majority of persons remain in relatively the same social status all their lives, moving neither upward nor downward. The exceptions are those who have been able to take advantage of opportunities for personal achievement.

## CHANNELS OF MOBILITY

As we have seen, social status is measured by a combination of criteria so that the person has a position in the total community and society. Social status, however, is not a mere abstraction. It is exemplified in and through people who are in association with others. The channels of mobility are the actual groups in which the individual participates. A person moves upward or downward only in relation to other persons with whom he is in some way associated and who can observe and judge the extent to which he possesses the highly valued cultural criteria.

In the major groups of every society there is successful and unsuccessful social striving. It is here that the individual enacts his social roles, and since his roles require the total personality they provide an opportunity for the scrutiny and judgment of social status of the whole person. The individual becomes the head of a family, the president of a college, the governor of a state, the bishop of a church. Whatever function he performs within these groups, he is seen to advance or regress in relation to other functioning individuals.

It must be further noted that these groups, like the individual himself, exist in concrete societies. We have seen that social mobility is relatively restricted in the communal type of society and relatively available in the associational type of society. This means that mobility does not go on at the same rate, and it does not affect the same proportion of people in all parts of any large society. The differences of rate and proportion do not rest in the individual so much as in the type of social and cultural environment around him.

Usually the stable, rural, village community does not have great class differences or a wide range of status. In the large industrial and commercial cities the number of positions and the opportunities for change are usually very great. In an associational society, dominated by the economic institutions, occupational mobility is an important criterion of shifting class position. This mobility is not always upward, especially where the institutionalization of occupational roles requires large assemblages of clerks, typists, stenographers, machine-tenders, and other semiskilled workers. People often get stranded permanently in one of these occupational categories.

Briefly stated, the urban milieu is more favorable for upward social mobility than the rural. The stratification system is greater in the sense that there are more layers or strata and a large differential from the top to the bottom. City people usually emphasize achievement of status more than ascription of status. This, together with the fact that the rewards are more numerous, motivates urban people to strive for higher status. Finally, the numerous secondary associations and groups open up more channels of upward mobility in the city.

## FACTORS OF UPWARD MOBILITY

We have seen that the various criteria of social status are intimately bound up with the social values existing in a culture. The possession of these valued criteria is the measurable determinant of the particular social status of the individual. It is obvious that the person who is striving for upward' mobility must have access to the objects that give high status. The conditions that help or hinder this access may be called the factors of mobility.

For any particular individual who has the personal abilities as well as the desire for upward mobility, the following conditioning factors must be taken into consideration. They exist, of course, in combination but any one of them may be more important than the others at a given time and place.

a. The policy and practice of immigration into a total society and into a local community will greatly affect the possibilities of upward mobility. If the immigrants are numerous and if they are mainly working people from abroad or from rural areas, they usually come in at the "bottom" of the social structure. This almost automatically pushes up some of the local natives and long-term residents so that they rise in social status.

b. Differential fertility of the social classes is also an important conditioning factor of mobility. It is sometimes said that there is "always room at the top," and this is probably true of occupational status in an expanding economy. In the general social structure, however, the upper class is always small. If these people have large families, the upward mobility of the lower classes is slowed down; if they do not reproduce themselves, mobility is accelerated.

c. The presence or absence of individual competition as a value in the culture significantly affects mobility. If competition is valued, there must be goals for which the successful competitor can strive. There must be opportunities for status advancement and social prestige for the "self-made" man. A competitive society actually encourages upward mobility but it also permits downward mobility of unsuccessful persons.

d. The availability of opportunities to prepare oneself for the competitive process is a secondary factor. If education is universally obtainable it may act as a shortcut to upward mobility in the sense that the individual can prepare himself for the business and professional roles that carry high prestige. It is necessary of course that the occupational positions be opened to those who best qualify for them.

**e.** The patterns of equality and inequality in a society have much to do with the chances of social mobility. If there is a categorical attitude of discrimination against a racial, religious, or ethnic minority, upward mobility will be slow, if not impossible, for people in these categories. Inequality of treatment on the basis of age and sex is also a hindrance as, for example, when young persons and women are held back from opportunities for advancement in role and status.

These factors must be studied in combination, as they function in real social situations. It may be said that the possibilities for upward mobility for the individual are greatest in a society in which the lower classes are increasing either by immigration or by birth and the upper classes are not reproducing themselves, and in which competition is encouraged and the opportunities for self-improvement are available to all without discrimination. Conversely, the degree to which these factors are absent from a society will indicate the lack of upward mobility.

MOBILITY AND SOCIAL PERSONALITY

To the extent that higher social status is the result of personal achievement there are as many channels of mobility as there are social roles the person enacts. The competence of the individual must be tested in the social groups in which he participates. Since each person has a key role, this is usually the one in which he does the most to achieve status, but all the groups and roles are possible avenues of mobility. A woman may move into a higher class by marriage or by competence in a profession. A man may achieve status through his political or educational activities.

Striving for higher status is often accompanied by certain strains and frustrations for the individual person. For example, it is not enough for him to have abilities, he must also show results that can be measured in terms of the cultural values. Results are particularly pertinent in the occupational role but are also necessary in political, religious, and other social roles. Furthermore, it is not always true that ability and efficiency are rewarded with higher prestige. There are frustrating situations for an individual in which another person is rewarded on the basis of unearned privileges that have little relation to his competence.

Another source of frustration occurs when the individual simply does not have the competence to achieve higher status even though he may have a desire and a drive for it, and the social pressure for upward mobility may be very strong. The demands and the expectations of group life are often "too much" for this type of individual. The competitive process in which social mobility is worked out is also a strain for him. Competition implies some rough equality among the competitors, and the less competent person finds himself pushed beyond his limitations. He desires higher status and the rewards that accompany it and he is frustrated in his failure to achieve it.

The attempt to achieve higher status in competitive groups sometimes results in an unbalanced social personality. This occurs usually when the key role, the main instrument of higher prestige for any individual, is emphasized at the expense of the other social roles. A balanced social personality does not imply that the individual's time, interests, and efforts must be distributed equally among all the social roles. This is sociologically unnecessary and psychologically impossible. The imbalance occurs when the individual neglects the demands of lesser social roles in order to concentrate on those functions and activities through which he can more successfully achieve upward mobility.

It must be observed that downward social mobility also carries its own social and personal costs. People who are "left behind" in the competitive struggle for social status, or who slip to a lower class, suffer strains, frustrations, and disappointments. If this happens in later adulthood, the person finds adaptation and readjustment to his new position very difficult. The "genteel poor" and the disillusioned clingers to the upper class suffer from this phenomenon.

### COMPENSATION FOR DOWNWARD MOBILITY

We must remember that social mobility is characteristic of the open, associational type of society and that social stability characterizes the closed, communal type. Since neither upward nor downward movement occurs to any extent in the latter kind of social structure, the strains and frustrations, rewards and compensations, are seldom present in it. On the other hand, "standing still" socially, or merely holding one's own, can be a frustrating experience in an associational society; and downward mobility is usually a disturbing experience.

Certain compensations, however, appear to be built into the cultural values of a society in which upward mobility is expected but in which the expectations cannot be universally realized. For example, the presence of large ethnic and racial minorities in the society assures the individual that he still has an appreciable degree of social status. Furthermore, the individual may still identify himself subjectively with the higher social status even though he has actually lost the objective criteria by which that status is measured.

a. The disappointments and frustrations of downward mobility are cushioned somewhat by the traditional conservatism of the middle class. This is especially true in societies where the middle class is large and important, and where many members of the middle class have satisfying recent memories of having risen out of the lower classes. The inclination toward conformity and the satisfactions that come from it help to compensate for some loss of social status by those who were formerly of a higher class. There are both strength and consolation in the fact that numbers of others share one's own social experiences.

b. Resentment over loss of status may never completely disappear from the individual, but it is modified by the fact that he need have little contact with his former associates of higher status. Constant association with people on the same social level can be satisfying for the normal personality. The demands of society are that everyone adjust himself to reality, and this adjustment is made largely subconsciously through social relations in real situations. The human environment, the presence of people who have similar aspirations and problems, tremendously influences a person to accept reality.

c. There is often also a rationalization of downward social mobility that helps to soothe the ego. A person in this situation may feel that there have been miscarriages of social assignment, that some people who have achieved higher status have not done so through honest effort and competence, and that some of those who have slipped from higher status have done so through no fault of their own. A curious twist to this rationalization is the opinion that the maintenance of social status is not worth all the trouble and worry it requires.

d. It is a compensation also for the person who has suffered downward mobility in a large industrialized society that there is little significant status visibility. The quality of his clothing may be different from that of higher-status persons but the style of clothing is seldom a mark of status. Unlike in a rigid, closed social structure, there are no caste marks on either the person or his possessions in an open, associational type of society. Many of the public activities and most of the public facilities are available to the persons of all social classes.

e. Finally, consolation derives from the belief that one's children may regain the social status that one has himself lost. A decrease in social prestige may be more or less permanent for the older person who has suffered it, but in an open-class society there is a strong drive to give children the advantages parents did not have or have lost. To the extent that parents attempt to "live again" in their children, they often spend less effort in improving or maintaining their own social status than they do in providing opportunities and advantages for their offspring's social progress. In this effort there is satisfaction for the person who has suffered downward social mobility.

## American Mobility

### 1. MOBILITY WITHIN THE CHURCH

The major social groups are the principal channels in which and through which upward social mobility takes place. One of the chief criteria of social status is functional utility, and since the American culture is dominated by economic institutions, most people think of their gainful occupation as the main index of social status. Because of this emphasis, there has been a neglect and perhaps a misunderstanding of other important groups in which upward mobility is possible.

The religious groups of the American society present a varied and complex area of research in this regard. A religious body obviously has a social structure, and the church members have possibilities for vertical social mobility within the structure. There are different strata within the official and formal organization of the church, and there are also certain informal criteria according to which social status is measured. A significant difference exists between the Catholic and the Protestant social structure, and some differences exist among the varieties of Protestant organizations.

In the social structure of the Catholic church there is a clear-cut distinction between the laity and the professional functionaries. The priesthood and sisterhood are traditional arrangements through which the individual "leaves the world" and is "set apart" from the laity. The persons who function professionally in these systems have a relatively high social status among their fellow Catholics. Although changes are occurring in this regard, such persons usually have a distinctive garb, are bound by sacred obligations, follow a certain rule of life, and receive deference, respect, and financial support from the laity.

There is less distinction between laity and ministry in Protestant and Jewish religious bodies, although the person who dedicates himself to God in these religions has higher status than the laity. There is a great variation depending upon other criteria of status: type and amount of education, attitudes toward wealth and family background, the kind of stratification within the religious body, and the social status the particular religion itself enjoys in the society.

The diocesan priesthood in the Catholic church is a striking example of opportunities for upward mobility within a religious structure. Theoretically, any competent boy from the lowest social class can be accepted into the seminary, receive holy orders, and climb to the highest position in the ecclesiastical structure. This is a peculiar characteristic of a church in which the son of an illiterate peasant can become pope. This potential mobility demands, of course, that the individual possess certain moral and intellectual qualities, specific kinds of knowledge and virtue, and an adaptive personality.

The concept of a "hereditary" ministry and of the influence of family on the admission and rise of the religious functionary also shows variations. It is not uncommon to find that a rabbi is a descendant of a long line of rabbinical ancestors. It is possible also for the son of a Protestant minister to follow in his father's footsteps. In the Catholic church the long-established custom of celibacy among priests, brothers, and sisters has prevented the establishment of hereditary privileges or of a self-perpetuating caste. In the United States the recruitment of candidates to the Catholic religious status is from all strata of society and not limited to any particular social class.

The Negro Protestant churches are a dramatic example of the extent to which social status can be achieved not only within the religious structure as such but also in the large community. The Negro preacher has long been an important figure as a leader among the people. The ministry itself has been an avenue to higher status for some who have become educators, labor leaders, civic leaders, and political officials. Many factors have made the religious group more important for Negroes than for whites, and this importance of the church has often attracted the socially aspiring and the more competent persons.

Since the laity form the largest portion of any religious body, the questions of religious mobility must include them. An interested, able, and active Protestant lay person has many avenues by which to raise his social status within the church. While there are many professional functionaries—bishops, superintendents, and ministers—there is also a wide opportunity for lay persons to participate directly in the activities of the church. Lay boards of administration with full power to fix policies, make rules, manage finances, and even with some power to influence moral and dogmatic teachings, are common among Protestant groups.

These opportunities for the upward mobility of lay persons appear to be more available in the congregational type of structure than in the presbyterian, and also in the sect or cult than in the denomination. Generally speaking, we may say that the religious body in which the status differential between the laity and the religious functionary is smallest is also the one in which the laity is allowed the greatest amount of direct participation in church affairs, but it is also one in which there is the least potential range of religious status.

There appears to be no comparable ladder of social mobility for the laity of the Catholic church. From a functional point of view there are few status-giving actions that the laity can perform. Until recently the lay person was not permitted within the sanctuary or in the pulpit; he has no voice in ecclesiastical government, and in the United States he has no direct participation in the administration of church properties.

To the extent that status is achieved through functions, the Catholic laity is at best an adjunct and auxiliary to the clergy. The able lawyer, physician, educator, and businessman, however, can make important auxiliary contributions to the nonsacred functions of the church. Since the ultimate responsibilities and decisions are in the hands of the clergy, these contributions can be advisory or they can be services under direction. Upward mobility, therefore, appears to be possible only for the laity who competently perform permitted actions in cooperation with the clergy.

This brief survey of the variant structure of American churches indicates how a prearranged stratified system affects the possibilities for upward mobility within a given religious body. The contrast is greatest within the Catholic church, where there exists no higher role and status for the layman but where any diocesan clergyman, starting from the lowest ecclesiastical status, may reach the highest possible position. The Protestant churches in general have much more direct lay participation in church affairs and provide both roles and status of high order for laymen. The Negro Protestant churches have an even greater advantage for both laity and clergy because they often provide a starting point for higher social status in the nonreligious groups.

## 2. DECLASSED PEOPLE

The concept of an organized social structure of status and class has no room for persons who have no social prestige and who are, as it were, outside the pale of society. The practice of ostracism is an ancient one, but the people so affected have usually been able to carry on their social relations in other groups within the larger society. In the United States there are at least three categories of people who are declassed, although they are commonly assigned by many observers to the lowest class. They are the habitual criminals, the hoboes, and the city bums.

a. Habitual criminals have been the subject of some intense sociological research in recent years. They constitute a large category of declassed people and suffer the accompanying disesteem, especially when they are in prison. Often enough, however, they do have connections "on the outside" even while they are serving their prison terms. With cooperation, effort, and a certain amount of good fortune, they may be able to regain their lost social status with their family and associates in the approved social structure.

Criminal society operates in ways similar to that of the normal social structure. It contains people of higher and lower social status, and some of the criteria employed in noncriminal society to determine social status are also used in it. Since, however, these people have much contact, communication, and social relations with noncriminals, and since much of their behavior is normal social behavior, it is difficult in every instance to term them outcasts, or declassed people. It appears that this term would be appropriate only when the individual has been removed from the larger society and is confined in prison.

**b.** Hoboes are vagrants who move about the country with no steady means of support. They drift from one place to another and perhaps take an odd job occasionally, but they are not like the migrant workers we have discussed above because they work as seldom as possible. They hitch rides on trucks and freight trains and are forced to take makeshift sleeping and eating arrangements wherever they are.

Most hoboes are only temporary tramps. They are usually unmarried males from twenty to thirty-five years old. During the economic depression of the thirties there were vagrants who were older than this, and there was also a considerable number of female hoboes. Generally speaking, the hardships of this kind of life are such that only younger men are able and willing to endure them.

The hobo is only temporarily declassed. Since he possesses so few of the criteria of social status, he is looked down upon by the more stable members of society. He does not associate with "respectable" persons in normal social relations. He is unwanted by people in any social class and he is harrassed by railroad detectives, state police, and town officials. Nevertheless, the hobo almost always has some place to which he can return, some connections with family or friends through whom he can again establish his social status and social relations.

It is to be expected that a restless, dynamic population like that of the United States would produce a certain number of "drop-outs" even during periods of economic prosperity. This is seen in the relatively recent phenomenon of "hippies" and self-styled "flower children" who remove themselves from conventional society and sometimes attempt to establish a less "artificial" mode of living. They are more likely than hoboes to associate in groups of people who share their philosophy of deliberate social protest. Like the hobo, however, they tend eventually to "come off the road" and settle down to normal living. Whether the spirit of adventure has been satisfied, or whether the hardships are too great, or whatever the reason, they reenter the social class system.

c. The city bum is quite a different phenomenon. He is usually a homeless male over fifty years of age. Since he has no post office address, no fixed domicile, no gainful employment, and no membership in formal social organizations, it is difficult to estimate the number of such men. City police estimate that there are thousands in every large American city. The city bum has experienced downward social mobility to its lowest terminal. He has skidded to the bottom of the social structure and is in some ways even outside the lowest social class.

Every large city in the United States has a Skid Row, a locality into which have drifted the social "has-beens." It is a terminal place. No one starts there; no one is born on Skid Row. It is the place where dirty and unkempt men, most of them suffering from malnutrition and alcoholism and dependent on the charity of others for food and shelter, live out their declining years in misery. Rescue missions have done much to alleviate their sufferings and are occasionally successful in reclaiming individuals to normal social living.

Skid Row is not the urban slum or ethnic neighborhood, which as we have seen has a certain degree of social organization, although it may be in the same physical place. Skid Row is an aggregate of people who have been heartlessly called the "offscouring" of society. Their personal histories show that each of them has descended from a previously higher social status. Some have been successful business and professional men; all have been at least accepted and acceptable members of society. They constitute the extreme American example of downward social mobility.

We have discussed these three categories of declassed people mainly from the point of view of social class, status, and mobility. They are social deviants also in some of the external manifestations of behavior. These people have gone through the socialization process in American society, and they can never completely release themselves from the influence of American culture. Even though they violate many of the mores and folkways and are visited with the negative social sanction that these violations entail, their basic behavior patterns are at least residually American. In this sense they still share in the American culture.

### 3. Education and Social Mobility

The amount and kind of education a person has constitute one of the most important criteria of social status, and this is basically in agreement with the fact of social mobility. Educational requirements are rising in all the major social groups, and most of the social roles in the American industrial society demand technical knowledge and competence. From the point of view of social mobility, however, there is a difference of educational effect upon those who receive education and those who dispense it.

a. Those who receive education may use it as a stepping-stone to higher social status. The elementary-school system, both public and private, has been a means of rapid socialization for immigrant children. Similarly, the city schools are now extremely helpful to the children of migrants from rural areas. In this way the school is a kind of short-cut agency for upward mobility, more effective than the family, neighborhood, or church. It provides the basic knowledge and training without which one could hardly hold his own, much less move upward.

Several other educational factors must be taken into consideration. One is the amount of education the individual has—a college degree has become almost an imperative in contemporary American society. The master's and doctor's degrees add significant prestige only in specialized and professional areas. Another factor is the content of the education; it is probably true that a person who majors in science or business, rather than in philosophy or the humanities, has a better instrument for future mobility. Similarly, the choice of a college or university is important since some have in themselves higher prestige than others.

**b.** Those who teach are affected differently, for they actually achieve their social status within the educational groups. Several serious changes have recently occurred in teaching. The social prestige of the teacher and educator is no longer as high, in comparison with other occupational statuses, as it once was. It appears that as the general level of education rises the American people no longer look upon the teacher with the same awe and respect.

Partly as a consequence of his lowered respect there are not so many young people who aspire to be teachers. This is due to other factors as well: the increasing school population, the relatively low salaries of teachers, the apparently increasing unruliness of pupils, especially on the public high-school level, and the attractive employment opportunities in noneducational areas. All these elements are lowering the high position the teacher once held in American society and are decreasing the attraction of the teaching role for young persons.

The social status of the college and university faculty is somewhat higher than that of the elementary or high-school teacher. But there are distinctions among the faculty. The general public often regards the college professor as a kind of impractical and fuzzy-minded person who lives in a world of ideals and who probably could not make a living in the world of reality. People in the business world frequently take this same attitude, especially if the professor is an "intellectual," like a philosopher, humanist, or social scientist. The social appraisal of physical scientists, laboratory experts, and accounting teachers is more approving.

Within the framework of the educational groups, the individual educator may aspire to higher academic rank, to positions as chairman, dean, and president, and to reputation and office in learned societies. These are all means of upward social mobility, and they add appreciably to the social status of the individual who achieves them. The necessity for the expansion of educational facilities, which first affected the elementary and high schools, also affects the colleges. Competent professors and administrators are at a premium, and lucrative offers are constantly being made to them from industry, business, and the professions.

Since faith in education is a deeply ingrained value in the American culture, it is probable that education will continue to be a means of upward social mobility for the students and the educators. No society in the history of the world has ever made the investment in education—in terms of personnel, energy, time, money, and effort—that the United States has. The fact that most important universities and colleges and many of the secondary and elementary schools were founded and maintained by private initiative indicates that the social value of education is not merely the result of formal and official policy. It is deeply imbedded in the culture, and as a widely accepted criterion of social status it logically remains an important channel of upward social mobility.

## 4. Migration and Social Mobility

The American people are said to be the most migratory in a physical sense, and the most mobile in a social sense, of all people on earth. Both these phenomena are related; but their mutual influence is seldom noticed. The reason people migrate is frequently that they are seeking higher social status and sometimes that they have actually achieved higher status.

Throughout most of its history the United States has encouraged the immigration of foreigners into this country. Millions of Europeans came to America to find a better way of life and to make opportunities for their children's upward mobility. Although certain regulations were set for immigrants in the latter part of the last century, real restrictions and quotas were not put upon them until after the First World War. After the Second World War these were somewhat relaxed to admit displaced persons and refugees.

The connection between migration and mobility is seen most clearly in the arguments American nativists have employed against the admission of foreigners. They have argued that the flood of immigrants was a threat to American standards of living, to high wages and job opportunities, to standards of education, and to the general cultural welfare of the people. It is immediately apparent that these are all criteria of social status; they represent the valued items people seek to possess as they attempt upward social mobility. The anti-immigrationists argued that the foreigners would "take these away," and the implication was that the native-born would suffer in their aspirations to higher status.

American history shows that the opposite has been the case. A foreign immigrant could seldom move into the same social stratum in the new society that he occupied in his native society. Individual scientists and professional people are sometimes exceptions. Immigrants to the United States have always as a body moved in at the level of the lower classes and have therefore "pushed up" the native-born. At the present time the migration of Puerto Ricans, Mexicans, and Negroes into the large American cities is met with the same kind of argument as that used against earlier immigrants. But because of their relatively low class-status, their presence has not impeded the social mobility of the native-born.

Another aspect of the relation between physical migration and social mobility is the phenomenal rate at which urban people change from one residence to another. Approximately one out of five American families moves to a new address each year. So much emphasis has been placed on the migration of rural people to urban areas that this internal residential movement of city dwellers has been largely overlooked. This change is frequently a factor of social mobility.

Every large city and its suburbs demonstrate the relation between residential mobility and social mobility. Traceable patterns of movement from poor to better residential areas can be made on any urban map. Sections where the "best" families once lived have gradually deteriorated physically. As lower or middle-class families move in, upper-class families move out. Then as these families move upward in the class structure they in turn seek more favorable residential areas. The tremendous migration of families to the suburbs has been largely by persons who can better express their improved social status in more acceptable physical surroundings.

With the growth and spread of large manufacturing and business concerns there has been a need for occupational mobility. The term "mobile labor force" refers generally to workers who are willing to move their place of residence as well as workers who are able to shift to other types of jobs in industry. In the ranks of sales and management the term "occupational mobility" refers usually to the opportunities for advancement within a company or industry. These people must be ready to move their residence when an opportunity for advancement is offered in another city. Unwillingness to migrate physically may cancel out the chance for higher social status and for occupational promotion.

We return to our original observation. Some people change their place of residence because they have already achieved higher social status and others do so because they are seeking higher status. A young man may seek his fortune in the city or in a foreign country. A rising junior executive may move his family to a better residential area as a manifestation of higher status. These examples demonstrate that physical migration may be both a cause and an effect of social mobility.

## 5. Success and Social Mobility

The American ethos contains a number of highly valued concepts that are directly related to the actual practice of social mobility. The high value placed by Americans upon activity, success, and quantity acts as a cause and an effect of upward mobility. If the possibility of upward mobility in the open-class society were not offered to people, these values probably would not exist. On the other hand, if we were not a "doing" society, constantly measuring our achievement by quantitative standards, we would not have people moving upward in the social structure.

a. The emphasis upon activity is seen in all the major groups of our society. It is strikingly apparent in the educational system, especially in the high schools and colleges, where there is a tremendous amount of extra-curricular activity. One has to strain logic to find the educational significance of fraternities and sororities, of proms and homecomings, or of highly competitive football and basketball programs.

Another example is that of the religious groups. The active church is one in which something is "always going on." This activity is to some extent directly spiritual, but the area in which the activity is most emphasized is usually only on the periphery of the spiritual. In either case, the value of activism prevails and the members of the congregation are constantly being urged to work for the church.

b. The value of performance does not stand alone but must be somehow related to success. The American people have long been avid readers of an endless series of books on how to be successful. The books that tell us how to do things stress the importance of doing the things successfully. The significant notion is that the best way to do anything is to do it successfully. The millions of relatively unsuccessful people in our society tend to be considered below par, perhaps even mentally subnormal.

The success ideal glows like a steady flame in the sky of the American culture. Educated urban people indoctrinated with this ideal have a special dread of failure. Success is expected and demanded in the raising of children, in the functioning of the household, in winning friends and influencing people, in salesmanship, in sports and recreation, and in all the institutionalized forms of social behavior.

c. A third value, about which we have already spoken, is that of quantity. The active, successful group is one in which large numbers of people perform frequently in a successful way. We look with respect at the biggest factory with the largest volume of products. We respect also the biggest university, political machine, hospital, church, and department store. There is even a certain pride in being an inhabitant of a big city.

From the point of view of social mobility, these values of activity, success, and quantity are extremely influential. Upward mobility means for any individual that he enjoys higher status than he previously had, and this change is in itself valued as an achievement. We have seen that the criteria of ascribed social status are numerous and that the functional role is only one of these. In American society, however, the status-giving property of the social role is greater than elsewhere, partly because the rewards in social prestige for the successfully functioning role are greater than elsewhere.

An analysis of this kind would lead us astray if we did not view it in the total ethical framework of the American culture. We must not have the impression that striving for higher social status is the all-absorbing purpose of American living. It is probable that the great majority of Americans are not consciously striving for, or are deliberately aware of, the relationship between upward social mobility and factors of achievement, success, and bigness. It would be a scientific error to assume that the people are grossly acquisitive or heartlessly materialistic in a naive pursuit of higher social status.

The success ideal places the emphasis on the rewards of achievement, and in the American context these are personal rewards for personal activities. But this competition is not merely a ruthless struggle which results in the survival of the fittest. The factors that help people to status and power and thus promote upward social mobility are not in practice divorced from the ultimate values of charity, brotherhood, democracy, personal and social rights, and human dignity.

A subtle distinction seems to escape many negative critics of the American culture. The American people do not interpret achievement, success, and quantity merely as practical means to higher social status. On the other hand, they do not interpret them as absolute ends in themselves. They assume the moral goodness and social propriety of achievement, success, and quantity. They believe it is both personally and socially beneficial to work hard, to succeed in work, and to have big measurable results to show for successful achievement. Upward social mobility is then assumed to be a logical corollary of these factors.

## Suggested Readings

Glazer, Nathan, and Moynihan, Daniel. *Beyond the Melting Pot*. Cambridge: Harvard-MIT Press, 1964.

Handlin, Oscar. *The Uprooted*. Boston: Little, Brown, 1952.

McClelland, David G. *The Achieving Society*. Princeton: Van Nostrand, 1961.

Sorokin, Pitirim. *Social and Cultural Mobility*. Glencoe: Free Press, 1959.

Thomas, William, and Znaniecki, Florian. *The Polish Peasant in Europe and America*. New York: Dover, 1958.

# 14
# Change

EVERY SOCIETY AND EVERY CULTURE, NO MATTER HOW
traditional and conservative, is constantly undergoing
change. This means that the subject matter of our study—
social and cultural phenomena—can never be completely
static. Change is inherent in its very nature. The central
unit of society, the social person, is subject to the universal
facts of birth, maturation, aging, and death; and eventually the total personnel of a society disappears and is
replaced by another. The minimum unit of culture, the
behavior pattern, while more durable than the persons
who perform it, is also subject to many factors of change.

Change is defined briefly as a variation from a previous
state or mode of existence. There is always something
that undergoes the variation, and this changed object
represents a reformation and combination of previously
existing modes. The social scientist here faces the old
philosophical problem of permanence and fluidity, of
unity in variety. We have seen that the basic sociocultural
phenomena must be permanently present, even though
they keep changing. The basic groups and institutions—
familial, educational, economic, political, religious, and
recreational—may change in form and content, but they
are necessarily present wherever there is organized social
life.

## RECURRENT AND NOVEL CHANGE

All the phenomena we have studied in this book—patterns and roles, status and values, processes and institutions, and others—are universally existent and comparable.
If this were not true there could be no reliable body of
knowledge called social science. Furthermore, these phenomena are always subject to change, and change itself
is a permanent phenomenon subject to sociological analysis and study.

377

For purposes of clarity and utility we must distinguish between recurrent permanent change and change that represents a shared modification of behavior. The changes of behavior patterns a child experiences as he grows up, or the change any adult undergoes when he meets a novel situation, are nothing new to society. Temporary fads and fashions, like those in speech, dress, songs, and games, are simply recurrent variants of the same phenomenon. Similarly, seasonal cycles in business, in clothing, in foods, drinks, and household arrangements are merely expected fluctuations of behavior. In the technical sense, it is only when some cultural element is accepted as a new arrangement and shared by many people that we can say a genuine cultural change has occurred.

This distinction between recurrent and novel change makes it possible for us to discuss separately social mobility in one chapter and deviation in another. Social mobility, as well as geographical migration, occurs to some degree wherever group life exists. Like social and cultural deviation, which is found to some extent wherever people live together, mobility is a relatively permanent phenomenon. Mobility and deviation are obviously kinds of change, and it is merely for purposes of analysis and clarity that we discuss them as constantly recurring changes distinguishable from novel changes.

## ASPECTS OF CHANGE

For a meaningful interpretation of sociocultural change it is necessary to understand certain general aspects from which change can be viewed. It is obvious that all change is *temporal*. The passage of time is an important condition under which change takes place, but time alone does not cause change. Sociocultural change is not analogous to the biological aging process in human beings; society or culture does not become tired or worn out. Time is required for both the renovation and the discarding of behavior patterns.

Change is also *environmental*; it has to take place in concrete surroundings that are both physical and cultural. The geographical environment is constantly undergoing changes, some of them induced by man's control over nature and others through the uncontrolled powers of nature itself. We have seen that cultural environment greatly influences the behavior of people and that it in turn is changed by them.

Insofar as it has sociological significance, all change has also a *human* aspect. The fact that people effect change and are themselves affected by it makes change extremely important. Furthermore, every society's personnel, viewed both as individuals and as pluralities, is constantly shifting. People move in and out of groups so that the size and type of group membership vary. Over a period of time the total personnel of any society is completely replaced by another.

In combination all three of these aspects of change are the necessary conditions under which change occurs. This is another way of saying that change must occur at some time, at some place, and with some people. At this point we discuss these aspects of change as conditions, not as causes. If we clearly conceptualize all three aspects as combined and necessary conditions, we shall find the study of change itself more meaningful.

SEQUENCE OF CHANGE

Change involves a question of the sequence of changing phenomena—what follows what—which in turn involves the question of the rate and direction of change. One may say that a total society is roughly in the transitional period between an agricultural and an industrial stage, or that a democratic culture is changing into a totalitarian culture, or that a kinship system is shifting from the consanguine to the conjugal type.

Most sociologists have abandoned the notion that there is an inevitable single direction of sociological change or that there are any universal laws of acceleration or deceleration of the rate of change. Earlier speculations concerning the evolution of society and culture through neatly arranged stages from lower to higher forms have lost their meaning. We need not be concerned with the vague historical assumptions, for example, that sexual promiscuity among primitives changed to group marriages, then to polygamy, then finally to monogamy; or that religion developed from magic to polytheism and then to monotheism. The empirical study of contemporary primitives has dispelled theories of this kind.

The comparative analysis of cultures has shown that the rate of change varies enormously. In fact, the rate of change has been one of the useful criteria sociologists employ in classifying societies. The difference between slow and rapid change constitutes a highly relevant index to the difference between a communal and an associational type of society, open and closed societies, rural and urban subcultures, and others.

The internal analysis of a society shows that change occurs at different rates of speed from one group to another. Even when we remark that an industrial urban culture changes very rapidly we must realize that some of its institutions remain relatively traditional and conservative. We have seen that the theory of cultural lag is based upon this observation. In a technologically successful society the economic institutions and groups change more rapidly than the religious and familial institutions and groups.

## PLANNED AND UNPLANNED CHANGE

Both the rate and direction of change depend largely upon whether the change is deliberate or nondeliberate. By induced deliberate change we mean that which is effected by social control, engineering and planning, by leaders, inventors, reformers, and pressure groups. From a variety of motives people foresee the direction in which they would like society and culture to move, and they make efforts to bring about the desired change. A manufacturer builds a factory to produce a new invention, for example. There are sometimes unanticipated consequences of these efforts, like slums in a rapidly expanding industrial city, but the general direction is intended to be one of forward progress.

The "great-man" theory of history is not an exclusive and universal explanation of social and cultural change;

every great reformer must work under favorable conditions. Nevertheless, there cannot be any doubt that individual men (saints, heroes, dictators) have been instrumental in effecting important changes. They have employed, in crude or refined forms, the various techniques of propaganda and pressure. Mass movements, inspired by these individuals, have swept across whole countries.

Nondeliberate change is generally unforeseen. It often occurs as the result of natural catastrophies like floods, droughts, and earthquakes, and the significance of its effects depends upon its severity and the ability of the society to absorb it or react to it. These catastrophies are in themselves sudden changes, and they usually require people to make rapid readjustments in their behavior. There are also certain nondeliberate biological factors of change like new diseases and even genetic mutations that cannot be traced to human agencies.

Any theory of determinism that attributes all social and cultural change to these nondeliberate occurrences must be scientifically suspect. Human and nonhuman agencies of change act and react upon each other. Blind, inevitable determinism, as the sole or even the principal factor of change, is no longer a scientifically respectable theory. As man through his technical knowledge and administrative competence gains more and more control over his physical environment, the importance of unplanned change and of "blind" forces of nature decreases.

## Factors of Change

Social scientists have discarded the early evolutionary notion of change through inevitable, progressive stages of development. Similarly they have abandoned the easy explanation of single causalty for changes in culture and society. Factors of change cannot be isolated and treated as though they were single, sufficient causes. There is a basic fallacy in selecting geographical environment, biological heredity, supernatural providence, or personal genius as the single complete cause of change. It is also contrary to the historical facts to emphasize a general principal cause of change as do the proponents of economic determinism, idealistic emanationism, psychic emergence, and others.

We have seen that change can be either planned and deliberate or fortuitous and nondeliberate. Single factors of change can be recognized and introduced, and certain minor changes in society and culture can be traced to these single factors. We know in general that changes in the law and its enforcement can have a wide influence upon the mores and folkways. We know that a change in the credit system or in mechanical production can start a whole chain of actions and reactions, some of them unforeseen. We also know with complete certitude that no one of these factors is an all-embracing cause that brings about all changes in society and culture.

Despite the available scientific and empirical knowledge in regard to multiple causality, there is still frequent and slipshod use of the single-factor theory. People still attribute the "present state of affairs," that is, the whole social and cultural system, to racial heredity, or geographical environment, or supernatural intervention, or to any number of mysterious factors like blind destiny, automatic evolution, and dire fate. It is true, of course, that physical factors like climatic shifts, droughts, and soil erosion, and biological factors like pestilence, lowered fertility, and increased senility may change the normal and expected course of a society. But the extent to which these factors can be and have been controlled lessens the force of their causal influence.

## CHANGE AND PROGRESS

The analysis of the direction of change immediately involves assessing whether any given change is an example of advancement and progress or of degeneration and regress. Induced change is generally intended to be beneficial and progressive, while nondeliberate and unanticipated changes may be either harmful or beneficial. The assessment of change appears to depend in most instances on what the people in a society consider desirable and undesirable. In most general terms, therefore, progress is a conscious movement in the direction of approved and desirable goals.

It is scientifically questionable, however, to employ exclusively a criterion of this kind. It means basing an estimate of progress on values, either those held privately and subjectively or those existing objectively in the culture. If a person measures social progress according to his own value criteria, he is in danger of private, relatively nonscientific interpretation. If he employs the common values of the culture, he is in danger of succumbing to the "fallacy of numbers," that is, of concluding that what many people desire is intrinsically progressive. He simply multiplies private interpretation into mass interpretation.

The way out of this dilemma appears to be the use of the goal-means relationship as a criterion of progress. For example, every major institution has as its goal the satisfaction of certain social and cultural needs of the people. The means used within each institution can be carefully analyzed, and a rough generalization can be made about the extent to which these institutional goals are being achieved in the total culture. Since no society stands still, the extent to which changes increase or decrease these cultural satisfactions is the extent to which society is progressive or regressive.

It must be noted, however, that not all goals can be clearly defined or objectively appraised. There are some institutional areas in which goals and means are not really understood, partly because there are large gaps in our scientific knowledge of society and culture and partly because people lack the willingness and ability to use rational means to intended goals. For example, in certain levels of the educational and political institutions, there is not only a conflict of values but a diffusion of purpose so that we cannot always say with accuracy that one line of achievement is more progressive than another.

Certain basic levels, however, of all the major institutions can be appraised by the goal-means relationship. If we recognize that the production of more goods at cheaper prices is an objective goal of the economic institution, we can readily see that mechanized production is superior to, and more progressive than, a system of hand labor. If we recognize that the assurance of justice and the protection of the law to the largest number of citizens are objective goals of the political institution, we can compare the degree to which different societies have achieved these goals.

It must be emphasized that rapid change is not synonymous with progress. It appears that the most rapidly changing cultures of the modern world are those that have made great advances in the technological, industrial, and material aspects of the society. The attempts to induce change through five-year plans in industry have resulted sometimes in the dislocation of the noneconomic institutions. This sort of experience indicates that the student of society must scrutinize the rate and direction of change in all the institutions within a society and then judge each on the basis of the goal-means relationship.

It appears also that an intelligent and fruitful comparison of cultures requires the study and appraisal of parallel institutions. Progress in the educational system of one society cannot be compared with the progress in the political institution of another or the economic institution of a third. This is precisely the area in which ethnocentrism and misinterpretation operate. The ethnocentric person uses the progress of a particular institution in his own culture as the measuring rod of the total culture of another society. It is a basic rule of logic that only comparable objects can be compared.

## FUNCTIONAL AND STRUCTURAL CHANGE

We have seen that there are wide differences in the patterns of behavior from one culture to another. The various ways in which different people pursue their social goals indicate that social and cultural functions are subject to change. Here again the rate and kind of change differ from one society to another. Communication at a distance may still be performed in some societies by means of smoke signals and drum beats, while in other societies it has changed over the course of a century from surface mail to airmail and to telephone, radio, and television communication.

The study of functional change within a culture is important to the sociologist. What people do and how they do it indicate the recurrent uniformities of social behavior that can be compared from one culture to another. Since culture is a dynamic reality, its principal changes and evolutions can be accurately traced by observation of the functions of the people in group life, that is, of people in their various social roles in the major groups of the society. Tracing the development of the paternal role, the worker role, the citizen role, and others over a period of time provides a meaningful insight into functional change.

The concept of social structure is not that of a rigidly static arrangement of parts. While every society has an orderly system of personal and group statuses and of interrelated social positions and strata, this whole structural system is a "going concern." In it are two kinds of simultaneous change: the movement of the total structure through time, and the movement of the parts in relation to one another within the structure. These two aspects of change are so closely intertwined that they can be separated only conceptually and analytically.

Structural change is involved in phenomena like the following: the development of bureaucracy, the shrinkage of the unskilled worker class, the expansion of the middle class, the multiplication of role specialties, and the shifting of social power from economic to political groups. These are all examples of the way in which the relative position of persons, classes, and groups undergoes change. A change in any one of these factors involves changes in other related segments of the society and a gradual realignment of the total structure.

This distinction between functional and structural change is sometimes roughly equated with the distinction between cultural and social change. The notion is that the cultural system is dynamic and the social system static; and this distinction may be useful in some aspects of sociological research. The fact is, however, that the components of a culture are structured in relation to one another and that the components of a society are functioning objects. It seems more logical to define cultural change as that which occurs among the units of the culture and the social change as that which occurs among the units of the society. Since culture and society in the concrete situation are closely allied, even this distinction has to be employed with caution.

## CONDITIONS OF CHANGE

There is sometimes an erroneous overlapping of meaning between the concepts of condition and factor. By the conditions of change we mean simply those circumstances in which change is likely to occur, and by the factors of change we mean those causes that can produce change. The passage of time is obviously a condition, not a cause, of change. The physical environment is from one point of view a condition of change, since all change must occur somewhere, but it may at times also be a factor of change.

Assuming the presence of the physical and biological environment as the circumstances in which change occurs, the social scientist focuses more directly upon social and cultural conditions. There are several general conditions under which sociocultural change is likely to occur:

a. The recognized needs of the people in any society are usually cared for by the traditional institutionalized ways of behavior. But when "new" needs appear—created, imaginary, or actual—they provide a situation in which change is often attempted, and perhaps effected. For example, the automobile complex has created a whole chain of needs which have been satisfied by superhighways, motels, drive-in theaters, auto clubs, collision insurance, and many other innovations. The creation of needs is especially characteristic of a mass-producing industrial and commercial society.

b. Need is closely aligned to readiness for change—the attitudes of expectation and anticipation people have in a society. Those who are more or less satisfied with the status quo and are suspicious of innovations do not provide fruitful conditions for change. Where people are eager for new and "better" ways to train children, to distribute income, to streamline government, or to promote religious values, they provide a condition favorable to change.

**c.** The accumulated store of knowledge is an important condition for change because new modes of doing things always build on already existing forms. The condition depends on both the amount and the kind of knowledge at hand. The extent to which this knowledge is rich, varied, organized, and transmissible will help to determine the basic starting point from which further knowledge is available. A culture in which the store of knowledge is rigid, conservative, and dogmatic does not provide a condition of easy change. Conversely, the greater the usability of the knowledge, the more accelerated the changes will be.

**d.** The type of dominant values that exist in a culture and the general attitude or orientation of the people toward them are significant as a circumstance of change. If the scientific spirit of inquiry is coupled with a pragmatic belief in social perfectibility, deliberately induced changes are almost inevitable. An emphasis on traditional, quietistic values provides a condition in which change occurs only slowly.

**e.** The degree of complexity of the social and cultural structure is also a condition for change. A society in which there is great differentiation and multiplication of status and class, specialization and division of functions, and a facile system of communication and transportation is one in which change is likely to occur.

It must be noted that all these conditions favorable to change are present simultaneously in a society where frequent change occurs; they complement one another. It is difficult to determine which is most important because any one of them, when taken separately, would probably not provide a sufficiently favorable condition for change. Futhermore, all these are in the realm of the "nonmaterial" culture, and they presuppose the favorable physical and biological environment of which we have spoken. In general, nonmaterial conditions are much more important and revealing than material conditions in the study of sociocultural change.

## INVENTION AND DIFFUSION

Although we have discussed both the factors and conditions of change, it is necessary to ask still a third question concerning the source of change. Since we are concentrating on the social and cultural, that is, the human, element in change, we are asking who originates change. The answer is that a new modification of behavior patterns is either invented or borrowed. It is only through invention within the culture, or through diffusion from another culture, that social and cultural changes occur.

Invention may be defined as a creative variation that puts into a new combination two or more elements already existing within the culture. Diffusion is the introduction of a behavior modification from another culture. These two sources of change are often studied as though they were different, but they have many common features. Contact and communication are essential for both, and the society that enjoys a great deal of intercultural contact is likely to be one in which changes are more numerous and rapid.

The crucial common factor in both invention and diffusion is, however, the way in which a society accepts an innovation. The comparative study of cultures shows that there is a selectivity of change, that societies do not accept all innovations, whether their origin is from within or from without the culture. There is no single criterion by which we can judge this cultural selectivity. Utility of change is a partial index, but there are occasions when a society rejects an obviously useful change. The appropriateness or fitness of change is also a partial indicator, but it is merely another term for the combination of conditions we have described above.

Internal invention and external diffusion are originating sources that have a cumulative, mutual influence on change. The society that shows a willingness to accept imported ideas, behavior patterns, and cultural traits from other societies is usually ready also to make its own innovations. An internally inventive society also seeks knowledge through contact with other societies. In a sense, every social change is strange and foreign, whether it originates at home or abroad. In spite of this strangeness, the exigencies of time and locality make the rapid acceptance of the domestic, rather than the imported, innovation more likely.

## RESISTANCE TO CHANGE

While it is true that change is a universal phenomenon, we must remember that societies and cultures are relatively permanent and durable. They differ widely in rate and direction of change, in the degree to which conditions are favorable for change, and in the way in which the factors of change are allowed to operate. The social and cultural functions and structures do not change suddenly even in the most dynamic populations. Certain resisters of change have become institutionalized.

The clearest intracultural demonstration of this resistance to change appears in the comparison between mores and usages. We have seen that mores endure because they are characterized by the widest conformity, the highest values, and the strongest social pressure. Those behavior patterns the society considers really worthwhile are the ones to which people must and do conform. Consequently, they offer the greatest resistance to innovation. Usages carry neither the same compulsion nor the same resistance, and they change more readily.

Similarly, from an institutional point of view, those major institutions in which the mores are deeply embedded are the most resistant to change. This helps to explain why the religious and familial institutions change more slowly than the other major institutions and why they have a greater strength than others through revolutions and natural catastrophies. It is the very nature of institutionalized mores that they are traditional, that through repetition and habituation they have endured the longest time.

## Some American Aspects of Change

### 1. Superstitious Explanations of Change

The difference between scientific prediction and general forecasting is well known to students of society. The first is based upon an accurate knowledge of the facts while the other is at best guesswork based on probabilities. Nevertheless, both are similar in that they are concerned with the factors, conditions, and explanations of change. One might expect the American people to be intelligent enough to prefer scientific prediction to the various sources of forecasting that are frequently used.

Superstition is defined as the attribution of supernatural or preternatural power to an object that does not have such power. In modern America there is a widespread and irrational belief that some objects or actions can, of their own power, influence the future course of action. This belief is different from that professed by crystal-gazers, tea-leaf readers, card manipulators, fortune-tellers, and other charlatans who simply claim that they can read the future without being able to influence it. They employ various objects as indicators, not as causes, of future occurrences.

Following are some of the more widespread superstitious practices current among Americans.

a. Certain forecasters pretend to find a causal link between the object they are "reading" and some future event. In this sense they are handling factors of change. Examples are palmists and phrenologists who forecast that because of certain physical characteristics the subject will act in certain ways in the future. The lines on the palm of the hand are supposed to be causes of future acts, and the variations in cranial structure are supposed to be explanations of behavior.

b. Diviners and spiritualists who act as a medium between the spirit world and their customers are for the most part tricksters. They fraudulently claim to have the power to bring messages from the outer world, but they do not personally believe in these superstitious practices. They do, however, constitute a culturally significant focus for the many Americans who employ their services and attend their seances. The customers are superstitious people who are not merely curious about extraordinary spiritual appearances but also seek guidance for the future. They believe they can learn what is going to happen and can take steps to change their behavior.

c. On a different superstitious level are the large numbers of people who carry good luck charms—a rabbit's foot, a horseshoe, a four-leaf clover, and many other lucky symbols. There are others who associate bad fortune with spilled salt, black cats, open umbrellas, stepladders, or think that thirteen is an unlucky number, or that three people should never light their cigarettes from the same match. Businessmen who wear a certain suit when closing an important deal, women who insist upon a certain chair when they play cards, athletes who lace their shoes a special way, are all examples of otherwise intelligent Americans who superstitiously believe they can influence the future.

d. The most curious of the superstitious practices is the modern revival of astrology. The influence of the stars and planets upon human behavior was once considered a reasonable scientific pursuit, but serious scientists have long since abandoned it as a field of study. Nevertheless, there are millions of literate and perhaps educated Americans who consult horoscopes, buy books and magazines on astrology, and study almanacs to make sure that the "signs are right" before undertaking anything important. Many newspapers carry a horoscope column, and the astrology business enjoys an annual income of millions of dollars.

It is a curious phenomenon that many Americans actually try to effect social change through superstitious practices. Americans have not learned all the secrets of nature; we have not reached the limit of inventions and discoveries; but our store of knowledge is sufficient to provide for us a reasonable methodology and an intelligent guide to social change. We maintain a tremendous, complex, and expensive educational system mainly for the purpose of teaching people how to live rationally. Our technological equipment and our scientific experience can be compared favorably with those of any modern society.

This contradiction between scientific and superstitious behavior is modified by the fact that the superstitious practices of most Americans are limited only to some areas of behavior. If the person has an intense desire for something—happiness in marriage, a raise in salary, victory in a game—he may follow all the intelligent steps to the objective, but add the strength of a four-leaf clover "just for luck." Especially if there is a strong element of chance, so that predictability is difficult, the individual may rely on charms. Finally, if there is a certain confusion or lack of knowledge in the area where the change is desired, he resorts to superstition. When these conditions are combined, they indicate that although superstitious practices persist among Americans, they are often merely supplementary behavior.

The incongruous presence of these irrational patterns of behavior side by side with the most advanced scientific systems in the world is a dramatic demonstration of the tenacious persistence of folklore. Even persons who do these things jokingly and without belief serve as carriers of traditional and outmoded practices. Sometimes they are also those who are the most critical of the magical rites of primitives, of Oriental beliefs, of peasant practices, and even of valid religious symbolism in their own society.

## 2. RADICAL SOCIAL CHANGE

In the sociological lexicon of the American people the term "radical" seems to have fearful overtones of destruction, nihilism, anarchy, and subversion. Part of the aversion for radicalism seems to be the notion that it is an alien importation, that only foreigners would promote schemes for sedition and insurrection that threaten to undermine the American way of life. The several versions of the Marxist ideology are looked upon as an international conspiracy to overthrow all the cherished traditional institutions of family and religion, education, government, business, and even our recreational and leisure-time activities.

Many Americans find it hard to believe that there may be some home-grown versions of radicalism, like those professed by certain militant Black groups and by the self-styled "campus radicals" in the larger American universities. Whether or not the ideology of these groups can be traced to foreign and anti-American origins, the fact is that the people involved in them are native Americans attempting to bring about radical change in American institutions. Without trying to assess or predict the degree of sucessful change achieved by these movements, let us analyze the meaning of radical social change.

a. One of the peculiarities of the radical movement is that while it plans its maneuvers to bring about change, it does not plan the goals of change. There is hardly even a vague blueprint of the "new society" that is to emerge as a result of radical change. The argument seems to be that society has suffered from too much planning, that the immediate focus must be the immediate removal of the plans and the planners that have complicated the lives of Americans. Scientifically controlled change requires some concept of both terms of the process, that is, where it starts and where it is going. Radical change is apparently non-directional in the sense that it presents no clear-cut substitution for that which is changed.

b. These American radicals have been called the New Left, and while they claim to represent the interests of the common man they do not constitute a mass movement, or a people's movement. According to the New Left, the people, including the majority of college and university students, are not yet ready for radical change; they have been seduced into an apathetic acceptance of the status quo and it would be useless to hold a democratic referendum by which their wishes might be ascertained. Radical change, therefore, is promoted as something that is good *for* the people, but not as something that will be promoted *by* the people in a mass movement.

c. The process of radical change is not conceived as a democratic process, and this fact is highlighted by what

are called "non-negotiable" demands. Only the "true be-
liever" is allowed to caucus about these demands while
they are being formulated, which means that whites are
excluded from the Black caucus, and liberals and conservatives from the radical caucus. Once the list of demands
is presented to the Establishment, there is no need for discourse, or compromise, or mutual agreement. This is
quite foreign to the accepted American practice of give-
and-take by which agreements are normally reached.

**d.** The fact that the radicals are unwilling to discuss matters with the Establishment results from a kind of principle of anti-institutionalism. When they say that the system
is corrupt and must be destroyed, they do not mean merely
that corrupt people must be removed from the system, the
organization, the institutionalized bureaucracy. They mean
that institutions are inherently evil. This indicates a remarkable ignorance of social science and of the basic fact
that all social life everywhere is institutionalized. From
this point of view, radical social change is self-con-
tradictory.

**e.** Since radical social change cannot be brought about
by the democratic process or by a popular mass movement, its proponents are willing to employ other means.
The intention seems to be an imitation of the nonviolent
civil disobedience of the civil-rights movement, but the
actuality is anything but peaceful. There is deliberate
provocation of social authority, particularly of policemen,
with the expectation that arrests and other penalties will
be forthcoming. But there is general unwillingness to be
a witness to the cause, as indicated by demands for immediate and general amnesty for all those involved in these
tactics.

One of the interesting aspects about radical social
change, as we have seen it in recent years, is that it has
been effective without being successful. Instead of destroying the institutions that the radicals oppose, the actions of the radicals have forced programs of reform within
these institutions. They have highlighted the defects that
would probably be removed from American institutions
over the course of some years, and these defects are now

being given immediate and serious consideration. This is
not the effect intended. Radical social change is aimed at
the removal of institutions, not their reformation.

### 3. LIMITS OF CHANGE

The adventurous and progressive "spirit" of the American culture, and the dramatic material success of the
American people, have led some foreigners to observe that
the United States is a country of "unlimited possibilities."
Some Americans share this naive faith in progress and the
future. The notion is particularly prevalent in the field of
material and technical changes that can be measured by
miles of concrete highways, underground telephone ca-
bles, and air-flight routes, and by numbers of automobiles,
television sets, and refrigerators.

The fact that this multiplication of material things has
been so phenomenal, has brought benefits to so many persons, and has been so rapid leads to the conclusion that it
has no foreseeable end. We have become habituated to
rapid progress, and we define progress in measurable
terms. Some Americans have come to the conclusion that
physical science has merely scratched the surface of the
potentialities of nature and that mechanical wonders will
never cease.

**a.** While it is not the sociologist's task to judge the limits
and potentialities of the physical sciences, a realistic scientific appraisal of social trends and changes indicates some
areas in which trends must end and changes are limited.
For example, if there is a long-term trend toward a lower
average age of marriage, there is also a point where this
trend must stop. There are not only biological barriers but
also cultural taboos against child marriage. The percentage
of married persons in our population has been increasing
for a long time but this too must reach a saturation point.
There is a limited number of possible sex pairs in any
society, and this is especially important in a system of
monogamous marriages.

**b.** Social change is limited by the readiness of the people
and the institutions to accept change. In many instances
this may be called a limit to the "suddenness" or rapidity

of change. It is commonly asserted that engineers have
already designed radically new automobiles, airplanes,
and trains, but that the public will not accept them now.
The limit of suddenness is seen in the twenty years that
have lapsed between industry-wide collective bargaining
and the guaranteed annual wage; there was also about
two decades between the admission of a Negro to a Southern white university and the universal prohibition of pub-
lic-school segregation, a prohibition that has not yet been
completely enforced.

c. Any trend that involves numbers of people and physical actions must necessarily have a limit. In the area of
cultural developments of a nonmaterial nature the limitations are not always present. If the increase in education is
measured by the number of years and of people involved,
it is certainly limited; if it is measured by the progress of
knowledge, there appears to be the possibility of continuing perfectibility. Similarly, if the improvement in group
relations is analyzed in terms of social virtues of justice
and love, there appears to be no point at which it must
be limited.

d. Social and cultural change is limited by the number
of forms the principal phenomena can assume. The number and kind of social roles an individual can enact and a
society contain are finite. The form the political institution
can take has certain outside limits; the possible major
variations in the institutionalized economic system are
relatively few. In other words, there are boundaries beyond which change cannot go; if it were otherwise, there
could be no reliable core of sociological science.

Generally speaking, however, the American people are
not interested in the so-called lateral variations of sociocultural phenomena. The basic forms of our major institutions and groups have become well-established; certain
internal variations are permitted and even encouraged.
The main interest is in the lineal, "forward and upward"
direction of trends and changes. The expectation is not
that capitalism, democracy, or Christianity will change to
some other essentially different economic, political, or
religious system, but that these institutions will continue

to "get better." The common notion seems to be that if
there are any limits to the benefits derived from these
institutions, we have not even remotely approached them.

In summary, we may make the following observations
about the limits of change in American society and culture.
**a.** Some trends have an obvious saturation point, as those
with biological bases in sex and age. In other trends involving the multiplication of material products, the level
of saturation is not so clearly seen.
**b.** Trends in the development of nonmaterial culture,
as in education, knowledge, and social virtues, appear to
contain the possibility of continual perfectibility.
**c.** There seem to be built-in limitations to the suddenness of change that result from the exigencies of time and
the readiness of people to accept change.
**d.** ·There is also a limitation to the number of major
institutional forms available to any culture. The American
people seem intent on improving those that are established
rather than exchanging them for others.

### 4. CHANGE BEGETS CHANGE

Belief in a single causality for social change is one of
the most widespread errors in social thinking among the
American people, and perhaps among most other people.
The perceptive student will recognize this error in daily
conversations. Many people appear to have a favored single solution for one problem or for all problems. We hear
that "the only way to solve the race problem is through
education," or that "world problems will disappear if you
get rid of the Communists."

This fallacy of the single solution is prevalent among
persons who want quick results and are ignorant of the
deep complexities of society and culture. This simplistic
approach ignores the demonstrable fact that every social
change involves a series of other changes, that the web of
action and reaction spreads more widely in more complex
societies, and that absolute stability and balance are impossible in any sociocultural system. These three facts help
us to understand why social change cannot be attributed
to single causality and cannot eventuate in total solutions.

a. Every change involves many other changes. People were mistaken who thought that political suffrage for women, gained through an amendment to the Constitution, would satisfy the women's movement for equal rights. Increasing numbers of women took gainful occupation, especially in white-collar, clerical, and office jobs. This had an effect on family relations, especially in the comparative status of husband and wife. The widespread use of dependable means of contraception has been another important factor in the change of women's status in America.

It is probably true to say that "one change led to another" in the matter of women's equal rights, but it is difficult to place all these factors on a continuum of successive change. Political equality may lead or follow occupational equality. The experience of coeducation may be as important as the achievement of independent income in changing the marital status and familial role of women. Legislation to guarantee fair employment for women may have unforeseeable consequences. The point is that there has been interdependent and mutual causality among all these factors of change.

b. The complex American society allows the causal web to spread widely. The American experience in racial desegregation exemplifies this point. Had the separate-but-equal doctrine been legitimate and workable it would not have required major social changes. Even when the school cases were decided by the Supreme Court in 1954, the process of racial desegregation had started or was occurring in many other institutions. The military had been ordered to abandon the policy and practice of racial separation. Professional athletics and commercial entertainment had opened up opportunities for Negro participants. Some labor unions, at least on the national level, promoted job equality across racial lines. Leaders in church and synagogue were preaching about the immorality of racial discrimination.

Whether we talk about the civil-rights movement or about some form of "black separatism," the point here is that change in American race relations affects all institutions of the cultural system. The answer could not have been found only in the educational system, and not elsewhere. What we have said earlier about the mutual dependence and interlocking of the whole society is demonstrated in the causal influence of social change. Differentiation of roles and functions always implies complexity, and this in turn requires relative uniformities in the total system. In spite of lags from one institution to another, the total culture tends to change as a whole. What happens in one major segment of society affects what happens in others.

c.  The third fact, concerning the impossibility of an absolute equilibrium, requires an understanding of the dynamics of sociocultural phenomena. Strictly speaking, balance can never be restored because there never was and never can be balance. Balance is a static concept not applicable to social science. People all over the country had to "adjust" to the large areas of change in the relations of men and women, and in the relations of whites and Negroes. What we really mean is that people had to change their patterns of behavior; they had to learn new ways of meeting new people and new situations. Equal rights have not yet been achieved either by women or by Negroes, and in neither case is there a "final" solution.

The American's sense of orderliness and efficiency is offended because causality does not work in the area of social phenomena as it does in that of material things. If he puts so many pieces of matter together according to a certain pattern he has a house. But if he brings so many persons together to form a group for a certain purpose, he has to be ready for any number of variable factors. If he has learned something about the causes, direction, rate, and extent of change, he is not likely to be disappointed or to expect neat, balanced, and permanent solutions.

This elementary analysis of the manner in which change affects a total society is of great significance to the ordinary citizen and the active social reformer. Confusion and frustration on the part of individuals seem to be traceable to an ignorance of the facts themselves. People living in the midst of an ever-changing culture are often obli-

vious to the meaning of the behavior patterns in which
they themselves participate. The reformer with more zeal
than knowledge is almost certain to be subjected to dis-
appointment and chagrin. Many of these difficulties can
be obviated by a closer study of the changing American
sociocultural system.

## 5. TRENDS IN KNOWLEDGE

Most Americans recognize that the day of the universal
scholar is over. One may well question whether the so-
called intellectual giants of the past would attempt to
embrace all knowledge if they lived in our day. The mental
capacities of man have not degenerated, for there appears
to have been neither mental evolution nor devolution in
the whole history of the human species, but the store of
human knowledge has increased tremendously. No modern genius can encompass more than a small proportion
of it.

This change in the amount of knowledge has demanded
a change in the approach to scholarship and education.
The age of the specialist has behind it a whole series of
interlocking causes. It is not merely the aftermath of human decisions to concentrate on segmental areas of knowledge; nor is it merely a simple imitation of the successful
rationalization of industrial production. The spirit of inquiry and the capacity for scientific thought have existed
throughout recorded history, but it is only in recent centuries that the store of knowledge has become unmanage-
able except through an increase of scholars and other
specialists.

In the United States it is possible to trace in rough
outline the change of emphasis and direction in three
major areas of teachable knowledge. The educationists
recognize three broad divisions: the humanities, the natural sciences, and the social sciences. Without attempting
to force all college courses and all research projects into
some one of these major categories, we are able to make
some generalizations about the kinds of change and the
reasons for change. If we recognize that the American
cultural values of pragmatism and progressivism are in-

fluential in institutionalized education, we may evaluate these changes according to the norms of utility and applicability.

a. As taught in our colleges and universities the humanities include the great literature of the past, the important ideas that have gone into the development of civilization. While the proponents of the humanities often stress knowledge for its own sake and insist upon philosophical thinking as a means for developing the intellect, their most effective argument appears to be that knowledge of the past helps us to understand the present and the future.

This is an important insight. The American culture is not geared to a "return to the past." The humanists and philosophers cannot seriously propose to Americans the restoration of historical grandeurs; nor do they attempt this. We have only to ask what happened to the Latin and Greek literature our grandfathers studied so laboriously in the original texts, to the systematic courses in philosophy and theology once considered essential for the educated man. These fields are no longer judged directly useful in our kind of society and culture.

b. The tremendous progress of the natural sciences has done much to change the concept of the educated man. These sciences have obtained results. They have taught man to master nature; they have given students the attitudes and skills that find outlet in the American industrial society; they satisfy and promote the cultural values we profess. It is no mere historical accident that they have in many colleges replaced the humanities as the focus of higher education.

The statement that the natural sciences are useful and practical does not mean that the resulting human product is merely a glorified mechanic. They require a high level of abstract thinking probably comparable in depth and breadth to that exercised by any humanist or philosopher. But it is the empirical approach and the empirical result that has "paid off" and has brought the natural sciences into the leading position in the American education scene. They appear to fit most aptly in our kind of culture.

c. The rise of the social sciences as a significant area of knowledge in higher education has been relatively recent. Several factors have been important in this change. One was the change of focus from historical speculation and social philosophy to an empirical and scientific approach. The further the social scientists moved away from the speculative generalization of the humanities and the closer they came to the methodology of natural sciences, the more successful they have been. The general and vague concern of Americans about the effects of technological advance on society and culture has brought increased interest in the social sciences.

Social science has advanced further in the United States than elsewhere in the world. As researchers and writers and particularly as teachers, our social scientists are answering a need in higher education. They have vastly increased the storehouse of sociocultural knowledge, have attracted an increasing audience of students and scholars, and have spread the conviction that this kind of knowledge is useful and practical for Americans.

In summary, it may be said that a society develops the kinds of knowledge it requires and deserves, and that its changes and trends in the areas of knowledge can be measured against its principal values. In this rough tracing of the American educational trends, we have mentioned only two value norms, pragmatism and progressivism. A mere reference to the total core of American values (including rationality, success, activism, freedom, tolerance, and others) would show that our cultural ethos is compatible with the changing status of three major areas of knowledge—the dominance of the natural sciences, the increasing importance of the social sciences, and the relatively diminishing position of the humanities.

## Suggested Readings

Barnett, H. G. *Innovation*. New York: McGraw-Hill, 1953.
Bennis, Warren G., and Slater, Philip E. *The Temporary Society*. New York: Harper and Row, 1968.
Etzioni, Amitai. *Studies in Social Change*. New York: Holt, Rinehart and Winston, 1966.

LaPiere, Richard. *Social Change.* New York: McGraw-Hill, 1965.

Mack, Raymond W. *Transforming America: Patterns of Social Change.* New York: Random House, 1967.

Moore, Wilbert E. *Social Change.* Englewood Cliffs: Prentice-Hall, 1963.

# 15
# Social Control

SOCIAL CONTROL IS AN EXTENSION OF THE SOCIAL-
ization process. We have seen that socialization, whether
of a person growing up in his own society or of the migrant into a different society, means ultimately that the
individual learns and enacts the expected patterns of
approved behavior. Persons and patterns are brought together so that a systematic way of group life can be
pursued. Self-control is the extension of subjective socialization. Social control is the objective aspect of socialization. It is the mechanism that perpetuates this process by
inducing and maintaining conformity of the people to
the behavior patterns.

It may be helpful to recall here what we have said
about social pressure. The range of behavior patterns from
strict mores to mere usages is measured by the three criteria of values, conformity, and pressure. When we analyze
social control, we are studying the ways in which social
pressure is exerted. Social control puts pressure on people
so that they will conform to the kind of patterns, roles,
relations, and institutions that are highly valued in the
culture.

A preliminary caution in the study of social control
is to avoid the restriction of this concept to the area of
governmental and political control. In contemporary society the dominant power of the state over individuals has
been recognized and feared. As a matter of fact, however,
the demands of the political institution are in most societies quite indirect and impersonal. The influence of other
groups is much more powerful, and it is axiomatic that
small primary groups have greater and more immediate
control over individual behavior than large secondary
associations.

404

LEVELS OF CONTROL

Social control exists on different levels of society and operates in different kinds of human relations. On the level of the social person, we tend to think of the control by the society or group over the individual. The total society influences all its members; but social control is exerted also by primary and secondary associations over their members. Since the social roles are the functional connecting link between the person and the groups in which he participates, the actual conformity of the person is recognized in the way in which he enacts these roles. Hence the role is the channel through which control is exerted on the person from his familial, economic, religious, and other groups.

Social control is not, however, directed only from the group to the individual. There is also a reverse control through which an individual, usually designated a leader, influences a group to conform to the patterns and values he promotes and approves. We shall discuss in some detail the function of leadership in society.

Besides the influence of the plurality on the individual and of the individual upon the plurality, there is also social control exerted by a relatively small group, or combination of groups, over the total society. Much has been made in recent years of the influence of the so-called "military-industrial complex" over the political destinies of the United States. Historically, social control of this kind has been exhibited by the dominance of a small upper class, or a rich and powerful political oligarchy, or by ecclesiastical leaders. Social control on this level operates more subtly, but often just as effectively, when employed by special interest groups and pressure groups. This latter type of group has in modern times perfected refined techniques of persuasion for getting the larger society to conform to the behavior norms and patterns it promotes.

KINDS OF CONTROL

The classification of social control can be made from

various points of view, depending upon the interest and purpose of the student of society. We discuss here briefly the three general classifications of positive and negative control, formal and informal control, and group and institutional control.

a. Certain positive mechanisms, like persuasion, suggestion, education, and rewards, are useful in influencing people to practice the behavior and to hold the attitudes that are socially approved. Other forms of control may be termed negative, like threats, orders, commands, compulsions, and penalties. They are employed to prevent people from antisocial behavior and attitudes.

Societies and groups try to get people to do certain things and to avoid other things, but this contrast between positive and negative controls can be made only in the abstract order. Both appear to operate together in the concrete order toward the goal of social conformity. Human motivation is complex, and the individual may act in socially approved ways either because he seeks rewards or because he avoids penalties, or because of both kinds of sanctions simultaneously.

b. A further classification is that of formal and informal controls. Every society and group institutes certain measures that are formally devised to bring about social conformity. These are the public enactments, ordinances, and laws established by political authority; they are the constitutions and by-laws of a country club, the regulations and commandments of a church, the official rules of a school or college. They are called formal because they are carefully planned, fully promulgated, and obligatory on all persons who submit to the authority of the lawmakers. There is also usually some sort of enforcement procedure of an official kind in formal controls.

Informal social controls are more subtle, but equally effective. They are employed to enforce the kind of behavior "everybody knows" should be performed and to prohibit patterns that are obviously socially disapproved. People usually know informally when their behavior is acceptable to others because they can sense the approval of their fellowmen even when it is not expressed in applause or congratulations. They usually also know informally when they are being snubbed or ridiculed or subject to some degree of social ostracism because of their nonconforming behavior.

c. The third classification, that of group and institutional controls, we shall analyze in more detail below. Briefly, group control achieves conformity through conscious, voluntary, and deliberate action on the part of both controller and controlled. The control may be positive or negative, formal or informal, but the distinguishing note is that it is deliberate and organized. Institutional control is the subconscious, often nonrational response of the individual to the cultural environment. The person carries out unthinkingly patterns of behavior to which he has become accustomed through long experience in his particular culture.

## The Person and Social Control

The person controlled is not an automaton. It is important to recall that people are not inert creatures of their culture or mechanical puppets of their society. Socialization is often stressed as a process that happens to the human person, and immediate situational interaction is often thought of as an influence upon a person, but we must remember that the person is an actor in both the process and the situation. He both acts in, and reacts to, socialization and cultural situations.

We have seen that a human being is a person because he is a thinking and deciding animal; he can store up abstract knowledge and has the ability to use it in planning and self-direction. It is scientifically absurd to suggest that he is nothing more than an unwitting victim of cultural forces. Nevertheless, it is obvious that man is a creature of social custom, that he does not stop to reflect and plan every thought and action, that he finds life much simpler when he accommodates himself to routines of behavior.

This patterning, or routinization, is quite different from the process of stimulus and response through which brute animals learn. In human beings self-control is an essential ingredient of social control. It is only in rare and extreme cases, where the individual has become "dehumanized" or "brainwashed" or rendered irresponsible through mental or physical torture, that one can speak of social control without self-control. For these individuals, and for mentally subnormal persons, the term social control is logically inapplicable.

Why do normal people constantly submit to social control? To say that man is a habit-forming animal is simply to go back to the socialization process through which his habits were formed. To say that he is by nature a conforming animal is simply to say redundantly that he submits to social pressure. The suggestion that man is a status-seeking animal is a retreat to another general catch-all explanation of human behavior, like utilitarianism or self-interest.

The social fact of conformity to cultural norms and pressures is so obvious that it requires no demonstration, but the conscious and intrinsic motivation behind it poses a problem of some complexity. There can be no doubt that human beings seek their own good, insofar as they consciously conform to norms and standards of approved conduct. They seek the recognition and approval of their fellowmen because these are the evidences of status, and because it is to the interest of the individual to preserve social status.

Together with all these motives, and deeper than any of them, is the fact that every normal social person has a developed sense of right and wrong. Most of the expressions of this sense emerge during the process of socialization, but the source of the expression is the human conscience. The social person learns how to use his conscience by living in society and by learning the cultural expectations. Like the inherent abilities to know and to judge, the basic feeling for right and wrong is a human quality. It is characteristic only of human beings, and therefore only of social persons; and it is the ultimate—though not the only—personal explanation why people submit to social control.

## GROUP CONTROL

It is essential to the maintenance of every group that some degree of conformity be achieved and that some type of social control be exercised. The primary groups need conformity more than the secondary associations, and there is also a difference between the two in the types of control they employ. The members of the primary group tend to display a voluntary, spontaneous, and informal submission to social control. In the secondary groups controls are more impersonal and formal.

A further distinction in control and conformity is found in an analysis of the major groups universal to every society. Each of these together with their numerous subgroups is interested in having people conform to its norms of behavior and belief. It is possible to rank these major groups according to the closeness and amount of control exercised in each, a ranking that depends to some extent upon the importance of the behavior patterns performed in each major group.

The mores valued by any group are more strictly enforced than its usages. This means of course that the group is not concerned with imposing conformity to all its behavior patterns. We have said that social pressure varies, and that it is greatest in those areas of conduct where high values are involved and wide conformity is attained. This is simply another way of saying that social pressure and social control have much in common. In highly ritualized behavior, as in secret lodges and fraternities and in some religious groups, exact conformity is often required even in minute and apparently nonessential details of behavior.

a. The closest control over group members is exercised in familial and educational groups. In these groups the socialization of persons is of greatest importance; social relations are most intimate; values engendered are high; and conformity to norms is a deliberate purpose of the group. In these groups there is relatively little variety and freedom of choice. The persons in authority are easily identified, and the members know that observing the rules is basic to the maintenance of the group and to the pursuit of their own welfare.

**b.** Economic and political groups rank next in the strength of their social controls. The conditions of gainful employment vary greatly but for the great majority of human beings they include obedience and conformity. The expectations concerning function, time, and procedure in economic activities are often rigid and formal, so that the individual has no choice except to conform or to resign. Politically, at those points where the citizen comes into contact with civic and public regulations he is compelled to relatively close conformity. The controls are as strong in political as in economic groups, but they are not applied as frequently.

**c.** Recreational and religious groups have the least amount of control over their members. These groups are in general more loosely knit than the others; there is much more freedom of movement and of choice by individuals; there is neither the need, nor often the possibility, of enforcing rigid conformity. The purposes of these groups are achieved more through voluntary cooperation of members than through strict social controls. This does not mean that there are no strictly disciplined and authoritarian religious groups, and even recreational groups. Here again social control and conformity are a matter of degree.

It must be noted that this ranking of groups from the point of view of social control may vary from society to society and from time to time. A totalitarian system would differ from a democratic one; it would tighten all controls and would shift the emphasis onto obedience to the political center. A culture in which religious values are high would probably deemphasize economic conformity and insist upon closer adherence to sacred norms. In spite of these variations, however, there is always discernible a rank-order of group control.

### INSTITUTIONAL CONTROL

Institutional control is the effective influence of the patterned cultural environment as exhibited by the subconscious response of the people of the group or society. In the conceptual framework of our study of sociology we have seen that persons use patterns, groups use institutions, and society uses culture. The cultural patterns and institutions show us not only what people do, but what they are expected to do. These expectations and demands of patterned behavior indicate that culture is in some sense self-enforcing. This is what we mean by institutional control over the people. Institutionalized behavior is the "thing to do" and this fact by itself exerts social pressure.

The analysis of social control requires an understanding of both group pressure and institutional pressure. The latter is largely impersonal and subconscious. It is a general environmental influence upon behavior rather than a specific personal ordering of an individual to this or that particular pattern of behavior. The two kinds of control go hand-in-hand. The group verbally demands conformity of the individual, but the group also gives an example of conformity because the institutionalized patterns are followed by everyone. But constant repetition of the same behavior patterns in relatively the same way develops social acceptance in people, and this is why we can say that custom both enforces and reinforces itself.

The ranking order of the degree and amount of social pressure exerted by the major groups of a society becomes clearer when we analyze it from the point of view of the institutions these groups employ. Shared patterns of behavior and close agreement on norms have to exist in the primary group more than in the secondary association. Similarly, mores identified with familial and educational institutions become more strongly patterned—and consequently exert greater pressure over a longer period of time —than those of the recreational and political institutions.

The institutional environment exerts control over the behavior of the person. From another point of view, however, institutions exert varying degrees of social pressure on one another and on the total society and culture. We have said that every culture contains a recognizable pivotal institution that demands more conformity and has more influence than any of the other institutions. Examples can be drawn from various cultures to show that in one the economic institution is dominant and that in another the political, or familial, or religious institution is the greatest influence. The environmental control exerted by the pivotal institution affects the institutionalized behavior throughout the culture. Since the major institutions must necessarily exist in every culture this control of the pivotal institution can never destroy or replace the other institutions.

Institutional control varies in its effectiveness from one society to another; it varies within the same society, and from one period of time to another. So-called tradition-bound people accept institutionalized restraints of long-established behavior patterns much more readily than the people of a restless, dynamic, individualistic society. Older people conform more steadily than younger people to institutional patterns. The dominance of a major institution may vary according to the exigencies of the time and the needs of the society, as for example, in large-scale warfare when the political institution requires great conformity and cooperation.

## LEADERSHIP AND SOCIAL CONTROL

From our observations about group control and institutional control we must not come to the conclusion that the deliberate influence of leaders is of little importance. The presence and action of dominant personalities are significant means for bringing about the conformity of people to the social norms and standards. Leaders can be classified in many ways, from the point of view of effectiveness, of techniques used, of types of groups served, and others. From the point of view of social control they are characterized as follows.

a. Positional leadership refers simply to the status dominance a person has in a group or society. This leadership is ascribed, since the person who is born into a royal or other prominent family, or who fills a position in a bureaucracy or hierarchy, has influence attributed to him by virtue of this fact alone. People who are asked to "lend their names" to programs and causes have this kind of leadership; it is abstracted from any particular skill or competence they may personally possess.

**b.** Personal leadership, on the other hand, is for the most part achieved. Its exercise as a means of social control depends upon the qualities of leadership the individual possesses. The person pursues a functioning social role, and because of his success in this role he can directly or indirectly influence the behavior of others. Three recognized general categories of personal leadership are as follows.

*Expert* leadership in a specific area of technical competence is enjoyed by specialists. The best brain surgeon, the best atomic physicist, and the best lawyer are persons who are leaders in their fields even though they may not be consciously striving to exert control over others. In most instances the wider importance of this indirect influence is through the transfer of leadership; for example, the expert mathematician exerts leadership by expressing his opinions in politics, religion, art, and other fields in which he is not an expert. His opinions are listened to in these other areas even when they are erroneous, because people tend to accept the statements of an "important" person.

*Charismatic* leadership evolves out of certain emotional qualities an individual possesses and exhibits. He is able to convince his followers that he is preordained, inspired, and enlightened in special ways. The charismatic leader inspires personal devotion to himself in others and depends upon it in the use of his influence. People intensely believe in him. The historic heroes, the founding fathers of a country, the crusaders in a great cause, the successful generals, the prophets and preachers, have been men in whom this special charism is recognized.

The most general type of leadership is *managerial,* which usually includes executive expertness and a touch of charism. The managerial leader has deep insight into complicated problems, a large comprehension of all the facets involved in them, an ability to make decisions and to carry them through to a conclusion. He knows how to delegate functions and authority to others and his executive ability is not confined to one profession or industry.

He is the superorganizer, the "troubleshooter," who can function expertly in government, industry, or any other organized system.

## COMMUNICATION AND SOCIAL CONTROL

The expectations of behavior must somehow be communicated to the people who are to conform to them. All the various mechanisms of socialization—written and spoken words, symbols, and examples—are used to convey the prohibition or approbation of behavior to people. If the group or the leader cannot get essential norms across to the members there is no possibility of conformity and control.

In any system of conscious, deliberate social control the edict is the most common form of communication. It is expressed by "do" and "don't." It may be a new law or a revision of an old law, a command, a regulation, or a decision by persons in authority. In most instances, especially in primary relations and informal groups, the edict is accompanied by reasons, explanations, and persuasions.

Advertising is one of the most carefully planned forms of obtaining social conformity because the advertiser must explain in precise detail what he wants people to do. He is attempting not only to build up a favorable attitude toward his product, he also wants people to purchase and consume his product. Propaganda is another deliberate medium for obtaining conformity to certain values and conceptual patterns. By its very nature and purpose it cannot be as detailed as the advertising medium, but it is nonetheless a powerful instrument of social control.

The educational process is the channel through which society transmits its culture to succeeding generations. The social purpose of education is to train persons to accept and conform to the highest behavior norms of the culture. Education works through formal systems and informal procedures, but its end product is a person who knows the difference between approved and disapproved behavior and who can take his place as a conforming member of the society.

## SOCIAL ENGINEERING AND CONTROL

Just as man occasionally thinks about his environment, himself, and his future, so also every social group does a certain amount of planning. Group members and especially leaders are conscious of the functions and goals of the group and of the fact that these are subject to design and direction. Even the informal primary group, which appears to be quite casual and spontaneous, requires the fore-thought and decision that are the basis of planning. Secondary associations construct budgets, hold meetings, arrange for elections and terms of office, issue statements of purposes and programs, and make analyses of their successes and failures. All this is a simple demonstration that planning is essential to organized groups and societies.

Social engineering means more than planning; it also means social action, the carrying through of plans. "Engineering" implies a detailed analysis of parts, a specific and technical design for making them workable, and a scheduled program for manipulating them toward the predetermined ends. This definition is, of course, a mechanical analogy and it can be interpreted only with the proper understanding of the strictly sociological phenomena involved. The basic units analyzed and manipulated are behavior patterns and social persons and their various combinations, and we have seen the conditions and limitations under which these function toward given ends.

From the point of view of social control, social engineering presents one of the central problems of group life. We have seen that socialization is the process through which the person is inducted into society and learns the patterns of culture. This results in general conformity to the accepted norms and standards. Social engineering goes beyond this and demands a more specific conformity to rationally planned behavior. The problem lies in the working relationship between the individual and the group. Engineering that minimizes the initiative and voluntary cooperation of the individual defeats its own purposes. Engineering that does not exert sufficient control over individuals to arrive at its end is meaningless.

It is possible to have social control for its own sake without engineering; but it is impossible to have effective social engineering without some control and conformity. An effective type of social engineering requires that the people have some participation in both the planning and the execution of the social design. The type of social goals set, the speed at which the plan is executed, and the kind of pressures and sanctions applied all require a general knowledge of pertinent trends. In addition to this knowledge, effective social engineering requires great understanding of the social personalities involved in the proposed change.

## Social Controls in America

### 1. RESISTANCE TO SOCIAL CONTROL

It is important to remember that even in a progressive and pragmatic culture like that of the United States there are many traditionalists among the people and many who resist social control. Every attempt at social reform, or induced social change requiring social control, engineering, and planning has been met by opposition. We must not think of the American society as a sort of pliant, fluid, passive system that is easily controlled and in which change takes place almost automatically.

Every major social reform which has required planning and control has had to overcome the opposition of those who said that change would do more harm than good. A list of reforms taken at random demonstrates this point: the shortened work-week, political suffrage for women, safety rules in mines and factories, infant and maternal care, public health benefits, public housing, old-age pensions, child-labor laws, extension of education, public parks and playgrounds, released time from school for religious instruction, fair employment practices, and many others.

All these have required a change in both conceptual and external behavior patterns, a conformity on the part of Americans to new social situations, and consequently a submission to social control. We cannot make an exhaustive analysis of the reasons why objections are raised to social reform, but we present the following as a partial explanation of resistance to social control.

**a.** The virtue of prudence is often invoked to bless and justify opposition to social reform. Correctly used, "prudence" is an essential virtue for every scientist who makes sure of his facts before drawing a conclusion. Incorrectly defined, the self-styled prudent man leaves the facts and the conclusions where they are and does nothing about them. An ill-defined concept of prudence is used as a rationalization against reform.

**b.** It is more comfortable to continue doing things in the same old way. Older people, especially, seem to magnify the costs of reform in terms of their own comfort and convenience. The creature of habit is disturbed at the prospect of changing his attitudes even in cases where no change in his external patterns is required. This inertia is characteristic of many people.

**c.** A more positive aspect of this characteristic is self-interest. The fear of losing status, or some of the criteria of status, motivates people to a staunch defense of the present order of things. This fear is part of the constant though often imaginary conflict between self-interest and public interest, between personal gain and social gain. It cannot always be demonstrated that what will benefit the total society will also benefit the individual, and the strong individualist is unwilling to experiment in order to discover whether this is so.

**d.** Ignorance of social trends is one of the strongest obstacles to social reform. Fear of the unknown, past and present, reinforces fear of the future. It is a curious fact that those who know least about the technical areas of society and culture are frequently the most dogmatic in prophesying exactly and in detail the harm that will ensue from any given proposal for social reform. Fortunately, the diffusion of social science knowledge among Americans is decreasing this obstacle.

**e.** Pressure groups are often positive means of social control, but they act in many instances as preventives of social change. The pressure group functions to protect the interests of some organized segment of the population and may exert an influence far out of proportion to its importance or its numbers. The notion that a proposed reform will do more harm than good usually implies that the group fears danger to itself rather than to the total society.

The traditionalists who are prophets of doom in the face of every proposed social reform display a curious set of reactions after the reform has been in effect for a considerable period. First, they learn to live with it, to conform to the change, and even to approve it. Second, they forget the fact that their worst fears were unfounded and that their dire predictions did not come true. Third—and this is most frustrating to the social reformer—they use precisely the same arguments ("it will do more harm than good") when a new program of further social reform is proposed.

It is probably true that certain types of social personality—authoritarian, ethnocentric, paranoid—are more likely than others to oppose social reform. At the present time we have no reliable studies to indicate whether these people are increasing in the American population. The hope and expectation of the student of society is that they are not increasing but that the spread of knowledge about society and culture is increasing the number of Americans who welcome and approve social progress.

## 2. VARIATIONS OF INSTITUTIONAL CONTROL

Institutional pressure varies throughout the culture. Although all the major institutions affect in some way the behavior of all the people, they do not have an even and equal influence on all. The total American culture is influenced more by the economic institution than by any other. This represents, however, only the general picture. There are many variations of pressure within the sociocultural system, and it may be useful to make a rough analysis of these variations.

a. From the point of view of the people in any group, the force of the institutionalized patterns differs according to the function and role of the individual. The inner and higher functionaries are forced by their position to adhere closely to the strongest mores of the group. Those who are relatively passive members and hangers-on have less pressure upon them, while outsiders are only lightly influenced. These generalizations are valid for all major groups.

b. There are also local variations in social control and pressure. Some parts of the country are more conservative and resistant to change than other parts. American farmers are more likely to be influenced by familial and religious mores, while urban people seem to be under greater pressure from the economic and recreational patterns. Local subcultures, especially those influenced by ethnic mores, also exhibit differences in institutional control.

c. The strength of institutional pressure differs from one social class to another. There is much talk of middle class, or "bourgeois," morality in the United States, indicating that behavior conformity is greater among class-conscious people and especially among those who are straining for higher status. Often enough, at least in certain areas of conduct, socially secure upper-class people take institutional pressure lightly. There are also examples of lower-class persons who disregard the educational and religious mores of the culture even though they yield to strong pressure from economic and political institutions.

d. There is an uneven age variable in the kind and the degree of institutional control. It may be said that controls are personally applied by the group more to young persons than to adults; but the impersonal institutional pressure is greater on adults than on youth. Older people are conformists by habit and by inclination; it is more convenient to conform than to resist. It is obvious also that the institutional environment of younger people is mainly that of the familial, educational, and recreational systems.

e. The time variable is noted by a glance at recent American history. During the Second World War and the Korean War there was an emphasis on patriotic mores, on military conduct, and on nationalistic behavior. Strong reaction to the war in Vietnam brought an upsurge of pacifism and focused attention on the domestic problems of housing, education, and poverty. In periods of national catastrophe and economic depression it is also said that the influence of the religious institution increases.

f. The social pressure from institutions varies also according to the values held in a culture, and there can be no doubt that the institutionalized economic values have taken precedence in the contemporary United States. Directly and immediately for the adult working population, and indirectly and mediately for the rest, there is a subsconscious feeling for the appropriateness of the economic mores. The number of people, the amount of time, the degree of interest, and the extent of subservience that surround the demands of the economic system indicate where the highest values of the American people lie.

This list of the fundamental variations of institutional control gives a hint of the complex network of social pressure. It makes us realize that institutional conformity is no automatic, evenly distributed result of a mechanically operating force. Not all Americans are affected in the same way by the same institutional pressures. There are times and situations when these pressures work in opposite directions, as when a conflict arises between familial and occupational patterns, or between political and religious norms. The tremendous increase in leisure-time activities in our society has raised the recreational institution to a force of ever-widening influence and has placed the values of work and play in contrast.

In spite of these variations and complexities it is possible for the careful student to obtain a general appreciation of institutional control in a given culture at a given time. Consideration of this control is necessary in any attempt to characterize the American people or any other society. Certain signposts point the way to generalizations without which the valid construction of a social science would be impossible. As we obtain more knowledge through sociological research on the American culture, we obtain also a clearer understanding of the workings of institutional controls.

## 3. IMPERSONAL CONFORMITY OF AMERICAN WORKERS

The increasing trend toward secondary relations and associations has interfered with personal and mutual loyalties in America. This decrease in personal involvement and in face-to-face relationships is apparent in all large-scale organizations—in educational, religious, and political associations—but nowhere is it more striking than in the occupational system. Mass production of goods in our industrial economy has required a disciplined conformity to the demands of the machine, demands different from those of any other work situation.

The fact that American workers do conform to this kind of system and produce successfully and abundantly is witness to the resilience of the social personality. From the point of view of social control this conformity is remarkable because it is mainly the result of technological planning and occurs largely without benefit of personal and mutual loyalty between employer and employee. Social reformers who decry the "inhumanity of the machine" and who rue the passing of both economic individualism and paternalism do not seem to realize that personal fealty to the employer is a practical impossibility in the present work situation.

Following are a few social facts that help to explain why American workers conform to the plans of employers without having deep personal relations with them.

a. The high cultural value of independence has characterized the American worker throughout our history and has been coupled with an aversion to paternalistic authority. The industrial worker rejects anything that resembles servitude, bondage, or peonage, and the society itself puts legal prohibitions on this kind of work arrangement. The absence of a docile and humble servant class in America is symptomatic of the general unwillingness of workers to become personally dependent upon employers.

b. As labor unions have become larger and stronger they have acted as an agent for the worker. They make collective agreements for him, arranging the details of hours, wages, seniority rights, and other conditions. They step between the employer and the employee and in this sense discourage the need for personalized relationships between the two.

c. To some extent the government has also helped to depersonalize this relationship. The successful functioning of our gigantic industrial economy is a national and federal concern. A certain amount of regulation and control is essential. Labor laws have been made and remade by the Congress and they deal in considerable detail with the content—the rights and privileges—of the labor-management relation.

d. The basic corporate structure of big industrial enterprises is necessarily a formal, legalistic, and impersonal arrangement. The thousands of owners of a large corporation are themselves represented by management in control of the business. Hired executives and specialized functionaries are themselves employees even though they are on the side of management in the direction of operations. Nevertheless, they often develop a loyalty to the firm difficult for the ordinary worker to achieve.

e. The mobility of the work force, or at least of a significant proportion of it, appears to be a permanent concomitant of our kind of industrial economy. A local solidarity and a set of close personal relations between worker and employer would interfere with this mobility. The relatively fluid labor force responds to the changes and pressures always at work in our economy.

f. The tendency to conceptualize labor as simply another cost item in the production of goods also has a depersonalizing effect. This is in line with the general commercialization of materials, goods, and services, and it must be remembered that the constant effort to cut down the cost of production has been a large factor in the increase of purchasing power of the consumer. A rigid and stable relationship between employer and employees, especially one of loyalty and personal solidarity, would have an effect upon this concept.

g. Finally, the specialization of functions compartmentalizes labor and separates the worker from the employers. The sheer quantity of technical knowledge required, especially on the higher levels of the industrial function, makes it impossible for a worker to be proficient in more than a few jobs within an industry. This means that his day-to-day social experience is narrowed to a relatively small circle of fellow workers.

This list must not be construed as a total explanation of the work situation in American industry. Sufficient research has been done in factories and plants to show that the impersonal conformity of workers to the demands of the job does not imply automatic or mechanical social relations. Peer groups of people with mutual respect and loyalty exist everywhere. Techniques have been devised for maintaining human relations within the factory, and many programs have been established as substitutes for personal employer-employee relationships.

As the present system of relations becomes more and more institutionalized, the workers become accustomed to it, take it for granted, and submit to it with only a vague realization of the "rules of the game." Most workers are conditioned to the kind of conformity their jobs demand, and as long as there are no patent injustices they probably prefer to have it that way.

## 4. POLITICAL CONTROL OF INDUSTRY

We have seen that the major institutions of the American culture are necessarily interlocking systems, mutually influential and interdependent. Persons who naively speak of complete separation of the political and religious institutions are usually those who also complain about the intrusion of the "welfare state" into the economic order. There are many points at which the government and the economy meet; and it is difficult to see how this merger could be avoided or to imagine that this avoidance could be sociologically helpful.

The notion that the government could be a mere arbiter among economic pressure groups, or that it could be an aloof umpire over the general economy, is as outmoded as the individualistic philosophers who first proposed it. The American government from its beginning has exerted control over the economy; and as the economic system grew larger and more complex this political control also had to increase. We may sketch very briefly the two directions of this relationship between the political and the economic institutions: implementation and regulation.

Probably the more important aspect of political influence is found in the tremendous service the government has rendered to American business. Our economy would be unworkable if the government did not control currency and counterfeiting, support the banking system, operate a patent office, set norms for the stock exchange, and provide a legal framework for everything from the establishment of corporations to the procedures for bankruptcy and reorganization. The enforcement of property laws and contract terms, the provision of direct subsidies, and the establishment of tariffs are all mechanisms the government provides in order to facilitate the operation of the economy.

For the benefit of the whole economy the government maintains research departments and information bureaus for almost every economic function. Mining, forestry, agriculture, heavy and light industry, and producers and distributors of all types are helped by these services. The physician who condemns farm subsidies gets assistance from the Public Health Service; the farmer who fears socialized medicine gets help from federal and state agricultural stations. The Securities and Exchange Commission aids investors; the Bureau of Labor Statistics gives information on employment trends; the Bureau of Standards does research for consumers.

Besides these and many other supportive mechanisms the government also regulates economic activities, primarily in order to restrain monopoly and promote competition. Government regulations have been made to prohibit deceptive business practices, misleading advertising, the bootlegging of trademarks, and so forth. These have been helpful regulations for which the great majority of honest and efficient businessmen have been grateful. Nevertheless, the cry of "interference" is almost always heard whenever the Justice Department suggests an investigation of monopolistic practices.

In recent years the government has been called upon by both sides to "balance" the power between giant corporations and giant unions. The attempts by Congress and the administration to promote industrial harmony have become major issues in each political campaign, enmeshing the political institution even more deeply with the economic institution. Because we have never developed a large American labor party, both of the major political parties contend for the labor vote.

These two aspects of political control, supportive and regulative, are not always initiated by the government. Farmers, workers, businessmen, and professional people are forced to comply with many government regulations and they readily accept government support. But much of this political "interference" has come at the request of pressure groups, lobbies, and interest groups. We seldom appreciate the fact that the decennial census is of great service to the economic system and that many of the questions asked in it are proposed by people with business interests.

Although for purposes of analysis we distinguish between political and economic functions, the concrete situation shows a close interlocking of the two. The cost of operating the government is ultimately paid out of the economic activities of the people, but it is safe to predict that the economy would collapse if there were any serious attempt to withdraw the political from the economic institution, or even to return to the government policies of fifty years ago.

From the point of view of our institutionalized value system, economic values have penetrated government more than political values have influenced the economy. Americans depend upon the government to promote prosperity and to take preventive measures against economic depression. Economic problems, like inflation and the high cost of living, have become a central concern of the government, and the American people apparently believe that only the government is "big enough" to do something about them.

## 5. Social Planning and Morale

America is one of the few large societies of the world without mass movements. The political apathy of Americans is particularly noticeable, and even much of the success of organized economic movements has come through the work of relatively small interest and pressure groups. Besides this lack of mass action there has also been a lack of confidence in any obviously dictatorial individual who has tried to assume control.

It may be said in general that, in the United States, deliberate social engineering succeeds best when it is promoted by small groups with high morale. This may appear to be an anomaly in a country where large-scale projects are carried out by big organizations requiring the cooperation of large numbers of people. The appearance is deceptive because we tend to look at the results of planning, that is, thousands of people in coordinated action, rather than the planning process that brings about such action. To discover the planning process we have to watch the committees, boards, bureaus, and small groups of people who are dedicated to change, reform, and control.

The quality characteristic of all these groups is high morale, which in turn is the result of a combination of factors. We have seen that teamwork is effective when three conditions are fulfilled: first, if the action to be performed is concrete; second, if the responsibility for performance can be fixed; and third, if the action to be performed is considered worthwhile by the participants. Morale among the members of the group is an added element, and even groups with excellent leadership and emotions of righteousness do not succeed without it.

Empirical research has shown that morale is present in a group where there is: (a) a clearly defined goal of real value to the members; (b) a deep conviction that the goal can be reached, or at least that a worthwhile portion of the end can be achieved; (c) some empirical evidence that they are making progress toward the goal; (d) a feeling of solidarity among the members of the group; and (e) an awareness of danger or threats from outside the group (external threats tend to unite and "uplift" the members).

These conditions of high morale can be recognized in all groups that successfully plan and execute social reform. This is exemplified in many instances in the American society: in the small group that engineered the prohibition amendment, in the group that fought for and won suffrage for women, and in any number of citizens' committees that have cleaned up vice, gambling, and political corruption in various cities in the United States.

One of the most dramatic examples of the effects of high morale is that of the small committee on industrial organization that formed within the American Federation of Labor in the 1930s. They had the whole tradition of the trade union movement as well as the most powerful labor organization in the country against them. They were a close-knit group, convinced that their goal was worthwhile and attainable, and they had almost immediate success in organizing the industrial workers. It is true that there were some defections, but these occurred only after the group had become the powerful Congress of Industrial Organizations.

The importance of high morale is demonstrated also by its absence in large numbers of unsuccessful social planners. The history of the country is dotted with abortive movements of social reform, and especially of groups that resisted strong social trends. The morale of many socialist and Marxist groups has been broken because one or more of the above conditions were not present. New groups have formed for the same purpose and have also been unsuccessful over the long term.

It appears that the intensity with which group values are held is in inverse relation to the size of the group, and that this high intensity is divisive, if not destructive, of group morale. This is most readily demonstrated in extremist groups of both right and left which demand pure and undeviating loyalty from their members. What happens here is that deviationists and revisionists are either expelled or they split off to form separate groups. High morale is often maintained in each splinter group but the general effect is a weakening of the thrust for social reform.

High morale ultimately makes the difference between mere social planning and genuine social engineering. One of the qualities of the leader is that he follows through in social action the ideas he proposes. Similarly, the test of the planning group is the endurance of its morale through the transitional period into the actual program of social reform. The members of the small planning group do not perform all the functions required in the total program. The program necessarily requires some cooperation from many persons. For progressive ideas to reach the engineering stage, the group's morale must remain high.

## Suggested Readings

Blau, Peter M. *Exchange and Power in Social Life*. New York: Wiley, 1964.

LaPiere, Richard. *A Theory of Social Control*. New York: McGraw-Hill, 1954.

Lemert, Edwin. *Human Deviance, Social Problems and Social Control*. Englewood Cliffs: Prentice-Hall, 1967.

Lenski, Gerhard. *Power and Privilege*. New York: McGraw-Hill, 1966.

Pound, Roscoe. *Social Control Through Law*. New Haven: Yale University Press, 1942.

# 16
# Deviation

In previous chapters we have noted that social change is any variation from a former mode of existence, and that social control is the process through which change to, or maintenance in, social conformity is effected. Both social change and social control are concerned with regularities and norms. Both are recurrent, routinized sociocultural phenomena, for change is inherent in social life and control is a necessary condition of society and culture. Induced social change is always directed toward the values and norms current in the culture, and deliberate control is directed toward the conformity of people to those norms.

## The Deviant and the Abnormal

Social and cultural deviation involves abnormalities and irregularities. The social scientist uses the term "normal" to refer to anything standardized, patterned, recurrent, and characteristic. This means, of course, that these regularities of behavior and structure are themselves employed as norms by which we discover and evaluate that which is "abnormal." It is assumed that normal behavior meets with the approval of society and abnormal behavior its disapproval, and that the study of deviation is related to the values of the culture. In strictly scientific terms, however, the recognition of deviation does not bespeak the subjective disapproval of the observer.

If social control is a mechanism for making people conform to the normal patterns of the culture, then deviation is a process in which people "get out of control." Persons who do not perform in normal ways, that is, who do not conform to the expected, recurrent regularities of behavior, are called abnormal or deviant. They are not normless, or anomic. Subjectively, every rational person entertains a set of behavioral norms, but insofar as these subjective norms differ from those commonly accepted in

429

the culture, he is a deviant. From the sociological point of view the normal persons in any society are those who share the commonly held patterns of belief and conduct. Those who depart from these patterns are deviant.

## POSITIVE AND NEGATIVE DEVIATION

Every culture contains both ideal and real patterns of behavior. The ideal patterns are interpretive of the highest values; they are expressed in the basic principles to which the society subscribes, but they are never fully attained. It is not these, but the real patterns of behavior, that we employ as a norm of conformity or deviation. Thus, the mores and folkways are the normal regularities and uniformities against which the social scientist must measure deviation.

*Positive* deviation is that which moves in the direction of the ideal patterns of behavior. It is an approximate conformity to those ideal norms the society itself considers superior and to those forms of behavior people term "more virtuous." The positively oriented and upwardly deviant person or group "rises above" the commonplace, often repeated, real patterns of thought and action. This kind of deviant is the extraordinary person, the saint, the hero, the exemplar of behavior. It is often easier to discern such a person in the literature of a people than to recognize him in concrete social situations.

There are many historical examples of persons who were called radicals and fanatics during their lifetime but who were later recognized as positive deviants. Political and religious revolutionaries were sometimes persecuted. Inventors and discoverers were often ridiculed by their contemporaries. Similar treatment was accorded to prophetic social reformers and to innovators in the fields of painting, sculpture, and architecture. These examples indicate that a time perspective is important in the recognition of positive deviants and that both tolerance and objectivity are required of the scientific social observer.

*Negative* deviation moves in the direction of disapproved, inferior, and inadequate behavior. It means conformity to modes of conduct that are substandard in the culture, that are "below" the real patterns. This substandard behavior is the most common form of deviation discussed in sociological literature. Books on social problems deal with negatively deviant behavior because it is a downward departure from the level of behavior acceptable in a society. Persons and groups who are negatively deviant are usually accorded low social status by their society in general.

It will be recalled that three indexes are employed by social scientists to distinguish among the mores, folkways, and usages in the culture. The real patterns of behavior are measured by the amount of social pressure exerted for their observance, the extent of conformity among the people, and the degree of value in which they are held. Similarly, the analysis of deviation becomes meaningful in a scientific way only when we have a knowledge of these three indexes and can measure the deviant behavior against them.

The difficulty of analysis arises from the fact that these indexes must be used in combination. Generally speaking, deviant behavior of a negative nature is that which is accompanied by low social values; relatively few people enact it or urge that it be enacted. Recognized criminal and other antisocial behavior readily fits this description. Positive deviation towards superior and more virtuous behavior fits the highest values in the culture but does not fulfill the two other qualifications. There are relatively few persons in the society who perform it, and there is little effective pressure to force compliance. Positive deviation, although in accord with the highest cultural values, must still be termed deviation.

## TYPES OF NEGATIVE DEVIANTS

The people who are deviants are different and abnormal compared to the average person and the average kind of behavior. But there are kinds of differences and degrees of abnormality in every society. People may be extreme nonconformists or only moderate nonconformists; they may be abnormal from the physical, mental, moral, or

cultural points of view. This approach classifies rather than explains, but at least a partial explanation of deviation may be surmised from the type of classification made.
**a.** The mentally defective and the psychologically unfit constitute a category of negative deviants. Their behavior is erratic in various degrees because they are unable to adjust themselves to the normally accepted ways of society. Included among these are morons, idiots, and simple-minded persons as well as those who suffer from severe psychotic and neurotic disturbances. Their antisocial behavior may range from that of the violent destructive person to that of the harmless, helpless person.

Negative deviants of this kind are said to be "out of touch with reality," and they require the care of society for their own protection and for the sake of others. Their behavior is random and eccentric since they cannot recognize and duplicate the real patterns considered normal in a society. Calling them "deviants" does not imply a moral or ethical judgment, since they are not responsible or accountable for their conduct.
**b.** The physically or organically handicapped are another category of negative deviants to the degree that they cannot pursue the normal patterns of life in society. These people are quite different from both the psychologically and the morally abnormal deviants. Deaf-mutes, the crippled and paralyzed, and the chronically ill constitute a problem for themselves and for society. Through training and personal abilities they may learn to participate to some degree in the culture and society, but they can never reach the level of behavior considered normal and acceptable.
**c.** Those who may be called dependent deviants are in a third category. In a sense, they are declassed people who have little or no social status within the normal structure and are dependent upon society. These are derelicts, drifters, dropouts, as well as genuine paupers and voluntary mendicants. This category includes dependent illegitimate children and orphans, although these latter may well pass through the socialization process to take their place as normal social persons in adulthood.

**d.** Criminal or delinquent deviants are subject to a different standard of judgment by society than are the mental, physical, and dependent deviants. Criminals are nonconformists who deliberately violate the value norms of the culture. It is only because they are accountable for their conduct that they are visited with penalties imposed by the society itself. Their deviant behavior ranges from serious to light offenses and their irregularities from relatively habitual to merely occasional actions.

## Deviation and Social Roles

Uniformities of behavior can be meaningfully analyzed from the point of view of social roles. When a person deviates markedly from the normal expectations of his social roles, we observe a lack of uniformity and regularity. Since the role satisfies a specific need and functions toward a recognized goal, it provides for us a clue to the cultural significance of conformity and nonconformity. The effective and integrated social personality is one in which all the social roles are functioning in normal and expected ways.

This approach through an analysis of social roles helps to avoid the oversimplification that a person is all good, or all bad, or that deviation is a total condition of the social personality. An adequate analysis of the role indicates that most nonconformists are only partial deviants and that most conformists occasionally act abnormally. An absolute conformist appears to be a sociological impossibility since both conformity and deviance are relative to the person, the role, and the culture.

From the point of view of role-content, society readily permits a degree of variation and deviation in the performance of usages. This permissive attitude tightens up in regard to folkways and turns into a prohibition in regard to mores. Thus, in the parental role the individual is permitted no choice on the level of compulsory duties toward children. Deviation here from the strict mores is not tolerated by society. But on the level of usages the parent has a certain freedom of choice, limited only by extreme eccentricities. The father may not starve his children, but he may restrict their eating of certain foods.

We have seen that the norms for social roles are developed not in the society as a whole, but in the various social groups in which the roles are enacted. In the socialization process, the individual does not learn merely a general total social role, but the several specific social roles in the major groups in which he participates. Logically, therefore, the normal uniformities of behavior are pertinent to the functions and goals of each group and differ from group to group. A man does not act in the same way in a golf foursome as he does in a church choir or at a sales meeting. The same set of behavior patterns that is perfectly normal in one situation would be deviant or abnormal in another situation.

## ROLE DEVIATION AND THE SOCIAL PERSONALITY

The acceptable social personality avoids deviation by learning not to "mix" his roles. The society judges him on his ability to adapt his behavior to given times, situations, and groups and to follow the behavior expectations of each role as it is enacted. Usually, however, deviation of the social personality does not occur merely by substituting one role for another, as playing the choir member's role in an economic group. This would be total nonconformity and would be considered outright abnormality by the other participants.

Role deviation is seen more frequently in the uneven enactment of the various social roles. A man may fulfill adequately his roles as husband and father and his recreational and political roles, but depart from the norms of behavior expected in his business practices. The adolescent daughter may conform normally in all her social roles with the exception of her student role. Conversely, the model student may be an incorrigible family member, conforming to the demands of school behavior but failing in the expectations of the familial role.

It is probably true that, comparing the internal social roles enacted by the individual person, all human beings are to some degree social deviants. Here again it is necessary to make the distinction among mores, folkways, and usages and to realize that deviation in most instances is a temporary aberration. Even the normal social personality is sometimes a deviant in some aspects of his social roles. A certain amount of elasticity is overlooked and even expected by society. A "slip" here and there is hardly noticed and sometimes even approved because it makes the person "more interesting." However, a person who is consistently a nonconformist in one social role, although he may fully conform in his other roles, certainly fits the definition of the social deviant.

## INSTITUTIONALIZED DEVIATION

Since patterns of behavior become institutionalized it is obvious that the normal person is one who conforms to the general demands of the institutions. The uneven enactment of social roles by individuals is often paralleled and sometimes caused by a certain amount of inconsistency among the various institutions of a culture. The highest values of the religious institution may be at odds with those of the economic or political institution. This institutional inconsistency, or impersonal deviation, probably exists in every culture; and since we define deviation as a lack of conformity, it is probably best evaluated against the norms of the pivotal institution.

Aside from the abstract level of the basic cultural ethos that seems to penetrate all institutions, the people tend to measure all institutional norms against those of the pivotal institution. If the culture is dominated by the values of family and kinship there is a tendency to bring all other institutional arrangements into conformity with them and to judge as a deviation those patterns that do not conform. In this sense deviation becomes a more or less static concept of inconsistency.

One of the knottiest problems of sociological analysis lies in the fact that every culture contains patterned, and apparently approved, deviations of conduct. Anthropologists report that primitive tribes countenance occasional orgies and that in simple societies these act as a psychological release of tension. Whatever the explanation, the fact is that even highly developed and complex societies permit similar deviations.

These institutionalized deviations are sometimes called "patterned evasions." They are more or less regularized ways of contravening the approved and established norms of conduct. They are deceptive and paradoxical and may be called "normal abnormalities." Surreptitious punishment and deprivation of racial and minority groups, the passive cooperation of the police in these practices, and the tacit approval given to them by upper-class people combine in an established pattern of deviation. Various forms of prostitution and illegal gambling, ticket-fixing, graft, fee-splitting, and similar practices are recognized as "undersirable" behavior. Nevertheless, they satisfy real or imagined needs of people, and even though they contradict the expressed values of the culture, they develop into systematized and institutionalized deviations.

DEVIANT SITUATIONS

Besides the more or less established forms of institutional deviation, the social scientist also recognizes the infrequent abnormal situation. This is a temporary phenomenon in which people tend to "forget themselves" and act almost completely out of their accustomed roles. For example, a panic or a crisis occurs and normal social persons act in strange and unanticipated ways. A riot or street fight may bring together people who have never met before and involve them in unaccustomed and uncoordinated behavior. The definition of a mob implies a plurality of persons in an abnormal situation.

Not every deviant situation of this kind is sudden and unexpected. Periods of increasing social friction and of tense human relations often precede the panic, riot, or mob action. A labor strike may be well organized, and the intentions of the pickets may be quite peaceful, but the situation sometimes lends itself to a social eruption. Similarly, a rebellion may be secretively planned over a considerable period of time, but when it does occur it creates an abnormal situation. The rebels themselves are nonconformists and the action they pursue is abnormal.

If we view sociocultural deviation as a situation in which socially disapproved behavior is performed by large numbers of people, we can distinguish three situational levels. The *first* is the more or less established routine of deviation, like the "fixing" of tickets for traffic violations, that is merely tolerated by the people. The *second* is the temporary and unexpected behavioral aberration that occurs in crises or panics. The *third* is the temporary, but often anticipated, social eruption, like that of violence and conflict. Numerous and varying influences are at work in each deviant situation in this tri-level analysis.

## Deviant Groups

The analysis of every society shows the presence of the major basic groups: the familial, educational, economic, political, religious, and recreational. It is rarely, however, that there is complete coordination and conformity of all the segments within each major group. The subgroups may range from those that comply with the highest values and norms to those that are almost extreme nonconformists. The latter we call deviant groups.

In a large, complex, and dynamic society numerous examples of deviant groups can be classified under the major groups. Cults and sects break off from the large religious bodies, and radical movements emerge and make demands for reform within the parent body. Political parties have their groups of internal dissenters who sometimes form splinter parties. In the business world there are positive deviants who venture into new systems of production and distribution and negative deviants who operate shady enterprises. Similar forms of organized deviations are found historically in the recreational, educational, and familial groups.

We have seen that social persons may be classified as deviants psychologically, physically, economically, or ethically. From the point of view of group classification, the ethically deviant groups are the ones that attract the most attention and present the largest problem to organized society. These groups are made up of lawbreakers, whether they are temporary aggregates forming riot and lynch mobs or relatively permanent associations of various kinds of criminals. Illegal and morally deviant groups, gangs, and even crime "syndicates" are present to some degree in every large society.

The student of society must understand that these criminal groups and associations are only partially deviant. An analysis of their functions and structures indicates that they exist and operate according to all the sociological generalizations we have made about nondeviant groups. The individuals perform patterns of behavior, enact roles, and have status within the structure. They require the various processes and relations, as well as control and administration. These groups are stratified, with leaders and followers; their shared behavior is institutionalized. They are sociologically different from nondeviant groups, however, because some of their values and actions differ from those approved and accepted in the larger society.

The goals of negatively deviant groups vary somewhat, but they point in the general direction of exploitation of the total society. It is probable that the main motivation of some of the youthful gangs is the desire for thrills and recreation, while that of the corrupt political machine may be a desire for power. Generally, however, the ethically deviant group exploits the society for material gain. In this sense they are economic groups seeking financial profit through illegal channels and in ways disapproved in the culture.

The distinction between the law-abiding and the lawbreaking groups in a society is not so clear-cut as this description may indicate. If sufficient data were available about individuals, we could construct a continuum of persons ranging from the full-time professional criminal to the honest, upright citizen. Yet somewhere along the continuum are numerous persons who are esteemed as honest citizens but who participate regularly in illegal activities. We have seen that every culture contains patterned evasions, or institutionalized deviation. For example, the whole area of "white-collar" crime contains deviant groups of people who enact these patterns.

## MARGINAL GROUPS

In terms of the accepted norms of the culture we have seen that persons and groups may be either positively or negatively deviant, that is, either superior to the patterned behavioral norm or inferior to it. Some persons, groups, and types of behavior are at the "margin" of the accepted limits of the sociocultural system. They are not completely within it nor are they completely outside it.

The concept of cultural marginality does not necessarily connote an ethical or moral judgment. The marginal man is one who has not been fully assimilated or accommodated to the social and cultural norms of the society in which he lives. The marginal person is different, and in this sense he is a deviant, even though he may be striving earnestly to follow the mores and to be accepted by the majority of the people.

Marginal groups are obviously minority groups, and from the broad view of the total society they are more technically termed "social categories." They are made up largely of immigrants and newcomers, who still exhibit the characteristics of their socialization in a different culture. Marginal categories may also be racial or religious minorities that, except for this specific characteristic, fully share the culture of the majority population.

Marginality is measured by the general criteria of social status, and in a large modern society this is necessarily a dynamic concept. The marginal person does not have in sufficiently high degree some of the valued items that increase status in the society, whether these are wealth, skin color, type of education, religion, or others. Most of these items change gradually in the persons who possess them, and their evaluation may also change over a period of time in the minds of the majority members. The marginal group is peripheral to the total culture and must be conceptualized as moving toward it, unless this is prevented by castelike arrangements in the social structure.

The degree of deviation of the marginal group depends

ultimately on what is considered normal in the total
sociocultural system. The deviant group can gain acceptance only to the extent that it can "achieve" normality.
The concept of achievement emphasizes the social role,
while the concept of ascription emphasizes social status.
The former is much more effective for the person or
group already contained within the major society, while
the latter is more important for the marginal person or
group. Marginality is consequently a special aspect of
deviation since the marginal deviants frequently cannot
do anything about removing the source of their deviation.

## SOCIAL PROBLEMS AND PROGRESS

Social deviation is a peculiar phenomenon in that it
creates both social problems and the conditions for social
progress. If society were a nicely balanced mechanism
functioning in an exactly repetitive way, it would be subject to neither abnormalities nor improvements from
within. Every sociocultural system is subject to internal
change and to deviation from previously accepted regularities and normalities.

Sociologists who employ the "value approach" define
a social problem as a discrepancy between the value
norms and the actual social behavior in a society and
imply also that there are always conflicts between different sets of values. Whether or not this approach is used,
the social problem appears always to be related to a deviation from the accepted standards of behavior. The list
of social problems ordinarily analyzed by the sociologist
—poverty, crime and delinquency, substandard housing,
ill health, and many others—suggests that a considerable
number of people do not, or cannot, participate normally
in the valued items of the culture.

It is obvious that the term "social problem" has to do
with negative deviation. Whether it is defined as social
pathology or as social disorganization, it is behavior that
swerves "downward" from approved and desired social
standards. The collective attempt at solution or ameliora-
tion of social problems must include the attempt to narrow
the gap between the behavioral norms and the concrete

situation. The deliberate effort to eliminate this deviation is an effort to "restore" the society to its level of normality.

Social progress is not simply the removal of social problems or a decrease in the amount of negative deviation in a society. Nor can one imagine even a relatively stagnant society in which permanent normalities exist. Social progress, no matter how one defines it, moves in the direction of positive deviation and has its source in positively deviant persons and groups. If cultural uniformities were rigid, if people repeated the same behavior patterns in exactly the same way, if human beings could not forsee, plan, and execute new programs of action, there could be neither positive deviation nor social progress. The accumulated experiences of people form the normal and expected patterns of the current culture, but they are also the basis from which new sociocultural patterns are projected.

Temporary novelties, like fads and fashions, are not significant deviations, although they indicate that a certain culture may be highly volatile. Important progress evolves from long-term, large-scale positive deviations that raise the level of normality. The extension of the protection of human rights to more and more people in the society is this kind of positive deviation. The introduction of new institutional forms through which group conflict can be lessened, the expansion of opportunities for social and cultural participation, the elevation of standards of family living—all these are examples of deviation in the direction of more acceptable and valued norms.

## Deviation in America

### 1. LEISURE AS DEVIATION

One of the most remarkable changes occurring in the American society is the development of a leisure subculture. The traditional emphasis on hard work as a means of material prosperity and eternal salvation has not been lost among Americans, but the continual advance of machine power has lifted much of the drudgery from manual labor. The Puritan notion that "idleness is the Devil's workshop" is still to some degree current, and even our leisure time has been filled with feverish activity. Roughly speaking, we may say that the previous emphasis on production has shifted to an emphasis on consumption.

This transition from an emphasis on a work culture to emphasis on a leisure culture is not, of course, a complete reversal. The work continues but the patterns of work have greatly changed; there has always been leisure, but new patterns of leisure are emerging. This emergence of institutionalized leisure may be called a form of social and cultural deviation. It is a departure from the standardized attitudes and behaviors that had previously existed in the recreational institution. It is a new direction forming new normalities and regularities, and it is having a tremendous effect upon the total culture.

The analysis of this recreational deviation shows several broad lines of conduct. These patterns are not rigidly set and probably cannot become so as long as our culture continues its rapid change, but they are sufficiently established to be recognized as quite different from previous patterns.

a. In the general field of entertainment there has been a marked relaxation from the so-called Victorian and Puritan standards. Movies featuring sexuality and nudity that would have been embarrassing to an all-male audience fifty years ago are now played in the neighborhood theater. The corner drugstore provides pornographic paperbacks in which the story often has overtones of sadism and brutality. Suggestive songs that would have shocked Americans of two generations ago are hummed by almost every adolescent.

b. In the general field of what the moralists call "self-indulgence" there have also been remarkable changes. We spend more money per capita for tobacco than for public education. The consumption of alcoholic beverages, especially of mixed drinks, has not only increased tremendously but has also directly affected patterns of entertainment for guests. Various changes in attitudes and conditions have permitted a sexual freedom never before possible in American society.

**c.** One broad category under which the new American leisure and wealth can be studied is that of conspicuous consumption. Pretentious standards of living have been used as symbols of status in many societies, but among Americans many items that were once luxuries are now considered necessities. Beyond this, however, we find people who never read books buying and displaying shelves of serious volumes; people who do not swim build a swimming pool in the back yard; people who need only one automobile build and maintain a three-car garage; and there are women who wear mink stoles when the temperature requires a light cloth-coat.

There are degrees of conformity to these newer forms of conduct, and there are differences among the deviant personalities who induce or accept the change. A strip-teaser is still considered a deviant personality by most people, as is the adolescent who commits a murder modeled upon one of the crime-magazine stories he has read. The upper-class drunkard is called an alcoholic and is treated with a certain amount of sympathy. The person who has a TV antenna on his roof but no television set inside the house, or the man who drives an expensive car he cannot afford, may be ridiculed by his neighbors, but he is a person who strives for the newer patterns of conduct.

Whatever one's moral judgment concerning the goodness or badness of these changes, the causes of the deviation are not simply good or bad people. Changed attitudes toward sin and virtue unquestionably have an effect upon external patterns of recreation, but the deviation in question is more than a personal matter. In a sense, the American people have had leisure "thrust upon them" and perhaps have not yet learned to live with it. There are signs of popular interest in music and painting, of developing patterns of self-help in handiwork in the home, of an appreciation of natural scenic beauty through touring and sight-seeing.

These three broad lines of development—entertainment, self-indulgence, and conspicuous consumption—must be kept in the perspective of our question of recreational deviation. It would be an error to exaggerate them as external patterns of behavior currently pursued by the majority of Americans. It is probably true that most Americans are in some way affected by them; they are therefore sociologically significant. From a negative point of view, they are deviations no longer protested by most people; and from a positive point of view they are deviations admired and desired by many people.

## 2. DEVIATIONS OF RELIGION

The American culture contains an extremely large number of internal religious deviations. Almost every known form of worship ritual can be found in practice somewhere among the religious bodies of our country. Most of the religious oddities and abnormalities, however, are practiced by relatively few people. Most churchgoers adhere to a few basic well-known patterns of worship.

Besides these internal deviations, which have been widely studied and commented upon, there is also the important aspect of religious deviation as an influence upon nonreligious institutions. Here we consider the ways in which behavior patterns accepted and practiced in a religious group are extended beyond the group as an attempt to reform nonreligious patterns. From the point of view of social deviation, this means that behavior considered normal within the religious group but abnormal by the great majority of Americans was introduced as a general pattern for the total society. Sometimes the new pattern was successfully established, and at other times it was not.

a. The best-known experiment along these lines was the eighteenth amendment to the Constitution, known as the prohibition law. Certain fundamentalist religions that taught the use of intoxicating beverages to be sinful were able to get sufficient political support to outlaw the sale of liquor. The real pattern of liquor consumption among the people was not changed into one of abstinence, and the national law was ultimately repealed. The drive against gambling, also promoted by these religious groups, has been successful in some places.

**b.** The question of the teaching of religion in the public school system has had some curious variations. All churches hold that children should be taught religion, but there are so many churches in the United States that there could be no agreement on what to teach. Even the Protestant version of the Bible is no longer taught in most public schools, and the system of "released time" from the public school for religious instruction and church attendance has been set up in many places. The pattern of religious instruction has been established, and the percentage of children receiving it has increased, but the people teaching it are not public school employees.

**c.** To some degree the churches have been successful in extending the concept of racial brotherhood into wider areas of American life. In many instances, churches had first to abandon their own internal patterns of racial segregation and to develop a doctrine of Christian solidarity before promoting this doctrine in the nonreligious structure. While the religious groups have not been the only agency of racial integration in the American society, the influence of religious leaders has been very great in establishing the new patterns. What were once considered peculiar local and group deviations in this regard are now gradually becoming accepted as standardized practice throughout the society.

**d.** On the level of conceptual patterns of economic justice, the principles of the papal encyclicals and of various other pronouncements by religious leaders have had wide acceptance. These principles have been realized through direct action of religious representatives, such as chaplains in industry and ministers acting as strike arbitrators, and through the religious services of Labor Day, the publication of labor papers, and the establishment of labor-management institutes. The notion that the religious institution has something to offer to the economic institution is no longer strange to most Americans.

The examples given here are a few indications of the ways in which induced change has been deliberately at-

tempted in order to carry over religious patterns into
other areas of life. The opposite trend, the so-called secularization of our culture, has often been pointed out. Other
examples can be given of the religious patterns that have
persisted as long-established customs—the celebration of
Christmas, Easter, Thanksgiving, and Memorial Day, and
the religious ceremonies observed for birth, marriage, and
death. These patterns can hardly be termed deviations
since they have long been accepted as normal behavior.

To some extent the acceptance of religious deviations
into nonreligious institutions involves the various phenomena of social change, control, and integration. It is probable that as the American culture grows older, its major
institutions will acquire closer coordination and more
interchange of patterns. This requires that some deviations be tolerated in the various institutions and that the
people who have deep convictions about these deviations
be permitted to propagate them. The American society
has provided a fertile field for experimentation in religious
beliefs and practices, and while most of the deviations
remain weak or disappear, some of them become accepted normalities in the total culture.

### 3. LAW DETERS DEVIATION

The American legal system acts as both a positive and
a negative control over social deviation because it promotes conformity to norms and employs formalized techniques for punishing nonconformists. The home, the
church, and the school are important instruments for
encouraging conformity, for instilling an appreciation of
the highest social values, and for standardizing the conduct of people. These and other institutionalized groups
succeed in promoting a respect for the law, but they do
not have the clear-cut definitions of behavior norms or
the apparatus of enforcement and punishment that the
law possesses.

In spite of their tradition of individualism and their
rapidly changing culture, the American people are by
and large law-abiding. Sensational reports about nonconformity, from the minor delinquencies of juvenile

gangs to the planned murders by organized criminals, overlook the fact that the large majority of Americans are never involved with law violations. Whether our rate of crime is higher or lower than that of other countries is beside the point here. We are interested in the fact that the law acts among us as an impediment to serious social deviation.

a. To the extent that the norms of other groups are ineffective, the law acts as the ultimate means of control. Punishment by a parent, expulsion from a school, excommunication by a church, or ostracism imposed by any other group or association may in particular cases suffice as a control mechanism. The individual may "return to the fold," or he may accept the uniformities of behavior prevalent in other groups; but if he persists in serious deviation, he must ultimately reckon with the law.

b. American law is more precise and detailed in the behavior norms it sets up than are any of the other institutionalized systems of control. Every formal association has rules and regulations, but these are limited to the immediate membership, are often vaguely and inefficiently worded, and are taken seriously only in crisis situations. The canon law of the Catholic church is a conspicuous exception in this regard, but it is in itself a legal system.

c. The laws that define prohibited and deviant behavior have been written and interpreted by technical experts and discussed and enacted by municipal, state, and federal assemblies deliberately constituted for this purpose. In no other area of human activity is it the precise purpose of a large body of persons to establish the norms of behavioral conformity and the criteria by which deviation can be judged. Nowhere else in society is such rational effort devoted to the elaboration of standards that tell us what is beneficial and what is harmful to society.

d. The law is a relative and changing system, but the legal norms at any given time tend to be absolutistic. While legislative and juridical lags may exist, there is still a demand for conformity to the legal norms. Since law can be changed and improved, it can cope with any new and large-scale deviations that may threaten the

American culture. The unchanging principles of the natural moral law are recognized as the basis of all American law, but the application of the law fits the needs and interests of the total society.

e. Strictly interpreted, the objectivity of the law requires that the criminal deviant be punished, not because he is antisocial or immoral, but because he has violated specific legal norms of behavior. In effect, however, the whole system of law and law enforcement, with its police and courts and prisons, provides pressure for conformity to minimum standards of behavior. It is essential to the welfare of society that this minimum conformity be maintained.

These statements concerning the utility of law as a deterrent to social and cultural deviation do not mean that all criminals are caught and punished or that all aspects of the legal system operate efficiently. The fact that a law is "on the books" does not mean that it is rigidly enforced or even that a majority of the people accept it. The body of laws in any society is not a reliable indicator of the actual behavior of the people. A severe code of laws may be only laxly enforced in one society while a less severe code may be rigidly enforced in another society.

The American legal system, therefore, can be sociologically analyzed only in relation to the actual behavior patterns of the American people. There is a certain amount of public corruption; there are occasional miscarriages of justice; there are fee-splitters and ambulance-chasers among the lawyers and incompetent personnel within the total system. In spite of these deficiencies the law continues to act as a preventer and punisher, and sometimes as a reformer, of criminal deviants.

It is probably true that a sociocultural system gets the kind of law it deserves. The pluralistic American society is in many ways tolerant of deviation; it has grown from groups that have had many variations in culture patterns, it has absorbed ideas and persons from many different societies. Tolerance of differences has certain outside limits, and it is principally the legal system that sets those limits when people and patterns appear to be getting out of hand.

### 4. THE PATTERN OF DIVORCE

The nineteenth-century traditions of the United States showed a remarkable record of marital durability. In the middle of the century the general and ideal pattern of marriage was one of permanence and indissolubility. There were, of course, also cases of unhappy marriages, infidelity, and even desertions. The churches were unwilling to remarry divorced persons, the law in general made it difficult to obtain a divorce, and cultural pressure was strong upon married people to remain together. By 1890 there was one divorce in about seventeen marriages; the current annual divorce rate in urban places is about one in four.

The contemporary pattern of divorce in America deviates from the normalities of the last century. The divorce laws in some states are extremely lax; many courts apparently allow collusion; the alleged causes for divorce are often trivial; some churches place little negative sanction upon their divorced members; and social disapproval is not always visited upon the divorced person.

The changed conception concerning divorce requires a changed conception concerning marriage. Thus there is really a twofold deviation involving the essential quality of the indissolubility of the marital contract. This solemn agreement appears in some places to be less binding than a mortgage contract or an agreement to pay for goods delivered. It is probable that most persons who enter marriage intend at the time to remain married permanently to their partner. The intended conditions of the contract appear to change under the pressure of experience, and because of these changed conditions the spouses often feel justified in voiding the contract.

Following are some aspects of deviation which are a general result of the spread of divorce.

a. Not all divorced persons are parents, and childlessness may sometimes be a contributing factor to divorce. Never-

theless, the children of divorced persons are required to
make numerous adjustments. Living with one parent and
paying a weekly visit to the other, or getting used to a
"new" father or mother at home with still another to greet
him on his weekly visit, can be a most confusing experience. Whether the child lives at home or is boarded with
foster parents, or lives in a children's institution, he is still
the product of a broken home and his socialization process
is deeply affected by this experience.

**b.** The divorced persons themselves must necessarily
make adjustments to the new situation. The patterns of
behavior of people who have lived together become quite
different, once they have parted from each other. The
woman, especially, is placed in a new category that appears to provide good opportunities for remarriage and,
consequently, provides difficulties for the divorcee who
does not believe in remarriage. The man is also faced with
new problems as he attempts to live as a bachelor again.

**c.** In spite of the relative independence of the conjugal
unit in the American society, marriage does develop a
loose system of contact and communication among the
blood relatives of both spouses. The longer the marriage
lasts the more likely are the inlaws on both sides to become
acquainted with one another. Divorce often causes an
awkward rearrangement of these social relations. If small
children are involved, some of the relatives become spon-
sors for their baptism or confirmation, and grandparents
also maintain interest in and contact with the children.
Few social arrangements are more peculiar than the wedding of children of divorced parents. No satisfactory
protocol for this situation has yet been established.

**d.** Similarly, but to a less embarrassing degree, divorce
requires a realignment of the friendship circles of both
spouses. Invitations to parties, to dinners, and other congenial gatherings now require selective care. Married
couples develop and maintain at least a small circle of
friends with whom they do things together. If the divorced persons remain in the same community and continue to belong to the same church clubs, country clubs,

and other primary groups, the contacts with their mutual friends may often be awkward.

The deviations in both marriage and divorce patterns may be rooted in the personal, rather than the social, aspect of the marital relation. An analysis of divorced persons and their children, relatives, neighbors, and friends, however, indicates that neither marriage nor divorce can be a purely personal affair. Even in the American system of the conjugal family that emphasizes the spouses rather than the total group of the consanguine family, there is need to recognize the broader sociocultural effects of marriage. Deviations in so basic a relationship as that of marriage are certain to effect deviations in the wider circle of people.

The emphasis on the self, on one's personal desires and privileges, which characterizes the divorce pattern contravenes an important American social trend toward collective morality. In almost all other areas of social problems there is progress toward better cooperation, more cohesive group relations, social justice, and guaranteed social rights to more categories of citizens. The increase of social welfare and collective action in American society appears to correlate with a wider acceptance of social values and a wider conformity to the virtues of love and justice.

The divorce pattern is a deviation in this respect, too. It not only causes new patterns of behavior in the divorced persons and in others, it also deviates from the general American trend toward social integration and cohesion.

## 5. Mental Abnormalities

We have indicated that most social deviants are only partial deviants, that is, they occasionally depart from the expected mores or they deviate in only one of their social roles. Mentally abnormal persons are also abnormal in their social behavior. They range from the total deviant to the person who is only moderately disturbed. The social scientist is not directly concerned with organic psychotics whose mental disease is traceable to some defect in the structure or physiology of the organism. These present primarily medical problems and only secondarily social problems.

The so-called functional psychotics constitute the largest percentage of Americans who suffer from mental abnormalities, and their psychoses have been traced to no known physical or organic cause. They are of interest to students of society not only because they involve all kinds of behavior aberrations but also because some of them appear to suffer from the effects of the social and cultural environment. Functional psychoses are increasing in the United States, and more than half the hospital beds at any given time are occupied by these patients.

The statistics concerning mental diseases in our country have caused considerable controversy. Large numbers of young men are rejected by the armed services for various forms of personality disorders, and the number of Americans being treated for these disturbances is increasing faster than the population growth. Whether this increase is due to the fact that more precise diagnoses are now being made and more attention is being paid to these mentally disturbed people, or whether there is an actual increase in the incidence of these diseases, has not yet been made clear.

Schizophrenics and manic-depressives constitute well over half of all Americans who suffer mental disorders, and these functional disturbances are said to be increasing. Such persons are sometimes roughly called "split personalities," although only manic-depressives exemplify extreme shifts of the personality back and forth from excitement to depression. Both these types not only occur more frequently but also remain under treatment longer than others.

More than a half-million Americans are resident patients in all types of mental hospitals. Some of them are curable; others are hopelessly and permanently out of touch with the realities and the normalities of behavior. All of them constitute a large category of Americans who are behavioral deviants. Their responsibility is decreased and they cannot be classified as moral deviants. Some of the possible sociocultural sources of these mental diseases are the following.

a. The rapidity of change in the American society is often alleged to be a causal factor of mental abnormalities. The need to adjust one's self to new situations, patterns, and values is said to cause mental confusion. The less endowed individual cannot keep up the pace; the frequent demands are too much for him, and he has a "nervous breakdown."

b. The United States has the most competitive culture the world has ever seen. Competition is itself a highly valued social process, and people are trained from childhood to be successful competitors. But competition implies that some persons must fail to achieve a desirable prize or goal. The losers are expected to accept defeat graciously but to try again; in some cases frequent failure leads to discouragement and mental unbalance.

c. The complexity of American society is an overwhelming problem to some people. There are so many factors that are too big and complicated for the individual to understand or control. War and peace, economic prosperity and depression, and political and religious mores do not lend themselves to easy analysis. The individual feels helpless before these gigantic problems, and this frustration may lead to mental disturbance.

d. The inconsistencies of the culture, either real or imagined, are also a disturbing element for many people. We have spoken of the patterned evasions and incongruities in many areas of American life. To many people these do not "make sense." They portray a kind of disorder that annoys and confuses the person who wants everything to be reasonable and neatly arranged. People of simple intelligence, particularly, are often very literal and precise in their expectations of others and are frequently disappointed and frustrated. They do not understand why the real patterns do not always coincide with the ideal patterns of our culture.

e. Much has been made also of the secularization of the American culture as a factor in mental disturbance. Human beings seem to require many moral supports to maintain a stable personality. For many people one of these supports has been a strong confidence in the providence of a supreme being. Secularization tends to deemphasize the reliance on prayer and divine grace. Curiously enough, the opposite can also lead to frustration, that is, a deemphasis on the secondary causes of the material world leads people to an unreasonable presumption upon the transcendent first cause. They anticipate miraculous intervention, and when they are disappointed conjure up their own miracles.

These are the social scientist's tentative explanations for the apparent increase of functional psychoses in the American society. Psychiatrists are paying more attention than ever before to the cultural environment as a factor in mental abnormalities. Since conceptual patterns are an integral part of the culture, there can be no doubt that at least in many instances a correlation exists between the personal, internal aspects and the impersonal, external aspects of the culture.

## Suggested Readings

Becker, Howard S. *The Other Side*. New York: Free Press, 1964.

Bienen, Henry. *Violence and Social Change*. Chicago: University of Chicago Press, 1968.

Clinard, Marshall. *Sociology of Deviant Behavior*. New York: Holt, Rinehart and Winston, 1968.

Liebow, Elliot. *Tally's Corner*. Boston: Little, Brown, 1967.

Matza, David. *Delinquency and Drift*. New York: Wiley, 1964.

Yablonsky, Lewis. *The Violent Gang*. New York: Macmillan, 1962.

# 17
# Sociocultural Integration

UP TO NOW IN THIS BOOK WE HAVE ANALYZED THE
various segments that constitute society and culture. While
carrying on this analytical "fragmentation," we have
also frequently pointed out that society and culture are
so closely intertwined that they must ultimately be
viewed as a total, single socioculutral system. This totality
—how it can be recognized and how it is achieved—is the
content of study in the present chapter.

## STATIC AND ACTIVE INTEGRATION

The term integration is often used synonymously with
terms like cohesion, solidarity, unity, balance, adjustment,
and harmony. All these terms have meaning to the social
scientist only if they include the kinetic as well as the
static aspects of sociocultural phenomena. In other words,
integration implies not only order and structure but also
action and function. In this final chapter we study the
integration of structure and function in society and culture.

Sociocultural integration does not mean strict homogeneity throughout the whole system of human relations.
We have seen that differentiation is an essential quality of
social relations and that it is a prelude to integration. One
cannot speak of integration unless there are different segments to be combined, ordered, and integrated. Integration does not refer to a highly formalized society of rigidly
obedient people. An authoritarian society may be only externally regimented, without inner, meaningful solidarity.
People and patterns that are identical with others are not
necessarily united to them.

The term integration often signifies social processes like
assimilation, amalgamation, socialization, and accultura-
tion. For example, the migrant from farm to city, or from

one country to another, goes through a process of socio-cultural integration as he gradually takes on the behavior patterns of the new environment and develops social relations with people who were formerly strangers to him. This example and others like it simply indicate that integration can be viewed as a process and a product and that the former is always going on because the latter can never be complete.

Because of the relativity and mutability of the socio-cultural system, several precautionary statements must be made concerning the concept of integration. (a) We cannot always say that a "well-integrated" society functions better toward its goal than a loosely integrated society. The best we can say is that a certain degree of integration is a necessary condition for social and cultural functioning. (b) The assessment of the degree of integration existing anywhere is not an intuition or a concealed value judgment. It requires a knowlededge of the recognizable conditions under which integration occurs. (c) This assessment cannot be made from a mere list of all cultural items that happen to coexist within the same territorial boundaries. We shall see that certain cultural phenomena have a greater integrative significance than others.

## BASIC REQUISITES

It must be clear from what we have said in this book that every sociocultural system requires for its existence two fundamental elements: the maintenance of cooperation and the satisfaction of needs. These are the minimum sociological requirements. They presuppose the presence of all the biological and physical elements, the presence of resources and people, and the geographical and material conditions in which social and cultural life occurs. Integration must be studied in sociological terms and not reduced to biological or physical factors.

a. The maintenance of cooperation means that persons are able to function with one another at least at that minimum level at which the system can be called a going concern. This minimum requirement refers to those social processes or basic forms of human relations we have called positive or conjunctive. Roles, statuses, groups, and social strata are fairly well coordinated through the associative processes without disabling interference from negative and dissociative processes.

**b.** The satisfaction of sociocultural needs means that the people have found systematic and acceptable ways to achieve the purposes of the major institutions and groups. We have seen that these means cannot be satisfied individually or in isolation and that they are found universally wherever people live together. A sociocultural system cannot exist—it cannot be imagined—unless it contains institutions and groups that fulfill in some cooperative manner the familial, educational, economic, political, religious, and recreational needs of the people.

These are basic requirements, and it is possible to measure roughly the extent to which the requirements are met. A society in which these sociocultural functions are poorly supplied is obviously one in which the people are not efficiently cooperative. The cause of this failure at any given time may lie outside the sociocultural system, in a lack of resources, in overpopulation, in changes of climate and other physical catastrophies. Aside from all these external factors, it is possible to measure the manner in which the people are trying to achieve the goals and the extent to which they succeed.

These basic prerequisites for integration operate through and with people. They exist in the real order of sociocultural phenomena, but they can be analyzed meaningfully only when they are abstracted from the concrete social situations in which they exist. We must study separately the integration of the culture and the integration of the society. It is in this way that we can bring together the segments of a vast and complicated system in which people behave toward one another in patterned ways.

## Cultural Integration

We have seen that the total culture is made up of major and subsidiary institutions and that each institution can be analyzed into its coordinated patterns of behavior. From this point of view the cultural system can be studied on three levels: behavioral patterns, institutions, the total culture. This appears to be a horizontal approach, but it must be understood that these levels are vertically coordinated. The institutions contain the patterns, and the culture contains the institutions.

a. The integration of behavior patterns means that the generalized uniformities of conduct are coordinated in each social personality and between one person and another. They make sense to both the actor and the observer. This notion is best demonstrated by its opposite. Random, erratic, and uncoordinated behavior is immediately detectable, and the individual who pursues it is often alluded to as a disintegrated or disoriented personality.

Since the social person is not an isolated individual and since social science deals only with shared and generalized patterns of behavior, we must note also the integration of relational patterns. A man regularly and in the same way fulfills the paternal roles in the family. The other members of the family know what to expect from him; they recognize the consistent and recurring uniformities and they respond with their own behavior patterns. Integrated patterns include consistent reciprocity. Integration is observable when the reciprocal behavior patterns of two or more persons meaningfully "fit together."

b. On the level of the institution itself we find integration when the segmental patterns and roles are consistently coordinated. Any one of the major institutions in a culture can be analyzed from the point of view of its numerous subsidiary institutions, which in turn must be interrelated if the larger institution is to be integrated. For example, the regularized behavior in courtship and dating, in the training and raising of children within the home, in the relations of husband and wife must somehow "fit together" if the familial institution is to be integrated.

Institutional integration is seen in the interdependence of the various subfunctions. A capitalist economy must have institutionalized ways of planning production, of assuring credit, of gathering stock piles of raw material, of cost accounting, and so forth. These and many other subsidiary institutions function together, and if any one of them suffers a serious breakdown the whole system tends to disintegrate. These are all differentiated functions, but they point toward the total institution. It would be physically impossible in an industrialized system for the same person to extract the raw material, finance production, build and assemble the commodity, and advertise and distribute it to the consumer. When all these functions are performed by different people, and when their functions are coordinated, the institution is integrated.

c. The integration of the total culture means that the various major institutions are mutually consistent and coordinated. A lack of integration on this level is one of the most serious problems a society can face. The functions and goals of one major institution differ from those of another, but in an integrated system they must ultimately serve the whole society. For example, the maintenance of public order through the political institution is not the same as the production of goods through the economic institution, but the fact that they pursue different immediate and mediate goals does not mean that they can be completely disconnected.

What we are saying in effect is that the integrated culture functions as a total system of distinct contributing patterns, roles, and institutions. Since the culture itself is a constantly changing system, there are always minor inconsistencies and lags. This is not to say that all parts of the culture change with the same rapidity or even move in the same direction. One institution may develop more rapidly than the others; the mores change more slowly than less important customs; certain roles become more demanding than others; some values are emphasized more than others.

## Social Integration

In the conceptual framework of this book we have seen that people enact behavior patterns, that groups use institutions, and that the whole society has a culture. The major segments of the society are its numerous groups, and each group is composed of social persons. Social integration, therefore, can be analyzed on the three levels of: the social personality, the major groups, and the entire society. Here again, as in the conceptualization of culture, we note that integration occurs both horizontally and vertically.

**a.** From the sociological point of view the integration of the social personality refers to the fact that the individual enacts his various social roles in a coordinated and consistent way. This approach presupposes the psychological definition of the normal, balanced personality, an area of study outside the field of social science. The integrated social personality exhibits no apparent conflict of behavior patterns as he moves from one group to another and as he carries out the functions of his different roles. His behavior in a recreational group is different from, but not contradictory to, his conduct in his family, his business, and his other groups.

**b.** Group integration means that the members of the group enact their reciprocal roles interdependently toward the goals of the group. An integrated group is one that achieves its purposes with a minimum of conflict. It is not only well structured, but the social relations of its members proceed in a productive and peaceful way. They emphasize the social processes of cooperation, accommodation, and assimilation.

The test of group integration is not external order and observable cooperative functioning toward common goals. External orderliness may result from the coercive power of a dominant minority, as in the case of a prison or a concentration camp. The absence of a disabling amount of overt conflict is not a sufficient proof of solidarity. There must also be, on the conceptual level, a consensual sharing of institutionalized culture patterns. This point we shall discuss later.

**c.** The integration of an entire society refers to the fact that not only the major groups but also the multitude of sub-groups are able to cooperate successfully. In the integrated society, the school, home, and playground do not pull the child in opposite directions. Business office, church, and political party are not at odds with one another in competing for the interest and loyalty of the adult. Within each of these larger areas, the smaller subgroups are necessarily coordinated if the society is integrated.

Social integration is not the result of the complete similarity of all the people in the society. Integration is a matter of structure and function rather than of identity or similarity. It cannot be emphasized too often that within any large society people differ and groups vary; statuses and roles are multiple. Thus unity is a logical concept and it means in society that the people and the groups are brought together in a meaningful way and that their social needs are satisfied in an orderly way. Social integration does not dispel differences; it coordinates and directs them.

## INTEGRATION OF CULTURE AND SOCIETY

It must be remembered that separate discussion of culture and society is possible only on an abstract level. Each can be studied in its various parts, as we have studied them throughout this book, but neither can exist in the real order without the other. The persons who are organized into groups in society are the people by, through, and for whom the cultural patterns and institutions are developed. Culture and society are inseparable entities, and this very fact indicates that there must be at least a minimum degree of coordination between the two.

That culture and society must somehow be integrated requires little factual demonstration. We need only compare two widely different sociocultural systems and attempt to interchange their cultures. For example, China has a culture and a society, and so has Italy. It would be impossible for the Chinese society to combine with the Italian culture and still remain the Chinese society. The ways in which the Italian people conduct their behavior patterns, social relations, statuses, groups, and institutions are very different from the Chinese ways.

Although culture and society are inseparable in existence, they do not have an equal mutual influence for integration. We have seen that it is possible to arrange, discipline, and direct a social aggregate like a crowd or mob into a form of external social cohesion. This aggregate of semiautonomous persons, as in a police state, may give the appearance of an integrated social order, but it does not have genuine sociocultural solidarity. In other words, the meaningful integration of the society depends more upon the integration of the culture than vice versa. From the point of view of total integration, therefore, the culture is a more influential factor than the society.

We may say that it is the culture that puts the society into action or that the action, both conceptual and external, of the people in society is the culture. Lack of cultural integration throws the whole society into confusion, depending upon the degree to which it is lacking. Without cultural integration the social persons cannot adequately enact patterns and roles, the groups cannot properly employ institutionalized forms, and the total society becomes disjoined into uncoordinated and even conflicting factions. We have seen that inconsistent behavior patterns result in split social personalities, and inconsistent institutions result in contravening roles and groups.

Sociocultural integration is not a rigid absolute. Although a degree of integration of the culture and the society must essentially and always exist, we must repeat the warning that sociocultural integration is a relative phenomenon. Human nature, as well as the very nature of social relations among men, prevents a rigid, permanent integration between society and culture. If integration were complete, there would be neither change nor progress; and while sociocultural progress is not inevitable, sociocultural change is a constantly present phenomenon.

ESSENTIAL FACTORS OF INTEGRATION

We have described in general the meaning of sociocultural integration and how the various social and cultural segments are interdependent. It remains now to answer the important question of how this integration is effected and maintained. What factors account for this integration? Here again we must note that not all the factors are of equal importance, since conditions and situations change. Nevertheless, we can attempt to arrange them in a rough order of importance.

a. Social scientists in general agree that value consensus among the people heads the list of factors for meaningful sociocultural integration. The continuing operation of any society, and its essential solidarity, require a minimal sharing among the people of an ultimate body of values and norms. The majority of the people conform voluntarily to a common set of significant values. The presence of value consensus excludes the simple hypotheses of either an instinctive gregariousness innate in all persons or a rationalistic and formal social contract emerging out of the dim recesses of history.

Consensus on common values does not imply total agreement upon all the detailed norms regulating specific social relations and patterns. We have seen that there is great diversity of conduct among the people of a large society but that there is also a basic and common adherence to ideal patterns of behavior. Many of these values are, and perhaps must be, vaguely formulated in terms like "loyalty," "democracy," "brotherhood," "progress,"' "opportunity," "equality," and "liberty." These values cannot be easily spelled out in concrete action but they supply the generalized meanings to which the people give consensus, and they appear to be the principal factor of sociocultural integration.

b. The sharing of common functions is another important factor of integration. People who together do things they believe are worth doing are drawn closer together. This simple conclusion is drawn from empirical observation by many social scientists. The reasons why people cooperate may lie deeply hidden in their motivation and probably involve the appreciation of values and goals as well as appreciation of the people with whom they share the function. Here again the degree of voluntariness is significant since we are not talking about external cohesion resulting from either force or automatic routinization.

c. The third factor of sociocultural integration is the multiple participation of persons in different groups with varying cultural patterns. This integrating factor is more conspicuous than commonly shared values, and it is empirically observable when persons share common functions. The same person usually enacts his different social roles in groups made up of sets of different people. Lawyers are most active in political and economic groups; clergymen are active in both educational and religious groups; the mother of a family may play active roles in recreational, religous, and other groups. The integrative element is therefore the social personality as it is expressed through the multiple roles in relation to other social personalities.

We are analyzing three factors that are inseparable in the concrete sociocultural situation. If the total combination is viewed from any of its three parts, it demonstrates mutual and reciprocal influence, as in the following three statements: (1) persons are integrated with one another because they share common functions and values, or (2) common values bring people together in the same functions, or (3) common functioning increases the participants' appreciation of each other and of the commonly shared values. Each of these three statements is empirically verifiable, and all three together indicate the most important integrating combination in the whole sociocultural system.

AUXILIARY FACTORS OF INTEGRATION

Besides these essential factors of integration there are several others that are auxiliary rather than essential factors.

a. One of them is the external pressures, threats, and dangers to which the members of a society respond. These threats are most obvious when they come from an enemy in time of war. If the danger is not overwhelming and allows a hope of successful resistance, the social reaction is an increase in cooperation. Under these conditions a society under attack from without is unwilling to tolerate deviants, shirkers, and traitors. Common sacrifices in a common cause, even when the sacrifice is unpleasant and

distasteful in detail, strengthens the culture and integrates
the society.

**b.** There are also numerous more or less deliberate mechanisms and techniques employed by society to ensure
sociocultural integration. We have spoken of these in the
chapter on social and cultural control. Conformity to
behavior patterns is reinforced through techniques of
authority and obedience. Social status and personal sanctions help to keep the primary groups integrated, and
systems of collective representation are an integrative factor in large secondary associatons. This network of overlapping techniques operates throughout the total society;
and its largest and most obvious exemplification is that of
a national system of formal laws.

**c.** A general recognition in a society of the interdependence of interest is still another factor for sociocultural
integration. Individuals and groups continue to interact
and to avoid conflict on the basis of gains each anticipates
from the maintenance of the social framework essential to
interaction. This is the empirical antidote to the hypothesis
that social progress and the general commonweal emerge
from the pursuit of self-interest. The interests and motives
of many groups are different and separable, but in the total
society many of them are interdependent. Even religious
bodies with conflicting dogmas have some interests in
common. There may be certain conflicting interests between an economic group and a political group, but they
also have some common interests.

These three factors—external pressure, deliberate techniques, and interdependent interests—are ancillary rather
than major factors of sociocultural integration. An understanding of them requires a certain amount of insight
into the structure and function of the total sociocultural
system. Their operation requires a certain degree of rational planning toward integration. This analysis goes beyond the crude and outmoded notions about the automatic balance of power, or the inevitable readjustment
of forces, or the blind play of symbiotic interdependence.
The sociological explanation of integration does not

lie in physical or biological factors; it is found in the persons and groups who constitute the society and who employ the culture.

## COMMUNAL AND ASSOCIATIONAL INTEGRATION

Although sociocultural solidarity is possible—and necessary—in every type of society, it differs in kind and degree from one society to another. We have seen that a culture is usually dominated by one of its major institutions and that a society gives greatest importance to one of its major groups. In this case the pivotal institution and group are a focus of solidarity for the total system. We may say, for example, that the Chinese society was integrated around its family system and that the people of medieval Europe were mainly united through their religious system. Similarly, a large modern society may find its principal focus of solidarity in its political or its economic system.

We have discussed also the further general classification of societies into the communal and associational types. Either one of these may be dominated by any of the major institutionalized groups. The small, simple, communal society is frequently a strongly familistic society in the sense that the kinship system is a weighty factor for sociocultural integration. This type of society also adheres to traditional values and is largely controlled by the mores; it is usually preindustrial and slow to change; it has a narrow range of stratification and little contact with outgroups. Together these elements help to develop subconscious, informal, and almost automatic sociocultural solidarity.

The large, complex, associational type of society is characterized by certain elements opposite from those of the communal society. Human relations are contractual rather than familial. Values are relatively volatile; social control is exerted through formal, legal systems; there are numerous classes and categories; and change is rapid. Solidarity must exist in the associational society if it is to maintain itself as a distinct and functioning sociocultural collectivity. But in this kind of society integration depends upon different factors and requires rational effort and planning.

The complex, large-scale society, with its numerous conflicting pressure groups, varying institutional values, and diverse goals, cannot depend upon the automatic and spontaneous operation of solidaristic processes. The greater the differentiation of roles and statuses, functions and goals, interests and values the more deliberate must be the techniques of cooperation. This does not mean that the communal society is "natural" or that the associational society is "artificial," but it does mean that some of the inherent advantages for solidarity present in the former are absent from the latter. These advantages have to be supplied by conscious, scientific, and technical effort. The people must discover, devise, and employ mechanisms that maintain sociocultural integration.

## Integration in America
### 1. LOYALTIES AND INTEGRATION

The United States has a pluralistic and heterogeneous sociocultural system. We have observed that all our people are of immigrant lines from various ethnic and racial sources and that much of our culture was originally imported from foreign places. For several centuries the processes of cultural assimilation and biological integration have been going on, and there has been an accelerated trend toward a relatively monistic and homogeneous sociocultural system.

Meanwhile there is still more heterogeneity here than there is in any other large country. We can identify in general two large (Protestant and Catholic) and one smaller (Jewish) religious orientations; and even among these there are many variations. There are in addition many minority groups. The disparities of national and ethnic backgrounds are gradually decreasing, but there are still recognizable categories of Spanish-speaking immigrants and of peoples from eastern and southern Europe. The differences in social class are not as sharp as they once were, as more and more people are absorbed into the expanding middle class.

The general goal of this trend toward integration seems to be that each person should become a "true" American. The belief of some observers, especially foreign visitors, has been that this goal is impossible because various and conflicting loyalties interfere with loyalty to the country itself. Americans, however, maintain their allegiance to all kinds of groups: family, political, religious, economic, and others. In this kind of society, in which authority is polyphasic and values are multiple, Americans find multiple allegiances not only possible but desirable.

Some of the factors that make this paradoxical situation workable are the following. They help to explain how Americans foster allegiance to many apparently contradictory groups and values and still maintain loyalty to the central cultural ethos.

a. A toleration of differences is apparently built into the American value system. The defense of individualism and independence has gradually brought about the realization that others must also be allowed their individualism and independence. Tolerance is the result of practical necessity. No single group, whether religious, economic, or political, has been large or strong enough to impose its own way of life upon all the other groups. Toleration of differences has been the necessary and positive compromise.

b. In concrete group relations there is rough procedural agreement on the "rules of the game." The competing groups are expected to grant one another a fair chance. Those that gain an advantage expect to be challenged again; and those that lose out are expected to accept the situation gracefully. This is, of course, a general attitude. There are instances of "poor sports" and "bad losers." In spite of bitter labor disputes, vicious political campaigns, and occasional recriminations among religious groups, the general attitude of sportsmanship that prevails in the recreational institution helps people to recognize and follow the rules of fair play in other institutions.

c. Multiple participation in groups is an extremely important and little-recognized factor of integration. Especially in the urban milieu, it is impossible for an adult

Catholic or Protestant or Jew to associate only with fellow religionists in his neighborhood, business, civic, recreational, and other activities. Americans do and must associate with other Americans who differ from them even in their deepest convictions. Given the general attitudes of toleration and procedural agreement mentioned above, this common functioning and face-to-face relationship constitutes a practical form of integration. The individual participates in each group with other individuals who share the values and functions of that particular group, even though they may refuse to share the values and functions of other groups.

**d.** The American people try to avoid overt disagreements by deemphasizing contradictory values. They seem to skirt controversial issues whenever possible. A conscious effort is often made to find areas of agreement, as when people of differing religious faith agree that "after all, we all believe in the same God; and we are all going to the same heaven." What may be merely superficial conformity and integration appears to be necessary in the pluralistic culture. Furthermore, external patterns of conformity tend to break down prejudices against other groups even when deep-seated value differences remain.

These four factors are at work particularly among urban, middle-class Americans. They bring about a kind of tactical integration that works as a temporary mechanism of cooperation even while individuals continue to maintain loyalties to numerous differing groups. If present trends of assimilation continue, this temporary and external mechanism may some day be abandoned. Certain lines of internal cultural integration have been developing for many decades, as we have seen in discussing the ultimate core of American values, but it is improbable that total integration will come about, or even be desirable, in our kind of sociocultural system.

## 2. War and Solidarity

It is sometimes observed that military conflict is a universal culture pattern and that the results of war are destructive and disintegrative. In the conceptual framework of this book we classify the preparation for and the conduct of war as a subsidiary institution contained within the major political institution. Except for the Civil War and the major frustration of the Vietnam War, the American participation in armed conflict has most often exerted an integrative influence upon our sociocultural system. Let us look at the evidence for this paradoxical assertion.

a. The two World Wars of 1917-18 and 1941-45 did more than any other events in our history to achieve cooperation among the American people. In both instances there were conscientious objectors throughout the struggle; there were many who opposed our entrance into war; and there were some traitors and shirkers. But by and large, the war effort with everything it entailed in training and fighting by the armed forces and in production and sacrifices by the civilian population, brought the American people together at a relatively high level of sociocultural integration.

b. It is an axiom of social science that the threat of external danger tends to unify a society internally. For purposes of cooperative functioning it was necessary of course that the people be aware of this danger. Hence the importance of propaganda to the home country; a constant stream of slogans reiterated the necessity of "saving the world for democracy" and of "keeping the world free of tyranny." Except for the persons in uniform, the immediate danger from the outside was not always apparent. A consciousness of the threat had to be aroused and maintained, and it is noteworthy that this was not the case in the more recent Vietnam War.

c. The First World War was the major test of the possibility of integrating the many ethnic and national strains of the American population. The unwillingness of Irish-Americans to fight on the side of England, of German-Americans to break their ancestral ties, and of other Americans to participate in a "foreign entanglement" they considered none of their business, was a source of considerable anxiety to the national leaders before the First World War. No large society had ever before faced this kind of sociocultural problem. The United States emerged from the First World War not only as a major international power but also as a society of united people.

**d.** The spirit of patriotic unity engendered by the war effort is necessarily a short-lived phenomenon. The cooperation is pointed to a precise goal—victory over the enemy— and the psychological intensity of the effort cannot be maintained at the same high level during peacetime. The notion of "getting the job done" is not expected to carry over after the job is actually done. We must note, however, that although the spirit of unity subsided somewhat after both world wars, the level of sociocultural integration was higher after each than it had been before.

**e.** These two major wars had an immediate effect in bringing together Americans from widely separated sections of the country and of various sociocultural backgrounds. The war factories drew workers from the rural, agricultural areas to the urban, industrial areas, while the induction centers and training camps brought persons together from all over the country. Many had never before experienced this physical mingling. Contact and communication, however, merely provided the necessary conditions under which the process of assimilation could occur. The essential factor was that these persons in factories and in the armed services shared common functions in the pursuit of common and valued goals.

**f.** One of the most far-reaching integrative effects of the Second World War was the deliberate plan to remove racial and religious discrimination within the armed services. This plan is an example of the manner in which intelligent leadership, through the use of approved legislative and administrative functions, is able to influence the real patterns of behavior. The executive order to remove segregation and discrimination came from the commander-in-chief, President Truman, after the war. It was carried out in all branches of the service—in the academies that educate and train officers as well as in all American military installations throughout the world. It was shown to work with fair success during the Korean and Vietnam conflicts.

The armed forces were not the only agency for this type of sociocultural integration. When we analyze a society and culture, we necessarily concentrate upon one segment of an institution or group at a time. Other changes were going on concurrently in educational, economic, and other areas at the time when integration was being planned and promoted in the armed forces. The fact that millions of young men of draft age had this practical experience of integration was most significant in its broad influence. It provided a sociological demonstration that persons of varying ethnic, religious, and racial backgrounds could function together in relative harmony. It affected these young men in their postservice experiences in schools, churches, factories, and communities.

The general and positive integrative consequences of war upon the American sociocultural system do not, of course, prove a universal means-end relationship. Given the circumstances and the trends in our country, as well as the fact that we have been fairly successful in waging war, the logical result has been a higher level of sociocultural integration. In other societies where the circumstances are different and the trends are in other directions, the effects of war are often likely to be destructive and disintegrative.

### 3. INTERNATIONAL COMPETITION

Every society suffers a continuing degree of internal inconsistency because of the discrepancy between its ideal and real patterns of behavior. The United States is no exception to this generalization. Our constitution, the Bill of Rights, and the general social philosophy of the people uphold ideals of conduct based upon the natural moral law. There have been, however, numerous patterned evasions of these ideals. The contemporary American trend seems to be in the direction of higher ideals, and one of the most compelling factors in this trend is our present status in world affairs.

a. At the risk of oversimplification we may say that the international factor of domestic solidarity emerges from the competitive roles of the ·American and Communist systems. Americans have been loud in their denunciation of authoritarian governments, critical of the denial of human rights in other parts of the world, and boastful of the freedom and prosperity that accompany the democratic system. People of other countries, with equal ethnocentrism, have been critical of America for preaching a sociocultural idealism it does not practice. The result has been a sharp reevaluation by Americans, especially by young intellectuals, of the inconsistencies between ideal and real levels of behavior.

**b.** American leadership has been forced to take cognizance of this international challenge. The Communists boast throughout the world that their system can bring economic security to all working people; various former colonies and protectorates are suspicious of Caucasian pretensions to racial superiority; smaller countries at a lower level of technological advancement demand respect, recognition, and independence from the two power centers, Russia and the United States. This situation has forced America to accelerate the trend toward the fulfillment of democracy at home and thus toward sociocultural solidarity.

**c.** America has been "put on the spot"; Americans are asked to demonstrate to the world that our sociocultural system contains the promises we claim for it and that those promises can be fulfilled. In concrete, measurable terms this demonstration includes numerous programs: practical plans to improve housing and health; extension and improvement of the educational system; enforcement of democratic principles of racial equality; the protection of workers' rights; an increase of purchasing power for more and more Americans; various programs for the economic relief of agriculture; and many other similar indications of sociocultural progress.

**d.** It must be noted that there is an intimate connection between these programs of progress and the American system of sociocultural solidarity. The ideals of freedom and justice are neither novel nor exclusively American principles, but in the American ethos they are closely allied to the notions of equality of opportunity, brother-

hood, mutual responsibility, and other solidaristic principles. Similarly, the striving for national prosperity and
for the material progress of the common people is not an
exclusively American invention, but in the American society these are considered the right of the people to be
obtained through democratic cooperation and participation.

e. If all these cultural threads are pulled together, we
perceive a network of interacting principles and ideals
supporting internal American solidarity. If brotherhood
and equality are translated into concrete social situations,
they imply both mutual responsibility of people and a
common sharing of social and cultural benefits. Democracy
is not a mechanical institution that automatically produces prosperity, nor does the material prosperity of the
people inherently guarantee the processes of democracy.
The political slogan that "it is people who make democracy work" means that there must be an effort to elevate
the real patterns of conduct closer to the ideal patterns.

In effect, this elevation has taken place during the so-
called cold-war period folowing the Second World War,
although it was challenged again in the 1960s. America
has been competing for the good will of other nations not
merely through economic, political, and military support
to them, but also by trying to develop an internal example
of democratic solidarity. Obviously, international competition is not the only factor at work in this process, but
the challenge of other societies does find a response in the
ethical sensitivity of the American people.

4. SECONDARY GROUPS

We have seen in other parts of this book that the American society is characterized by a trend away from primary
relations and groups toward secondary relations and associations. We have seen also that the individual person
learns the mores, appreciates social values, and develops
solidarity in small face-to-face primary groups. The family
and neighborhood, the work and play groups, are essential
to the ongoing society, and they are essential also to the
socialization of the individual. The sociologist sees an

American dilemma: if the decline of primary groups is making individuals less solidaristic, how can the increasing number of large secondary associations develop a satisfactory solidarity for the total society?

**a.** Secondary groups are numerically large; social relations are formal and impersonal; the social structure is loosely organized; social control operates through rules and regulations. These characteristics are seen in urban America with its gigantic labor unions, business corporations, political parties, large-scale recreational centers, and even religious associations. On the upper layers of these organizations individual persons and subgroups are represented in common functions rather than participating in them.

**b.** From this perspective of large-scale organizations the importance of the millions of interacting basic primary groups can be appreciated. Psychological security for the individual is anchored in these smaller units—families, work groups, friendly meetings and activities. Through them the individual escapes the anonymity that appears to be a concomitant of secondary associations, and in them he participates in sociocultural integration with other individuals. The basic layers of primary groups are in many ways related to the larger and broader layers of secondary groups. The same persons are present in both primary and secondary groups, but the manner of their social relations is notably different at each level. The total aggregate of people cannot participate directly in the higher centers of administration and communication.

**c.** The type of sociocultural integration differs at these two levels. In the primary groups, solidarity is taken for granted; it may be called spontaneous, natural, and subconscious; the individuals do not deliberately work at its achievement. In the secondary associations, solidarity is deliberately contrived; it is often arbitrary, planned, and devised. The recognition of this difference is an important insight into the nature of the sociocultural integration characterizing the United States. The observation of solidarity on the level of secondary groups reveals two facts: first, there are professional people whose function it is to plan and execute integration and, second, the major decisions of these top people must take cognizance of the total society.

**d.** The fact that professional coordinators are becoming increasingly important in American society means that integration is in part a strictly technical problem. We have seen that occupational roles are becoming more and more institutionalized and that bureaucracies are necessary in these large associations. There can no longer be a reliance on "nice" personalities, on hit-or-miss techniques, or on old-fashioned paternalistic relations to integrate the persons and roles in large organizations. Skillful practitioners with a knowledge of social science, like labor specialists, psychologists, sociologists, statisticians, and social workers, are employed for the purpose of applying the techniques of solidarity.

**e.** Paradoxically, the most successful of these experts in human relations are those who have studied the workings of primary groups within the large secondary organizations. For example, a detailed knowledge of the mores and folkways, the status aspirations, and the prejudices and preferences of the members of small factory groups has been of great value in understanding and implementing the total structure of solidarity. This kind of painstaking research has produced more integrative results than the philosophical maxims, moral exhortations, and peremptory edicts of employers. Similar comparisons can be made of the scientific analysis of social relations in churches, schools, hospitals, and other large organizations.

These experts are employed mainly by large corporations and industries and to some extent in educational, political, and religious associations and even in athletic organizations. They are not numerous at this time, and the body of reliable knowledge with which they can work is only beginning to emerge from the various research projects constantly being conducted by social scientists. Nevertheless, they are contributing invaluable service in dealing with the problems of conflict and tension that occur within large secondary associations and with the larger problems of public relations and communication on the national level.

f. It is true that within the total sociocultural system these large secondary associations pursue different goals —the objectives of a medical association differ from those of a lumbermen's organization, and these again differ from the objectives of a political party, a ministerial alliance, or an automobile workers' union. It is true also that large associations within the same major institutional framework—like rival automakers, religious bodies, and educational groups—are imbued with competitive and often conflicting values. At the top level, however, they are gradually developing techniques of negotiation, arbitration, and compromise. They often achieve voluntary coordination among themselves and sometimes have it forced upon them by public opinion or even by the intervention of political and legal authority.

This brief analysis of the relationship between social solidarity and secondary associations introduces an area in which much research is being conducted. We must realize that primary groups are necessarily functioning within the large secondary associations. Both the kind of goals pursued and the type of integration achieved are on a different level from those of primary groups. Nevertheless, the work of the scientific researchers and of professional coordinators indicates that a relatively successful form of integration can be achieved in secondary associations.

The degree of sociocultural integration attained among Americans appears to depend ultimately upon the integrative success of the large secondary organizations. It is fatalistic to suggest that these large groups must necessarily "gobble up" the smaller groups, or that they will inevitably crumble from their own gigantic size, or that they can achieve solidarity only by developing into an authoritarian and totalitarian political system. These negative and hypothetical apprehensions are belied by the obvious fact that their dire prophecies have not been fulfilled during the past half-century.

## 5. SYMBOLIC INTEGRATION

The American likes to think of himself as a hardheaded, reasonable, practical kind of person who knows what he is doing and where he is going. Social scientists, however, have presented enough evidence to indicate that this self-evaluation is somewhat inaccurate. Perhaps we Americans are not so susceptible to the influence of slogans and symbols as people of some other societies; it is certainly true that we are influenced by different types of slogans and symbols. We feel there is something odd about the political banners and heroic posters in Communist countries, but we blithely accept advertising jingles and commercial slogans.

On a more serious level Americans are drawn together by certain symbols of national unity without precisely defining their ideological content. The integrative effect of the sharing of common symbols requires only a vague reference to their specific meaning. In our kind of pluralistic culture we would probably find many grounds for disagreement if we attempted to define, for example, what the national anthem really means to the different people in an audience while it is being played.

a. The Star-Spangled Banner had great symbolic value when it was frequently played during wartime. The custom of using it as kind of invocation before public gatherings has carried over into peacetime. A reverent hush falls over the crowd; everyone faces the flag; men remove their hats. The pledge of allegiance to the flag itself, as well as the songs written in honor of it, provide a kind of psychological security. It is as though people were saying, "Here at least we have something upon which we can depend and about which we do not disagree."

b. The Constitution acts as another common symbol that has important integrative effects. The symbol is not the Constitution in detail with all the interpretations and definitions worked out by scholars, legal experts, and judges during our national history. The integrating symbol is the general notion of the Constitution as a kind of sacred focus of reverence that somehow or other protects us all and remains a dependable bastion in a hectic and changing world. Even those who disagree violently with the findings of the Supreme Court cling tenaciously to the Constitution and sometimes challenge these judicial interpretations as an "assault" upon the Constitution.

c. Historical heroes, and to some extent political figures, act as a common symbol of integration for Americans. Washington and Jefferson, John Paul Jones and John Pershing, exemplify the supposed national virtues. The highest political officials—the president, governors, and senators—make a deliberate effort to represent all their constituents, or at least they create the impression that they are doing so. In this case, the common symbol of unity is more frequently the public office itself rather than the holder of the office. The fact that high governmental office is closely associated with other symbols like the flag and the Constitution reinforces it as a factor of generalized solidarity.

There are other types of heroes who, because they represent successful achievement of common aspirations, act as a symbolic focus of integration. Successful businessmen, well-known scientists, eminent literary and artistic figures, and even athletic heroes and entertainment stars are in this category.

d. Certain inanimate physical objects in our country are often endowed with meaning and value. National parks, monuments, and buildings, as well as "natural wonders" like Niagara Falls, the Grand Canyon, and the Mississippi River, have the trademark "America" stamped on them. These objects are operative in subtle and subconscious ways as symbolic integrators of the American people.

e. In spite of differences in creed and of numerous people who are not directly church-affiliated, the common fatherhood of God acts as a symbol of unity to many. The meaning of the Lord's Prayer is sufficiently generalized to be acceptable to people of almost any religious persuasion, and there is a vague notion even among nonchurchgoers that it is a "good idea" to have a Father in Heaven. Innumerable public and official meetings are opened with prayer for divine guidance, and this action is, if nothing else, a satisfying formula for a generalized unity.

The immediate connection between sociocultural integration and these various kinds of common symbols has not been studied with scientific precision. To understand the validity of this connection, however, it is necessary to distinguish the specific and interpretable content from generalized and vague symbolism of these phenomena. Group cleavages are numerous on the level of specific interests and values within our society, but there does exist in America an observable type of sociocultural unity, and one of the factors that influence it is found in the common symbols.

## Suggested Readings

Argyris, Chris. *Integrating the Individual and the Organization*. New York: Wiley, 1964.

Bell, Daniel. *The End of Ideology*. New York: Free Press, 1960.

Claude, Inis L. *Swords into Plowshares*. New York: Random House, 1961.

Drucker, Peter. *The Age of Discontinuity*. New York: Harper & Row, 1968.

Nisbet, Robert. *The Sociological Tradition*. New York: Basic, 1967.

Parsons, Talcott. *Structure and Process in Modern Societies*. New York: Free Press, 1960.

# Name Index

# Subject Index